P9-CQB-790

HISTORICAL KNOWLEDGE,
HISTORICAL ERROR

Historical Knowledge, Historical Error

A CONTEMPORARY GUIDE TO PRACTICE

Allan Megill

with contributions by Steven Shepard and Phillip Honenberger

The University of Chicago Press ‡ CHICAGO AND LONDON

WINGATE UNIVERSITY LIBRARY

ALLAN MEGILL teaches history at the University of Virginia.
STEVEN SHEPARD is a graduate of the University of Virginia.
PHILLIP HONENBERGER is a graduate of the College of William and Mary.

The University of Chicago Press, Chicago 60637
The University of Chicago Press, Ltd., London
© 2007 by The University of Chicago
All rights reserved. Published 2007
Printed in the United States of America

A Russian version of this book, translated by Marina Kukartseva, V. S. Timonin, and V. E. Kashaev, is slated to be published in December 2006, under the title Историчекая зпистемология [Historical epistemology], by the Moscow publisher Kanon+. Peking University Press is slated to publish a Chinese version, translated by Han Zhao, in January 2007, under the title 历史知识 —— 历史谬误：当代实践导论 [Lishi zhishi—lishi miuwu: dangdai shijian daolun].

16 15 14 13 12 11 10 09 08 07   1 2 3 4 5

ISBN-13: 978-0-226-51829-9 (cloth)
ISBN-10: 0-226-51829-9 (cloth)
ISBN-13: 978-0-226-51830-5 (paper)
ISBN-10: 0-226-51830-2 (paper)

LIBRARY OF CONGRESS CATALOGING-IN-PUBLICATION DATA

Megill, Allan.
    Historical knowledge, historical error : a contemporary guide to practice / Allan Megill ; with contributions by Steven Shepard and Phillip Honenberger.
        p.   cm.
    Includes bibliographical references and index.
    ISBN-13: 978-0-226-51829-9 (cloth : alk. paper)
    ISBN-10: 0-226-51829-9 (cloth : alk. paper)
    ISBN-13: 978-0-226-51830-5 (paper : alk. paper)
    ISBN-10: 0-226-51830-2 (paper : alk. paper)
    1. History—Philosophy. 2. Knowledge, Theory of. I. Shepard, Steven, 1978– II. Honenberger, Phillip. III. Title.

D16.9.M299   2007
901—dc22   2006021624

♾ The paper used in this publication meets the minimum requirements of the American National Standard for Information Sciences—Permanence of Paper for Printed Library Materials, ANSI Z39.48-1992.

For Rita and Maria, again

I would figure out why Martin Guerre left his village and where he went, how and why Arnaud du Tilh became an impostor, whether he fooled Bertrande de Rols, and why he failed to make it stick. This would tell us new things about sixteenth-century rural society. . . . It turned out to be much more difficult than I had thought.

NATALIE ZEMON DAVIS, *The Return of Martin Guerre*

For the simple truth is that truth is often hard to come by, and that once found it may easily be lost again.

KARL R. POPPER, *Conjectures and Refutations:*
The Growth of Scientific Knowledge

CONTENTS

Some years ago the American historian David Hackett Fischer published an amusing and troubling book, *Historians' Fallacies: Toward a Logic of Historical Thought*. Although it appeared in 1970, it remains in print today, a minor classic. It is read by laypersons interested in how historians go about their jobs, and teachers of historical method have long assigned it to history majors and first-year graduate students as a salutary warning of the pitfalls of the discipline. Fischer catalogued 112 different "fallacies," sorted into twelve types, and then found a wide array of historians of the 1920s through the 1960s guilty of committing them—indeed, he seems to have left no eminence unstoned.

I cannot rise to the level of Fischer's refreshing wit, but I do take inspiration from his work. My concern, now rather unfashionable, is Fischer's concern, and my question is Fischer's question. In short, my central interest in this book is in the substratum of argument and justification that allows an answer to the question, What grounds do we have for accepting the accounts of the past that historians and others offer to us? Or, to put this in a slightly different way, How can we best avoid historiographic error? Historical epistemology—or, if you will, epistemology for historians—is concerned with detecting and avoiding such error. But no one can understand the argumentative or justificatory side of historical research and writing without an understanding of other, related topics. Hence this book also deals with the role of memory in—and against—history; with description, explanation, and interpretation in history; with objectivity and the place of speculation (or "abduction") in historical research; and with framing assumptions in historical research and writing that are offered, usually surreptitiously, by notions of "paradigm" and "grand narrative." This book also attacks a few blatant solecisms—most notably, the widely held notion that the historian should strive to give us an "immediate" experience of the past.

Some signposts are called for. I should note first of all that the chapters are not connected in a lock-step way. There are intertwinings, but usually one chapter does not pose a problem that is then resolved in the next. This is not that kind of book—nor does the subject matter lend itself to such a treatment. It is not my intention to offer a theory of historical writing, because I do not think that a single theory, either of historical writing in general or of historical epistemology in particular, can be offered. At any rate, no *acceptable* theory can be offered. Rather, this book offers a set of theoretical reflections on historical epistemology—that is, on the problem of the limits and conditions of historical knowledge. The theoretical reflections arise in the course of examining particular examples. The payoff will be found more in the general reflections offered in—and I hope also prompted by—this book than in the illumination cast on the specific examples. The aim is less to contribute to a philosophical examination of epistemological issues than to alert (or re-alert) practicing historians—and especially beginners—to the epistemological aspect of their practice. I often return to the same issue from different angles. I hope in this way to stimulate the reader's own reflections. Above all, I hope that readers will take what is offered and apply it to their own reading and writing of history.

In the introduction, "The Need for Historical Epistemology," I reflect on instances of good and bad epistemological practice in history, taking examples from the so-called new cultural history that has recently played a dominant role in professional history-writing in the United States. In particular, I contrast the sense of epistemological responsibility to be discerned in Natalie Z. Davis's *The Return of Martin Guerre* (a riveting account of an instance of "identity theft" in sixteenth-century France) with what I take to be the epistemological irresponsibility manifested in a recent "experiment" in Web-based, or "digital," history relating to slavery and the U.S. Civil War—an experiment that, in my view, generates negative results. This, too, is a contribution to historical knowledge, at least if we recognize that we should now move on in different directions.

Part 1, "Memory," pursues issues brought to light in the introduction. The two chapters in this part are both concerned with casting doubt on the frequently heard claim that history is simply a form of memory. Chapter 1, "History with Memory, History without Memory," attacks this assumption directly, yet argues at the same time that we cannot simply dispense with "memory." We can view history in two ways that are polar opposites: as having an affirmative function (affirming some particular human community) and as having a negating function (criticizing the myths that this community has made for itself). Neither of these two poles can justifiably be rejected. The chapter ends, however, by preferring the critical pole, as the one more necessary at the present time, when affirmation of the reigning collectivities is strongly expressed, and when multiple forms of memory challenge a history that is often seen as yet another self-interested and self-regarding form of intellectual "discourse."

Chapter 2, "History, Memory, Identity," adds "identity" to the mix. In the last generation identity has become both a problematic and a highly valued category in American culture and elsewhere. Identity is closely tied up with memory, and both identity and memory have a complex relation to history. The fact that history's relation to memory is actually, in many respects, a *negative* relation has unfortunately been largely lost from sight. Certain important distinctions have also been lost from sight. One of these is the distinction between memory, which is deeply rooted in present-day subjectivities, and tradition, which is connected to an objectively existing set of cultural artifacts or articulations. Another is the distinction between memory and nostalgia. In empirical reality, such categories often overlap. However, we cannot think clearly about them unless they are distinguished at a conceptual level. Moreover, historians and others who confuse history with memory, tradition, or nostalgia are destined to fall into error. They will always be tempted to turn the authenticity, usefulness, or attractiveness of such and such a claim about the past into a reason for holding that the claim in question is true.

Part 2, "Narrative and Knowledge," addresses the cognitive dimension of historical narrative. Chapter 3, "Does Narrative Have a Cognitive Value of Its Own?" starts out from Louis O. Mink's suggestion that it is possible to discern "conceptual presuppositions" embedded within narrative. In Mink's view, this gives narrative a cognitive value. Chapter 3 both affirms and denies Mink's claim. It notes the ubiquity of narrative—how it keeps popping up again and again even when it is supposedly in crisis. This suggests that narrative has value for human beings, and part of that value is surely that it helps people to see their way around in the world. At the same time, different people or groups of people give their allegiance to mutually incompatible narratives. The chapter concludes that we need to deploy epistemological criteria if we are to decide what to accept or reject of particular narratives.

Chapter 4, "Narrative and the Four Tasks of History-Writing," casts light on the cognitive side of the historian's enterprise by parsing out the main tasks of historiography. It also offers a redefinition of narrative that is intended not so much to *replace* the usual definition (namely, a chronologically ordered account) as to *clarify* it, by focusing not on the manner of telling but instead on what narrative conveys (characters, settings, actions, happenings). Chapter 4 contends that history has four main tasks: description; explanation; argument, or justification; and interpretation. From the perspective of historical epistemology, the most important point is that historians cannot simply *assert* that such and such claims are true about the past. Rather, they must put forward arguments and evidence that justify our agreeing that the claims in question are true. "Simply telling a story" isn't good enough: we need more than "simply a story" if we are to regard a historical account as epistemologically responsible.

Part 3 turns to the interconnected topics of objectivity and speculation in history. Chapter 5, "Objectivity for Historians," argues that objectivity is an inherently complex conception, for instead of having a *single* meaning at its core, it has four different but related meanings. All four senses of objectivity are essential to the doing of history: they constitute a kind of "factor X" that allows the work to be history and not mere propaganda. To be sure, historians are motivated by commitments that we can refer to, for the sake of verbal economy, as "political" (taking *political* in a broad sense, to include religious, philosophical, aesthetic, cultural, and other similar commitments, as well as *strictly* political ones). Without such commitments, historians would have no drive to write history and no perspective from which to do so. And yet political commitment is a dangerous poison in the absence of an equal commitment to objectivity.

Chapter 6, "A Case Study in Historical Epistemology: What Did the Neighbors Know about Thomas Jefferson and Sally Hemings?" (co-authored by Steven Shepard, Phillip Honenberger, and Allan Megill), addresses a problem that historians always face in their work—the problem of what social scientists fondly call "bad data." One way to deal with bad data is to take a position of agnosticism, making no claims about the past unless one can be quite certain that they are true. But historians following such a strategy would be able to offer their readers only "scattered empirical fragments," as the nineteenth-century historian and theorist of history J. G. Droysen put it. In order to produce any worthy history at all, historians need to speculate.

Our claim in chapter 6 is that historians ought to speculate in a self-aware manner, and that, further, they ought to signal to their readers how they are going beyond the evidence. In this chapter we consider one historian's assertions about rumors that allegedly circulated in Albemarle County, Virginia between 1790 and 1802 about a sexual relationship between the American founding father Thomas Jefferson and one of his slaves, Sally Hemings.

In the course of examining the evidence for and against this historian's assertions, we show the role that "inference to the best explanation"—also known as *abduction* or *abductive inference*—plays in historical research and writing. Indeed, even such apparently obvious historical assertions as "Napoleon existed" or "World War I began in 1914" are known to us not empirically, and certainly not deductively, but only by abductive inference. We also claim in this chapter that an epistemologically responsible history requires that historians make comparative judgments, canvassing the arguments both for and against the hypotheses that occur to them.

Chapter 7, "Counterfactual History: On Niall Ferguson's *Virtual History* and Similar Works*," reflects on the place of one species of speculation, counterfactual reasoning, in the researching and writing of history. It does so by looking at the explicitly counterfactual genre of "virtual" or "imaginary" history. It distinguishes between the legitimate, indeed essential, role of counterfactuality in any attempt on the part of the historian to make claims about what caused what in history, and another use of counterfactuality that is closer to imaginative literature than to history.

Part 4, "Fragmentation," turns to the splitting up of the historical field that has come about within academic historiography. This fragmentation has occurred as different interpretive perspectives have arisen and come into conflict with each other. Indeed, fragmentation seems to be an inevitable consequence of the interpretive nature of historical research and writing that is noted in chapter 4. I contend that an epistemologically responsible historiography needs in large measure to go along with such fragmentation.

Chapter 8, "Fragmentation and the Future of Historiography: On Peter Novick's *That Noble Dream,*" looks at the fragmentation of history in relation to the final part of Peter Novick's well-known 1988 book, in which he describes an American historical profession in which, at the time that he wrote, there was "no king"—that is, no dominant consensus. Some readers of Novick's book saw him as lamenting this fact. I contend, on the contrary, that there was and is no reason for lamentation.

Chapter 9, "'Grand Narrative' and the Discipline of History," is a much longer and heavier chapter, but I hope that it will repay the attention that it requires. It offers a number of distinctions and perspectives that are essential to understanding the nature of historiographic coherence. We can think of the coherence of the historical account as occupying four distinct levels: there is the coherence of narrative proper, of master narrative, of grand narrative, and, finally, of metanarrative. Further, we need to consider notions of the coherence of the historical world as rooted in four distinct attitudes toward history—attitudes that can coexist, but that also have a historical progression. We can hold that there is a single, unified history and that we know what it is now; that this history will only be known later, after "further research" is done; that such a history is a purely regulative idea and will never actually be known; or that the notion that we ought to aim for a single history is unjustified and limiting. Chapter 6 also explores the options that follow when the idea of a unified history is abandoned.

In spite of the evident multiplicity of interpretive perspectives that are now being brought to the historical past, a strong drive toward the "re-coherentization" of history persists. Chapter 10, "Coherence and Incoherence in Historical Studies: From the *Annales* School to the New Cultural History," examines this tendency, focusing on one response to the retreat of the notion that historical scholarship will eventually underpin a unified account of the historical world, a "universal history." The most widely influential school of historical research and writing in the second half of the twentieth century was the so-called *Annales* school in France. Such luminaries of the *Annales* school as Lucien Febvre and Fernand Braudel longed to write a "total history" (or, as Febvre once called it, a "totalitarian history"). Their effort failed. Subsequently, a new generation of historians, linked closely to the *Annales* school, invented the "new cultural history." These historians no longer aspire to write total history, for they well understand that the past holds far more to write about than will ever be accommodated in a single, "total" view. Yet they still look to coherence—an *imposed* coherence, for which they find justification in Thomas S. Kuhn's notion that scientific disciplines are usually unified by the adherence of all competent researchers to a single "paradigm," or model, of scientific research. Chapter 10 points out that the paradigm notion is itself unjustified—as some of the more astute proponents of the new cultural history freely acknowledge.

In the conclusion, "Against Current Fashion," I reflect briefly on how history is and is not valuable for the present. In particular, I call attention to the unjustified, un-self-aware, even arrogant character of the popular assumption that the historian can and ought to aim at making the experience of people in the past available to us in its raw immediacy.

Some of these chapters are quite demanding, whereas others are more accessible. Readers unfamiliar with historical theory may wish to begin by reading the introduction, chapters 3, 5, 7, and 8, and the conclusion before tackling such weighty chapters as 4, 6, 9, and 10.

Ivy, Virginia, January 2006

ACKNOWLEDGMENTS

In my thinking about history and how it should be written I have been influenced by many people. In previous writings I have thanked a large number of them for their help. Here, in a minimalist spirit, I shall mostly desist from naming names. Still, I must mention the following for their readings of the manuscript or parts thereof: Babak Ashrafi, Malachi Hacohen, John Holloran, Michael Holt, Erik Midelfort, Peter Onuf, David Pickus, Brad Whitener, Perez Zagorin, and two anonymous readers for the University of Chicago Press. I thank my editor, Doug Mitchell, and his assistant, Timothy McGovern, for their commitment to this project, and Nicholas Murray for his expert copyediting. I am also indebted to four people I encountered during fifteen years spent at the University of Iowa: the late William O. Aydelotte, Deirdre McCloskey, John S. Nelson, and Alan B. Spitzer, all of whom have written on issues addressed in this book. Two classes that I currently teach on historical theory grew out of a graduate class on the philosophy of history that Bill Aydelotte taught for many years; I was privileged to attend Aydelotte's final offering of that course and to continue it after him.

Phillip Honenberger was a helpful assistant in the writing and revision of this book. Besides pushing the work along, he entered into the spirit of a paper by Steven Shepard that formed the basis for chapter 6, bringing his own important contributions to it. Consequently, he is listed as second author of that chapter.

I thank collectively the many students at the universities of Iowa and Virginia who have taken my classes on philosophy of history, historiography, and related topics. They have greatly contributed to the working out of my ideas.

The University of Virginia gave me time off from teaching in the spring semesters of 1994, 2000, and 2005, as well as some summer support and help with research expenses. Without these semesters free of teaching my writing would have proceeded more slowly (however, teaching has usually helped more than hindered my research). The book collection and superb service provided by the University of Virginia's Alderman Library also contributed to the completion of this book. The earliest support for this project came in 1986 in the form of a summer grant from the University of Iowa's University House (now the Obermann Center for Advanced Studies).

My greatest debts are to Rita Felski and Maria Felski, and I am also glad for the constant support of Jason, Jessica, and Jonathan Megill.

Parts of this book have appeared in different versions elsewhere, although all previously published material has been revised, some of it extensively. I thank my earlier editors and publishers for their faith in my work and for permitting its republication. The original titles and places of publication are as follows: "History, Memory, Identity," *History of the Human Sciences* 11, no. 3 (1998): 7–62 [chapter 2]; "Does Narrative Have a Cognitive Value of Its Own?" in *Dimensionen der Historik: Geschichtstheorie, Wissenschaftsgeschichte und Geschichtskultur heute: Jörn Rüsen zum 60. Geburtstag,* ed. Horst Walter Blanke, Friedrich Jaeger, and Thomas Sandkühler (Köln: Böhlau, 1998), 41–52 [chapter 3]; "Recounting the Past: 'Description,' Explanation, and Narrative in Historiography," *American Historical Review* 94 (1989): 627–53 [chapter 4]; "Four Senses of Objectivity," *Annals of Scholarship* 8 (1991): 301–20, reprinted in *Rethinking Objectivity,* ed. A. Megill (Durham, NC: Duke University Press, 1994) [chapter 5]; "The New Counterfactualists," *Historically Speaking* 5, no. 4 (March 2004): 17–18 [chapter 7]; "Fragmentation and the Future of Historiography," *American Historical Review* 96 (1991): 693–98 [chapter 8]; " 'Grand Narrative' and the Discipline of History," in *A New Philosophy of History,* ed. Frank Ankersmit and Hans Kellner (London: Reaktion Books, 1995), 151–73, 263–71 [chapter 9]; "Coherence and Incoherence in Historical Studies: From the *Annales* School to the New Cultural History," *New Literary History* 35 (2004):207–31 [chapter 10]; and "Are We Asking Too Much of History?" *Historically Speaking* 3, no. 4 (April 2002): 9–11 [conclusion]. In addition, I have reused in this book a small bit of material from my paper, "What Is Distinctive about Modern Historiography?" in *History of Historiography Reconsidered: Essays in Honor of Georg G. Iggers,* ed. Q. Edward Wang and Franz L. Fillafer (New York: Berghahn Books, 2007).

In an earlier form, chapter 1, "History with Memory, History without Memory," was presented as a "Tuesday Lecture" at the Institut für die Wissenschaften vom Menschen/Institute for Human Sciences in Vienna in the spring of 2000.

The Need for Historical Epistemology

In the past twenty-five years historians have changed how they study the past. Perhaps the most significant shift has been a turn to cultural history. The rise of the new cultural history has broadened the vision of historians, bringing into view aspects of the human past that were once ignored or underrated. For example, one widely noticed book was Natalie Davis's *The Return of Martin Guerre*, the story of a sixteenth-century French peasant woman, Bertrande de Rols, whose husband, Martin Guerre, disappeared from the village in which they lived and then, eight years later, apparently returned a much better person—only to be exposed as an impostor when the *real* Martin Guerre finally came back, minus a leg lost while fighting as a soldier for Spain.[1] Davis tells us much about Bertrande's situation and speculates about what she must have been thinking when she made the choices she did. But Davis always clearly identifies her speculations *as* speculations: "perhaps" this happened; people "must have," or "would have," or "would probably have" done this under this set of circumstances; Bertrande "may have been" helped by so and so; "perhaps" she thought this; "perhaps" she accepted the false Martin Guerre for such and such reasons; "as a 'thought experiment,' let us imagine what might have taken place"; the couple "probably worked out a strategy"; and so on. In all of this, Davis is careful to tell us what the evidence is for the claims she makes and the possibilities she proposes. She never dumps this evidence on us. She tells us why she thinks the evidence in question leads to the conclusion she has reached. She *argues*.

Recently, however, some historians show a tendency to lose sight of the kind of care in evidence and argument that Davis exemplifies. There is no doubt that Davis wrote with the concerns of American feminism of the second half of the twentieth century in mind. As a result, she asks questions about the consciousness of a sixteenth-century French peasant woman that historians previously had not asked. One can infer from *The Return of Martin Guerre* a feminist commitment on Davis's part. But she is never careless of evidence and never murky in her claims and arguments. Nor does one ever have the impression that she puts a thumb on the scale. To be sure, there is a fine narrative intelligence at work in *The Return of Martin Guerre*. Let's face it: it is a great story, one that has been told and retold several times, most notably in a 1982 movie starring French actor Gérard Depardieu. But although Natalie Davis shows real delight in the story, she is always clear about how the story relates to the evidence. She shows, in short, an epistemological care, akin to the care that the cofounder of Western historiography, Thucydides, recommends at the beginning of *The Peloponnesian War*. No doubt she had a personal agenda, but her history is not subordinate to the agenda. There are lessons for the present in the book, but they cannot be given one exclusive form: one cannot exactly *say* what they are. In sum, *Martin Guerre* is a history, and not something else. It is an attempt to get at historical truth. It is an imaginative construction or reconstruction that Davis undertakes in the hope of getting us to engage with a reality different from our own (although also similar to it). She carries out her work with an attentiveness to the rules—sometimes tacit and sometimes explicit—of what I call historical epistemology.[2]

To think clearly about historical epistemology, one needs to have some sense of what is distinctive about the historian's approach to the past. Here the tradition of historical writing that goes back to Thucydides and to his fellow, fifth-century BCE Greek, Herodotus, can give us some help. In *The Peloponnesian War,* as well as in *The History* of Herodotus, one finds something that also runs, like a red thread, through the subsequent historical tradition, distinguishing it from the traditions of philosophy and science. One can call this "something" by various names. I prefer to call it an *unresolving dialectic* or *unresolving tension*. I mean to suggest by these terms that a true historian—one who is faithful to the tradition of history—is happy to leave her mind suspended between conflicting attitudes or claims. It is not the historian's task to articulate a single unequivocal position, let alone a single consistent theory, concerning the world as it is. We can leave such a task to those philosophers, natural and social scientists, and other theorists who wish to take it up.

This is not the place to run variations on the notion of an unresolving dialectic. But examples are in order, and so is a statement as to the relevance of this notion to historical epistemology. One can hardly do better than to begin at the beginning: with the first "father of history," Herodotus.[3] According to tradition, Herodotus traveled through the eastern Mediterranean world gathering material for his great account of the wars that the Persian Empire carried out against the Greeks—wars that led to the defeat of Persia and to the preservation of what we like to think of as "Western culture." The people Herodotus interviewed told him many stories. Some stories Herodotus could check, others not. He was willing to go a long way with stories of whose truth he was uncertain. His procedure in such instances might well appear epistemologically irresponsible. But it is not, for in recounting uncertain stories he announces his own uncertainty: "I must tell what is said, but I am not at all bound to believe it, and this comment of mine holds about my whole *History*."[4] He is interested in the stories themselves apart from their factual truth, and he hopes that we will be too. Yet he is also interested in what really happened and will contradict a story when he thinks it wrong: "But they lie; . . . it was one of the Delphians who put that inscription on it. . . . I know his name but will not mention it" (1.51). To state the matter in present-day terms, Herodotus rejected the notion that history should be identified with what people today sometimes call "memory." But he also rejected the notion that history should *exclude* "memory." Rather—and somewhat paradoxically—history should be both history and memory.

A different tension appears in Herodotus' successor and competitor Thucydides. To be sure, Thucydides rejected Herodotus's love of stories: near the start of *The Peloponnesian War,* he declares that he wants to avoid *muthodes*—a word related to *myth*.[5] Instead, Thucydides attempted to find out for himself what had happened, and to report only what he could be sure of. (He could conceive of proceeding in this way because the Peloponnesian War occurred during his adult lifetime and was still going on as he was writing. Moreover, he himself had been a general in it until the Athenians held him responsible for a defeat at the hands of the Spartans and exiled him.) Thucydides is not unresolved as to the factual truth of his account: on the contrary, he is solidly persuaded that he has the story right. The tension in Thucydides's work appears, rather, in his willingness—indeed, eagerness—to report at length the conflicting views and policies of the different parties involved in the war. Thucydides' *own* views, on the other hand, are kept modestly or cunningly in the background. He is not a propagandist, although he clearly had commitments of his own. He is not a political scientist trying to give us a theory of warfare or of international relations. He is a historian, trying to tell a true story, and therefore a complex one. This is why, as the classical scholar Daniel Mendelsohn points out, present-day writers who try to turn Thucydides into the purveyor of direct lessons for the present are wrong to do so. For example, according to Mendelsohn, the Yale classicist Donald Kagan gives us a reading of Thucydides that could be taken to support "a very twenty-first-century project . . . a unilateralist policy of preëmptive war." Mendelsohn suggests that by offering such a reading, Kagan flattens out Thucydides's account of the war—"stripping away the many voices and points of view that he worked so hard to include." Thucydides is not trying to give us a policy prescription; Kagan is.[6]

The unresolving dialectic that characterizes historical thinking is closely related to historical epistemology; for one aspect of this attitude—very different from that of the theorist or scientist—is that it preserves a breach or gap between the past reality that the historian describes and the world of the present. (It is not that past and present are *totally* disconnected—only that they are different.) The true historian is not a propagandist or cheerleader, not someone who wants her history to be "useful." Rather, her ruling passion is to explore the unvisitable foreign country that is the past. This passion is connected with historical epistemology, because the historian can only be true to it if she takes seriously the relation between historical evidence and the words she is writing. Attentiveness to historical evidence helps keep the historian honest, and hence less likely to impose her own prejudices and good wishes on the past. Conversely, too great an interest in the uses of history in the present is likely to make the would-be historian inattentive to historical evidence. Davis, in *The Return of Martin Guerre,* is exquisitely attentive to the need to write an account that connects with the evidence that is there. This does not mean that her book is beyond criticism, nor does it mean that hers is the only possible historical story that could be told about sixteenth-century peasants, or even about the strange case of Martin Guerre and Bertrande de Rols. In fact, the true historian *cannot* claim exclusivity for her account: this is Herodotus' insight. (Claims that "anything goes" and that what *really* happened does not matter are equally faulty: this is Thucydides' insight.) The claim to know the past with certainty violates the principle of historical irresolution. It turns the historian into some other sort of knower outside the tradition of history-writing. Or, worse, it might turn him into a purveyor of error and even of immorality (for example, by fostering smugness, arrogance, and pride with regard to the past, the present, and the relations between them). An exclusivity-claim would also sin against historical epistemology, for singular events or "existents" in the past are not susceptible to the kind of justification that would support a historian's claim that her own account is true and all other accounts are false.

The claims that I am making are already known to all true historians, although perhaps not quite in the form offered here. I write the present book against a different view, one that has come to center stage in recent years—the view that the true function of history is *to support the good cause in the present*. In this view, history is politics—and even war—by other means. Of course, it is not surprising that people with an axe to grind and the capacity to impose their own will or preference should hold to this view. Those who have the money to pay the bills will naturally expect historians to earn their keep. What is disturbing is that such views have recently attained some following among professional historians, who ought to know better. And a remarkable inattentiveness to questions of evidence often accompanies the notion that history ought to serve the good cause.

Consider an "electronic article" by William G. Thomas III and Edward L. Ayers, "The Differences Slavery Made: A Close Analysis of Two American Communities," that appeared in the *American Historical Review* and on an associated Web site in December 2003. The article purports to give readers "full access to a scholarly argument" concerning the relation between slavery and the United States Civil War.[7] In brief, the authors maintain that slavery was "more central to the Civil War than we have thought," because it exerted a "determining influence" even in parts of the South where there were no cotton plantations or African-American majorities.[8]

In support of this claim they point to a "digital archive" that they have assembled, "The Valley of the Shadow: Two Communities in the American Civil War" (http://valley.vcdh.virginia.edu), which contains a considerable amount of information about two counties in roughly comparable geographical settings, one north of the Mason-Dixon line (Franklin County, Pennsylvania) and one south of that line (Augusta County, Virginia). On the basis of this two-county data set, supplemented by various other "strands of historical argument and evidence," Thomas and Ayers make another claim, which is more emphatic and specific than the claim to "centrality" and "determining influence": "*The experiences of our two counties show that slavery drove all the conflict that brought on the Civil War* but not in a simple way based on modernity, not in the way many imply when they speak of "economics" causing the war or of the "industrial" North against the "agricultural" South [emphasis added]" (*AHR* 1302). The question that we need to ask here is, What is the evidential basis for this claim?

We should note that the initial collecting and digitizing of a large part of Thomas and Ayers's data preceded the writing of their article by a number of years. Originally, Ayers and his assistants collected data concerning Augusta County, Virginia, only, making it available on the "Valley of the Shadow" Web site.[9] Thomas and Ayers then cast about for a northern county to compare with Augusta County. Deciding on Franklin County, they entered data concerning Franklin into the data collection. Then, recognizing that one cannot proceed directly from data, however fetchingly organized, to more general historical claims, the authors crafted their Internet article—we infer—as a way getting from one to the other. The Internet article tries to mediate between "archive" and claims, purporting to offer the "scholarly argument" (*AHR* 1299) supporting the above claims as to the centrality of slavery in the coming of the Civil War. (More accurately, the Web site offers a "Summary of Argument" [TAS1].) The material in the "Valley of the Shadow" Web site and in the Internet article (in the section entitled "Evidence" [citation keys beginning with E]) will be interesting to anyone with a desultory curiosity about wealth, economic activities, population, religious institutions, political and social views, and so on in two relatively similar communities north and south of the Mason-Dixon line in the period just before, during, and just after the civil war. In short, it seems clear that the data in the "Valley of the Shadow" Web site and in the Internet article have a kind of descriptive interest that is distinct from any attempt to infer broader conclusions from these data.

However, the authors never actually *make* the argument to which they purport to offer "full access." In fact, they do not make an argument at all: their "Summary of Argument" is all we have. Although the word *argument* appears frequently in their piece, they have the habit of using it as a synonym for *claim* or *assertion*. But if *argument* means *claim,* then no claim needs an argument for it. It is an odd foreshortening, and it leads to the scholar's equivalent of the lovers' alleged license to never have to say one is sorry. Of course, a large amount of what the authors *call* evidence is present in the Internet article and in "The Valley of the Shadow" data collection. The authors say that they give "the evidence for" their "scholarly argument," by which they mean the evidence for their claim, or claims, about slavery and the Civil War (*AHR* 1299), but they fail to understand what is required for something to be "evidence" for something else. It is strange, and deeply unsupportable, to imagine that one presents "the evidence *for*" a "scholarly argument." This is to imagine that evidence is one thing and a scholarly argument something else. But this is not so: when we make an argument, whether in history, law, physics, or any other field, the supporting evidence appears as a seamless part of the "argument." To put it another way, there is no such thing as unmodified evidence: evidence is always evidence for or against a particular claim, and it becomes evidence for or against that claim by virtue of the argument that the historian, attorney, or physicist constructs.

The authors also fail to understand the requirements for making an argument that goes beyond just describing a past historical reality (see chapters 4 and 7). They write of "the determining influence" of slavery and of "the differences slavery made"; they also say that slavery "drove all the conflict that brought on the Civil War." These are explanatory and not just descriptive claims: the authors are saying that slavery played an important causal role in American society and politics at the time. It seems highly probable that slavery did affect American society in important ways. But to go beyond what has now become a truism and make "a scholarly argument," the authors must provide evidence and arguments to support the claim. One crucial point is that a scholar is obligated to present not just the evidence "for" a given causal claim, but also the evidence against it. For instance, in order to assess whether X had any "determining influence" on Y, and what sort of influence that was, we must also consider the possible impact of W, V, U, T, and so on, on Y. Causation does not occur in a vacuum: hence it is always a matter of assessing the relative strengths of various different *possible* causes. (Doing so always involves engaging in counterfactual reasoning, as I suggest in chapter 4.) Scholars must also be precise about terms, but Thomas and Ayers are remarkably imprecise. For example, they could have entitled their Internet article, "A Comparison of the Characteristics of Two American Counties in the Civil War Period, with a Supporting Data Collection." This would have been a legitimate historiographic project. Instead, they claim to address "the differences slavery *made*" without showing any understanding of how a historical investigation of slavery's differentiating impact might actually be carried out. They choose to regard as "determinative" one element in the complex reality of the time, and then (vaguely) purport to lay out "the differences" it brought about. The result is confusion. The authors have not seen what form of reasoning is required for the claims they make.

The form of reasoning in question can only be analytical. Thomas and Ayers do appear to understand this at the level of lip-service, since in the "full electronic version" of the article they lay out what they call "points of analysis" that are supposedly relevant to their argument (TAF1-47). But it turns out that their "points of analysis" are not "points of analysis" at all. Rather, they are claims of various sorts. The claims in question always have something to do with the historical reality of Augusta or Franklin County in the nineteenth century, stating a fact or set of facts about one or both of the two counties. For example, one such "point of analysis," set off in bold type in the Internet article, reads as follows: "In Augusta, almost every group of white people owned property and homes worth more than their counterparts in Franklin, most of it tied inextricably to slavery" [TAF05]. In principle, this claim ought to be easy to confirm: after all, it appears to be a simple descriptive claim, not a claim about causation.[10] But the paragraph that immediately follows the above sentence stops us short: "The difference was most pronounced for personal property. Since slaves constituted an entire category of wealth prohibited in the North, the average farmer in Augusta owned three times as much personal property as the average farmer in Franklin. Slavery seemed responsible, at least in the eyes of whites, for a standard of living that benefited all whites" (TAF05).

What is wrong in this paragraph? Consider, first, the assertion that "the average farmer in Augusta owned three times as much personal property as the average farmer in Franklin." Thomas and Ayers expand on this claim as follows: "In Franklin, personal property amounted to less than a third of the value of real estate. In Augusta, by contrast, personal property, mostly held in slaves, added up to $10.1 million, nearly three quarters of the $13.8 million of farmland, town lots, and hotels in the prosperous county" (TAF05). Thomas and Ayers overlook an important conceptual problem hiding behind the comparisons they make here between personal property in Franklin and Augusta counties, and between personal property and real property in each county. Since the problem is obvious to any intelligent, active reader, one wonders why they fail to address it. The question that arises in the intelligent reader's mind is this: given that North and South were under two different property regimes—one that allowed some human beings to be the personal property of others and one that did not allow this—how can we compare the two regions with respect to personal-property valuation without taking into account the difference in regimes?

Their direct comparison is deeply misleading because the slave component of the personal property held by some people in Augusta County had no direct equivalent, *as property,* in Franklin County. Slave-owners in Augusta County owned the labor represented by their enslaved workers, whereas employers in Franklin only rented labor, by paying wages to unenslaved workers. The inclusion of the value of slaves in the figure for the value of personal property in Augusta County generates, Thomas and Ayers report, a figure for average holdings in personal property that is higher than the figure for Franklin County. But the difference between the two figures does not demonstrate that, with respect to personal property, "the average farmer" in Augusta was better off than "the average farmer" in Franklin. Rather, the difference between the value of slaves in Augusta (substantial) and the value of slaves in Franklin (zero) is a marker of the difference between the two property regimes.

In order to establish the different values of personal property enjoyed by "the average farmer" in the two counties, Thomas and Ayers would have had to engage in a *real* work of analysis. Instead, all they do is offer us lists of figures describing various economic attributes of each county. To compare in a meaningful way the wealth of "the average farmer" in the two counties, they would need to derive comparable figures from data that, in a raw form, are not comparable. In sum, the authors would have had to calculate the value of the labor provided by both enslaved and unenslaved workers—for slaves and hired workers were presumably purchased or hired for the value of the labor they provided. Such a comparison would necessarily involve much analysis and inferential reasoning. But it is the only way of rendering comparable the raw incomparables that Thomas and Ayers nonetheless attempt to compare.[11]

I eventually found my way to the "Chambersburg and Staunton City Tax Records" in the "Valley of the Shadow" database. Tax-assessment records offer a good deal of information not found in the census data. But here as elsewhere, Thomas and Ayers's use of the data seems more decorative than evidentiary. Thus they assert that "while the tax collector visited every home in the county, *we have chosen to include only the records from the two county seats* [emphasis added]" (http://valley.vcdh.virginia.edu/Reference/citytax/citytax.intro.html). But why? Arbitrary selection makes the data useless for supporting Thomas and Ayers's claims about the two counties in general. I therefore infer that the data are included because they provide interesting decoration, not because they allow justified generalizations about the two counties.

It has long been understood, as an elementary point of social science method, that in order to make comparisons, we must compare things that are comparable. Why do Thomas and Ayers fail to engage in the analytic work needed to derive comparables from figures that in a raw form are incomparable? One possible explanation emerges from their statement that "slavery seemed responsible, *at least in the eyes of whites* [emphasis added], for a standard of living that benefited all whites." The words I have emphasized are puzzling, for Thomas and Ayers start off in this "point of analysis" (TAF01) by making a claim about the objective situation in Augusta in the Civil War period. In other words, they begin by sounding like Thucydides, who wanted to write an account of the Peloponnesian war as it really was. But in the sentence just quoted, they shift gears and refer to what people at the time *believed* was the case—as Herodotus did in recounting the stories of the Persians, Greeks, and so on, whether they were true or not. To their credit, both of the Greek founders of history were clear about the difference between what was the case in the past and what people in the past believed was the case. They focused on either one or the other, and when they shifted between them, they signaled the shift. Thomas and Ayers seem intent on blurring this salutary and important distinction. It is unfortunate that this should happen within the framework of professional historiography: it is a decided step backward.

Of course, as noted, the authors provide a great deal of "evidence." (Printed out, the "Evidence" section of the Internet article [E01–E156] amounts to 386 pages in PDF format—and this leaves aside the links in that section to "The Valley of the Shadow" data collection.) But the article's so-called evidence often seems more like decoration or (perhaps better) like heavy furniture designed to impress by its size and weight. Thomas and Ayers tell us that they want to "fuse the electronic article's form with its argument, to use the medium as effectively as possible to make the presentation of our work and its navigation express and fulfill our argument" (*AHR* 1299). Perhaps what they are doing will be "effective" for audiences looking for entertainment and for a certain quantum of edification. After all, their work gives us a chance to lament again the role that slavery played in the history of the United States. But in making effective presentation the fundamental desideratum of their work—and it seems clear that this is indeed what they are doing—the authors are giving us history-as-propaganda without straight-out telling us so.

Still, they come close to telling us. Consider the following claim, which appears in the Internet article's introduction, at TI3, just before TI4. Here Thomas and Ayers provide some suggestions as to what future "digital scholarship in history," building on their own pioneering work, "might concentrate on":

· how to present narrative more effectively
· how to represent event and change
· how to analyze language more precisely
· how to create visualizations as compelling and complete as narrative

In the first, second, and fourth of these suggestions, Thomas and Ayers are really talking about how to produce maximally effective propaganda. As for the third suggestion, their article is not a good model of precise analysis. They do insist that their article "takes advantage of the [digital] medium's possibilities for precision" (*AHR* 1302). If this is precision, one wonders what imprecision is.

Since, as any historical epistemologist knows, "evidence" does not exist independently, we must avoid the solecism of equating *information* with *evidence*. Information becomes evidence only when used in the service of an argument that seeks to show that the information in question supports or undermines some claim. The ideologically oriented historian avoids asking the question, "How can the claims I am making be supported or undermined?" Rather, she *assumes* that her claims are true, or at least socially useful, and then attempts to present them as "effectively" and in as "compelling" a form as possible. The historian who is concerned with historical knowledge and with the retrenching of error proceeds differently. This historian assumes that her claims are legitimately in question. This historian knows that she needs to offer arguments (not just summaries of arguments) for holding her claims to be true. This historian is always asking what evidence supports each claim that she makes. Such inquiry imposes an intellectual discipline that encourages precision. But Thomas and Ayers deliberately separate the claims they make from the historical data, previous historiography, and analysis that would be needed to support them.[12] It is hardly surprising that, having unburdened themselves of the discipline of arguing with real or imagined critics, they should fall into imprecision.

In recent years it has become fashionable to insist that *history is narrative*—that it is just a matter of telling a story. It is certainly true that by far the greater part of historical writing is primarily narrative in character. Indeed, in a broad sense (to be explicated in chapter 4), almost all history—not just the greater part—is narrative. But history is not *only* narrative. The French classical historian and historical theorist Paul Veyne has suggested that history is "a truthful narrative."[13] Let us insist here on the word *truthful*, which does not mean "true" in any absolute sense, but does mean "justified," by a mode of justification appropriate to history. The alternative to the view that history is truthful narrative is one form or another of history-as-propaganda.

I am not asserting that the broad claims of Thomas and Ayers in their *American Historical Review* article are false. Rather, I am asserting that the authors fail to justify those claims. Instead, in their journey through "The Valley of the Shadow," they ask us to accept their broad claims on faith. (By "broad claims," I mean, for example, the claims that slavery was "more central than we thought" and that it had a "determining influence" on the whole of the South. As for the specific factual information that they organize and reproduce, I have no reason to doubt that the 1860 census, for example, actually reports what Thomas and Ayers say that it reports.) The critical historian is a bit handicapped by the imprecision of these broad claims: what exactly do Thomas and Ayers *mean* when they say that slavery was "more central than we have thought" and when they say that it had a "determining influence"? It is also unclear what they have added to the existing historical literatures on nineteenth-century United States history. (A likely reaction among specialists is that, beyond their descriptions of Augusta and Franklin counties, they have added nothing—that their broad claims are already accepted by most historians in their field.) Thomas and Ayers assert in only a muted way that their work on the coming of the Civil War is original: by their own account, they are saying only that slavery was "more central" to the Civil War than previous historians thought (thus these previous historians must have seen slavery as *somewhat* central). Clearly, Thomas and Ayers do not think that their work makes its contribution at this substantive level. Instead, and very emphatically, they claim that they have pioneered a wonderful new way of doing historical scholarship.

Does this claim stand up? If the historian has an obligation to offer arguments and justifications for the claims she wishes to make, it does not. If, on the other hand, the historian is obligated only to write interesting and socially useful narratives, one might reach a different conclusion. But would it be good to do so? Let us imitate Natalie Davis and engage in a thought experiment. Thomas and Ayers's central substantive claim is that, with regard to the United States Civil War, slavery "made the differences," to evoke the title of their work. Imagine, now, Nazi Germany in 1935, but with a computer technology like ours. Propagandists for the regime would be assigned the task of demonstrating that "the Jews are the source of our misfortune [*die Juden sind unser Unglück*]." Vast reams of data would show how Jews dominate large sectors of the economy and culture far in disproportion to their numbers. Such claims would be very persuasively made, with a huge digital archive putting all the wealth of German Jewry on display. And thus the case would be "proved." How, on an epistemological level, would this hypothetical exercise in digital history diverge from the mode of scholarship now being recommended by the *American Historical Review*? My claim is that, fundamentally, there is no difference. Of course, we might object that these Third Reich propagandists were immoral and self-deceived. But what we want and need is a historiography that will stand up independently of the morality, good will, sense of political responsibility, and so on of the historian and scholar. We can have this kind of history only if we pay serious attention to issues of historical epistemology. The alternative is to bring in tests for morality, benevolence, correct political orientation, and so on for historians or would-be historians. Were such tests to become general, historical scholarship would be finished.

My premise in this book is that historians have an obligation to argue in a clear way. Clear argument includes putting the evidence where it belongs, engaging in conceptual and counterfactual argument where it is required, and always attempting to match the strength of one's claims to the strength of the evidence supporting them. Hypothesis and speculation are acceptable in a work of history—indeed, they are unavoidable (as several chapters in this book attempt to show). But hypothesis and speculation must be so identified, and we need good intellectual reasons for their presence. Anything else is hype.

True historians have adhered to my view for a long time: I claim no originality here. It was the view of Herodotus, the teller of competing stories whose truth he held in suspense. It was the view of Thucydides, the paragon of factual research. (Scholars traditionally believe that after his fellow Athenians exiled him in 424 BCE, he spent a good deal of time traveling, in order to consult what documents there were and to interview war veterans.) The professionalization of historical writing that began in the early nineteenth century emphasized rules of historical method—both formalized rules and rules of thumb. In many areas of the profession these rules still hold sway. To be sure, historians are among the most untheoretical of scholars, and so the rules are often not articulated in an explicit way. But they are *lived* by any historian or group of historians who subject their draft manuscripts to the methodological criticism that professional colleagues—at their best—can provide.

All this is known—at least, it is known to many. It was known to those older generations of historians who gained their sense of historical method from traditional historical seminars, or who learned rules of method from social science. (Social science method is not quite historical method, but it can teach historians much.) The present book is not addressed to such dinosaurs, but to a younger generation, a generation that, if it obtained any epistemological guidance at all, obtained it by default from Michel Foucault—a historian-philosopher whose brilliance and originality are undeniable, but whose insistence that knowledge is nothing but a manifestation of power is a simplifying and ultimately very dangerous claim. To those who are persuaded by Foucault's version of anti-epistemology, or who, independently of Foucault, believe that history is and ought to be a mode of propaganda and cheerleading, I can say little. In short, I address this book not to those who already know the true historian's devotion to letting the chips fall where they may, nor to those who see themselves as cheerleaders. Rather, I intend it for the as yet uninitiated, as an introduction to the issues that are at stake.

PART I

Memory

History with Memory, History without Memory

Many people just naturally assume that history ought to be a form of memory. They assume that a central task of history-writing—maybe even *the* task—is to preserve and carry forward memory. The assumption has ancient precedent. In the first sentence of his *History,* Herodotus tells us that he wrote his work so that "time may not draw the color from what man has brought into being, nor those great and wonderful deeds, manifested by both Greeks and barbarians, fail of their report."[1]

The assumption that history equates to memory persists today, in various and conflicted ways. Consider two examples akin to that of Herodotus, in that both are concerned with the memory of war. In 1994–95 a controversy exploded over an exhibit proposed by the Smithsonian Institution commemorating the dropping of the atomic bomb on Japan fifty years earlier. The original exhibit, scheduled to open in May 1995, was canceled when veterans' groups, political and cultural commentators, and politicians objected to the interpretation that it offered of the war and its ending. The question at issue in the public debate was whether President Truman was justified in using atomic bombs against Japan. Critics of the planned exhibit charged that it failed to emphasize that Japan had been the aggressor in the war, that it failed to make clear the reasons for using the bomb, and that it emphasized Japanese suffering over the suffering of those whom the Japanese had attacked. On another level, the controversy between veterans' groups and their defenders on the one hand and the Smithsonian on the other had to do with issues of memory. Whose memories were to be valued in this exhibit—those of American veterans or those of Japanese bomb victims? Relatedly, should memory give way to the later constructions of historians and museum professionals?[2] Powerful forces in the culture held that it should not. A similar demand for the right kind of memory arose from the Vietnam War and led in the early 1980s to conflicts over the

National Vietnam Veterans Memorial. At the time, Maya Lin's proposed design for the memorial failed to satisfy the sensibilities of many veterans and veterans' organizations, some of whom condemned it as a "black gash of shame."[3] Similar complaints and demands have arisen and will no doubt continue to arise out of the attack on the World Trade Center and out of the "war against terrorism" that followed.

A common, current question is, Who owns history?[4] It is an astoundingly inadequate question. In many instances, what is really being asked is, Who has the right to control what "we" remember about the past? Or, to put this another way, Whose "political, social, and cultural imperatives" will have predominance at any given moment in the representation of the past?[5] The demand that the past should be remembered *in the right way* is an insistent one, and historians are expected to do their part, by those who pay them and by those who feel that their own political, social, and cultural "imperatives" are the deserving ones. To shift our focus now from a past that has allegedly been wrongly remembered to one supposedly forgotten, some people say that the Germans in the first generation or two after World War II, and the Japanese even today, suppressed and continue to suppress the memory of the atrocities that their nations carried out in the course of that war.[6] They also say that what the Germans needed, and what the Japanese still need, was and is memory—the more, the better. Some suggest, further, that historians should be engaged in the task of making up the "deficit of memory" that exists in such situations. So conceived, history would be primarily a continuation of memory—in this case, the continuation of memories that, for one or another reason, have been cast aside.

MEMORY VERSUS HISTORY

Something like the opposite of these claims is closer to being true: that is, far from being a continuation of memory, true history stands almost in opposition to memory. In other words, it is a mistake to hold, as many people do these days, that the central function of history is to preserve and carry forward memory. To be sure, history and memory have been linked together for a long time, as we see from Herodotus. But Herodotus's memory is not the same as memory in the modern dispensation. With Herodotus, and with historians operating in a similar mode in later times, the "memory" that is in play is subsequent people's memories of deeds done in the past. We gain these "memories" through engagement with the works of historians, who offer accounts of the way things were. But in the modern dispensation a new kind of "memory" has come dramatically into play. (Some might call it a "postmodern" kind of memory, although the term *postmodern,* because it is vague, protean, and likely to become entangled in polemics, must be used with caution.) In this new view, memory is an object of value in its own right, not simply a way to gain or keep a greater knowledge of the past than we would have without it.

The new, memory-valuing dispensation has an affinity with something we do see in Herodotus, namely, his tendency to become fascinated by the sense-making stories that his interlocutors in different cultures told him. Herodotus loved to repeat these stories. He found them interesting in themselves and also for the light they shed on how the people who told them saw the world and how they behaved in it. But he was not interested in memory as such. He was interested in understanding how other peoples saw the world and in how the world actually was. He wanted to recover and to tell us about the "marvellous deeds" carried out by both the Greeks and the Persians during the conflict between them. He was interested in the deeds themselves—not in the mode of their remembering. Second, as he also says at the beginning of his *History,* he wanted to show "the reason why they fought one another." In short, his focus was on the reality of the deeds and on the real background to the war that called those deeds forth.

Much of the preoccupation with memory as an object of value—indeed, as an object of reverence—in the recent past emerged as a response to the events that we now call the Holocaust, or Shoah. A preoccupation with memory arose in this context in the wake of the recognition, which became intense by the 1970s, that soon all survivors of the Holocaust would be dead. Accordingly, if victims' recollections of their own experiences of being victimized by the machinery of the Holocaust were to be preserved, they had to be preserved soon. Archives of audio- and (later) videotapes were set up for this purpose by Yad Vashem in Israel, by Yale University, and (most famously, if belatedly) by the filmmaker Steven Spielberg.[7] The collection of the testimonies of "witnesses" and "survivors" went far beyond what would be needed for historians' reconstructions of past events. It is not simply that there are so many testimonies (more than fifty thousand in the Spielberg archive alone) that each additional testimony is unlikely to contribute anything to historical understanding. After all, there is always the chance that, beyond all expectation, the next piece of evidence might provide a surprising insight into what happened. The problem is rather that the testimony gives a far from adequate account of what happened. The events were deeply traumatic and often glimpsed in circumstances where careful observation was impossible. Moreover, many of the testimonies were collected decades after the events being described, so that the memories could both fade and undergo modification by dint of rethinking and retelling. It is well known that even testimony collected right after the events being recollected has to be treated with great caution.[8] When time is added, the situation usually becomes worse. People become unable to distinguish between what they actually saw and what they only heard about. They also incorporate into what they think were their own memories information that only became available later. To take only one instance, the survivor testimony presented in Israel in 1986 in the trial of the former concentration camp guard John Demjanjuk turned out to be wrong on many points. It is all but certain that Demjanjuk was not, as the prosecution claimed, the cruel and demonic "Ivan the Terrible" of the Treblinka camp. The witnesses who were certain that he was were wrong.[9]

In fact, the massive collecting of Holocaust testimonies has little if anything to do with establishing a more accurate record of the Holocaust. Rather, the testimonies are collected because they have come to be seen as having something of the character of sacred relics. In *The Holocaust in American Life,* historian Peter Novick has written tellingly of the "sacralization" of the Holocaust that occurred after the mid-1960s.[10] The sacredness of what is being recounted justifies the massive number of testimonies that have been collected. The sacral character of the testimonies also makes their unreliability as evidence irrelevant. From such a perspective it does not matter that a videotaped testimony offered half a century after the end of World War II, in response to questions posed by an interviewer who most likely knows little of the place and time about which the witness speaks (possibly not even knowing the language or languages in which the events unfolded), can hardly be said to contribute to historical knowledge. The ritual of the gathering, preserving, and reception of the testimony, not its evidential content, is the important thing.

This kind of testimony-collecting is far from the Western (or perhaps any) tradition of history-writing. It is far from Herodotus, who was certainly interested in how a number of peoples culturally distant from the Greeks perceived the world. It is even farther from Herodotus's successor, counterpart, and competitor, Thucydides. Thucydides insisted that he was concerned with recounting what *really* happened in the past, and he made a special point of his desire to avoid "the unreliable streams of mythology." (Thucydides used the word *muthodes,* which means "legendary" or "fabulous"; it is derived from *muthos,* which variously means "speech," "report," "plot," and "story" and, as already noted, is related to our word *myth*.[11]) Early in his book Thucydides complains that people are inclined to accept the first story that they hear. Determined to get at the actual truth, he "made it a principle not to write down the first story that came my way, and not even to be guided by my own general impressions." Rather, he resolved to write only about events in which he himself had participated, or about those of which he had knowledge "from eye-witnesses whose reports I have checked with as much thoroughness as possible"—for he was deeply aware of the fact that "different eye-witnesses give different accounts of the same events, speaking out of partiality for one side or the other or else from imperfect memories."[12]

In other words, memory was not something that Thucydides found interesting for its own sake. Rather, it functioned as his most important source of evidence. He interviewed eyewitnesses, gathering their memories of the events of the war, and then, if we can trust his account, he attempted to check those recollections against each other, against what he himself had seen, and presumably against whatever other sources he could find. For Thucydides, in short, it was not a matter of preserving memory at all. If anything, it was a matter of *correcting* memory, including his own, by using the defective memories of all as a check against the defective memories of each. Thus the historian uses memory in order to get beyond it. This was not only Thucydides's view—until recently, it was also unquestioned in the mainstream of professional historical scholarship.[13]

In contrast, the new, memory-oriented dispensation promotes what I call a "double positive" focus on memory. I label it "double positive" because it values memory in two ways. First, it values the recollections of past historical actors and sufferers "for their own sake"—that is, quite independently of their accuracy. Second, it values our knowledge of these recollections, a knowledge viewed not as cold and distant, but as itself a form of memory, one that links past, present, and future in a common framework of recollection. Memory-oriented historiography is a special case of a more general category that we can think of as *affirmative* historiography—affirmative because its fundamental aim is to praise the particular tradition or group whose history and experiences it is recounting. It seems clear that we must have an affirmative relation to a particular tradition—a wish to support that tradition, to be its friend and promoter—in order to feel justified in undertaking the considerable effort of collecting the memories of participants in past events simply for the purpose of preserving them for the present and future. Note that I am not claiming that such an activity is illegitimate. I am only claiming that it is deceptive, even dishonest, not to present it for what it is, namely, an exercise in piety. Both producers and consumers of history need to be aware that the cognitive value (or lack of value) of such recollection is an issue that is entirely separate from the emotional and existential impact that it may well have on us.

Memory-oriented, affirmative historiography is a version of the "ordinary" or "vulgar" understanding of history that Heidegger identifies and discusses in a late section of *Being and Time*.[14] We need not worry here about the technicalities of Heidegger's view of history, for my basic point is simple. Affirmative historiography subordinates the past to the projects that human beings are engaged in now. It lacks a critical stance on the memories it collects and on the tradition it supports. Indeed, it not only lacks a critical stance on its favored memories and traditions but actually tends toward a mythification of them. (Here Heidegger's "falling" for National Socialism offers a negative lesson of considerable importance.) To focus on past historical actors' memories "for their own sake" (that is, to see the memories as valuable in themselves), and to think of historical research and writing as offering a continuation of such memories, is to put in abeyance the kind of critical procedure of which Thucydides was perhaps the first practitioner.

Should a central task of history-writing be the preserving and carrying forward of memory? We might think so, from the way the task of history is presented by politicians, school authorities, the popular media, and some historians. But my argument here is that history ought rather to counter the harmful effects of an excessive preoccupation with memory. The failure on the part of some people in some countries to come to terms with aspects of their own pasts is not best thought of as amounting to a "deficit of memory" that ought to be corrected by the addition of more memory. The first problem with such a view is epistemological. However we define *memory*—and it has a considerable range of commonly accepted meanings—it does seem to have, as Collingwood has suggested, the character of being "immediate." In other words, if a person sincerely asserts "I remember that P," we have no adequate grounds for challenging the assertion: we pretty much have to accept that this is indeed what the person remembers. History is different, for here we must bring evidence into play. As Collingwood memorably puts it, to say that I remember writing a letter to So-and-so is "a statement of memory" and not a "historical statement": whereas if I can add, "I am right, for here is his reply," I am talking history.[15] Admittedly, we might want to attenuate in some degree Collingwood's sharp distinction between history and memory as being too insensitive to the emotional force of memory in human life. But the undeniable importance of memory for our individual and collective lives as they are actually lived does not justify the claim that history should be equated with memory.

This leads us to a second problem, which is both existential and practical. This second problem is, in addition, a manifestation in real life of the epistemological distinction between history and memory. It is clear that in many situations people suffer not from a deficit of so-called memory but from too much of it. Most notably, the "memory" of allegedly ancient conflicts often feeds into and intensifies violent conflict in the present. Consider the role of "memory" in the Israeli-Palestinian conflict, in the Balkans, and in northern Ireland, to take only three examples. When "memory" comes up against "memory" in such situations, people are all too often stuck in a contest of memories that is without issue and that cannot be adjudicated in any clear way. It is important for historians not to join in such contests of "memory." In most cases, the contests are unresolvable: one group "remembers" in this way, another in that way. But what is more important is that these contests are, or ought to be, irrelevant to whatever *real* issues lie at hand. The real issues almost always pertain not to ancestral conflicts, real or imagined, but to differences in the present and in the recent past. The emphasis on memory in these fields of conflict is something that historians should certainly take note of, but it is not something that they ought to emulate. For memory both abets such conflicts and is a symptom of failure on the part of the people involved to deal with the causes of conflict in the actual situation within which they live.

We can, of course, find situations where a deficit of historical *knowledge* has prevailed and has discouraged a confrontation with the real issues of the present. One of those issues is how to deal with the residue of past crimes. In the year 2000 I spent six months living in Austria, and I could not fail to notice the case of Dr. Heinrich Gross, a Viennese physician who was responsible for euthanizing a large number of handicapped children during World War II. After the war he had a long and lucrative career as a professor at the University of Vienna and as a well-paid psychiatric expert witness in the Vienna court system.[16] Although his background was known to people in positions of authority, this did not harm his career. A serious attempt to bring him to justice came about only in the late 1990s. Was the failure of the courts to deal with the Gross case in a timely and effective way, and the failure of Austrian historians to notice this or other instances of Austrian collaboration in Nazi crimes, the result of a "deficit of memory"? No. These linked failures do not in any sense result from a lack of memory. In the Gross case, there was a good deal of memory present, both on the side of Gross's protectors and on the side of surviving relatives of the murdered children. Rather, the essential problem was a *critical* failure—primarily a critical failure on the part of the Austrian historical profession.

No doubt this failure resulted in part from decisions made outside the historical profession, concerning funding and appointments to professorships (historical research requires financial underpinning if it is to be carried out well, or even at all). But these decisions were clearly not made entirely outside the historical profession, which in Austria as in other countries tends to be closely—sometimes too closely—intertwined with everyday politics. One function of the historical profession is to resist the political commonplaces of the day wherever they come from and to investigate the past with rigorous care and accuracy, letting the chips fall where they may. Obviously, this does not always happen. In any case, the failure of either the Austrian legal system or historians of Austria to address adequately the case of Dr. Heinrich Gross was not the result of a lack of memory. Influential people in Vienna had all too much memory concerning the outlines (although not, perhaps, the details) of what had happened. Many people in Austria were eager to maintain the myth that Austria was innocent of the crimes of the Third Reich.[17] There was a deep disinclination to delve too deeply—or at all—into what had actually been done in Austria and by Austrians during World War II. Had the real past been brought out and confronted, it would have been possible much earlier to see what sort of judicial and political action was needed in order to put Austria's Nazi crimes definitively into the past.

To be sure, without the faculty of memory there would be no history. This is manifest in at least two ways. First, historical investigation and writing are closely tied up with the experience of temporality, a point that Paul Ricoeur has made emphatically. Without the human experience of time—without the sense, at the most elementary level, of a distinction between what happened before, what is happening now, and what will happen afterward—there could be no historical writing. And it is also clear that the human experience of time could not exist without memory. Indeed, we might say that memory is one mode of our experience of time—the mode of our experience of time that is focused on the past. Thus memory makes a basic conceptual precondition of history-writing possible for us, since without memory we would have no experience of time, and without the experience of time, we could not situate events and "existents" in the past, as distinguished from an actual or eternal present.[18] Second, history and memory are related at the level of content. Among other things, history deals with historical facts. (History also deals with perspectives or interpretations, but we can leave this matter, which I address later, aside here.) The registering of facts in historical records, and the registering of the facts conveyed by the records within the minds of historians, would be impossible without memory.

However, to say that memory is history's *conditio sine qua non* is not to say that memory is a foundation of history, let alone that it is *the* foundation. It is deceptively easy to leap from the first kind of claim to the second. Thus it is common to see memory as the source or root of history, and to regard history as starting out from memory and in some sense never leaving the terrain of what memory offers it. This is the position that Jacques Le Goff appears to take in his book *History and Memory,* when he characterizes memory as "the raw material" of history and suggests that "mental, oral, or written, it is the living source from which historians draw."[19] To this, we must say "yes, but," for it is potentially very dangerous to take memory as the sole source of historical facts. Consider the following: It is well known that the "memories" (that is, the testimonies) of Holocaust survivors are marked by inaccuracies—some trivial, some not so trivial. As noted already, students of evidence have long been aware of the unreliability even of immediate eyewitness accounts of events. It is also well known that memories change as time passes and as rememberers become more distant from the events they recount and more influenced by things they heard or read later. It is easy for rememberers to be wrong about details, for example, about the precise location or number of gas chambers or crematory ovens. Rememberers also have a tendency to integrate into their memories of events facts or interpretations that only became available after the events themselves occurred. If we overvalue memory, we open the door to bad-faith attempts to use the errors of recollection that inevitably go along with memory to discredit *completely* what the rememberers are saying. This has been a favorite tactic of Holocaust deniers. Accordingly, there are pragmatic grounds for avoiding an overemphasis on memory.

There is also a well-developed theoretical argument against relying too heavily on memory—or, more accurately, on the testimonies by which memories are articulated and made known to others. The modern historical tradition distinguishes two basic types of historical evidence. Although they exist on a continuum, they are readily distinguishable from each other on a conceptual level. The conceptual distinction is one that no self-respecting historian can avoid making: there are historical *traces* and historical *sources*. A trace is anything remaining from the past that was not made with the intention of revealing the past to us, but simply emerged as part of normal life. A source, on the other hand, is anything that was intended by its creator to stand as an account of events. This second category of evidence, which we might also call "testimony," clearly relies more heavily on memory than do traces.[20]

It is easy for persons unaccustomed to thinking clearly about theory and method to underestimate the role that nonintentional evidence plays in historical research and writing. An example of a trace in its pure form would be the wear visible on two sets of steps leading to different doorways, which would allow us to make inferences as to the relative number of people using each entrance (just such an inference plays a role in one of the Sherlock Holmes stories).[21] The train schedules produced by the directing office of a railway system are another, less obvious, example of nonintentional evidence. Unlike the writers of, say, medieval annals, the people who work up these schedules do not do so with the intention of leaving a historical record. They do so, rather, because schedules are necessary in order to move trains around efficiently and without having them crash into each other. Although such records were not constructed with the intention of allowing subsequent historians to reconstruct the operations of the railway, historians can in fact do this. Thus central European train schedules during World War II count as evidence of the Holocaust, even though the makers of these schedules certainly did not intend them to serve this purpose. A later historian, reading a schedule from September 1942, can see that a train was sent full to an obscure siding in Poland and that it was empty when it left the siding. The historian can then make inferences from these facts.[22] The inferences have nothing to do with anyone's testimony. Here it is not memory but the inadvertent remnants of the past that stand as the "raw material" of history.

Normally, both kinds of evidence—inadvertent and intentional—enter into the construction of a historical account. Although the point may seem counterintuitive, there is a sense in which inadvertent evidence is a far more solid foundation for historical knowledge than is the evidence that people in the past have intended to stand as evidence. The reason is that a source is inevitably mixed up with past people's conceptions and misconceptions as to what was happening, whereas a trace, at least in its pure form, is devoid of such admixture. Sources are always already interpretations of events, whereas traces are not. To be sure, "traces" do not offer us facts in a pure state—nothing does. But by virtue of being only inadvertently evidence, traces are insulated from people's conscious or unconscious wishes to remember and testify in a particular way. Memory lacks this kind of objectivity.

HISTORY AND THE PRESENT

Yet it would be too simple to stop our reflections at this point, for history involves wider matters than simply establishing historical facts accurately. Facts are important, but they are only one aspect of a good historical account. A central feature of any historical account worthy of the name is its attempt to situate facts within a larger framework. To put this another way: historical accounts deal in *part-whole relations*. A fact may be considered a "part," and the part is meaningless unless it is situated within larger frameworks that give it meaning. Such frameworks are partially rooted in the historian's present world. One question that we must ask when trying to articulate a notion of historical thinking is, In what specific ways can historical accounts be related to the present world? Here I want to argue that it is best to think of history-writing as something that can be oriented in three possible ways to the present world. Two of these are close to being polar opposites; the third is something of a synthesis between the two.

One polar position sees history-writing as having the function of binding together and affirming the community, group, *Volk,* state, nation, religion, political commitment, and so on out of which it arises. The opposing position sees history as having a primarily critical and negating function with regard to the community out of which it arises and the past that it studies. Between a historiography that affirms and a historiography that engages in critique, there is a third, didactic position that seeks to guide the *Volk,* or the flock, in the direction of a better future. It might be expected that I would choose the middle, didactic position as my own, because of its attempt to mediate between the other two positions, those of affirmation and critique. But in view of the weight of the present (and of the past that is attached to it), history ought in fact to chart out a critical role for itself. Didactic historiography is an honorable but underjustified attempt to make history do what it does not have the authority to do, that is, be preceptor as well as critic.

My opting for a critical over an affirmative or didactic historiography in part accounts for the weight that I give to various distinctions that bring a certain clarity and directness to the matter of understanding the past (in contrast, affirmative and didactic approaches are inclined to leave in darkness, even to deliberately hide, the framework of assumptions and justifications by which they operate). Most important, if we opt for a critical historiography, we *must* distinguish history from memory. Obviously, memory is not simply the reproduction of the past—far from it. So we cannot claim that memory is passive—on the contrary, it is an active faculty, as we know from the forcefully creative way in which it orients itself toward known facts of the past. But it is not a critical or reflective faculty, as becomes glaringly obvious when different "memories" come into conflict with each other (as tends to happen whenever, for example, different ethnic groups—Israelis and Palestinians, Serbs and Croats, Bosnian Serbs and Bosnian Muslims, and so on—manufacture different "historical" justifications for their own dominance). At the level of memory itself, the conflict of *different* memories cannot be adjudicated.[23] The critical resolution between conflicting memories can only come at a different level, where criteria other than mnemonic ones are deployed. To put this another way: memory cannot be its own critical test. The criticism must come from outside memory. The criticism of "memories," insofar as it makes claims about history and about the relation of this supposed history to the present, can only come from methodologically sound historical research, and from a thinking that is sensitive to the relevance—*and irrelevance*—of that research for present issues.

But we must distinguish not only between history and memory. We must distinguish also between different concepts that in recent discussion have been promiscuously blurred together under the single rubric, "memory" (which explains why I have at times enclosed *memory* in quotation marks). The basic sense of memory is what we can call the "experiential" sense. In its experiential sense, "historical memory" denotes the experience of people who actually went through the historical events under discussion. More accurately, historical memory denotes the *recovery* and *conversion into narrative* of that experience. (Thus, only people who were actually affected, in the period 1933–45, by the machinery of the Holocaust can be said to have a "memory" of the Holocaust in the experiential sense of the term *memory*.) Obviously, some of the interest in historical memory that has emerged over the last quarter century treats memory in this sense. The videotaping of interviews with Holocaust survivors amounts in major part to preserving the memory of the experience of being caught up in the Holocaust. As already noted, this massive videotaping has almost nothing to do with the project of collecting more evidence about the workings of the Holocaust. It is the experience *itself* that is the focus of attention.[24] Lest anyone think that the Holocaust is an entirely special case, we should note that a concern with memory, and with experience as memory's ultimate object, also enters significantly into other current genres of history, including "history from below," history of everyday life, and the dominant versions of cultural history, wherein the focus is on the process of culture far more than on its content.

Use of the term *memory* to designate accounts offered by participants of their experience of the past is entirely legitimate. So also, in its proper context, is another term widely used in current historical discussion—*collective memory*. Properly speaking, a collective memory is what arises when a number of people experience the same set of historical events. These people can then be said to have a "collective" memory of those events, not in the sense of a memory that exists supra-individually—for there is no such thing as memory apart from individuals—but in the sense that each person has, within his or her own mind and within her own reports, an image, or gestalt, of an experience that other people also underwent. Moreover, these images, or gestalten, overlap in large degree—otherwise the memory would not be "collective." Survivors of the Holocaust can thus be said to have had a collective memory of their experience of what only later—during the 1960s—came to be known as the Holocaust. Each of their accounts of that experience was different, but most accounts narrativized the same general set of events in quite similar ways. The same will no doubt be true of the many people who experienced, in one way or another, the events of September 11, 2001.[25]

The question that concerns us here is not whether we can justify an interest in how people experienced the historical past or in how they have preserved their experience in memories and testimonies. The answer to that question is obvious. Rather, the question is what the historian's attitude toward these historical memories should be. Here we find an interesting distinction among four different attitudes toward historical memory, or—perhaps more accurately—among four different ways of *using* historical memory. Three of these fit inside the field of historical research and writing; the fourth goes beyond historical research and writing into different territory.

First, historical memory—or, more accurately, the narrations of the past that rememberers have produced—can serve the historian as evidence for what objectively happened in the past—that is, for what happened in the form of externally observable events. After all, historians use both "traces" *and* "sources" in their constructions or reconstructions of the past. "Memory," in the form of participants' recollections, is one kind of source for the historian's building of an account of the past. Sometimes memory is important in providing historical evidence that would otherwise be unavailable. Thus, witnesses' accounts might be virtually the only evidence we have of an uprising in a *Vernichtungslager* (extermination camp). Still, it is better when this kind of evidence can be checked against nonintentional evidence.

Second, historical memory can serve the historian as evidence for how the past was experienced by the people who later recorded their memories. In other words, the historian might shift her attention from what happened in the past in the form of externally visible events to what went on in the minds and feelings of the people who were involved. In short, the historian would attempt to construct or reconstruct *the experience of historical participants* (in such and such a set of historical events). Ideally, this sort of historical investigation, focused on participants' experience, needs to be brought into dialogue with other forms of historical investigation focused on such things as structural and material conditions and determinants, philosophical and religious assumptions and commitments, scientific theories, technical practices, views as to the best way of organizing political and social life, and so on.

Third, historical memory can serve the historian as an object of historiographic attention in its own right. That is, the historian can focus, not on the externally visible events of the past, and not on the experience of participants, but instead on participants' ways of remembering their experiences later—for which, of course, the recorded memories *themselves* are the evidence. Clearly, how people have remembered the past is also a legitimate object of historical investigation, and this is so independently of the question as to whether their remembrances are accurate.

Fourth, there is a way of approaching the recorded memories of past events that takes us beyond the ambit of the historian. Here, the recorded memories of past events—or, more accurately, the narratives based on those memories—become something akin to objects of religious veneration. They become valued objects in their own right. We see this development above all in relation to memories of the Holocaust, but something of the same sort has certainly happened in other contexts as well.

When veneration comes in, memory in its basic, experiential sense tips over into something different: *memory* becomes *commemoration*. I take memory generally to be a matter of the carrying forward into the future of the personal experience either of individuals or of groups of individuals who underwent a common experience of some sort. Memory begins in a more or less spontaneous remembering of lived experience. While memory and commemoration are closely akin, they are also sharply different. Whereas memory is a by-product of past experience, commemoration is something *willed in the present*. Commemoration arises in the desire of a community, existing now, to affirm its communality and commonality, strengthening its bonds through a shared orientation to past events, or, more accurately, through a shared orientation to a *representation* of past events.

The events in question may or may not have actually occurred. It is no accident that commemoration is an important element in some religions: consider Passover in the Jewish tradition and Christmas and Easter in the Christian tradition. Commemoration is about holding together a community, the community of the commemorators. Some commentators, taking seriously the etymological link between *religio* and *religare* (to bind), see religion's function as the preservation of community. In this view, commemoration has close affinities with religion.

CONFLICTING ATTITUDES TOWARD THE PAST

Should historical research and writing have this same binding function? That is, should historical research and writing have as an important function the binding together of a human community by the affirmation of its (possibly mythic) common experiences? Should history, in other words, be fundamentally affirmative of the community from which it arises? This is an important question, and one that appears in a different light in different times and places. It is tempting to say that, yes, of course history should have an affirming function. It is tempting to say this because, *as a matter of fact,* the historical discipline has generally affirmed the political order that pays its bills. Affirmation of the community out of which it emerges seems to be a permanent concomitant of organized historical writing. The only thing that appears to change is the particular emphasis and direction of the affirmation.

The discipline of history in the nineteenth century was closely connected with the extension of the power of the European nation-state. In Germany, France, and England, as well as in the United States, the newly professionalized discipline of history tended to serve as an ideological support for the state: in the German-speaking lands, for the Prussian state and its extension (or, alternatively, for its competitors); for the secularly-based French republic, with its *mission civilisatrice,* that emerged after France's defeat by Prussia in 1871; for England and its Empire in the same period; and for the national and then imperial pretensions of the United States as well. In each case there was a "master narrative" that was seen as running through the nation's history—the master narrative of the nation's movement from its early beginnings, through the rise of national self-consciousness, to its current struggle for recognition and success. Behind the master narratives, there lay a larger "grand narrative"—a secularized version of the Christian narrative of pristine origin, struggle, and ultimate salvation.[26]

The relative solidity of these master and grand narratives gave historical writing a particular shape and feel. Except for those historians who stood outside the disciplinary framework (one thinks especially of the Swiss cultural historian and art connoisseur Jacob Burckhardt), the focus was overwhelmingly on political history of a particular kind. The dominant story was the story of the increasing actualization of freedom. Sometimes the story was told in a liberal register, with emphasis placed on the increasing freedom of the individual to pursue his private interests and to have a voice in the running of the state; sometimes it was told in a conservative or authoritarian register, with emphasis placed on cultural cultivation (*Bildung*) and on the freedom and power of the state itself. What is obvious today is that these variant master narratives, and the grand narrative that underpins them, are lacking in essential authority. Indeed, they have been lacking in essential authority from roughly the time that it began to dawn on people that the war of 1914 was turning into a vast slaughterhouse. To be sure, we cannot say that *nobody* believes in the old grand and master narratives any more. For example, I am often struck by the extent to which many Americans still believe in the great American narrative of the "city upon a hill" that stands as the "last best hope of mankind"—"the hope of the world," as President Nixon once put it.[27] But for most people who think about such matters—and even for many people who do not—neither the old national master narratives nor the grand narrative of freedom and *Bildung* is persuasive any more. Instead there prevails what Jean-François Lyotard has called an "incredulity" toward such overarching narratives.[28]

In the absence of belief in an authoritative narrative of human advance, one finds a number of attitudes toward the past circulating in contemporary culture, especially in contemporary American culture (see fig. 1.1). Each of these attitudes is a way of denying or evading history. Prominent is an attitude of historical nescience, or unknowingness, which might be defined as simply the absence of any explicit, or even implicit, orientation toward history. One might think of historical unknowingness, in temporal terms, as amounting to the collapse of the horizon of history into the one moment of the present. Or, in cognitive terms, one might think of it as a great discarding, where all forms of knowledge *of* the past are either ignored or deliberately cast aside as irrelevant. To be sure, one needs to make a distinction here between knowledge *of* the past and knowledge *from* the past—for knowledge *from* the past is not discarded at all, as long as it is seen as useful for action in the present. But knowledge *from* the past readily coexists with a complete ignorance as to the contexts within which knowledge taken *from* the past was previously situated.

Although it will perhaps sound condescending to reflect on historical unknowingness, I do not intend to be condescending but only factual and descriptive. The use of the term *History* in popular parlance in English to mean "dead and gone, irrelevant, passé"—as in the classic line from a "cool" 1980s television series, *Miami Vice,* "Drop that gun or you're history!"—is indicative of a wider mind-set. This mind-set is perhaps more distinctively American than non-American, and perhaps more prevalent in

HISTORICAL NESCIENCE. Ignorance or rejection of history. History, if thought about at all, is seen as the needless study of the "dead and gone."	THE AESTHESIS OF HISTORY. History is identified with beautiful (or sublime) aesthetic objects. Context is rendered as, at most, an afterthought.
HISTORY AS TRADITION. The function of history is to carry forward from the past into the future the traditions of specific groups, especially ours.	HISTORY AS: (A) MEMORY. The function of history is to promote the "memories" of specific groups, especially ours. (B) COMMEMORATION: The function of history is to assist us in honoring our dead (the "greatest generation," etc.).

FIGURE 1.1 Four ways of evading history

certain Americas than in others. One associates it with the America of the suburbs and housing developments; with the America that is addicted to television; with the resolutely optimistic America of "have a nice day, now" and of entrepreneurial get up and go. It is an old story, one of the true myths of America, the myth of pulling up one's stakes and moving westward into the wilderness that is to be conquered, leaving the old behind. And then leaving the old behind again, and again. The departures in question are not even necessarily geographical or even physical. They can be conceptual, technological, economic, political, scientific. What they have in common is a failure to think of historical experience at all, or, if there *is* thought of historical experience, a failure to attend to the contextual differences that separate past from present and that radically change the meaning of the historical particulars that are the most immediately visible aspect of the past.

Historical unknowingness is not specifically American or specifically new. Knowledge of history has surely always been, in the main, one of two things: a cultural luxury good having something of the status of an acquired taste (with some oversimplification, think Herodotus here), or else a would-be instrument for forwarding the interests and assisting in the work of actual or prospective rulers (think Thucydides and his intellectual heirs). People not in a position either to purchase such a luxury good or else to participate in the workings of power will have nescience and indifference toward history as their normal stance, at least in the absence of a grand narrative of progress or some functional equivalent to such a narrative. Grand narrative can give a justification to knowledge of the past by allowing historical particulars that otherwise would seem irrelevant to find their place in a broader story, and it can also serve as a support for the master narratives attached to particular ethnic, national, religious, and other groups. In the absence of a grand narrative able to give space and meaning to historical particulars, historical unknowingness becomes something like the normal human position.[29]

A second attitude toward the past that is present in contemporary culture (and that figures in the undermining of master and grand narrative in recent times) is one that we can designate as the *aesthesis of history*. In the real world the aesthesis of history is often closely intertwined with other, related attitudes toward history. But at the theoretical level one can define the aesthesis of history quite precisely. The aesthesis of history amounts to an aesthetic orientation toward objects that are left over from the past, or that appear *as if* they are left over from the past. These objects are seen as in some way *standing in for* the past. The fundamental orientation toward these objects is one of delight or admiration. In the aesthesis of history the focus is on the sensual aspect of the objects being contemplated. The aesthesis of history is not primarily an operation of intellectual or ethical judgment. It fosters no interest in the broader contexts within which the objects in question are situated—unless those contexts, too, can be aesthetically contemplated.

Examples are in order. The ones that I am most familiar with are close to the place where I live, Ivy, Virginia. I think of the architecture of the central core of the University of Virginia, the "Academical Village," with its Rotunda, pavilions, and student rooms all designed as an ensemble by Thomas Jefferson. I think also of Jefferson's house, Monticello. These monuments— but especially Monticello—stand out all the more because they were originally set within a largely natural environment and still bear marks of that environment today. These monuments prompt a sensuous appreciation, but one that is different from a pure, Kantian appreciation because it is tied up with the historicity that the monuments possess and that the natural environment, to all manifest appearance, does not.

In sum, the "aesthesis of history" shows itself in a positive, appreciative, orientation toward historical monuments. Such an aesthesis is to be found in the "preservation movement," which strives to preserve old buildings and to protect them from changes that are not in the spirit of their earlier use. It is to be found in the marking, throughout the United States, of such remnants from the past as old battlefields, native American ruins, and so on. Perhaps paradoxically, it is to be found in its purest form where the object of aesthetic-historical contemplation is a completely *invented* object. A paradigm case would be the reproduction of the ship "The Titanic," centerpiece of the popular movie *Titanic* (1997). Here an immense amount of effort was reportedly expended to ensure that the plates and silverware on the set were exact replicas of the tableware on the original "Titanic." Another example of the aesthesis of history would surely have been "Disney's America," the theme park that in 1994 the Walt Disney Company proposed to build four miles away from Manassas National Battlefield Park in northern Virginia, in the vicinity of Washington, D.C. Here an artificial, constructed past, which no doubt would have been much prettier and more upbeat than the original, was seen as conflicting too blatantly with the real historical events that had taken place in the vicinity—and the project was never built.[30]

A third attitude that has arisen in the wake of the collapse of the authority of grand narrative involves an identification of history with memory and with commemoration. Historical unknowingness negates history by declaring historical knowledge to be irrelevant to the life of the present and future. The aesthesis of history negates history by turning the physical furniture of the past into beautiful objects existing on a "set" that fundamentally has nothing to do with history. In both cases, there is an attempt to reduce our consciousness to the horizon of the present: in the first case, by the declared irrelevance of anything that is not *of* the present, and in the second, by the declared irrelevance of anything that cannot be presented beautifully *in* the present. The same processes are at work in the identification of history with memory and commemoration. When history becomes simply what people remember or commemorate, this amounts to a reduction of history to the framework of present thought and action. Memory tells us as much about the present consciousness of the rememberer as it does about the past. Memory is an image of the past constructed by a subjectivity in the present. It is thus itself subjective; it may also be irrational, inconsistent, deceptive, and self-serving. It has long been clear that, without independent corroboration, memory cannot serve as a reliable marker of the historical past.

A fourth attitude toward the past, likewise amounting to an evasion of history, also deserves to be considered: tradition. To a striking extent, much current talk of "memory" is really talk about tradition (with commemoration standing as a kind of middle point between the two). It is a mistake to blur together memory and tradition: a fundamental lack of clarity arises from doing so. Memory is subjective and personal; it is deeply experiential. Tradition certainly needs to be experienced in order to be possessed, but it is more than subjective and personal. It is suprasubjective; it is suprapersonal. Tradition implies, not the passing on of personal experience in its supposedly unique character and subjectivity, but something that is much more distanced from the individual, something that has a collective weight and existence *over* individuals. We must be educated *into* tradition. Each person and generation must actively appropriate tradition. It thus has a kind of distance, and a connection with a process of learning, not found in the notion of memory.

History is closer to tradition than it is to memory and commemoration. With historical knowledge, matters proceed in somewhat the way they do with tradition. In one of its aspects, historiography is a ship sailing on the dark seas of time and oblivion. It is in part an active effort to resist time and oblivion. In this respect history closely resembles the workings of those kinds of religious schools in which students are taught, and come to make their own, the texts of a particular religious tradition. And yet history, in modern understandings, is *not* tradition. On the contrary, the modern European tradition of historiography arose, in the late eighteenth and early nineteenth centuries, out of a breaking up of tradition. When the grand narrative offered by religious tradition lost a large element of its authority, a space was opened for the emergence of a *discipline* of history, which stood in continuity with the religious tradition, but which nonetheless separated itself from that tradition and from tradition generally. Obviously, the claims to a kind of absolute objectivity that the nineteenth- and early twentieth-century discipline of history made cannot be sustained today. This is one reason why the boundaries between history on the one hand and memory and commemoration on the other have been obscured and why in some instances the latter have arisen almost as substitutes for history.

HISTORY'S LEGITIMATE ROLES

It is dangerous when history takes its primary cues either from the idea of preserving personal memory or from the idea of functioning as a mode of commemoration. And we ought not to view history as a form of tradition either, in spite of the affinities between history and tradition. The submergence of history into memory, commemoration, and tradition tends to wipe out history's critical function. For example, what reasonable and sensitive person could stand at the Vietnam War Memorial in Washington on Memorial Day and deliver a sustained critical account of American involvement in that ill-fated war? It would not suit the occasion. Memory and commemoration have their place, but merging history with memory and commemoration subordinates history to the mnemonic and commemorative functions. History-writing ought to be more critical of the present order than affirmative of it, and for a simple reason: most of what appears in the culture of the present already affirms that culture. We need an orientation toward the past that stands apart from the present because so much of our orientation toward the past does not. To say that historiography ought to be critical of the order that funds it is not, in the wider picture, to privilege criticism over affirmation. It is simply to recognize that affirmation thrives in the normal course of things, and criticism does not. The matter is all the more difficult in that criticism must also be critical of the received critical (or so-called critical) ideas of the present time.

In short, the blurring together of history and memory is deeply problematic. If the historian enters into the service of memory, the consciously or unconsciously self-interested and self-serving memories of individuals and groups become the final arbiter of historical knowledge. This is dangerous. The task of the historian ought to be less to preserve memory than to overcome it or at least to keep it confined. One can of course imagine historians including in their works testimonial accounts of the past by historical actors—for example, by American soldiers in World War II or in Vietnam, to take two cases where entire books filled with such testimonials have been published.[31] But clearly, historians need to proceed beyond this genre.

Should historiography be didactic? That is, should history-writing attempt to offer lessons from the past for the edification of the present? Some philosophers of history do recommend a didactic function for history. In Germany in particular—for reasons connected with the troubling reality of the Third Reich—quite a lot has been written under the general heading of "historical didactics."[32] The difficulty with the notion of a didactic function for history is that historians *qua* historians do not appear to have the authority to prescribe for the present and the future. Their expertise has to do with the construction and reconstruction of the past. Insofar as they do this work well, they are remarkably well equipped to criticize politicians, and citizens generally, who misrepresent the past in an attempt to support such and such a line of legislation or policy. For example, a historian who has written a book about the internment of Japanese-Americans during World War II would be remarkably well equipped to speak out against a politician using a distorted account of that sad policy in support of a similarly cavalier approach to civil liberties now.[33] But the historian would be ill-advised to proceed as if her own normative political preferences in the present have any grounding in the historical record. History can provide cautionary tales against political arrogance in the present. But it cannot support such and such a proposed policy. It can only show how such and such past policies pursued by a variety of historical actors played out over the course of historical time.

Relevant here is Kant's *Conflict of the Faculties* (1798).[34] In this work Kant distinguishes between the "lower," philosophical faculty, which he says ought to be devoted to the pure search for truth, and the higher faculties of law, medicine, and theology, which are intended to serve the interests of the state and community. Accordingly, the higher faculties are not allowed the pure freedom of research and teaching granted to the philosophical faculty. However, the advantage is by no means all to the philosophical faculty. The professor of theology is constrained to follow the dogma of the established state church: in this respect his freedom is restricted, whereas the freedom of the professor of philosophy is not restricted. But the professor of theology has behind him the power and authority of the established dogma. On the one hand, the professor of theology is restricted in what he can say; on the other, his prescriptive words have an authority that the words of the professor of philosophy lack.

The historian belongs more properly to Kant's philosophical faculty than to his theological faculty. To be sure, I would not say that engagement in a didactic enterprise, an enterprise of edification, is entirely beyond the pale for the historian. But such an enterprise presupposes dogmatic commitments that must be kept explicitly in mind, that should be announced up front, and that should not be confused with historical knowledge. Moreover, in Germany historical didactics has been part of an attempt to root out the remnants of National Socialism. It is thus oriented critically toward Germany's past. In the United States a didactic history is very likely to be affirmative in the course of its being didactic.

Hence—I contend—the historian ought generally to be critical in orientation. In this regard the French historian and philosopher of history Michel de Certeau offers an exemplary model. De Certeau argues that modern Western historiography is built on the notion of a breach or break between past and present. The historian cannot directly access the experience (or memories) of the past; this is an "other" to history that remains beyond comprehension. De Certeau also insists on a breach between the historian and his or her present. In a brilliant paper, he explores the complexities of "the historiographical operation," an operation whose practitioners know that their work deals with margins, discontinuities, and differences far more than it deals with continuities and similarities.[35] In this sense history is unlike "memory," which in both its experiential and its commemorative senses fosters the comforting illusion of a commonality and continuity between past and present.

Admittedly, some objection could be raised to the view of history that I offer here. When I delivered the first version of this paper as a lecture, a

Czech philosopher objected that there are certain situations—such as when the need emerges to build a new, or newly democratic, state—in which affirmative history-writing is not only permissible but necessary. But I am not persuaded that in the long term the affirmative role is a good role for history to play. It is in the first place a usurpation of and confusion with the role of tradition (and perhaps also of and with the role of religion). Second, what is essential to tradition is only loosely connected to, and not at all justified by, the historical past at all (the same applies to religion). During my early childhood years, the Canada in which I grew up (which was emphatically English Canada rather than the very distant French Canada) justified its existence in part on the basis of a traditional connection to the British Crown and to the British system of government. In retrospect, I think that what was valuable about this tradition were things that could have been, and often were, stated in the form of specific principles or claims (most often defined by contrast with the United States). One claim was that parliamentary government is superior to presidential government; another, that individual rights ought to be subjected to the test of the common good, "peace, order, and good government" offering a better guide than "life, liberty, and the pursuit of happiness."

If we view the tradition to which I am referring as amounting to a set of implicit and explicit claims, it acquires the shape of a vaguely stated political theory. It was a political theory wrapped in the clothing of an *apparently* historical narrative. This British-centered narrative could hardly stand up to serious examination, especially given the ethnic composition of the country even then, and it ended up prompting a backlash in the form of a separatist movement in Québec. But the narrative was ultimately dispensable. What was really important, and could actually be discussed in a reasonably intelligent manner, was the validity (or not) of the claims and principles. These claims and principles were not narratives concerning the past. Rather, they were guidelines or frameworks for organizing the present and future.

Surely, we ought not to look for the basis of the state in historical narratives. The problem is not just that such narratives violate the "separation" principle, namely, the principle that history worthy of the name carefully distinguishes between past and present. More compelling is that such narratives are quite likely to be defective as the basis for political systems. For example, if the real basis of the French polity is French history—*nos ancêtres les gaulois*—this may well end up excluding from the present and future France people who do not happen to look like inhabitants of ancient Gaul. In a broad sense, such a tradition might be considered a "cultural memory." But even if it were a true memory—even if it were true that the French state goes back in a continuous line to the Gauls—this would be a perhaps interesting and surprising fact, but it would be nothing on which one could legitimately base the French state now. And the same surely applies to *all* attempts to provide "historical" justification for the current order. Either the narrative will be a defective foundation for the present and future order, *or* it will be so void of legitimate historical content as to be no longer a legitimate historical narrative at all.

A critical historiography has to stand at a distance from memory in all its senses, and by the same token it must be both connected to and estranged from the present. A critical historiography does not prescribe for the present. It only shows what is different and surprising—astounding, even—in the past. If history-writing lacks the quality of surprise, it lacks scholarly, scientific justification as well. Such a history can reinvent itself as memory, or commemoration, or tradition. None of these is a bad thing in itself, but none is distinctive of historiography's project. Alternatively, such history-writing can turn into a paradigm-subservient, time-serving, unoriginal, unstimulating form of professional historiography—something to be avoided like the plague. When, to the contrary, history brings to the fore a hitherto unknown past, it causes people to see how the horizon of the present is not the horizon of all that is. In short, history both needs memory and needs to go beyond memory. If we wish to set out to write history, we must hope to find things that common understanding will see as surprising. When the historian stays within the framework of memory, confirmation rather than surprise is the likely result.

History, Memory, Identity

The terms *identity* and *memory* are in wide and contentious circulation at the present moment. Identity has been turned into a site of commitment and also of dispute and uncertainty. Not unconnectedly, memory has been seen as a privileged discourse having peculiar claims to authenticity and truth. What can the uncertainties that surround memory and identity teach us about the project of historical understanding? Conversely, what can history teach us about memory and identity?

Historical research and writing are caught between commitment to the universal and the claims made by particular identities. This seems to be one manifestation of the unresolving tension or dialectic that characterizes all truthful history.[1] The universal dimension of historical research and writing is rooted in the commitment of historians to a set of procedures designed to maximize the chances of arriving at justified historical claims and to minimize the chances of error. The particularistic dimension, which has gained some outspoken advocates in the wake of Michel Foucault and other theorists who equate knowledge with cultural power, attaches itself to the good cause in the present (we are expected to know at each moment *which* cause that is). Since historical particularism is often articulated in the language of memory, a tension is set up between history and memory. On the one hand, "history" appears as a pseudo-objective discourse that rides roughshod over particular memories and identities, which claim to have an experiential reality and authenticity that history lacks. On the other hand, memory appears as an unmeasured discourse that, in the service of desire, makes claims for its own validity that cannot be justified.

How can we square this circle? We cannot: the dialectic does not resolve. But we can arrive at some clarity concerning the history–memory tension and concerning the relation of both to identity. This chapter examines certain salient features of the history–memory–identity relation. My aim is less to be definitive about the matter—for no single theory can satisfactorily embrace everything that is in conflict here—than it is to show where the crosscuts lie. It is not a question of a simple opposition: history vs. memory. Nor it is a question of another simple opposition: discipline vs. desire. Rather, it is a matter of both writing and living in a situation in which some certainty can be achieved, but in which, finally, a background of uncertainty persists. Let us now explore these points in a manner that is more concrete and specific, and hence more capable of being grasped and retained.

IDENTITY AND THE MEMORY WAVE

A memory wave has swept through much of contemporary culture. Its most important site, although far from the only one, has been the United States. Appearing in the 1980s and reaching something of a peak in the mid-1990s, memory invaded a wide variety of fields, often in the company of its evil twin, amnesia. By the end of the 1990s some of the more extreme forms of memory preoccupation had retreated, but in many respects memory continues as a major preoccupation in contemporary culture. So pervasive is the concern with memory that it seems needlessly restrictive to limit the list of examples. But limit it we must, if there is to be any chance of making conceptual progress. Among a multitude of possible examples, the following will give some concrete sense of what "memory" involves.

1. In many therapeutic circles in the United States, therapists have placed great emphasis on the need for psychologically troubled persons to recover the "repressed memories" of the childhood abuse that allegedly led to their problems: several groups believe strongly that the recall, through memory, of past evil is (as Ian Hacking has put it) "a critical source of empowerment."[2]

2. Memory therapies have entered into the American judicial system as elements in divorce proceedings, in civil lawsuits of other kinds, and in criminal prosecutions for child abuse (and in one celebrated case, for murder), sometimes on the basis of no physical or other evidence contemporaneous to the alleged crimes.[3] By the mid-to-late 1990s a growing sense of skepticism about cases of this sort had become evident. Nonetheless, hysteria, an ignorance or willful ignoring of epistemological standards, and, above all, the truly appalling failure of the Roman Catholic Church to confront real child abuse on a large scale meant that there still remained people willing to believe every accusation, even those "recovered" from a repression so deep as to have kept the alleged memories completely blanked out.

3. Going beyond the United States, we note the ethnic conflicts that emerged in the wake of the fall of the Soviet Union in 1991. The cases that are of interest here are those where conflict had little or no basis in outwardly visible differences between ethnic groups and much to do with so-called "collective memory." The former Yugoslavia is a good case in point.[4]

4. We note, in the United States and elsewhere, a preoccupation with the memory of the Holocaust. Almost all people who were involved in the Holocaust, whether as victims, perpetrators, bystanders, or mere contemporaries, are now dead; soon no one will be left. Because the Holocaust has become important for Jewish identity, the question of what would happen to the "memory" of the Holocaust—of how that "memory" would be preserved—became and remains a matter of concern to many people.[5] The Holocaust also figures in remappings of German history, although what is at issue in Germany is far less the preservation of Holocaust memory than the embarrassment of the Holocaust's having happened.[6]

Obviously, each of these examples is situated within specific material, institutional, and cultural contexts and has its own particular set of causes. Yet the examples seem to have a generic similarity. Why, in such radically different contexts, do "memory" and its opposite come up? Why is Alzheimer's disease perhaps our greatest health horror? Why do legal proceedings get recast as exercises in remembering? Why do popular movies deal so much with matters of memory and forgetting—to mention only a few, *Blade Runner* (1982), *Total Recall* (1990), *Primal Fear* (1996), *Men in Black* (1997), *Memento* (2001), and *Eternal Sunshine of the Spotless Mind* (2004). Why do we need to possess again the hurts of childhood? And why must the Holocaust be so desperately and deliberately remembered? The common feature underpinning most contemporary manifestations of the memory craze seems to be an insecurity about identity. In a world in which opposing certainties constantly come into conflict with each other and in which a multitude of possible identities are put on display, insecurity about identity may be an inevitable by-product. Such a situation provides ample reason for "memory" to come to the fore. We might postulate a rule: when identity becomes uncertain, memory rises in value.

We can address identity on both a philosophical and an everyday level. The two levels seem to have some affinity: perhaps there is even a causal relation between them. In *An Essay Concerning Human Understanding,* John Locke posed the classic philosophical problem of identity. For Locke, the problem was to figure out how anything that we might call personal identity can persist over time: as is well known, Locke concluded that personal identity is sustained by a persisting consciousness. Noteworthy is the untroubled thinness of Locke's account. Strikingly, when Hume, in *A Treatise of Human Nature,* concluded that one cannot find the self-consciousness that Locke held to be the sole constitutive property of personal identity, and that personal identity is a fiction, he did not consider the conclusion troubling.[7] In general, until the twentieth century, identity itself was not seen as problematic. Only with the emergence of an existential tradition in philosophy did the deep constitution of the self arise as a central problem.

Charles Taylor has argued at length that the retreat within modernity of generally agreed-upon theological and religious assumptions has had an effect on "the modern identity": this retreat, he contends, has deprived identity of a larger framework in terms of which it could define itself.[8] Certainly, in the existential tradition and elsewhere, reflection on the self is manifestly related to the decline of the notion that man was created *imago dei*. It is related also to the decline of subsequent equivalents to that notion, above all the conception of a human nature that defines the individual. We can postulate that when such external supports are absent, individuals and communities have the opportunity to fashion their own identities. In the ideology of high modernity this "self-fashioning" was to be carried out in a spirit of creative self-confidence.[9] Nietzsche, who was perhaps the foremost theorist of modernity, evoked the self-confidence of Goethe, who "disciplined himself into wholeness . . . *created* himself. . . . Such a spirit who has *become free* stands amid the cosmos with a joyous and trusting fatalism."[10] Still speaking speculatively, we can posit that, more typically, such self-fashioning would be ringed by anxiety and hence would require some form of justification. When Goethean or Nietzschean self-confidence is lacking, there would be a motive to appeal to the past—or rather, to a certain image of the past, which we might call memory.

Such a line of thinking is not merely a matter of abstract speculation. On the contrary, one can find analogues to it in real life. In significant parts of the contemporary world (those parts where there is relative economic sufficiency and where the media are ubiquitous and influential), identity has *in fact* been problematized. That is, identity has been rendered variable and in that degree also uncertain: it has become a matter of various and sometimes conflicting roles that people can choose. Under such circumstances, identity is not necessarily a matter of empirically verifiable statements that can be seen to be unequivocally either true or false. Admittedly, some identity-related statements *are* either true or false: thus it is true or false that I am 5′9″ tall or that I have four children. But many identity-related statements that people make are not, or at least are not unambiguously, of this type.

We might call identity statements that are not unambiguously true or false "self-designations." Self-designations are not physical or statistical facts. Self-designation is how "we" choose to name ourselves, how "we" designate ourselves in language.

Thus the United States is a country of three hundred million people and "Americans" (as the term is usually employed) are citizens of that country. But the United States is also "the land of the free and the home of the brave," the "city upon a hill," "the hope of the world," and so on. Similarly, as individuals we define ourselves by self-designation. There are limits to the reception of such self-designations—limits of a material and institutional sort. At least among persons inclined to ask for evidence, we could not succeed for long in claiming to have physical characteristics, institutional affiliations, or personal attainments that we do not in fact have. But it is also clear that many milieus of contemporary society offer much leeway regarding what one can claim to be. It is hard to know how such statements as "I am a searcher for truth and justice," "I am a Christian," and so on could be empirically tested in any definitive way. Consequently, we often find ourselves accepting such identity statements without significantly questioning them.

Identity is constrained in some ways but not in others. It is marked by an element of arbitrariness or contingency, a certain freedom or at least a "freedom effect." The putting on and taking off of identities is a common experience in the contemporary world—underpinned by the mobility of a capitalist economy and by the myriad examples of possible identities presented in the media (clearly, this is not a *universal* experience: its precondition is a certain degree of freedom from the most compelling demands of material need). But in a relatively prosperous, media-saturated social context, people have available to them a surfeit of models of self-designation, which they are able to, and are even invited to, consider as possibilities for themselves.[11]

There is an important relation between the process of self-designation and images of the past. "Memory" arises as a special preoccupation in situations where people find themselves engaged in self-designation, for it serves to stabilize and justify the self-designations that are claimed.[12] The characteristic move of self-designation is a statement of the type, "I am an X," with "X" being any sort of designation of identity. While someone would have difficulty claiming, in any literal sense, "I am a six-footer" when he is not close to six feet tall, other kinds of self-designation can indeed be "taken on." That is, a person can adopt a self-designation that is significantly different from the way that he has seen himself or been seen by others up to now. Of course, self-designation can be conceptualized as a complete break from the old designation: Paul's conversion on the road to Damascus is paradigmatic. In the presence of the conviction that the new identity is authorized by God, there is perhaps no need to support the new identity with the claim that it already implicitly existed before the turn: in any case, the old identity is seen as unredeemed, tied to a world dominated by sin. However, in contemporary culture a different linguistic and conceptual move seems more prevalent. The statement "I am an X" is often supplemented and extended in the following manner: "I am an X, *and I have always been an X.*" For example, people undertaking gender reassignment often make such a claim. Here the memory of having always been an X supports an identity that might otherwise seem insufficiently justified. When such a move is made, issues of "memory" and "history" come directly into play.

A sense of weak or threatened identity seems to be a common feature uniting evocations of "memory" in ethnic conflict, in the recall of deeply troubling communal events, and in the recovery of traumatic or supposedly traumatic events of personal life. In short, there seems to be a fact here, and there also seems to be *prima facie* justification for regarding the fact as significant. The phenomenon of self-designation is in no way incompatible with the sense that identity is weak or threatened: on the contrary, an identity that has been brought into visibility by means of self-designation would be all the more likely to need justification of the sort that "memory" can bring. The memory wave and uncertainty concerning identity go together.

IDENTITY, MEMORY, AND HISTORICAL UNDERSTANDING

The question now arises of the relation between current concerns with identity and memory and the project of historical understanding. There exists a large literature on history and memory, one that has burgeoned since its beginnings in the late 1970s.[13] But while the literature has cast much light on the history–identity–memory relation, it has largely failed to explore the relation of historical understanding to the problematizing of identity. The literature has focused much more on how history and memory have functioned to consolidate and carry forward identities already assumed to exist. It has not much considered the possible volatility of these identities.

We must begin with the French sociologist Maurice Halbwachs (1877–1945). Halbwachs was the first scholar to discuss systematically the relation between history and memory, devoting several works to the subject: *The Social Frameworks of Memory* (1925); *The Legendary Topography of the Gospels in the Holy Land* (1941); and the posthumously published synthesis *The Collective Memory* (1950). For a long time Halbwachs's work on memory went all but unnoticed in the wider intellectual world; only in the late 1970s did it begin to attain some fame.[14] It is a matter, here, of the articulation of a set of ideas within one context and their reception within another, sharply different context.

A major representative in France of the nascent discipline of sociology, Halbwachs wished to show that memory is a social and not merely an individual phenomenon, and hence is properly the object of sociological investigation. His central claim was that the memory of individuals is heavily determined by categories of understanding coming from society. In *The Legendary Topography of the Gospels in the Holy Land* he applied this sociological conception of memory to a specific case, namely, interpretations offered, from the early Christian period onward, of the relation between the physical and human geography of the Holy Land and events described in the New Testament. Thus he also suggested that historical interpretations in particular are subordinate to the consciousnesses of the groups producing them.

Crucially, the Halbwachsian model holds that memory is determined by an identity (collective or individual) *that is already well established*. Halbwachs's work on memory—both his account of memory in general and his account of historical memory—is primarily about the construction of memory by such identities. His account of historical memory deals with how an identity, whose integrity at a certain moment is assumed, goes about inventing a past congruent with that identity. Time and again Halbwachs underscored this assumption: for example, "in each epoch" memory "reconstruct[s] an image of the past that is in accord . . . with the predominant thoughts of the society," and "the various groups that compose society are capable at every moment of reconstructing their past."[15] He also insisted that the groups in question are "delimited in space and time."[16] The essential point here is that, for Halbwachs, the social identities in question already have a determinate existence before the collective memories that they construct. To be sure, over time an identity will undoubtedly be reshaped by the collective memories that it has constructed, but fundamentally identity *precedes* memory.

In contrast, the most characteristic feature of the contemporary scene is a lack of fixity at the level of identity, leading to the project of constructing memory with a view to constructing identity itself. The appropriate model for understanding such a context is less Halbwachs's than Benedict Anderson's. In Anderson's evocative phrase, it is a matter of "imagined communities"; we might think of imagined communities as imagined identities.[17] Of course, every community beyond a very small group is in some strong sense "imagined." The more a community is imagined, the more it finds that "memory" is necessary to it—and so is "forgetting."[18] Conversely, the less rooted the community is in extant and well-functioning practices—that is, the more problematic its identity—the more constitutive for it is its "remembered" past.

It is important to note what the "memory" in question is not. First, it is not nostalgia. For purposes of the present analysis, let us define *nostalgia* as attraction to—a homesickness for—a real or imagined past. But one finds in many of the appeals to memory in contemporary culture a lack of attraction to the past at issue. Think, for example, of Holocaust memory and the memory of child abuse. The difference between nostalgia and memory, as here defined, is that whereas nostalgia is oriented outward *from* the subject (the individual person; the group), focusing attention on a real or imagined past, memory is oriented *toward* the subject and is concerned with a real or imagined past only because that past is perceived as crucial for the subject, even constitutive of it. Whereas memory, as understood here, is connected with insecurities concerning the present-day identity constructing those memories, nostalgia is connected with a sense of complacency about the present-day identity bearing the nostalgia. Much of the historical nostalgia that exists in the United States (nostalgia for old battlefields, for the houses of former presidents, indeed for historical relics of any kind) is untouched by any deep insecurity about identity. As for the French *lieux de mémoire,* explored by Pierre Nora and his collaborators during the 1980s, many of these "places of memory" are as much places of nostalgia. The historians' treatment of "places of memory" is often most interesting when it highlights the complex dialectic between memory and nostalgia that these "places of memory" reveal.[19]

Second, memory as understood here is also not quite tradition. Let us here define *tradition* as an objectively existing set of cultural artifacts or articulations. Adherents of a tradition that is confident of its own validity are unlikely to make an appeal to memory: instead, when required to defend the tradition, they characteristically appeal to nonsubjective factors—to a canon, to a set of philosophical or religious truths, to alleged historical events, to an existing institutional structure. An identity that solidly exists has little need for an explicit, thematized appeal to memory. When memory approximates to tradition, it approximates to *weak* tradition. In other words, an appeal to memory—that is, an appeal to what is subjective and personal—is likely to arise only when objectively existing supports are felt to be inadequate. For example, it is hard to imagine any pope who maintains a strong belief in the solidity of the traditions and institutions of the Roman

Catholic Church appealing to "memory" as he defends and promotes that church.

Admittedly, on an empirical level, memory often overlaps with nostalgia and with tradition. But memory on the one hand and nostalgia or tradition on the other remain significantly different phenomena. Consequently, on a conceptual level, we must retain the distinction between them. To fail to distinguish these different phenomena is to risk obscuring the important relations between memory and identity, and the important tensions existing between memory and history.

The problem that is raised for the historian and for the philosopher of history has to do with the character of the claims made in the name of memory. These are often tied up with the deepest convictions of present identities. Two examples will illustrate this abstract point.

FIRST EXAMPLE. In May 1995, I judged history papers written by upper-elementary and junior-high-school students who were finalists in the Virginia "National History Day" competition. I was thus obliged to read the National History Day competition rule book, which I take to exemplify widely shared views concerning the character of historical understanding. The rules required students to distinguish in the bibliographies of their papers between primary and secondary sources. The rules defined a *primary source* as "material directly related to a topic by time or participation. These materials include letters, speeches, diaries, newspaper articles from the time, oral history interviews, documents, photographs, artifacts, or anything else that provides first-hand accounts about a person or event."[20]

Any historian who has thought about issues of evidence will recognize that the definition of a primary source offered here is entirely unsatisfactory. Although historians are not always explicit in their thinking about such issues, there is nonetheless a traditional consensus that allows them to distinguish the two types of sources in particular cases. The basic point is that a primary source should be contemporaneous to the event that it describes.[21] But the National History Day rules allow a source to be designated as primary on the basis of its being "material directly related to a topic" by time "or" participation, and the rules include, without qualification, "oral history interviews" in the category of primary source. As a result, the rules widen the boundaries of a primary source far beyond what a properly trained professional historian can accept. For example, the rules allow one to regard as primary an "oral history interview" with a Holocaust survivor carried out many years after the events themselves. While I do not want to absolutize or in any way glorify the notion of a primary source, the long-standing historians' consensus that excludes a testimony offered fifty or sixty years after the fact from being considered "primary" is justified by everything that we know about the selective and discriminative character of memory.[22] Two points are important with respect to the distinction between primary and secondary sources: (1) The distinction is relative rather than absolute. For example, while a testimony offered in 1994 about events that occurred in 1944 is not "primary," it could be considered primary if the object of investigation was not events in 1944 but consciousness in 1994. (2) On a *theoretical* level it is hard to justify the distinction, for *all* testimony is in some degree subsequent to the historical reality being reported upon, and thus cannot in any complete sense be "primary." But whatever the theoretical difficulty, as a *methodological rule of thumb* the distinction is indispensable.

What grounds can there be for extending the notion of a primary source in such a way that the memories of a Holocaust survivor told to a grandchild in 1994 would count as a primary source? Two connected assumptions would certainly justify such a position. One assumption is that personal experience of historical events has a validity in itself, quite apart from any external standard, because it is "authentic."[23] The related assumption is that memory likewise has "authenticity," and hence validity, overriding any problems of accuracy arising from an original misperception or from distortions introduced in the lapse of time. However, the authenticity in question here is clearly not the kind of authenticity that one attributes to a document from the past whose provenance one has verified. It is rather authenticity in an existential sense, deriving its force from the alleged fact that it emerges directly and immediately from the subject's encounter with the world.

SECOND EXAMPLE. My second example, unlike the first, can lay no claim to typicality, but it is nonetheless revelatory. It manifests a cast of mind that, although usually expressed in less extreme ways, has had a significant hold on parts of the therapeutic community in the United States, and has also had some impact on American culture generally. The example in question is a book, *Ritual Abuse: What It Is, Why It Happens, and How to Help,* by the pseudonymous "Margaret Smith."[24] Smith contends that ritualized child abuse — involving black masses, the murder of children, the eating of children, sexual abuse of children, forced ingestion of urine and feces, mutilation of corpses, being forced to have sex with dead bodies, and other similar activities — is widespread in the United States. Smith herself claims to be a survivor of such abuse.

Smith reports that "a child's first reaction to this sort of abuse is to deny what is happening" (34). The abuse is so traumatic that the psyche does not remember it. But the body does, for the truth is preserved in the form of "body memories": "After the trauma has ceased, the physical sensations will recur in the body as *body memories.* . . . The body remembers exactly what happened" (35). Smith contends that severe abuse gives rise to multiple personality disorder. "During severe physical trauma, there is a point where the mind and the body split" (34). "Alter personalities" develop to relieve the contradictory feelings that ritual abuse survivors experience. Smith lists several types of alter personalities: the internalized perpetrator/persecutor; protectors; killer/torturers; child molester/rapist; the intellectual (who finds words to stop the pain); and guardian angels, helpers, comforters, and nurturers (36–42). Clearly, Smith here describes a severe dissociation of the personality.

Smith's evocation of multiple personality disorder (MPD) is extremely important and relevant, for it gives a specific content to my claim that memory has become closely tied up with identity and that memory is particularly important in situations where identity is threatened or uncertain. Could the weakness of an identity be more vividly rendered than by patients' insistence that they have not one, but many personalities (selves, parts, alters)? It is often said that persons suffering from multiple personality disorder do not have more than one personality, but less than one.[25] In viewing videotapes of a multiple personality individual being interviewed by a clinical psychologist conducting a forensic evaluation, I came to think of the person in precisely that way.[26] The alleged possession by the interviewed subject of a multitude of personalities seemed to serve as a means of avoiding responsibility for the actions that this person had carried out. Secure possession of *one* personality would have made possession of multiple personalities unnecessary. The clear impression in this case was that the different personalities were cardboard boxes within which the individual could hide. When one hiding place was threatened, there would be a leap to another.

Precisely because possession of the self is insecure, the subject insists that the claims being made are not simply *ex post facto* interpretations that make sense of a difficult personal history by giving an identifiable face to poorly understood terrors, but are literally and factually true. It is a question of self-validation: to validate the self in its current self-presentation, the subject insists on a particular story about how the self got that way. The author puts the matter well when she laments that "many people do not believe ritual abuse survivors. People are more concerned with evidence or proof of abuse than with the feelings of the victims. Many people think survivors are crazy, others blame survivors for their own pain" (33). Smith rejects such responses; in her view, "Survivors need supportive people in their lives who believe them and who do not blame them for the abuse" (179).

To return to the sphere of modernist theory: such insistence on the authenticity *and validity* of memory is far from the model of the relation between identity and memory that one archetypal modernist, Nietzsche, envisaged. Nietzsche's most important discussion of this relation occurs at the
beginning of the second treatise of *On the Genealogy of Morality,* entitled
"'Guilt,' 'Bad Conscience,' and Related Matters." In the first two sections of
the essay, he addresses the creation of a particular kind of subject, namely,
a subject that is capable of keeping promises.[27] He discusses memory not,
as one might imagine, because promises must be remembered to be kept,
but because memory enters into the creation of the subject. In these sections
Nietzsche writes not just about memory but also, and with equal intensity,
about forgetting. Clearly, forgetting has no positive relation to the keeping
of promises; on the contrary, on a manifest level its relation to the keeping
of promises is negative—a forgotten promise cannot be kept. Nietzsche
discusses forgetting because, along with remembering, it is essential to the
creation of the subject (in particular, Nietzsche is interested in the creation
of a certain *kind* of subject, namely, one that takes as its responsibility the
keeping of promises). Forgetfulness is what allows a subjectivity to emerge,
in the face of the constant flow of impressions into the soul.

As Nietzsche puts it, "forgetfulness . . . is an active and in the strictest
sense positive faculty of suppression (*Hemmungsvermögen*)" that allows
our consciousness to be disturbed as little as possible by our experience as
it is being absorbed. The result is "a little stillness, a little *tabula rasa* of
consciousness so that there is again space for new things, above all for the
nobler functions and functionaries, for ruling, foreseeing, predetermin-
ing." This "active forgetfulness" is "a doorkeeper as it were, an upholder
of psychic order, of rest, of etiquette." With the aid of memory, "forgetfulness is disconnected for certain cases—namely, for those cases where
a promise is to be made." Further, Nietzsche holds that memory, like forgetfulness, is "active." Memory is "by no means simply a passive no-longer-
being-able-to-get-rid-of the impression once it has been inscribed, " but
rather "an active no-longer-wanting-to-get-rid-of, a willing on and on of
something one has once willed, a true *memory of the will*: so that a world
of new strange things, circumstances, even acts of the will may be placed
without reservation between the original "I want," "I will do," and the actual discharge of the will, its *act,* without this long chain of the will breaking" (35–36).

It is clear from Nietzsche's account that he did not put a high value on
memory as such. Indeed, his reflections suggest an almost oppositional relation between memory and subjectivity. He is far from being the only thinker

on subjectivity to come to such a conclusion: one thinks immediately of Freud's harsh dictum that "hysterics suffer mainly from reminiscences."[28]

But many therapists, and others influenced by psychoanalysis, currently take a different view: while acknowledging that memories may be traumatic, they also see memory as a marker of the lived experience through which the self's identity has come into being, and hence as possessing an authenticity of its own, however distressing its contents. Hacking goes so far as to suggest that memory has come to serve as "a surrogate for the soul."[29] Why would this be so? In an earlier dispensation that included widespread adherence to an authoritatively grounded teleology or belief structure, the identity of the individual was seen as deriving its coherence and meaning from a larger framework of relations, as Droysen suggested (see n. 8, above). But in a disenchanted world the "soul" has no such definition or support. It is reduced to mundane experience, and the continuity of that experience is defined by, and dependent on, memory. It is a return to John Locke, but in a different, more desperate key.

Consequently, at a deep, experiential level, memory is crucial to us. As noted above, we are terrified by Alzheimer's disease. We are morbidly fascinated by memory disorders of the sort that the psychiatrist Oliver Sacks has described.[30] We treasure family photographs. None of this has much to do with "science," but it has a lot to do with our sense of ourselves. A high valuation of memory tends to enter into historiography (and into public interest in history) at those points where historical events and circumstances intersect with personal and familial experience. Our personal experience with history is a matter of "memory." Familial experience with history — say, the experience of grandparents who escaped the Holocaust, now narrated to and passed on by their descendants — is often designated as "memory," although in a strict sense it is not. The literary critic Geoffrey Hartman has written of the desirability of changing history into memory. The point here is not whether one agrees or disagrees with Hartman, but that, in calling for such a change, he acknowledges and participates in the high valuing of memory (and likewise the focus on identity) in contemporary culture.[31]

HISTORY, MEMORY, AND THE UNKNOWN

In the face of memory's high valuation, what should be the attitude of the historian? More important, what should be the attitude of any intelligent person? At the present moment there is a pathetic and sometimes tragic conflict between what "memory" expresses and confirms, namely, the demands made by subjectivities, and the demand for proof that is essential to

any scientific discipline. There is an impulse today within the wider culture and even within the academy to "de-emphasize the epistemology of
evidence and instead stress its erotics," to cite another literary critic, Eve
Kosofsky Sedgwick.[32] Obviously, evidence never speaks for itself, objectively: it always speaks *from* a subject position, *to* subjectivities, in an argumentative context established *by* subjectivities. In short, there is no such
thing as "pure" evidence. Moreover, the "erotics" of evidence is certainly a
necessary moment within a larger structure because without desire (which
I take to be the core of "erotics") there would be no impulse to construct (or
reconstruct) the past at all—as Ranke, Michelet, Burckhardt, and many
others have understood. But unless there are checks on desire, the past envisaged becomes merely a projection of the subjectivity imagining it. In a
fundamental sense, nothing is learned from the exercise: only if subjectivity
is checked can it learn to engage itself with opposing subjectivities and with
the social and material worlds within which those subjectivities operate.

To put this another way: it is easy to imagine that we ought to *remember*
the past. But we do not remember the past. It is the present that we remember: that is, we "remember" what remains living within our situations
now.[33] We *think* the past: that is, we construct or reconstruct it on the basis
of certain critical procedures. The relevant motto is: "Remember the present, think the past." "Je me souviens" ("I remember," the motto of Québec)
relates to a subjectivity that is present, not to a past that is thought. Almost
invariably, when historical understanding is described as "remembering,"
we can infer that we are confronting an attempt to promote some presumably desirable collective identity in the present.[34]

It would be easy—but also completely mistaken—to dismiss out of
hand the subjective, remembering side of this dialectic. Claims to possess
the perspective of absolute objectivity—to offer a "God's-eye view"—are
unsustainable (see chapter 5, below). But it is also a mistake to turn history
into merely an offshoot of struggles for identity in the present. Recent work
in the philosophy of history offers much serious reflection on historical understanding. This work does not resolve the conflict between the demands
of subjectivity that are linked to particular identities (of race, class, gender,
nation) and the demand for proof, but it does situate the conflict. With respect to the problems of valuation and knowledge raised here, there are two
conflicting tendencies in the literature. One tendency is best represented
by R. G. Collingwood and Paul Ricoeur; the other, by Hayden White and
Michel de Certeau.

The first tendency sees the past as fundamentally knowable. Such a tendency is present in Ricoeur's conception of historical narrative as something

that embraces heterogeneous phenomena within a synthesis—a "synthesis of the heterogeneous," as Ricoeur puts it.[35] But it is manifested far more emphatically in Collingwood's *The Idea of History,* most obviously in the chapter entitled "Historical Evidence," almost half of which is devoted to examining the question "Who Killed John Doe?"[36] Here Collingwood recounts, in detective-novel fashion, Detective Inspector Jenkins's investigation of the murder of John Doe, the next-door neighbor of an Anglican clergyman. (It is a purely fictional story, but I shall take the liberty of treating it as if it were about an actual murder.) The investigation culminates in the discovery that the murderer was the clergyman himself. For years John Doe had been secretly blackmailing the rector by threatening to reveal publicly an affair that the rector's wife, now dead, had had years before, just before her marriage. Doe's blackmailing had absorbed the whole of the rector's private fortune, and now Doe was demanding an installment of the late wife's fortune, which had been left to the rector in trust for the daughter of the marriage. When the rector saw that the detective inspector was closing in on him, he took cyanide and thus cheated the hangman.

Collingwood's account of the solving of the John Doe murder case (which he presents as paradigmatic of historical investigation in general) is marked by a glaring absence. He passes over in complete silence the trauma that must have wracked the rector and his family. It is clear that pain and concealment were endemic in it. During all the time that the rector was paying blackmail, he did not know that the man who had seduced his wife was the blackmailer himself. The rector's wife presumably did not know that her husband was paying blackmail to protect her name. Likewise, the rector's daughter, born six months after her parents' wedding, did not know that she had been fathered not by the rector but by John Doe. Collingwood is simply not interested in what must have been the deeply troubled relations between the rector and his late wife, between the rector and his daughter, between the late wife and the neighbor, and so on. In short, he leaves out the entire *cultural* history of the family. It is as if the trauma and repression that must have shadowed these people did not exist. In effect, Collingwood defines trauma as not part of history: he excludes it entirely from the historical field.

Collingwood conceived of the historical past as something constructed by the historian, following the rules of historical investigation. In Collingwood's view, historical investigation yields *one* true and objective conclusion. Indeed, quite wrongly, Collingwood claims that a historical argument ought to "follow inevitably from the evidence" and that it proves its point "as conclusively as a demonstration in mathematics" (262, 268).[37] Similarly, for the detective inspector, only one story acceptably explains the murder, and once he discovers the story, he is utterly confident in maintaining its truth. But the historian-detective is able to arrive at such certitude only by excluding all engagement with trauma.

The second tendency in the philosophy of history sees an unknowability in the past. In *The Writing of History,* de Certeau insists that a confrontation with death and with the Other is crucial for the emergence of modern Western historiography; that there must be a break between past and present for history to be written; and that history as a discipline has an obligation to recognize that there are things it cannot grasp—irremediable gaps and absences, an otherness that it nonetheless strives to represent.[38] Hayden White, for his part, sees truthful history as irrevocably marked by the sublime—that is, by that which is too terrible to be known. In sharp contrast to Collingwood, who maintained that the historian reenacts the past in his mind, White leaves room for what in the past is too horrifying to be reconstituted. As White puts it, misguided attempts to "beautify" the past "deprive history of the level of meaninglessness that alone can goad living human beings to make their lives different for themselves and their children, which is to say, to endow their lives with a meaning for which they alone are fully responsible."[39] In White's view, "historicality itself is both a reality and a mystery"—and the mystery cannot be gotten round.[40] In other words, White offers us a historical noumenon—that is to say, a conception of the limits of historical knowledge.

One can conceive of the historical noumenon in a number of different, although related, ways. In the broadest sense, it can be thought of as a zone of incomprehensibility lying behind what we *are* able to know. In this sense, the historical noumenon amounts to a principle of historiographic humility. It is akin to the humility of Herodotus, who often repeated stories told to him by his informants while holding himself at a distance from the claim that the stories were true.[41] However, White's view is only akin to that of Herodotus, not identical with it: for the notion of the historical noumenon implies that there is indeed a Truth behind the stories, testimonies, memories, and the like, even though we may be blocked from knowing it. More specifically, the historical noumenon can be conceived of as a domain inhabited (a) by what is too traumatic to be put into language; (b) by what is too foreign to be understood in the present; and (c) by what cannot be constructed or reconstructed for lack of adequate evidence.

The notion of a zone of incomprehensibility helps us to unravel the difficult relations between memory and history by suggesting another horizon that lies behind *both* memory and history. It is a mistake to see memory and history as continuous with each other: a mistake, for example, to think of memory as the raw material of history. It is likewise a mistake to think that history is simply the sum of all possible memories: *pace* Tolstoy, the Battle of Waterloo is not to be reconstructed by bringing together all memories of it. But it is equally a mistake to see history and memory as simply opposed to each other. On the one hand, far from being history's raw material, memory is an Other that continually haunts history. Memory is an image of the past constructed by a subjectivity in the present. It is thus by definition subjective; it may also be irrational and inconsistent. On the other hand, history as a discipline has the obligation to be objective, unified, orderly, justified. Yet it cannot entirely be so, for there is always a residue of incomprehensibility behind what is known, and an engagement with subjectivity that cannot be eliminated.[42]

With his proclamation, "God is dead," Nietzsche the modernist sought to characterize an important aspect of modernity. Nietzsche appears to have meant that modernity has succeeded, or will soon succeed, in separating itself from the Other: faith, revelation, metaphysics, transcendence, and anything else that is opposed to reason. Yet Nietzsche also acknowledged—in a move that is often overlooked—the anxiety caused by the expulsion of the Other: "How shall we comfort ourselves, the murderers of all murderers?"[43] It may be that memory has emerged in part as a response to an anxiety arising from the failure of modernity, with its focus on the pursuit of the new, to provide an adequate account of what is past yet continues to haunt the present.

Consider, for example, the relation of the discipline of history, which has Western, Christian, monotheistic roots (see chapter 9), to one of its Others, namely, those parts of the globe and of experience that are not part of "the West." Ashis Nandy has argued that the historians' history of the non-West "is usually a history of the prehistorical, the primitive, and the pre-scientific" that keeps open "only one option—that of bringing the ahistorical into history." The aim of such histories, Nandy claims, is "nothing less than to bare the past completely, on the basis of a neatly articulated frame of reference." This is, of course, a thoroughly Collingwoodian conception of the past. As Nandy goes on to say, "Enlightenment sensitivities . . . presume a perfect equivalence between history and the construction of the past; they presume that there is no past independent of history."[44] In this sense, the collective memory of non-Westerners becomes the Other of history, excluded from its domain.

But in actual fact this Other can be quite close to history, or at least to historians. One member of the "subaltern school" of historians of South Asia,

Dipesh Chakrabarty, has noted how the subaltern enters into the formation of the Westernizing middle class itself. People from the "subaltern" classes have been physically present, as servants, in the familial and formational space of the middle classes, and consequently aspects of their culture have been present there as well. These cultural experiences have entered, or at least *can* enter, into historiography. As children, many members of India's middle classes encountered the magical tales of the subaltern, which explained the world and provided a comprehensive understanding of it. The collective memory of the South Asian subaltern classes stands as an Other, opposed to history. It is an Other that, as adults, South Asian historians might well seek to understand—and some have.[45]

However, if memory is the Other of history, we must also say that history is the Other of memory. The claims that memory makes are only possibly true. In its demand for proof, history stands in sharp opposition to memory. History reminds memory of the need for evidence coming from eyewitnesses (*autopsy*) and from material remains.[46] Memory is a domain of obscurity: it is not to be trusted. Yet one should not think that history is by this token the domain of light, for along with the relative light of history and the relative darkness of memory, we must acknowledge a vast domain of historical unknowability. This lesson arises from the uncertainty of identity in our time, for in undermining the notion that a single authoritative perspective exists to which we can have access, the uncertainty of identity also undermines the arrogance of *both* history and memory: on the one hand, the arrogance of definitiveness; on the other, the arrogance of authenticity.

The limits of history and of memory are perhaps most clearly manifested in an important twentieth-century phenomenon, namely, trials of alleged perpetrators of state-sponsored brutality, when the trials are intended both to arrive at truth/justice and to help in shaping a new collective identity through the formation of collective memory.[47] What is striking is the simultaneous necessity and impossibility of the dual project that is envisaged: how can it be done? How can it *not* be done? Courts and commissions seeking at the same time to discover historical truth and to reconstruct collective identity are relevant in the present context as a manifestation of the general theoretical points that I have tried to articulate, which can be put in the form of several propositions:

1. The uncertainties of history, identity, and memory are mutual.
2. History and memory are sharply different, as manifested above all in the radically different histories that different people or groups remember.

3. The boundaries between history and memory nonetheless cannot be precisely established.
4. In the absence of a single, unquestioned authority or framework, the tension between history and memory cannot be resolved.

In the time of grand narrative, the presence of History meant that history could always conquer memory: History trumped "histories." In the time of grand narrative's collapse, this is no longer so. Thus it is hard to know how the tension between the historical and the mnemonic can ever be overcome. It is certain that the sum of memories does not add up to history. It is equally certain that history does not *by itself* generate a collective consciousness, an identity, and that when it gets involved in projects of identity-formation and promotion, trouble results. Thus a boundary remains between history and memory that we can cross from time to time but that we cannot, and should not wish to, eliminate. Perhaps the more disturbing tendency in our time is the tendency to eliminate oppressive History in favor of authentic memory. But truth and justice, or whatever simulacra of them remain to us, require at least the *ghost* of History if they are to have any claim on people at all. What is left otherwise is only what feels good (or satisfyingly bad) at the moment.

— PART II —

Narrative & Knowledge

Does Narrative Have a
Cognitive Value of Its Own?

CHAPTER THREE

Does narrative have a cognitive value of its own? The question is not easy to answer, at least not in any definitive way. Two answers suggest themselves, the simplest of all possible answers: yes, and no. Yes, narrative does have its own cognitive value. The truth in question resides in the *form* of narrative, not in its specific content: in the words of the philosopher of history Louis Mink, "the cognitive function of narrative form . . . is . . . to body forth an ensemble of interrelationships . . . as a single whole." This "bodying forth," Mink holds, makes us aware of things that would otherwise be inaccessible to us. In Mink's view, narratives "express their own conceptual presuppositions." In consequence, they are "our most useful evidence for coming to understand conceptual presuppositions quite different from our own." For example, we best understand the Greek idea of Fate through the plots of Greek tragedy, given that the Greek idea of Fate "was never explicitly formulated as a philosophical theory and . . . is far removed from our own presuppositions about causality, responsibility, and the natural order."[1]

We may raise the following objection to Mink's claim: How can we know, from any particular narrative, that the "conceptual presuppositions" that we discern in the text were generally held by persons in the empirical reality existing outside the text? In fact, the narrative itself cannot provide this knowledge. But narrative's "bodying forth" of relationships and its "expressing" of conceptual presuppositions nonetheless need to be taken as truthful in the sense that, even if our only evidence for some sort of commitment to those presuppositions lies in one narrative and in one narrative alone, we must acknowledge those relationships and presuppositions as *possible* ways of making sense of the world. In other words, narrative makes available to us an image of the world that we must acknowledge *as* an image of the world precisely because it is there in the narrative. By virtue of the narrative's existence, we know that the image or images of the world that it embodies likewise exist.

But the opposing answer is also true. No, narrative does not have a cognitive value of its own. The truth of narrative always needs to be justified by evidence outside narrative. The plausibility of a narrative—which we can conceptualize as the sum of (a) its coherence as a story and (c) its noncontradiction of the world outside the story—does not guarantee its truth. That is, a story that is "a good story" *and* that does not manifestly contradict anything that we currently know about the world outside the story may well be untrue. The "no" answer—that is, the claim that narrative does not have a cognitive value of its own—is likely to be preferred by the experienced and disabused judge, who again and again has heard testimonies that turn out to be false, and who therefore does not believe a story simply because it is internally coherent and does not contradict what we currently know about the world. For the judge knows from hard experience that close inspection may prove such stories to be false. People lie, and people can be mistaken.

The "no" answer, in its skeptical attitude toward the beautiful illusions of narrative, is the more prosaic answer. It is also the less interesting one. Not accidentally, for most historians up to now, it has also been the more compelling answer. No, narrative does not carry its own truth with it; it does not stand as its own warrant or gauge of truth. "No" is the answer more acceptable to historians because it pays attention to minute particulars—that is, to the specific facts and contexts that historians, when they are doing their job properly, most directly attend to. The "yes" answer is less acceptable because narrative form, in which the alleged cognitive value of narrative resides, connects with entities that historians, given the generally empirical bent of their discipline, are less well attuned to. The "form" of narrative connects with totalities rather than with particulars: it connects with views or perspectives. Perspectives are often unnoted by those who entertain them, having the status of unconscious presuppositions rather than conscious assumptions. This is especially true when it is a matter of considering the investigator and the context out of which she comes, for the interpretive perspective of the investigator will often be the one thing left out of the investigation.

It thus seems clear that both answers to the question, "Does narrative have a cognitive value of its own?" are true. It also seems clear that the relations between the "yes" and the "no" answers are not symmetrical, for they occupy different conceptual territories. To say that narrative has a cognitive value of its own is to evoke totalities rather than minute particulars. To accept the "yes" answer is to see historiography as aimed primarily at confirming or modifying people's ways of looking at and acting in the world. Conversely, to accept the "no" answer is to see historiography as aimed primarily at offering specific, justified descriptions and explanations of past reality, not at confirming or modifying people's "structure of historical consciousness," to use Mink's phrase.[2]

The present chapter explores and criticizes the "yes" answer. Historiography's role in helping to configure our ways of seeing and living in the world is indeed essential (falling under the heading of what, in chapter 4, I call "interpretation"). The "yes" answer embraces the indubitable fact that historiography is connected to the time of the historian and her readers as well as to the time that the historian investigates. The "no" answer embraces the recognition that the historian is under an obligation to make descriptive and explanatory statements that are true *about the past*. But these statements are situated within an interpretive framework connected to the present. Thus the "yes" answer is the one that is the more *broadly* true. Yet having said this, I must also note that the "yes" answer not only offers a bow to narrative but also invites critical reflection on it. Hence my concern here is with the epistemological limits of narrative. Narrative *qua* narrative has a seductive power that tends to carry the listener and reader along in the very telling of a story. In the cognitive domain this power becomes problematic. People can tell stories for all sorts of reasons, not all of them related to the work of finding historical truth. In view of the aesthetic fact that narrative *qua* narrative tends to satisfy us as human beings, lies and self-deceptions are easily given a pleasing form. The pleasing form of narrative tends to lend it a cognitive weight that it does not deserve.

Since the publication in 1973 of his *Metahistory,* the name of Hayden White has been at the center of a great deal of discussion among philosophers of history.[3] I am not interested here in engaging in debate over White's specific claims, which involve the bringing about of a rapprochement between history and fiction. Rather, I am interested in the *fact* of that discussion, for the wide (if controversial) notice that White's work has received among persons interested in theoretical issues in historiography is itself indicative of a considerable recognition of the power of narrative (and of related literary forms), and a recognition also that unresolved theoretical questions arise therefrom.

The character and implications of that compelling force need to be better understood. In part, narrative has an *aesthetic* force, by virtue of tying events together into patterns that people find interesting and pleasurable. It likewise has a *cultural* force. Thus narrative has been valued because of the way it carries, and clothes in specific and vivid images, important aspects of our ways of being together within the social order. For this reason, in the last thirty years or so, many have raised their voices in favor of re-narrativizing many fields of inquiry, as a means of investing them with moral purpose, common sense, marginalized voices, substantive rationality, democratic ideals, and so on.[4] We should further note that narrative is also capable of imparting and arousing a certain kind of *intellectual satisfaction*. When puzzling events "fall into place," becoming part of a coherent story, the puzzlement tends to disappear. Conversely, when we find ourselves unable, as inquirers and as actors in the world, to discern a narrative framework that would "make sense of" the phenomena we are confronting, we are likely to have precisely the opposite feeling—a certain sense of intellectual *dis*satisfaction.

All of these issues deserve further consideration. But I focus here on only two matters—on the so-called "crisis of narrative," and on the epistemological limits of narrative.

THE "CRISIS" OF NARRATIVE

By *narrative,* I here mean an account that is chronologically ordered and has a recognizable beginning, middle, and end (I offer a somewhat different definition of narrative in chapter 4). This classic definition is deceptively simple, and it requires two clarifications. First, there is the question of chronological ordering. As structuralist theorists of narrative have taught us, the events of a narrative are rarely, if ever, told in strict chronological order: on the contrary, all sorts of backtrackings and foretrackings take place on the level of the telling of the story (the level of "discourse," as structuralist narrative theorists call it). The important point, however, is that beneath the level of "discourse," the reader can discern a chronologically ordered "story."[5]

Second, just as narrative diverges from strict chronological order in greater or lesser degree, we must also note an insufficiency or divergence in the categories of beginning, middle, and end. For it is clear that beginning, middle, and end are never totally present in the text. Consequently, the claim is not that they must all be present for a narrative to exist. The claim is rather that, whether present or not, we can *project* each of the three categories from what is present in the text. Accordingly, we may still regard a truncated or fragmented narrative—that is, an account in which one or more of the three categories is missing—as a narrative.

As early as the 1930s, some commentators began to suggest that narrative is passé, even in crisis. Some have regarded narrative as threatened by the

conditions of modern life; some have regarded it as beneath the level of gen-
uinely scientific knowledge. To consider in detail the question of the alleged
crisis of narrative is beyond the scope of this book, but a few comments are
necessary, for narrative's alleged crisis is certainly relevant to questions of
evidence and truthfulness.[6]

A good place to begin is with the alleged crisis of "grand narrative"
(which I discuss in chapters 8 and 9). A "grand narrative" is an account
that purports to be the authoritative account of history in general; to this
notion we can add the closely allied notion of a "master narrative," which is
an account that purports to be the authoritative account of some particular
segment of history—say, the history of a nation. Famously, Jean-François
Lyotard argued in *The Postmodern Condition* (1979) that ours is an age of
"incredulity" toward "grand narrative." By this he meant that the cultural
authority of the unified history of humanity that Westerners once accepted
more or less implicitly has been profoundly shaken. In the nineteenth century it was still easy to believe that there was a unified history of humanity
that had freedom, cultivation (*Bildung*), or some combination of the two as
its *telos;* by the late twentieth century this belief was much more difficult to
sustain.[7]

But note that, however threatened grand narrative may be, its predica-
ment does not call into question narrative *tout court*. Indeed, it appears that
in the absence of a "master" or "grand" narrative that would make sense of a
particular nation or of humanity in general, human beings are all the more
driven to tell "little narratives" to make sense of their own individual situations.[8] Perhaps the presence of a "grand" or "master" narrative to some extent relieves people of the need to narrate their own situations. For example,
taking the Christian salvation story as the guide for their lives, individuals
or groups might well feel no overwhelming compulsion to invent and dis-
seminate particular life-stories of their own. We can plausibly hypothesize
that the absence of "grand" or "master" narratives tends to drive people to
"narrativize" their own situations—that is, to invent life-stories as a means
of making sense of who they are. In other words, the question of whether
any particular narrative is generally accepted as authoritative has no necessary connection to the question of whether narrative in general is in crisis.
Grand narrative can be cacophonously denied by the hybridity and variety
of a culture, while narrative itself, in the form of a multitude of *petits récits,*
flourishes.

Some might argue that all narrative, not just grand narrative, is in crisis. In part this seems to have been Lyotard's argument in *The Postmodern
Condition,* for he there describes a movement from a situation in which one

or another narrative legitimizes a society and its various institutions to a situation in which the "performativity principle"—that is, the optimization of a system's performance—is what offers legitimacy.[9] In the literature more generally, scholars have seen narrative as threatened both practically and theoretically. On the practical level, some have seen it as threatened by the linked realities of technology and bureaucracy. Walter Benjamin, in *The Storyteller* (1936), argued that technology threatens narrative and suggested that the transmission, within communities, of inherited stories, myths, legends, and the like is being replaced by the more anonymous and instantaneous transmission of information. In the same year, in "The Work of Art in the Age of Mechanical Reproduction," Benjamin argued that mechanical reproducibility removes the artwork from "the domain of tradition" within which it formerly resided.[10] Computer databases are often seen as having precisely this sort of infinite reproducibility; and a problem is also raised by the sheer mass of preserved information, which is so great that it is hard to imagine how it could ever be put into the coherent form of narrative.[11]

As for bureaucracy, its commitment to universally applicable procedural rules tends to departicularize individuals and to make irrelevant their attempts to justify their claims by recounting their own stories. Kafka's *Trial* brilliantly exemplifies this point: *The Trial* could not have been better couched to make clear the irrelevancy of Josef K's story to his fate (one must of course understand that the "court," in *The Trial,* is actually a caricature of a bureaucratic tribunal, and not a court as traditionally understood in the Anglo-American judicial system). Anyone who has had to deal with extremely large and remote governmental agencies will grasp the anti-narrativist impulse—for the determining factor, where a depersonalizing bureaucracy holds sway, is the fit of the individual to a particular bureaucratic category. For example, if the individual is a foreign professor for whom an American university wants to obtain a "green card," the university might find itself having to prove that the professor fits the category of "outstanding professors and researchers." In such instances, unless the person's story can be made to serve the purposes of classifying her, the story is irrelevant. Further, in the American bureaucracy, it is said, "governmental workers rarely read beyond the second page."[12] Compression carried out to this degree makes narrative exposition difficult.[13]

For its part, the theoretical attack on narrative appears in two opposing forms. One form of theoretical attack emanates from positivism. Here, an insistence on the necessity and importance of universal laws and theories leads to a manifest rejection of narrative. This scientistic form of anti-narrativism was articulated explicitly by the logical empiricists. Although long dead as a position in philosophy, logical empiricism considerably influenced the methodology of the social sciences, and its insistence that only laws and theories are truly scientific continues to hold sway in vast areas of the social sciences even today. The basic claim is that science should speak the language of law and theory, not the language of narrative. One thinks especially of Carl Hempel's account of the cracking of an automobile radiator on a cold night, to which I turn in chapter 4: the account is resolutely non-chronological, but consists instead of statements of initial and boundary conditions combined with statements of empirical laws.[14]

A second form of theoretical attack on narrative derives from entirely different preoccupations. This second form of attack casts the *continuity* of narrative as the villain: for by portraying an entity as having a sustained existence over time, it is said, narrative confirms the authority of that entity. In short, here narrative is rejected on the grounds that it serves to justify the central subject of the narrative. The argument is in some ways fundamentally Nietzschean, resonating to Nietzsche's claim in *Human, All-Too-Human* (1878) that "the whole of teleology is constructed by speaking of the man of the last four millennia as of an *eternal* man towards whom all things in the world have had a natural relationship from the time he began."[15] But Nietzsche never raised discontinuity to an explicit principle. It became such only in the twentieth century—most famously with Foucault, whose *Archaeology of Knowledge* (1969) presents itself as, among other things, an attempt to formulate "a general theory of discontinuity" to put up against the "continuous history" that is "the indispensable correlative of the founding function of the subject."[16] We should also note that in his "Theses on the Philosophy of History" (1940) Walter Benjamin insisted that historians ought to "[stop] telling the sequence of events like the beads of a rosary."[17] Note, however, that Benjamin's compressed formulation is hardly a clear statement of the anticontinuity argument.

We thus find an array of attacks (or alleged attacks) on narrative. At the practical level narrative is alleged to be the victim of technology and of bureaucracy; at the theoretical level it is the butt of attacks by proponents of a universalizing scientific method and by antihistoricist historicists like Foucault or Benjamin. Yet neither the technological attack, the bureaucratic attack, the scientistic attack, nor the anticontinuist attack is as threatening as it appears at first glance. On the contrary, time and again narrative returns, reappearing even in those situations where it seems most seriously threatened. Speaking speculatively and relying on evidence of a somewhat scattered and anecdotal character—for a detailed study is not possible here—I can suggest something of the character of this return.

Consider, first, the supposed attacks on narrative that are seen as arising on a practical level. Technologically, we do appear to live—as Lyotard suggested more than a generation ago—in "computerized societies."[18] It is likewise true that digital technology most often manifests itself in non-narrative ways. For example, information in a computerized database is not organized narratively. Similarly, the Web makes information available to us along a vast multitude of separate branching and rebranching paths: there is no single line, and the lines that do exist are in any case not chronologically ordered. Yet what is striking is the degree to which people seem driven to *construct* narratives out of scattered fragments of information. For example, the Web has been the matrix out of which conspiracy theories have been constructed—such as the alleged conspiracy to suppress the alleged fact that Trans World Airlines Flight 800 from New York to Paris on July 17, 1996, was shot down by a missile, possibly one launched by the United States Navy (other conspiracy theories, burgeoning after September 11, 2001, abound).[19] A conspiracy theory, of course, is nothing other than a tightly ordered narrative. Similarly, persons confronted by the bureaucratic order of the modern state customarily tell stories about themselves in an attempt to argue that they fit such-and-such a bureaucratic category. Narrativization appears to be a normal human response both to complexity and complication, and to the bureaucratic drive to oversimplify.

As for the theoretical attack on narrative, neither its scientistic nor its anticontinuist version is as opposed to narrative as it appears to be at first glance. In each case, would-be antinarratives are easily construed, by little more than a twist of the kaleidoscope, as narratives after all. For example, Hempel offers an account of what led to the cracking of the radiator via a series of singular statements, such as "The car was left in the street all night," and another series of general statements, such as "Below 32°F., under normal atmospheric pressure, water freezes." But although on the level of discourse Hempel's account is certainly not a narrative, readers can readily construct these statements *as* a narrative, discerning the story behind the discourse. And this is in fact what readers do. It is the same with the anticontinuist attack on narrative. Consider Foucault's account in *The Order of Things* (1966) of the succession of *epistemes,* or systems of thought, in the West: Renaissance, "Classical," modern or "humanist," and post-humanist. Foucault claims in that work that the movement from one *episteme* to the next has the character of a radical and inexplicable "mutation."[20] In short, Foucault denies that there is a narrative continuity in the succession of epistemes—but readers construct a narrative nonetheless, one emphasizing discontinuity rather than continuity.

In brief, it seems that narrative always returns, even when it is under the most severe attack. The repeated return of narrative suggests something of its power as a mode of organizing our perceptions of the world. It appears that human beings are constituted in such a way that, in orienting themselves to the world, they come back again and again to narrative. This is a point on which many prominent narrative theorists agree. For example, Roland Barthes, in his "Introduction to the Structural Analysis of Narratives," claimed that narrative is "intentional, transhistorical, transcultural: it is simply there, like life itself." Although he differs from Barthes in many ways, Paul Ricoeur, in *Time and Narrative,* makes almost the same point: "I see in the plots we invent the privileged means by which we re-configure our confused, unformed, and at the limit mute temporal experience." Mink notes that "storytelling is the most ubiquitous of human activities." W. B. Gallie emphasizes the "followability" of stories, and sees people as having a natural desire to be carried along by the stories that are told. Finally, Hayden White observes that "to raise the question of the nature of narrative is to invite reflection on the very nature of culture"—for the impulse to narrate is so "natural" that "narrativity could appear problematical only in a culture in which it was absent." Hence, White claims, "narrative and narration are less problems than simply data."[21]

Our discovery here of a crisis of narrative that turns out not to be a crisis underscores the point that these narrative theorists make: namely, that we human beings find stories deeply attractive. Of these theorists, Ricoeur is least suspicious of the powers of narrative. While it is sometimes difficult to pin down Ricoeur's own position in the midst of his extended commentaries on other writers, he does give a strongly positive valuation to narrative: we might even say that he mythologizes it. The other theorists noted above show a greater sense of reserve. In Gallie, "followability" does not in any sense amount to truth. In Mink, there is a clear sense that narrative goes beyond what the evidence of particular events can supply. And White, although he is not generally regarded as an epistemologically oriented writer, has emphatically suggested that we *impose* narrative on the world. We need not accept the position that White has sometimes seemed to contend for, namely, that the human world is at base chaotic, to accept the skeptical attitude toward the truth of narrative that White's position authorizes.

THE EPISTEMOLOGICAL LIMITS OF NARRATIVE

The ubiquity of narrative—its uncanny capacity to return from rumored death, its aesthetic and persuasive force as a way of making sense of the world—brings us back to the central question of this chapter: Does narrative have a cognitive value of its own? Narrative's ubiquity brings us back to that question by underscoring its importance. As noted above, one can answer both yes and no to the question: at the empirical level, we answer no; at the level of interpretive wholes or totalities, yes, for narrative bodies forth a view *of* the world—or a way of being *in* the world—that, if it did not exist prior to its appearance in that narrative, comes into being when the narrative comes into being.

Why does narrative continually return, even when it is programmatically refused? Why is narrative "natural" to human beings? The answer seems clear: narrative is intimately connected with the processes by which individuals and groups make sense of themselves—even define themselves. When we speak of such self-definition, there immediately enters into play something that is closely connected to narrative and that habitually manifests itself in narrative form—memory. When self-definition is in play, the question of how narrative is related to truth tends to resolve itself into the question of how memory is related to truth. We can think of the truth in question as primarily an identity-related truth, a truth that will sometimes converge with and sometimes diverge from another kind of truth that we can think of as a world-related or intersubjective truth.

In situations where memory's account of the past is unchallenged by some contrary account, and where we have no particular reason to doubt the reported memories, we customarily accept memory-based truth-claims. Under such circumstances we may more or less identify memory with (truthful) history; we may find ourselves speaking, regretfully, of a memory deficit (*Defizit an Gedächtnis*) when what we really mean is a history deficit (*Defizit an Geschichte*).[22] But at the present historical moment, the extent to which memories stand in conflict with each other is striking. Just as the solidity of a particular field of expertise becomes doubtful when representatives of that field contradict each other in the courtroom, so the solidity of memory becomes doubtful when different memories conflict with each other. This amounts to saying that the truth of the narratives that recount these memories is called into question. To put the matter another way: identity-related truth finds itself called into question by world-related truth.

What we must avoid is a romanticization of memory—which amounts to a romanticization of identity-related truth. The temptation is to take at face value the narratives that issue from memory. Where the mind in question is rational and attentive, the divergences may be slight between an account of the world that this mind narratively recalls and the construction of an account out of "traces" and "sources" (chapter 1). But the mind is not always rational and attentive, and when the deepest desires of individuals or groups are bound to a particular image of the past, the matter becomes even more difficult. In some situations today, memory is seen as confirming, justifying, and perhaps even grounding whatever identity a person has adopted. Where memory is seen as grounding identity, a deep commitment to the narrative that memory tells is likely, along with a correspondingly deep hostility to anything that would undermine that narrative.

It is possible to speak entirely in the language of memory and forgetting. Thus one could speak of a combined *Defizit an Gedächtnis* and *Übermaß an Vergessen* (excess of forgetting) prevailing in, say, Germany, or the Balkans, or in other regions, at certain (quite recent) times in their histories. But I wish to suggest (it is a Nietzschean point) that memory and forgetting are so closely tied up with each other that they are inseparable—that every remembering is also a mode of forgetting and every forgetting a mode of remembering. Thus, although I contend that the opposition between memory and forgetting does have a rough validity and usefulness, the interpenetration of the two categories means that it makes far more sense to speak rather of the acceptance or rejection of certain narratives—each of which is itself a bundle of rememberings and forgettings. The question then becomes, What criteria should one deploy in deciding to accept, reject, or partly accept and partly reject the narratives in question?

What seems manifestly clear is that the criteria *must* be epistemological and that they *must* reside outside the framework of narrative itself. We have a duty to be skeptical about the truth of the specific assertions of fact that enter into a narrative, especially in situations where such narratives play an important role in validating identity. This is not to deny that narrative may well have a heuristic importance for the historian. Historians in the midst of their research commonly find that the "premature" construction of a hypothetical narrative (or narratives) that attempts to "cover" the particular historical reality under investigation can offer insights. In constructing such narratives historians come to see more clearly what gaps still remain in their research—and thus the process of research is carried forward. Perhaps even more important, the historian may thereby come to see what aspects of the topic do not need to be researched (*limiting* one's research is essential if any research at all is to be finished). But claims as to the truth of the narratives in question must still be held in abeyance until the disagreements between competing accounts have been investigated and argued out.

Extreme cases often highlight problems that are hard to discern or even invisible in "average" cases. In short, extremity has a heuristic value, as narrative itself does. Consider the four extreme cases that follow.

CASE 1. As an undergraduate student in Saskatoon, I lived, one year, in a private house in which two upstairs bedrooms were rented out to students. The landlady, who was obsessively thorough about keeping the house locked up, told me an interesting story. She claimed that a gang of thieves was at work in Saskatoon, a gang with a peculiar *modus operandi*. The thieves would steal pieces of property and cunningly replace them with other objects of identical appearance but lesser value (one might imagine, here, an entire treatise on the metaphysics of theft). My landlady informed me that the gang had stolen various items from her house, *including the bathtub*. To my knowledge, no other person in Saskatoon was aware of the work of this gang of thieves, and its activities were never reported in the local newspaper. Skeptical about the existence of the gang, I attempted to persuade my landlady that she must be wrong, and that, in particular, the bathtub in the house was undoubtedly the very bathtub that had been in the house since its construction many years before. My efforts at persuasion failed utterly.[23]

CASE 2. In a celebrated case that has been discussed by the literary critic Terry Castle, two English academic women, Charlotte Anne Moberly and Eleanor Jourdain, claimed to have seen an apparition of Marie Antoinette and several members of her court in the gardens of the Petit Trianon near Versailles on August 10, 1901. In fascinating detail, Professor Castle recounts and analyzes their story. What is most striking in Castle's account is the ease with which Moberly and Jourdain found confirmatory details for their claim to have seen the late French queen.[24]

CASE 3. In the early 1990s a professor of psychiatry at Harvard Medical School, John Mack, worked extensively with nearly one hundred people who remembered being abducted by space aliens. He reached the conclusion that these people were not suffering from mental illness and had not merely imagined the encounters, but had had real encounters with non-human intelligent life. In Mack's words: "I am as careful as I know how to be in my diagnostic discriminations. I have exhausted all the possibilities that are purely psychological, even psychosocial, that could account for this."[25]

CASE 4. This is in fact a myriad of examples. From the early 1980s through much of the 1990s in the United States, many alleged cases of "repressed memory" related to "satanic" or "ritualistic" sexual abuse arose (memory of this abuse was allegedly restored thanks to the intervention of therapists).[26] The phenomenon still continues. However elicited, the material invariably takes the form of narratives that become more detailed and ramified as they are "worked on" and repeated. Large numbers of people in the "therapeutic community" in the United States regard such narratives as self-justifying. On occasion, gross miscarriages of justice have resulted. One of the most flagrant cases, briefly noted in chapter 2, is that of Paul Ingram, of Olympia, Washington, who in 1988 was accused by his daughters of having ritually abused them. Bizarrely, he was induced to "remember" episodes of such abuse, and in consequence he entered a guilty plea, which—too late—he attempted to retract. After fourteen years in prison, he was finally paroled in April 2003.[27]

What can we learn from these cases, and from the countless similar cases that could be adduced? They all underscore how evidence is far from being "evident." On the contrary, evidence is a frail reed, liable to be bent by subjectivity and undermined by carelessness and an uncritical attitude. Above all, the cases noted above suggest how easily evidence can be trampled underfoot by acknowledged or unacknowledged desire. Sometimes it is the desire to see oneself as such-and-such a kind of important or interesting person (a defender of hearth and home; a person important enough to be an onlooker at an Old Régime ceremony; an alien abductee; a protector of "the children"). Sometimes it seems to be nothing more than the desire to adhere to a simple and satisfying story of events. Perhaps, in the absence of simple and satisfying grand and master narratives, people's desire for such stories has fixated at another, more specific level, leading to a kind of allegiance very different from the national allegiances of old. Or perhaps it is simply a continuation of the hype and snake-oil salesmanship that tend to flourish in any commercial, market-driven society, where there are significant material rewards available to people who have a talent for persuading their fellow citizens of the truth of X, Y, or Z on grounds that ought not to be persuasive.

It would be easy if history were a matter of definitive truth, of an apodictic certainty admitting of no disagreement. In one of the least happy passages in the "Epilegomena" of *The Idea of History*, Collingwood asserts that "genuine history has no room for the merely probable or the merely possible; all it permits the historian to assert is what the evidence before him obliges him to assert."[28] Would it were as simple as this! But it is not, as chapter 6, below, attempts to make clear. Indeed, Collingwood himself knew better: in another passage he asserts that no achievement in history is ever final, that the evidence changes "with every change of historical method," that "the principles by which this evidence is interpreted change too," and that consequently "every new generation must rewrite history in its own way"

(248). I only need to add that this does not mean—cannot mean—that "anything goes," or that every "generation" (school, national group, paradigm) is equally justified in its writing of history. Collingwood also writes in this same passage that there is "variation in the competence of historians." Such a statement presupposes a capacity on our part for judging levels of competence. Doing so is one part of the task of historical epistemology. But it is also one of the tasks of history proper, since matters of argument and justification, and not narrative alone, make historical research and writing what it ought to be.

We all know the power of a good story. It is hard to define in a general way what the elements of a "good story" are. It is much easier to recognize a good story when one encounters it, especially when it already bears the imprimatur of time. Myth and literature are certainly two fields that are replete with stories so attractive that they are told and retold for hundreds and even thousands of years. We should also be aware—and this is the important point here—of the awkward juncture between the fictional constructions of myth and literature and assertions concerning literal truth in the world. One of the reasons that many works of literature and myth appeal to us is that they offer us a coherent fictional world—a world that, for all its peripeteia, finally is shown to make sense.

Gossip—which, evidentially, we can characterize as unsubstantiated hearsay—has a similar appeal. When we enter into the world of gossip, we move beyond the actions and sufferings of fictional characters (or characters whom we today *take* to be fictional) to those of real human beings. And here one risks entering into the territory of both epistemological and ethical transgression. One of the virtues of the time-tested epistemological practices of history is that these practices call upon us to consider the evidence for *and against* the claims that we might find pleasure in making. The problem with the evidence offered by the creator or proponent of a particular narrative is that it is often too integral to the narrative itself to be fully trustworthy. Thus we need not only *evidence,* but *evidence of evidence*: or to put the matter differently, we need concurrence among different pieces of evidence and forms of evidence. This is part of the reason why history must be not only (in some of its aspects) an aesthetic practice, but also a *discipline*—that is, an organized pursuit of knowledge by collectivities committed in principle and practice to the precise, methodical, and unending construction, dismantling, and reconstruction of the historical past. So long as the Certeauvian breach between past and present is maintained, the historian is better placed than are the practitioners of most other human sciences to carry forward the critical dimension of understanding. The stance of the historian implies a distance from the objects of her attention that *may* foster the idea that we really ought to try to get things right, even if no *practical* consequence hangs on doing so.[29]

———

In response to the question, "Does narrative have a cognitive value of its own?" the first answer must be affirmed. *Of course* narrative has a cognitive value of its own, in the sense that the coherence of narrative is the coherence of a possible world. Whether or not the vision projected by the narrative has an *actual* existence, it exists in the narrative, and it may well exist within the mind that conceived the narrative. But at the same time, and perhaps more emphatically, we must also say that narrative does not have a cognitive value of its own. What it has, rather, is a seductive power—a power that can easily be deployed in order to present the narrative's *possible* vision as an actuality. Here, we must say no to narrative: against its beautiful or sublime seductions we must bring to bear the deflating force of method and criticism. Among other things, this means that historians must proselytize by example, trying to be as careful as they can about matters of historical knowledge and as open as possible to the processes of argumentation and proof by which we test and refine historical and other claims—for it seems obvious that *the* truth will never be discovered.[30]

Narrative and the Four Tasks of History-Writing

W hat distinct tasks are involved in historical research and writing? Historians are not as clear about this question as they ought to be. Admittedly, rigorous conceptual clarity is not always compatible with the writing of coherent historical narratives. Moreover, scholars who fuss about the precise boundaries of the concepts they deploy may well end up becoming so interested in the concepts that the very idea of writing a history disappears from view. Yet at the end of the day we are obliged to say, with Francis Bacon, that "truth emerges more quickly from error than from confusion." [1] If historians wish to be something more than mere cheerleaders for this or that good cause, they had better be clear about what they are doing. Many historians undoubtedly learn to be clear about their own assumptions and practices by virtue of high intelligence and attentiveness to their work of research and writing. Nonetheless, it is usually best to reflect on such matters in an explicit way. What *are* the tasks of history-writing? Further: How do the different tasks fit together? These are the questions that I seek to answer in the present chapter. I enter into the subject by way of an erroneous opinion, the analysis of which will help us see our way to a conceptual truth about the writing of history.

As recently as the 1980s it was a widely held view among professional historians that the one truly serious task of history, making it a contribution to knowledge and not a triviality, was the task of "explanation." (I put *explanation* in quotation marks because we, reader and writer, have not yet come to an understanding as to what meaning to attribute to this word.) To be sure, the view that explanation is the central task of history-writing tended to fall by the wayside in the 1990s, when the "new cultural history" became widely fashionable within the discipline, and earlier commitments to social and social science history declined in prominence and influence (I discuss the rise of the new cultural history in chapter 10). Whereas social science historians took "explanation" as their main concern, new cultural historians emphasized "description" (preferably, "thick" description) and "interpretation."[2] Yet the older opinion—namely, that the primary task of history-writing is "explanation"—nonetheless persists, even occasionally among advocates and practitioners of the new cultural history. It persists as well among many theorists and practitioners of many of the social sciences, whose impact on history can hardly be discounted. But even if the opinion were no longer held at all, it would still be worth investigating, because some of the theorists and methodologists who focused on explanation managed, sometimes unwittingly, to clarify even the nonexplanatory tasks of the historian.

EXPLANATION AND DESCRIPTION

The view that explanation is the central task of disciplinary understanding—whether in history or in any other discipline—was most forcefully expressed by scholars who saw themselves as social *scientists,* and who viewed science in the light of theories articulated by logical empiricist philosophers.[3] In the methodological culture that followed from logical empiricism and was influential in the period from the 1940s to the 1970s, explanation had a privileged place. Note that I here use the term *explanation* not in the broad sense of "to elucidate" or "to make clear," but in the sense customary in philosophical and social science circles, where in most contexts to "explain" something means to say what caused it. That is, to "explain" something, as I am using the term in this chapter, is to offer an answer to the question, "Why?" (using "Why?" in the sense of "What caused it?" or "What brought it about?"). I have no objection to people using the word *explain* in other ways, for that is certainly their privilege. But if we are to think clearly about things, it is best that we not confuse different meanings of the same word. Hence my focus here on a single meaning of *explanation.*[4]

It is easy to find evidence of the privileged place of explanation, defined as I define it here, in Anglo-American philosophy of science. Philosophers of science in the 1940s, 1950s, and 1960s were overwhelmingly concerned with "explanation," which they viewed as the answering of the "Why?" question, taken in the causal sense.[5] Theorists and methodologists of social science followed the lead of these philosophers of science. Many methodological handbooks influenced by the logical empiricist dispensation proclaimed explicitly that the core task of social science is explanation. Such standard texts as Stinchcombe's *Constructing Social Theories* are clear on this point.[6] The handbooks are not always precise about what they mean by explanation, but usually the core, if not the exclusive meaning, is the answering of a causal question. Conversely, within this methodological tradition little attention was paid to "description," which was seen as essentially uninteresting. For example, the authors of *A Research Primer for the Social and Behavioral Sciences* maintain that "case study" type research has only a *preliminary* status: at most, it may suggest hypotheses for further research and may possibly provide "anecdotal evidence to illustrate more generalized findings."[7]

A generation or two of practicing historians appear to have shared the view that *the* task of historical research and writing is to explain historical events, while discounting or ignoring other possible tasks. To be sure, to find out what historians really were—and are—thinking about such matters would require a research project of impossible complexity, and the results would be problematic because historians do not always think clearly, or at all, about issues that are so theoretically oriented. The best we can do is look at what some historians have *said* about explanation. I ask readers to consider whether they agree or not with the position that each historian here quoted appears to be articulating.

In a 1961 essay, "Causation and the American Civil War," Lee Benson made use of E. M. Forster's distinction between "story" and "plot." A "story," as defined by Forster, is "a narrative of events arranged in their time-sequence": for example, "The king died and then the queen died." As for a plot, it is "also a narrative of events, the emphasis falling on causality": for example, "The king died and then the queen died of grief." Benson built on Forster's story/plot distinction as follows:

> Using Forster's criterion, we can define a historian as a plot-teller. Unlike the chronicler, the historian tries to solve the mystery of why human events occurred in a particular time-sequence. His ultimate goal is to uncover and illuminate the motives of human beings acting in particular situations, and, thus, help men to understand themselves. A historical account, therefore, necessarily takes this form: "Something happened and then something else happened *because*. . . ." Put another way, the historian's job is to explain human behavior over time.

Consider, second, E. H. Carr's assertion in *What Is History?* that "the study of history is a study of causes" and his repeated characterization of a proper historical account as one that gives the reader "a coherent sequence of cause and effect." Consider finally David Hackett Fischer's contention in *Historians' Fallacies* that "history-writing is not story-telling but problem solving" and that historical narration is "a form of explanation."[8]

The statements by Benson and Carr assume that the essential connections in a historical account are causal, concerned with articulating what brought about the next occurrence in the sequence of events. The revealing of causal connections is what I (and they) define as explanation. Fischer's position is ambiguous, for his definition of explanation embraces elucidation generally, not just causal analysis.[9] Nonetheless, Fischer's insistence that history is "not story-telling but problem solving" (a notion also advanced, as we shall see, by the French *Annales* historian François Furet) seems to confirm the presence here, too, of a bias toward explanation.

Of course, Carr, Benson, and Fischer are only three historians among thousands. But a bias toward explanation seems to be present *generally* among historians attracted by analytic philosophy or social science methodology. In short, it seems reasonable to regard the statements just quoted from Carr, Benson, and Fischer as symptoms of a larger commitment among historians. Other observers have noticed this same commitment. Thus the historian and theorist of history Paul Veyne observed in his *Writing History* that "there is . . . a widespread idea that a historiography worthy of the name and truly scientific must pass from 'narrative' to 'explanatory' history." Similarly, in the early 1980s the philosopher Paul Ricoeur declared, on the basis of his study of *Annales* school historiography, that in "history as a science . . . the explanatory form is made autonomous."[10]

The bias toward explanation among some historians and—even more—among social scientists is something that itself needs to be historically understood. First, in the twentieth century much philosophical and methodological thinking about science was influenced by the history of Newtonian physics. Logical empiricism, and much of analytic philosophy more generally, took a fact concerning that history and converted it into a principle. Physical science in the eighteenth and nineteenth centuries was marked by attempts to extend Newtonian theory to ever more phenomena. Within the Newtonian framework, the cutting edge of science was not to be found in "mere" description. To take the best-known counterexample, this was unlike the situation that prevailed, before the Darwinian revolution, in Linnean natural history, where kudos were to be gained by the discovery and classification of ever more types of organisms (only *after* Darwin did biological description come to be tied up with an explanatory project). In contrast, the payoff in Newtonian physics did not come in the ordering of phenomena into descriptive types. Rather, in extending Newtonian theory by discovering more laws of nature (or by showing how laws already discovered were more generally or intensively applicable than had been previously thought), physicists were engaging in what was ultimately an explanatory task. In laying out laws of motion, for example, they were showing why, under such-and-such physical conditions, a cannonball would follow such-and-such a trajectory. Nor did there seem to be an *interpretive* dimension to physics. Until the 1890s the Newtonian interpretive framework was almost universally held to be unequivocally true. In sum, it was not perceived as an interpretive framework at all, but as a rendition of the way the world (absolute time, absolute space) really is.[11]

Second, when we turn to the context of the human sciences specifically, we find that a striking feature of secular, modernist academic culture has been its commitment to metaphors of verticality—with surface reality playing off against a deeper, hidden reality. (The metaphor of verticality can equally well be thought of as a metaphor of *differential visibility,* and is akin to such contrasts as those between foreground and background and between on-stage and off-stage.) The use of such a metaphoric, which was perhaps most glaringly evident in Freudianism (id vs. culture) and Marxism (base vs. superstructure), was ubiquitous in twentieth-century social science. It is a common trope of modernist inquiry that things more or less directly observable are not the "real" reality at all. In this view, the task of inquiry is to get down to what is hidden—to "underlying" determinants, to the "fundamental" features of the situation. Metaphors of verticality tend to privilege the explanatory project. David Hume's demonstration that we cannot observe causation underpins the view that explanation is "deeper" than "description." When the philosopher of social science Philippe Van Parijis claimed that "any explanation assumes the operation of an *underlying mechanism,*" he unwittingly reported the presence of this same metaphor. Discussing Progressive social thought in America, Richard Hofstadter detected the assumption that "reality" is "hidden, neglected, and off-stage," a similar trope with an identical function.[12] When such metaphors are in place, the most striking insights will be those that claim to show how "on-stage" or "superstructural" things and events arise from previously invisible economic, sociological, or psychological conditions. These insights have an explanatory character, for they are answers to the question, "What caused it?"[13]

Base/superstructure metaphors are in no way contrary to the advance of knowledge, as long as they continue to produce new insights and as long as their heuristic, limited character is kept in view. But disciplines tend toward sclerotic self-satisfaction. Methodological rules articulated in one context are often inappropriately applied to other contexts. Interpretive frameworks all too often come to be seen as *die Sache selbst* ("the thing itself").

Consider the bias for explanation as expressed in logical empiricism. While logical empiricism gave way long ago to various neo- and post-positivisms, logical empiricist formulations remain important for two reasons. First, they express emphatically and with precision notions less clearly expressed elsewhere, and, second, many nonphilosophers, including a few historians, still cling to logical empiricist dicta of many decades ago and trot them out whenever they want to appear rigorous and methodological.[14]

In the first sentence of their once widely cited paper, "Studies in the Logic of Explanation" (1948), Carl Hempel and Paul Oppenheim declared, "To explain the phenomena in the world of our experience, to answer the question 'why?' rather than only the question 'what?' is one of the foremost objectives of empirical science." In a similar vein, Ernest Nagel asserted in *The Structure of Science* that "it is the desire for explanations which are at once systematic and controllable by factual evidence that generates science; and it is the organization and classification of knowledge on the basis of explanatory principles that is the distinctive goal of the sciences." As a final example, consider the following assertion by a number of self-consciously "rigorous" historians, appearing in a work that aspired to set the agenda for social science history in the United States, the Social Science Research Council's "Bulletin 64": "The truly scientific function begins where the descriptive function stops. The scientific function involves not only identifying and describing temporal sequences; it also involves explaining them."[15]

None of these authors denies that "description" is part of empirical science; such a denial would, of course, be anti-empirical. But, by the same token, they all hold that "explanation"—which they define essentially as I do here—is "the truly scientific function." Given the rhetorical prestige that attaches to the word *scientific,* we have no choice but to read these statements as manifestations of an explanatory bias.

Two mistaken prejudices supported—and to some extent continue to support—this bias. One is the prejudice for universality; the other is hermeneutic naïveté, or the belief in immaculate perception.

The prejudice for universality elevates explanation over "description" because in the logical empiricist view "description" is tied to the merely particular, whereas explanation is seen as universalizable. In the immediate background to logical empiricism stands the still remarkably influential opposition, first proposed by Wilhelm Windelband in 1894, between the "nomothetic" sciences, concerned with the search for general and invariable laws, and the "idiographic" sciences, whose focus of attention is held to be particular entities.[16] At least in principle, Windelband accorded equal status to nomothetic and idiographic investigations: in his eyes, both were science (*Wissenschaft*). Positivists, in contrast, restricted the name and status of science to nomothetic investigations, to those fields producing, or claiming to produce, general laws.

Because they often confuse "general laws" with other kinds of generalizations, historians sometimes miss the full force of the idea that a field is scientific only if it produces general laws. By *generalization,* historians usually mean a broad statement that is nonetheless still tied to a particular historical context. In historians' language, the following invented statement counts as a generalization (whether the statement is correct does not concern us here): "As a result of the growth of towns and trade, feudalism gave way to incipient capitalism in late medieval and early modern Europe." The "problem of generalization," as historians conceive of it, is usually the problem of how to get from fragmentary and confusing data to such larger assertions.[17] But such assertions are not what the logical empiricists, or Windelband before them, had in mind when they spoke of general laws. In nomothetic science, the desired generalizations *transcend* particular times and places, as in, for instance, the following invented statement: "*Whenever,* within a feudal system, towns and trade begin to grow [we would likely find enumerated further conditions, along with statements concerning their interrelations], *then* feudalism gives way to capitalism." In short, the generalizations in question are laws (which can be formulated as "if . . . then" statements) and assemblages of such laws brought together in theories.

The Windelbandian distinction between the particular and the general has often been equated with the distinction between "description" and explanation. Consider the following passage, which is the start of Hempel's famous paper of 1942, "The Function of General Laws in History":

> It is a rather widely held opinion that history, in contradistinction to the so-called physical sciences, is concerned with the description of particular events of the past rather than with the search for general laws which might govern those events. As a characterization of the type of problem in which some historians are mainly interested, this view probably can not be denied; as a statement of the theoretical function of general laws in scientific historical research, it is certainly unacceptable.[18]

As anyone willing to pause over this passage long enough to absorb its dismissive irony can see, Hempel is really making two moves here. First, he rejects Windelband's suggestion that historical research and writing ought to be defined by its "idiographic" character—that is, by a concern with particulars as distinguished from what is universal (namely, laws). Hempel concedes that "some historians" (we should read this as "unfortunately, almost all historians") are deeply interested in particulars. As a good logical empiricist, Hempel views such an interest as actually quite trivial. What is truly *serious,* in his view, is the articulation of laws and theories, to which the reliable "description" of particulars is related in the way that the pre-liminaries to sex are related to sex itself. Second, Hempel links "description" to the particular. These two moves add up to a profound downgrading of "description," but a downgrading that Hempel seems to have regarded as so implicitly justified that it required no explicit justification at all.

How so? Consider again the two invented passages, offered above, con-cerning the transition from feudalism to capitalism. Here is the first: "As a result of the growth of towns and trade, feudalism gave way to incipi-ent capitalism in late medieval and early modern Europe." This statement has both "What?" and "Why?" components. Clearly, the statement is de-scriptive, answering a "What?" question, for it asserts what was the case (or rather, what it *alleges* to have been the case) in late medieval and early mod-ern Europe: towns and trade grew, feudalism gave way, capitalism began. The statement is also explanatory, for it offers an account of what caused the transition from feudalism to capitalism: it took place because of the growth of towns and trade.

More precisely, the statement *claims* to offer a "description" and an ex-planation of something in the past. I say that the statement claims to do so, because it offers nothing that justifies our believing the claims. For example, it offers no evidence or arguments to convince us that the growth of towns and trade caused capitalism to emerge. To be sure, we might well find that passage in a history textbook, where it is hardly possible to provide support-ing evidence. But the epistemologically attentive reader demands that un-justified claims be *justifiable* (by evidence and argument), even though there may be grounds for the absence of evidence and argument from a particular historical work. Historians ought to be able to offer evidence and argu-ments for their historical claims, and to do so in a specific and not merely a vague, ostensive way.

We should also note that explanatory claims demand a different sort of justification than do descriptive claims. Any claim that is causal—that is, any claim concerning what brought about such-and-such a state of af-fairs—*must* involve counterfactual reasoning, as I contend below and in chapter 7 (although my assertion here is hardly controversial among those who have thought about the matter). Presumably, people will agree that the claim that feudalism's giving way to capitalism "resulted from" the growth of towns and trade is true once they have been persuaded by a consideration of the arguments for and against that proposition.

Let us turn now to the second statement: "Whenever, within a feudal system, towns and trade begin to grow, . . . feudalism gives way to capital-ism." This statement is very different from the first, for it "describes" no particular reality. Rather, it states a universal claim, a theoretical claim. Its relation is to concepts: feudal system, growth, cities, capitalism. When it is applied to a particular reality—say, Europe in the fourteenth century or Down-in-the-Boondocksland in the twentieth—it has an explanatory payoff, at least if the audience in question accepts the stated laws as true and agrees that the concepts in question are appropriate to that reality. "Why was there a transition from feudalism to capitalism in Down-in-the-Boondocksland in the twentieth century? Well, it is because whenever . . ." And so we have a form of explanation that has a portability, a universalizability, that mere "description" cannot have.

Where there is a prejudice for universality, people accord explanation a higher value than "description." It is widely held in philosophy and in social science that only knowledge of the general or universal (as distinguished from the local or particular) is truly scientific; all else is inferior. The prejudice for universality has roots in Greek thought, in Plato and (even more influentially for science) in Aristotle. In his *Metaphysics* and elsewhere, Aristotle contended that knowledge of universals is the highest form of knowledge.[19] In the *Poetics* he noted the implication for history, observing that "poetry is something more philosophical and of graver import than history, since its statements are of the nature rather of universals, whereas those of history are singulars."[20] In the modern world the universalizing commitment is still alive, although in modern thought it derives more directly from Hume and from Kant than from Aristotle. Poetry has dropped out of the circle of universal knowledge, which is now restricted to mathematics and the natural sciences—and social science insofar as it follows the natural science model thus projected.[21]

So the first mistaken reason for a general privileging of explanation over "description" is the prejudice for universality. The second reason, hermeneutic naïveté, leads not to the elevation of explanation but to the debasement of "description." By hermeneutic naïveté, I mean the mistake of thinking of the historical account as if it were a "view from nowhere," instead of—as it decidedly is—a view from some particular interpretive perspective. Modernist academic culture, particularly when it claimed the prestige of science, tended to repress the interpretive dimension. Both Marx and Freud were notoriously prone to such repression, but their offense is far from unique. Once again, logical empiricism provides an especially clear expression of a widely held view. Consider Hempel's "Function of General Laws in History." Historian-readers of Hempel's widely known paper will remember its centerpiece, the cracking of a car radiator. Hempel offered an explanation in a deductive-nomological form of the event, such that from certain initial and boundary conditions (for example, the bursting strength of the radiator metal, the temperature overnight), and from certain physical laws (for instance, concerning the freezing of water), we can deduce the cracking of the car radiator. The statement of initial and boundary conditions constitutes, of course, a "description." Ironically, at the end of his paper Hempel came to the proto-Kuhnian conclusion that the separation of "pure description" from "hypothetical generalization and theory-construction" is unwarranted. Presumably, then, every "description" is already permeated by "theory," as fact is permeated by paradigm in Tom Kuhn's image of science. Yet, in dealing with the radiator example, Hempel failed to take account of his own conclusion. Instead, he proceeded as if "pure description" were indeed possible.[22]

Hermeneutic naïveté is intertwined with the notion that "description" is intrinsically uninteresting. When the hermeneutic dimension is excluded, "description" gets reduced to data collection. On this point, positivism holds to a position that most historians will recognize as faulty. Yet even among historians of some sophistication, there remains a tendency to underrate the force and scope of the hermeneutic insight that all perception is perspectival. Richard J. Bernstein has usefully (if schematically) distinguished between pre- and post-Heideggerian notions of the so-called "hermeneutic circle." In many standard characterizations, the circle runs between part and whole within the reality that the investigator seeks to understand. For instance, a historian or a textual critic will come to understand one sentence of a document in light of the document as a whole. But in its wider, post-Heideggerian sense, the circle runs between the investigator and what is being investigated. The investigation will be prompted by the traditions, commitments, interests, and hopes of the investigator, which will affect what the investigator discovers. Conversely, the process of historical research and writing will change both the investigator and the audience—at least, it will do so if the inquiry is more than trivial.[23] To come to grips with the interpretive aspect of inquiry, we must make a reflexive move, looking at the way the inquirer's point of view enters into the investigation. The long historiographic tradition that holds to the fiction of an objective narrator feigning to be silent before the truth of the past resists self-reflexive sensitivity.[24] The tradition goes along with an underrating of the "descriptive" project, which, as we shall see in relation to Fernand Braudel's great work, *The Mediterranean and the Mediterranean World,* is far more complex and interesting than a hermeneutically unaware perspective acknowledges.

You will have noted that I have enclosed the term *description* in quotation marks, the intellectual equivalent of rubber gloves. Unfortunately, the word is tied almost umbilically to the notion of "*mere* description"—to the underrating of the project that it is meant to name. The project is the answering of the question, "*What* was the case?" rather than the question that is the hallmark of explanation, "*Why* was it the case?" (or "What *caused* it?"). Given the infinite variety of perspectives from which we can write a historical account, both projects embody an infinite number of difficulties and possibilities.[25]

Accordingly, a term not so suggestive of the mere copying of some external model is called for. Thus I favor *recounting* as an alternative term for designating answers to the question "What was the case?" Linked to the French *raconter,* the term encourages us to model the answering of such questions on the telling of a tale—in this case, a tale whose truth we affirm by means of various arguments, documentary and otherwise. There is clearly more than one way to tell a tale; by the same token, there are different ways of constructing or reconstructing the historical past. The term *recounting* helps us to appreciate that "description" is not a neutral preliminary to the *real* work of explanation, not mere data collection. It helps us to see that we cannot give description and explanation a differential importance in abstraction from the aims and audiences of particular historical works.

Those who miss the importance of recounting adopt (usually more or less unconsciously) one of two related positions. Either, while preserving a distinction between description and explanation, they see description as uninteresting (as when it is taken to be a mere preliminary to scientific knowledge); or they blend the two together, but in such a way as to reinterpret description as being nothing other than explanation. Both positions exclude recounting from the circle of valued knowledge.

The deprecation of recounting is closely bound up with questions concerning narrative and its validity. Narrative blends description and explanation. One of the effects of the bias for explanation and of the related bias for universality has been a deprecation not just of "description" but of narrative. The celebrated "revival of narrative" of the last thirty years had to work against the prevalent suspicion that narrative *as such* is epistemologically defective. When Lawrence Stone remarked in a 1979 article that narrative "deals with the particular and specific rather than [with] the collective and statistical," he seems to have been motivated in this assertion (which, as stated, is false) by the uneasy thought that narrative is incapable of the theoretical universality that explanation in terms of laws and theories promises, which would make it scientific. Thus narrative's alleged revival was shadowed by a deeply held prejudice working against narrative.[26]

We can get at the questionable nature of these views by looking at their articulation by François Furet, who dismissed both description and narrative for reasons closely connected to the philosophical and social scientific prejudices noted above. In "From Narrative History to Problem-Oriented History," originally published in 1975, Furet chronicled the rise of a new, analytical, conceptual, "problem-oriented" historiography, and alleged a "possibly definitive decline of narrative history."[27] He approved of these developments, for narrative, he held, is logically and epistemologically flawed: "Narration's particular kind of logic—*post hoc, ergo propter hoc*—is no better suited to the new type of history than the equally traditional method of generalizing from the singular."[28] Admittedly, Furet revealed himself to be a *disabused* positivist, for he denied that the transition from narrative history to "problem-oriented history" suffices to bring history into "the scientific domain of the demonstrable." Such a goal, he suggested, is probably unattainable, but at least the transition brings history closer to it.[29]

To what extent is Furet's characterization of narrative adequate to reality? Two points are of interest. First, like Stone, Furet alludes to narrative's supposed attachment to singulars, but unlike Stone, he gives the attachment an explicitly negative cast by linking it to the empirical error of faulty generalization. But the status of Furet's statement remains ambiguous, for he did not actually say (although his words appear to suggest) that narrative and generalizing from the singular have some special affinity for each other.

Much clearer is Furet's other assertion, namely, that narrative follows the (il)logic of *post hoc, ergo propter hoc*. The same assertion has been made by some other writers as well—including the literary theorist Roland Barthes, whose own brief comments on the allegedly fallacious character of narrative help to gloss Furet's rather clipped statement. In an influential essay, "Introduction to the Structural Analysis of Narratives" (1966), Barthes held that narrative is characterized by a "'telescoping' of logic and temporality": "Everything suggests . . . that the mainspring of narrative is precisely the confusion of consecution and consequence, what comes *after* being read in narrative as what is *caused by*: in which case narrative would be a systematic application of the logical fallacy denounced by Scholasticism in the formula *post hoc, ergo propter hoc*."[30] Even though Barthes's statement may seem puzzling at first reading, the basic point is simple. Barthes is suggesting that narrative is a sequence of stated causes and effects. In short, he is making the same assertion about narrative that, above, we found Lee Benson and E. H. Carr making about historiography. By the same token, he is suggesting that narrative is essentially explanatory.

Another causal/explanatory construal of narrative is to be found in the work of the American philosopher Morton White. In his *Foundations of Historical Knowledge* (1966), he contended that "a narrative consists primarily of singular explanatory statements," and that a history is "a logical conjunction of statements most of which are singular causal assertions." White distinguished history from chronicle, which is "a conjunction of noncausal singular statements." He then complicated matters by an explicit admission that a history may contain elements of chronicle and still be a history: this is why a historical narrative is only "primarily" causal or explanatory.[31] But he did not go on to consider what impact the presence of chronicle might have on the structure of historical narrative. Implicitly, he thought of chronicle as *mere* chronicle, just as historical "description" tends to bear the guise of "mere description." History proper is causal/explanatory.

The Barthes and Furet formulation of this idea is easily subjected to empirical test, for it makes a clear statement about the extant things that we call narratives. Narrative, Barthes suggested, confuses "consecution" and "consequence," leading us to see whatever it is that comes "after" X as being "caused by" X. Barthes's suggestion would be correct if narrative were indeed a chain of stated causes and effects, A causing B causing C causing D, and so on. If narratives actually do invite their readers to equate consecutiveness with consequence, *post hoc* with *propter hoc,* it follows that narrative does function as a chain of causes and effects. Further, if this is the case, narrative will be adequately understandable in terms of the category of explanation alone. Conversely, if we do not find that the *post hoc, ergo propter hoc* fallacy is prominent in actual narratives, this will suggest the need for precisely that attention to nonexplanatory elements in narrative that the recounting/explanation distinction encourages.

As it turns out, instances of causal-temporal confusion in narrative are fairly difficult to find. Admittedly, in a perhaps unexpected narrative sphere, the cinema, Barthes's suggestion is illuminating, for it casts light on how viewers make sense of film action. When a camera shot shows one person pointing a gun and firing it, and the next shot shows another person falling to the ground and lying motionless, skilled viewers normally assume that the second person fell to the ground not only after the firing of the gun but also because of its firing. But the cinema is in some ways a special case of narrative, for there is usually no narrator's voice telling us the story; instead, the film feigns to *show* the story. In consequence, cinema seems to depend especially heavily for its coherence on viewer-inferred causal connections.[32] In written fiction it is difficult to find instances of causal-temporal confusion in the absence of a narrator of a certain sort—one who, perhaps out of a stylistic commitment to parataxis, prefers to insinuate causal relations instead of stating them outright.[33] Written fiction thus makes clear to us that causal-temporal confusion is not an essential part of fictional narrative but results instead from the narrator's adoption of a particular style of narration. As for historiography, we can show clearly that, contra Furet, causal-temporal confusion arises not from the act of narration itself but from lapses in argument or justification—the third aspect of the historical account (and the third task of history-writing), beyond recounting and explanation.

In short, it is an epistemological-methodological lapse on the part of the historian—not a problem inherent to narrative—that leads to *post hoc ergo propter hoc* mistakes. Consider the following passage, from Nathan Rosenberg and L. E. Birdzell Jr.'s *How the West Grew Rich*: "It is easy to imagine business enterprises formed among companions who learned to trust each other at war or at sea, for it happens often enough in our own times. (The generation which fought the American Civil War in their twenties, for example, invented the epitome of enterprises not based on kinship, the modern industrial corporation, in their forties.)"[34] In the second, parenthetical sentence, Rosenberg and Birdzell appear to be making two distinct statements. They tell us straightforwardly that the invention of the modern industrial corporation followed the Civil War experience. At the same time, they insinuate that the invention of the modern industrial corporation was caused by the Civil War experience. Lay readers may find nothing wrong with this piggybacking of an insinuation on an assertion. But competently trained professional historians, when they encounter such a move, are likely to become suspicious and to ask for evidence. For example, how many of the inventors of the modern industrial corporation actually served in the Civil War? How close a connection can be drawn between such experience and their founding, two decades later, of corporations? What other factors might have prompted the development of corporations? The causal-temporal confusion in this text has nothing to do with the "particular logic" of narrative. It results from failure to adhere to a tacit rule in professional historiography against ambiguous assertion. One sees here an argumentative lapse, not the manifestation of an intrinsic property of narrative.

To sum up: narrative itself is not a scientifically disreputable application of the fallacy of *post hoc, ergo propter hoc.*[35] This is not surprising. What is surprising is that a view contradicted by the reading of almost any good narrative historian—Thucydides, for example—has been asserted without serious challenge. Perhaps this indicates the depth of the bias for explanation. The sociologist Arthur Stinchcombe suggested that "as the professional tone has taken over history (from the praising and damning tone . . .), the normal linguistic effect is to make the narrative *appear* causal."[36] Concluding that narrative is more than causal assertion, we are forced to attend to what is other than causal assertion in it.

NARRATIVE AND BRAUDEL'S *MEDITERRANEAN*

Furet's attempt to deny that narrative history is a legitimate form of knowledge-production is closely connected to the distinction between narrative history and "problem-oriented history." But Furet did not originate the distinction: it was proposed by Fernand Braudel in the same year, 1949, that the first edition of his *The Mediterranean and the Mediterranean World* appeared. At stake in the distinction between narrative history and problem-oriented history is a scientific mythology that long shadowed the so-called *Annales* school of French historians (discussed in chapter 10). In a review of Charles-André Julien's book *Les Voyages de découverte*, Braudel articulated the contrast between an *histoire-récit* that "too often hides the background of economic, social, and cultural facts" and an *histoire-problème* that "dives deeper [*plonge plus loin*] than events and men, a history grasped within the framework of a living problem or of a series of living problems clearly posed and to which everything that follows is subordinated, the joy of recounting [*raconter*] or of bringing the past back to life, the delights of making the great dead live again."[37] How are we to characterize the *histoire-problème* that Braudel recommended? J. H. Hexter offers an answer in a wittily parodic article on Braudel. Hexter rightly identifies *histoire-problème* as history in which the question "Why?"—in the sense of "What caused it?"—is uppermost in the historian's mind. In short, it is history that looks for explanations. As an example of *histoire-problème,* Hexter cited Edmund Morgan's article, "The Labor Problem at Jamestown, 1607–18," which set out to answer the question why, in a colony that by 1611 was on the verge of extinction, the colonists were to be found "at their daily and usuall workes, bowling in the streetes" instead of raising the crops needed to keep them alive.[38]

Hexter had to go to Morgan for an example of the kind of question that *histoire-problème* asks because *The Mediterranean and the Mediterranean World* is not *histoire-problème.*

First, the work poses no single, overriding causal question. For example, it does not ask the question, "What caused 'the Mediterranean world' to come into existence?" Of course, even to think of this question is to recognize the extreme difficulty of answering it. What about causal questions of a more specific sort? Hexter cited three instances: "Why did banditry flourish in the Mediterranean toward the end of the sixteenth century?" "What accounts for the considerable flood of Christian renegades into the service of the Turk and the Barbary states?" "Why did the Spanish ulti- mately expel the Moriscos?"[39] There are many more, but seen in relation to the work as a whole—1,375 pages in the English translation—they play a relatively minor role. They appear intermittently. We may read for sev- eral pages—even, exceptionally, for a dozen pages or more—and not en- counter the answering (or even the asking) of a "Why?" question. Then a question and perhaps an answer will appear. But one has no sense that the explanation, whether offered or only called for, in any way determines the general shape of the text. The explanations seem embedded in something much larger that is not explanation. For example, in the first three sections of chapter 1 of part 1, which take up sixty pages in the English text, I find only three clear instances of explanation-seeking questions.[40] While Braudel poses such questions somewhat more frequently elsewhere in the book, the early sections are not greatly atypical.[41]

Second, we are concerned not simply with the intermittency of Braudel's explanations but also with the range of the explanations offered. I have al- ready noted the affinity between explanation and metaphors of verticality. The metaphors are obviously present in Braudel's conceit that there exist three historical levels: the superficial, fast-moving, easily visible level of event; the more profound and slowly moving level of conjuncture; and the deepest geohistorical or structural level, which hardly moves at all and whose impact on human history is easily missed.[42] Moreover, he accepted the challenge that the conceit offers to the historian of explaining by con- necting one level to another. His most explicit statement of this aim oc- curs at the end of the preface to the second edition (1:16), and he also sug- gests it in his review of Julien. But as every serious commentator on *The Mediterranean and the Mediterranean World* has observed, Braudel failed to connect the different levels. Hexter noted that *histoire-problème* provides an answer to the problem "of bonding event, conjuncture, and structure."[43] But the answer is refused—to such a degree that the sociologist Claude Lefort, reviewing *The Mediterranean* in 1952, saw in it a "fear of causality": "The condemnation of the causal relation leads [Braudel] into a pointillism that seems contrary to the sociological inspiration of the work."[44]

Braudel himself seems to have recognized that *The Mediterranean* did not fit the *histoire-problème* mold. In the new introduction to part 3 written for the second edition, he suggested that recent research has made it possible for historians to choose from "two fairly well established 'chains'" in recon- structing the past—the chain of economic events and conjunctures, and the chain of political events. A fully explanatory history would presumably reduce one chain to the other. But he went on to assert that "for us, there will always be two chains—not one" (2:902). In the same introduction, he refers to the "bedrock of history" that is geography, and then immediately suggests that "the metaphor of the hourglass, eternally reversible" would be a "fitting image" of the work (2:903). In short, he himself deconstructed the metaphor of verticality that accompanies his notion of *histoire-problème*.

To what genre, then, does *The Mediterranean and the Mediterranean World* belong, if not to the professional genre of *histoire-problème*? Following Braudel himself (2:1238), Hexter suggested that it is "total" or "global" history.[45] This characterization begs to be filled in. In another important contribution to the Braudel literature, Hans Kellner showed that the totalizing aspirations (inevitably unfulfilled) of *The Mediterranean* help to identify it as an "anatomy" or "Menippean satire." In his authoritative—and self-reflexive—account of this literary form (the best-known manifestation of which is perhaps Robert Burton's *Anatomy of Melancholy*), Northrop Frye noted some of its most striking features: it engages in "dissection or analysis"; it is "loose-jointed"; it manifests "violent dislocations"; and it is apt, through the "piling up [of] an enormous mass of erudition," to turn into an "encyclopedic farrago" to which "a magpie instinct to collect facts is not unrelated."[46] Even those who have only leafed through *The Mediterranean* should feel a sense of recognition. But the anatomy, as Frye also pointed out, is "a loose-jointed *narrative* form," manifesting "violent dislocations in the customary logic of *narrative*."[47] In short, *The Mediterranean and the Mediterranean World* is a work of narrative history.

It would be an understatement to say that *The Mediterranean* is not usually seen as narrative. But this is because *narrative* is usually taken to mean "the organization of material in a chronologically sequential order," to quote Lawrence Stone.[48] Stone follows a venerable tradition. His definition of narrative has roots in Aristotle's *Poetics,* where Aristotle gives primacy to plot (*muthos*) over the other elements making up a tragedy.[49] But if, as is usually done, we take "plot" to mean the sequence of actions within a work, the notion of plot focuses on only one aspect of narrative. "Action" implies an agent, and it also implies a setting within which action takes place. Accordingly, to consider "chronologically sequential order" as the defining feature of narrative is to engage in an arbitrary exclusion. To be sure, "traditional" historiography does tend to focus on action, and in consequence history has often been thought of as the story of actions—as the *historia rerum gestarum*. But we should not allow what is only an aspect of narrative to define narrative as a whole.

More than a century ago, Henry James called into question "the old-fashioned distinction between the novel of character and the novel of incident."[50] The difference between the two extremes is a matter of degree, not of kind. We can imagine a continuum, running from fast-paced plots of incident (as in, say, some TV cop show series) to the novels of, say, Henry James. But the distinction between incident and character must be further broken down. Building on the Russian Formalist tradition, the narrative theorist Seymour Chatman distinguished between action (carried out *by* an agent) and "happening" (an impingement *on* a character). We must distinguish further between character (which acts) and setting (which impinges). The interaction of the four elements produces the narrative. Two of the elements (action and happening) *occur;* two (character and setting) simply *are.* The first two we can call *events;* the last two (to invent a term), *existents.* (Of course, existents can come into being, but this is no denial of the distinction between the emergence of an existent, which falls under the heading of event, and the existent itself.) Emphasis on one of the four elements perforce limits the attention given to the others. One might express this idea by means of a formula:

$$(AH) \times (CS) = k$$

(action times happening [that is, "events"] times character times setting [that is, "existents"] equals a constant).[51] It is simply tradition, when it is not uninformed prejudice, that insists on identifying narrative history with actions and happenings, for characters and settings can also in principle serve as the foci of a narrative as here defined.

Accordingly, the crucial question to ask, in deciding whether a given work is best seen as an instance of narrative history, is not, "Is this text organized in a chronologically sequential order?" It is rather, "How prominent in the text are the *elements* of narrative?" In *The Mediterranean and the Mediterranean World,* they are indeed prominent, even though only part 3, dealing with the "brilliant surface" (2:903) constituted by political events, is chronologically ordered. Succinctly put, *The Mediterranean and the Mediterranean World* is a work of narrative history that (except in part 3) focuses not on events but on existents. Braudel turned the historical setting and the divisions and subdivisions of that setting into a vast collection of characters. These characters make up the single, all-embracing character that is "the Mediterranean and the Mediterranean world" itself.

Many of Braudel's commentators have pointed out his penchant for personification. In an early review Lucien Febvre remarked that Braudel promoted the Mediterranean to "the dignity of a historical personage." Hexter observed that Braudel populated the *longue durée* with "non-people persons—geographical entities, features of the terrain"; towns have intentions; the Mediterranean is a protagonist; even centuries are personalized. Kinser noted that Braudel treated space as "a human actor energetic and prompt to change costume."[52] But we do not need to depend on the commentators, for Braudel himself was explicit about what he was doing. Consider the following passage, in the preface to the first edition: "Its character is complex, awkward, and unique. It cannot be contained within our measurements and classifications. No simple biography beginning with date of birth can be written of this sea; no simple narrative of how things happened would be appropriate to its history. . . . So it will be no easy task to discover exactly what the historical character of the Mediterranean has been." (1:17)

The Mediterranean and the Mediterranean World is best seen, then, as a vast character analysis, in which Braudel broke down "the Mediterranean," which begins as an undifferentiated entity, into its constituent parts, with growing attention over the course of the book to the human processes carried out within this geohistorical space. By the time he was through, "the Mediterranean" had become a massively differentiated entity. This is what we learn: that "the Mediterranean speaks with many voices; it is a sum of individual histories," as Braudel wrote in the preface to the 1972 English edition (1:13). *The Mediterranean* tells us what "the Mediterranean" was and, to some extent, what it still is. Braudel's explanations are contributions to this end. The work is a vast recounting, into which explanations are stuck like pins into a pin cushion. It is likewise a vast narrative, although more an anatomizing narrative of character than a sequential narrative of action.

THE FOUR TASKS OF HISTORY-WRITING

The force and implications of this chapter's distinction between description and explanation, and of its demonstration that Braudel's *The Mediterranean* is in fact a work of narrative, are likely to be misunderstood by many readers. Some may carry in their minds awareness of an earlier polemic, heavily marked by political commitments, concerning the desirability or undesirability of "narrative history."[53] Some will be inclined, wrongly, to see my attack on positivism's *a priori* privileging of explanation over description as, in some way, a rejection of the legitimacy and importance of historians' explanatory efforts. Finally, some will misunderstand the nature of the distinctions that the chapter poses. They are *conceptual* distinctions, aiming at clarity of thought about historical research and writing. To say that we can make a distinction in thought is not to say that we can always clearly mark out in practice the elements thus distinguished. In fact, the distinction between description and explanation is partly reader-constructed, but this is no denial of its reality, for the reader's active involvement with the text is a necessary condition of understanding.

As suggested at the beginning of this chapter, description and explanation are but two of the four tasks of history-writing. *Describing* some aspect of historical reality—telling what was the case—is the first task. A work in which this aim dominates will inevitably be ordered in narrative form, as defined here—that is, historical actions, happenings, characters, and settings will play (but in varying proportions) a prominent role in the text. Following on description is the *explaining* of some aspect of historical reality. If explanation becomes the historian's main concern, the work, in its focus on connecting *explanans* and *explanandum,* may well diverge from a primarily narrative form (although narrative does accommodate explanations).

Third, the historian claims that his descriptions and explanations are true: otherwise, we would conventionally regard him as something other than a historian (a place-keeper; a propagandist; a liar; a fool . . .). Thus the historical account has a third aspect, that of *argument* or *justification*. It is quite possible for a historian to turn aside from offering a first-order representation of the past: he might think, for example, that enough first-order representations, offering in each case some combination of description and explanation, have already been proposed. In such a case, the historian might well become fixated on justifying a particular representation of the past against one or more contrary representations. Here his account would have the form of an expository argument. Alternatively, the historian might come to fixate on "the sources," with description and explanation again receding into the background as he focuses on offering a commentary on, or analysis of, the source texts. Here the historian's account would begin to look a lot like literary criticism. In both instances the offering of a narrative of the past would recede into the background, for the *elements* of narrative (character, action, setting, and happening) would be presupposed rather than laid out in detail.

Finally, the historian necessarily *interprets* the past, for she both views it from a particular present perspective and addresses her work to people in the present or future. Perspective permeates all that the historian writes: we have access to no *regard de fin du monde,* and even if we did, it would be one interpretation among others, God's interpretation as distinguished from all the rest. Since the historical account is necessarily written from a present perspective, it is always concerned with the meaning of historical reality for people now and in the future—even if, on an explicit level, it denies that it has any such concern.[54] To the extent that the concern with present meaning comes to the fore, the historian becomes not simply a historian but a social or intellectual critic as well. Here, too, the historical account may well cease to be primarily a narrative of past events and existents.

The limits of this set of distinctions need to be kept in mind. The claim is not that the resulting schema is sufficient to underpin a *complete* analysis of works of history but only that the four interrelated tasks that it identifies are very important for the historiographic enterprise.

Consider the following sequence of statements excerpted from a freshman college history textbook—a sequence that, both in the usual definition and in the definition offered here, is an instance of narrative history:

1. In 1839, along with the other great powers, Britain had signed a treaty guaranteeing the neutrality of Belgium.
2. The Germans planned to attack France through Belgium.
3. They demanded of the Belgian government permission to send troops across its territory. . . .
4. Belgium refused. . . .
5. The kaiser's legions began pouring across the frontier [anyway].
6. The British foreign secretary immediately went before Parliament and urged that his country rally to the defense of international law and the protection of small nations.
7. The [British] cabinet sent an ultimatum to Berlin demanding that Germany respect Belgian neutrality, and that the Germans give a satisfactory reply by midnight.
8. The kaiser's ministers offered no answer save military necessity. . . .
9. As the clock struck twelve, Great Britain and Germany were at war.[55]

Each of the nine statements tells what was the case. But, taken collectively, they are more than just a sequence of descriptions, for they offer an answer to the explanation-seeking question, "Why did Britain go to war against Germany?" Once readers have passed through the descriptions, they will be positioned to see that the text offers an explanation as well. (One of the difficulties that weaker students have in reading such textbooks lies in their failure to make this leap.)

Explanation is dependent on description. To explain, as defined here, is to give an answer to the question, "What caused it?" In order to ask the question, we need an "it." Thus the question, "What was the case?" is primal: it precedes the explanation-seeking question. But the explanations offered will themselves be recountings of what was the case. Assume that an audience has been brought to an elementary understanding of, say, the French Revolution. The audience has been offered an outline of the Revolution: that it began in France in 1789 with the meeting of the Estates-General; that its first important symbolic event was the Oath of the Tennis Court; that the Estates-General became, soon thereafter, the National Assembly; that the storming of the Bastille happened soon after that; that there was a war and a Terror, and so on. Part of this recounting will include explanations of historical events and existents. The explanations, once accepted by an audience as persuasive, will become part of its image of what was the case—part, that is, of a representation of the past. But images of what was the case always make possible further explanation-seeking questions. These further explanations, if accepted as persuasive, will also enter into the image of what was the case and will make possible still more explanation-seeking questions.

Accordingly, what counts as an explanation in one context may count as a recounting in the next. The process is like the winning of land from the Zuider Zee. First, there is that part of the historical account that the audience—whatever audience it is, amateurs or the most "advanced" professional historians—simply accepts as what was the case, not (or not any longer) calling it into question. This is like land won from the Zuider Zee and now solidly under cultivation. Second, there is that part that the audience is inclined to ask further explanation-seeking questions about. This is like the present shoreline of the Zuider Zee. Persuasive answers to explanation-seeking questions are like pumps and dikes that will turn this part, too, into dry land—into what is accepted as what was the case. There is next that part—not knowledge but nescience—that is too far from accepted recountings to permit explanation-seeking questions, but which may become an object of explanation in the future. Here we have the deeper parts of the Zuider Zee, still hidden beneath the waters. Finally, not to be forgotten, there is the wider society within which historians write. This is like the North Sea, whose storms may overwhelm the dikes and inundate part or all of what had been won, with apparent security, for cultivation. When this happens, the old descriptions, and the explanations subsidiary to them, will come to seem mistaken; or, if not mistaken, misguided; or, if not misguided, at least irrelevant to the important concerns of the present and future. In response to the evacuation of what once seemed to be their inherent persuasiveness will come demands for a revision of the past.

Yet, for all the interweaving of description and explanation, the distinction between them is justified and important. Consider another passage from the same textbook:

"The Coming of the Revolution"

Faced with serious challenges to centralized power from the resurgent noble elites as well as popularly based political movements in the eighteenth century, only the ablest absolutist ruler, possessing in equal measure the talents of administrative ability and personal determination and vision, could hope to rule successfully. The French king, Louis XVI, possessed neither of these talents. Louis came to the throne in 1774 at the age of twenty. He was a well-intentioned but dull-witted and ineffectual monarch. . . .

Conditions in France would have taxed the abilities of even the most talented king; for one with Louis XVI's personal shortcomings, the task was virtually insurmountable. Three factors, in particular, contributed to the breakdown that produced revolution.[56]

Clearly, on one level, this passage offers us a descriptive recounting—a series of statements as to what the authors believed was the case in France in the period preceding the French Revolution. But on another level, the authors are beginning to offer an explanation as to why, in their view, the revolution occurred. While the distinction between description and explanation is not always clearly marked within historical texts, a clear marker is present here, in the form of a "contrary-to-fact conditional," or "counterfactual." As philosophers have long known, statements about causation presuppose counterfactuality. A historian who states that C caused (led to, occasioned, brought about) E is simultaneously implying that without C there would have been no E, all other things being equal.[57] In telling us that "only the ablest absolutist ruler . . . could hope to rule successfully," the authors of the passage quoted above explicitly introduce the counterfactuality that is present at least implicitly in all explanation. Historians who remain unaware of how explanation, in its appeal to contrary-to-fact conditionals, differs from description tread on shaky epistemological ground.

Description and explanation do not exist alone; rather, they fit within the fourfold matrix suggested above. Often in historiological discussion we make a distinction between "narrative" and "analytic" history. But the narrative/analysis dichotomy is too crude to contribute much to understanding. Braudel's *Mediterranean* shows that some narrative is heavily analytic—that is, it engages in the differentiation of hitherto undifferentiated entities. Conversely, much analysis proceeds in (conventionally) narrative form, following "chronologically sequential order": a model instance is Marx's *Class Struggles in France*.[58] The term *narrative* is often used confusedly, although the negative task of unpacking the confusions cannot be undertaken here. As for analysis, it takes place in quite different intellectual contexts, established by the four tasks of description, explanation, justification, and interpretation.

We have seen already, in connection with Braudel's *Mediterranean,* that analysis can occur in the context of description. It occurs also in the context of explanation: thus Marx's detailed analysis of the class structure of French society in 1848 aims at explaining why the French revolution of 1848 turned out as it did. Finally, analysis also occurs in the contexts of justification and interpretation. In the former case, the resulting focus on the texts out of which history is written may cause the writer-inquirer to be seen more as a literary critic than as a historian.[59] In the latter case, the resulting focus on the significance of the past for the present may cause the writer-inquirer to be seen more as a social critic and cultural commentator than as a historian.

Related to the narrative/analysis distinction is the distinction between "narrative" and "problem-oriented" history that Furet developed out of Braudel. In "From Narrative History to Problem-Oriented History" Furet seemed to imagine a breaking free of "problem-oriented" history from "narrative" history. In the introduction to *In the Workshop of History* Furet complained that the British historian of France, Richard Cobb, "turns history into a laboratory for a purely existential preference." Hating "ideas" and "intellectualism," Cobb transformed the quest for knowledge "into a passion for novelistic narrative." Lacking "intellectual constructs," he was a social historian for whom "only individuals exist." His narrative was guided by a sympathy for the "life" of the period he described. But according to Furet, sympathy, which seeks to displace "the explicitly formulated question" as a guide to research, "belongs to the realm of affection, of ideology, or of the two combined." Thus history à la Cobb "remains purely emotional," failing to maintain "cultural distance between the observer and the observed." The product of such a history is "erudition"—not, we are given to understand, the true seriousness of a "problem-oriented history that builds its data explicitly on the basis of conceptually developed questions."[60]

Yet, in his neo-positivist commitment to a universalizable (or at least a comparable) history that will supersede the current "proliferation of histories,"[61] Furet swept under the rug the fact that, on nicely "conceptual" grounds, explanation cannot be autonomous. Moreover, like many in the positivist tradition, he has forgotten that the explanatory theories he wants historians to deploy presuppose particular interpretive standpoints that the theories themselves do not bring to light. Descriptions (and explanations as well) must be offered from some place and for some motive. The interpretive dimension is thus inescapable. The first words of *The Mediterranean and the Mediterranean World* are telling on this point: "I have loved the Mediterranean with passion."[62] Braudel's words are as "affective" as anything in Cobb, and his history just as "erudite." These facts might be taken as excluding *The Mediterranean* from the true ranks of disciplinary history. In a review in 1953, Bernard Bailyn criticized the book for being "an exhausting treadmill," ruined by the fact that "there was no central problem Braudel wished to examine," painfully lacking in "proper historical questions."[63] But precisely at issue is what constitutes a "proper historical question."[64] To focus on explanation alone is to exclude this issue—and yet it perpetually returns.

To say that explanation presupposes description is to say that it presupposes a presentation of narrative elements. But historiography is a collective enterprise, and an individual historian may choose to forgo, in greater or less degree, the telling of a narrative that is already largely known. Indeed, such a forgoing is often necessary if historical knowledge is to advance. To the extent that a basic narrative is not told but presupposed, the elements of narrative will tend to fade into the background. In such cases, there is a genuine departure from narrative history. Thus, in rejecting the narrative/analysis contrast, I am not making the empty gesture of declaring that all history is narrative history.

The historian who is clearest on this matter is Alexis de Tocqueville. Consider the beginning of *The Old Régime and the Revolution*: "This book is not a history [*histoire*] of the French Revolution, whose story [*histoire*] has been too brilliantly told for me to imagine retelling it. It is a study of the Revolution."[65] Tocqueville is true to his word. Time and again in *The Old Régime and the Revolution* he refers to historical events and existents without recounting them in detail, relying instead on the reader's knowledge of them. His relative neglect of recounting frees him to move forward on the three remaining fronts. He addresses head-on the explanation-seeking question, "What caused the revolution?"[66] He argues explicitly against those representations of the revolution that saw it as essentially an attack on religious and political authority. He is likewise explicit about the interpretive dimension of the book and hence about the social criticism that it offers. As he observes, "I have never entirely lost sight of our modern society." Thus, among other things, he sought to highlight "those manly virtues which are most necessary in our times and which have almost disappeared."[67]

――――⊃⊂――――

An intellectual historian associated with the turn in the late 1980s to the "new cultural history" (see chapter 10) once suggested that intellectual history "must address the issue of explanation, of why certain meanings arise, persist, and collapse at particular times and in specific sociocultural situations."[68] Of course, this particular exercise in explanation, and explanation generally, is certainly part of what intellectual historians do. This suggestion is on the mark only if we understand that explanation is but *one* of the tasks of historical research and writing. Sometimes explanation will come to the fore; sometimes description; sometimes the task of argument and justification, by which historians seek to clarify how they know what they claim to know about the past; and sometimes the task of interpretation, by which they seek to reflect on the significance of the past for people now and in the future.

To grant priority to history's explanatory task is to put into the background the framework of assumptions that every explanatory project presupposes. These assumptions derive from the historian's own traditions, commitments, interests, and experience, which finally cannot be historicized, cannot be subordinated to an authoritative representation of history-as-a-whole. The conservative critics of historiography are correct: history is (in part) about values. Historians qua historians, given the largely unreflexive character of their discipline, do not seem especially well equipped to deal with this fact. Nonetheless, historians can at least know what they are doing when they are contributing to knowledge. It is not simply that they explain. On the contrary, they first of all describe, in delight or fascination or horror or resignation. Upon descriptions, explanations arise.[69] Descriptions and explanations presuppose an interpretive perspective, and in the best histories they modify and enrich such a perspective. The articulation of perspectives is a contribution to knowledge that historians too often overlook or view with discomfort.

For these tasks, argument and justification—and the historical epistemology that these presuppose—are a *sine qua non*. To the belief that history ought to be socially useful ideology, we must counterpose a critical pluralism that relies on standards of evaluation appropriate to the forms of knowledge being sought.

PART III

Objectivity & Speculation

Objectivity for Historians

—————⇒ CHAPTER FIVE ⇐=====

Is objectivity passé? A well-known historian of modern Germany, Geoff Eley, suggested in an essay of a few years ago that history ought to meld itself into the *"un*-disciplined" domain of cultural studies loosely defined (including such fields as women's studies, African American studies, ethnic studies, gay and lesbian studies, film studies, and so on). In Eley's view, such a mode of "un-," "inter-," or "cross-" disciplinarity "means transgression, . . . disobeying, . . . rule-breaking, . . . making trouble, . . . shaking things up, . . . being experimental, trying new thoughts, taking risks"; and it also has to do "with unsettling our customary conditions and habits of understanding, with the release of meaning rather than its predictable accumulation." Eley's unsettling "release of meaning" seems aimed at promoting whatever progressive political causes the undisciplined historian favors. Reviewing the volume in which Eley's essay was published, another historian, Thomas Haskell, noted that Eley has much to say "about the political perspectives that graduate students should want to embrace," but "scarcely anything . . . about the constraints that objectivity might entail."[1] "Release of meaning"—but how do we choose *whose* meaning? Is it essentially an arbitrary choice? And why should the "meanings" in question have any authority over us?

OBJECTIVITY AND COMMITMENT

One implication of the present book is that it is impossible to take seriously historians' (or anyone else's) blithely confident claims to have attained *the* truth of things. A related implication is that the disciplinary isolationism that arises from such confidence is unjustified. After all, historians do not have access to the authoritative narrative that would establish *the* right frame for understanding the general basis and direction of history. Nietzsche's assertion in *On the Genealogy of Morality* is correct: down here on earth, "there is *only* a perspective seeing, *only* a perspective 'knowing.'"[2] Accordingly, we must ask how historians are to choose between one perspective and another.

It is a hard choice to make—or rather, a hard choice to justify. One position is that the choice ought to be made on grounds that are in a broad sense political. That is, the perspective we choose ought to be one that can contribute to progressive change in the present. There is more than a hint of this in Eley's reflections on "historians and social values," as well as in some of his historical writing.[3] However, while Eley favors transgression, disobedience, and rule-breaking (all in the interest, it seems, of encouraging progressive change within the context of a discipline, history, that he sees as "more conservative than most"), he is also committed—as his words say and his work shows—to what he calls "the normal rules and protocols of evidence and argument."[4] In fact, the preeminent advocate for putting scholarship in the service of commitment was the French historian-philosopher Michel Foucault, rather than Eley or other advocates of a politically engaged "new" cultural history. Foucault exemplified his more extreme position in his life, and articulated it in two ways in his works. He wrote historical or quasi-historical studies, such as *History of Madness* and *Discipline and Punish*, that were primarily aimed at a radical transformation of attitudes and institutional practices in the present, and he also offered methodological (more properly, *anti*-methodological) reflections—in his book *The Archaeology of Knowledge*, in interviews, and in short essays—that were likewise aimed at radically transforming the present.[5]

I believe that the Foucauldian view is a mistake. It amounts to a recipe for the writing of works that are better seen as subjective encounters with the past than as history. There is no denying the brilliance of much of Foucault's writing. Notably, he was a master of the striking image or set piece. One thinks of his evocation of the alleged "ships of fools" that allegedly sailed up and down the waterways of Europe in the late medieval period. He uses this image to highlight his claim that in the late middle ages, far from being locked up in madhouses, the insane were allowed to wander about. One thinks also of the horrific set piece with which he begins *Discipline and Punish*, the execution of the would-be regicide, Damiens, in 1757. Even Foucault's rather abstract history of thought, *The Order of Things*, is enlivened by striking images, from the oddly illogical "Chinese encyclopedia" that he describes at the beginning of the book to the erasure of man by the rising tide of language at its end.[6]

But what exactly *is* the objectivity that Foucault attacks and that other historians give obeisance to? While various workable suggestions have been made, the actual content of the notion of objectivity remains elusive. It is often easier to begin by saying what objectivity is *not* than what it is. For example, Haskell entitles a review essay devoted to Peter Novick's *That Noble Dream* (see chapter 8) "Objectivity Is Not Neutrality."[7] Here Haskell is distancing himself from the notion that objectivity means attaining a perspective that is completely detached from the world of human commitments and desires (below, I give a name to this notion: "absolute" objectivity). In highlighting the idea that objectivity and neutrality should not be equated, Haskell means to suggest that commitment to objectivity does not exclude political or other commitments. On the contrary, in Haskell's view objectivity is perhaps most clearly discernable in instances where the historian has a "strong political commitment." The challenge for such a historian is to achieve, in the pursuit of an adequate understanding of the past, a measure of detachment from her own personal commitments. Such an understanding requires that we "strive to see things in a detached light," freeing ourselves from "life's most seductive illusion," namely, that "the world centers on me (or on those with whom I choose to identify)."[8]

Much could be added to what Haskell says here, but I will confine myself to two points that are not obvious. First, in seeing objectivity as coexisting with commitment rather than as achieving freedom from it, Haskell is pointing to an aspect of historical thinking that I alluded to in the introduction to this book, namely, its "unresolving" character. Second, he is here highlighting an important difference between what (good) historians aim for and what we find in the engagement of many theorists and social scientists (not to mention polemicists) with the past. "Detachment from one's own commitments" also means detachment from the project of trying to demonstrate the truth of one's own theory concerning human society. Philosophers, political theorists, social scientists, and others often mistakenly look for a conclusiveness in the work of historians that is simply not compatible with the project of doing history. They wrongly assume that the historian's work has as its determining aim the advancing of some particular political or theoretical position. Thus, when I published a book on Karl Marx, some people who encountered it assumed that I must have had the aim of either attacking or supporting Marx's views, when in fact my aim as a historian was to understand what those views were and how and why Marx arrived at them. The distinctive aim of the historian is not to show the truth or desirability of some particular theory or political orientation, although his work, if it is of any significance, will likely be relevant to such issues. Rather, the historian's distinctive aim is to illuminate the past.

Objectivity, then, is not neutrality—although it does involve a measure of detachment from one's own commitments. Another thing that objectivity is not is "balance," although in popular discourse today *objectivity* and *balance* are often seen as closely related, if not identical. For example, two slogans used by the Fox Television News Channel in the United States are "Fair and balanced" and "We report, you decide."[9] The implicit claim here is that an "objective" news channel is one that reports the different opinions or perspectives that are current concerning a subject and then allows viewers to draw their own conclusions. In sum, "objectivity" would be tantamount to neutrality between the different perspectives in question. By the same token, it would be "objective" for secondary school systems to give equal time, in the teaching of high school biology, to evolutionary and anti-evolutionary views.

The "balance" view of objectivity implies that objectivity is attained when all points of view are recognized, each finding its appropriate spokesperson. In this view, no particular account of reality can count as objective. Rather, objectivity is asymptotically approached *within the situation as a whole* as more and more perspectives are given voice. This is a position suggested by Nietzsche in *On the Genealogy of Morality,* where he tells us that "*the more* affects we allow to speak about a matter, *the more* eyes, different eyes, we know how to bring to bear on one and the same matter, that much more complete will our "concept" of this matter, our "objectivity" be."[10] This is an odd conception of objectivity, partly because it says nothing about the stupidity (or not) of the different competing perspectives and partly because it cannot be located in any particular work or statement. It is not surprising that Richard Rorty, in his own version of this Nietzschean position, argues that we do not need a conception of objectivity *at all*—that objectivity is completely reducible to social solidarity.[11] This is a logical development of Nietzsche's view as stated above, but it likewise says nothing about the stupidity, not to mention the mendacity, of the various competing views in circulation. It has no response to the observation that a hundred Fox News Channels, each cacophonously devoted to its own "point of view," are likely to get us no closer to "truth" and "objectivity" than one Fox News Channel. "Balance" between one stupid ideological position and another stupid ideological position does not equate to "objectivity," any more than does a "balance" in schools between a scientific theory like the theory of descent with modification (evolution) and a position grounded in religious faith (the Creator created all organic beings as they are now at or near the beginning of time).

However, "balance" can be understood in another, different way that does not amount to the offering of a supposedly "balanced" articulation of competing positions. Haskell puts this nicely in his 2004 review of the book in which Professor Eley's reflections appear, Leerssen and Rigney's

Historians and Social Values. Here Haskell suggests that the "balance" that historians ought to seek amounts to a "balancing act." More precisely, it is a balancing act between the ideal of excluding value judgments from scholarship and the view that the only thing that counts is striking a blow for one's own values. In other words, the balance is not between the different committed positions that are in play (a balance that of course includes the historian's own position or positions). Such a task would be nothing short of mind-boggling: How, after all, is one to "balance" the potentially infinite number of competing orientations—liberal, conservative, anarchist, syndicalist, radical, communist, socialist, monarchist, Catholic, Protestant, Islamic, Buddhist, Hindu, and on and on? It is rather a balance between commitment to the (disciplinary) value of objectivity and commitment to one or more extra-disciplinary commitments. In fact, the true historian needs to be committed to *both* objectivity and commitment, because "discernment of multiple perspectives is a condition of understanding human affairs," and thus is "also a prerequisite of attaining reliable historical knowledge." Haskell rightly notes that "this leaves the historian on a high wire, . . . grappling with the crosswinds of perspective and objectivity without any explicit instructions about how to proceed." The high wire act that Haskell evokes refers to one aspect of the unresolving tension that is part of—and in some measure peculiar to—historical study. Haskell is quite right to add that "those who will settle for nothing less than algorithmic solutions are best advised to seek alternative forms of employment."[12] Let them become mathematicians, analytic philosophers, or political "scientists."

Haskell's "balancing act" view of objectivity is nicely congruent with his earlier insistence that objectivity is not neutrality. Objectivity is not neutrality because some measure of commitment is necessary if we are to "see" the historical object at all (thus, gender issues in history were not "seen" until some historians developed a commitment to feminism). I would only emphasize that the historian's pursuit of the right kind of balance does not require putting forward a moderate, consensus-oriented, middle-of-the-road view. On the contrary, angularity of perspective can bring out aspects of historical reality that would remain obscure from more "moderate," "middle of the road" points of view. One can liken history-writing to the work of a photographer, who may sometimes light a surface from a sharp angle in order to bring out, by means of the heavy shadows that the light casts, features of the surface that would otherwise be difficult to see. Angular perspectives are not neutral, nor are they "balanced" in the sense of taking a "balanced view" of things. But such perspectives are certainly compatible with commitment to the project of discovering truth about the past. Natalie Davis's feminist commitment helped her to grasp the situation of the sixteenth-century peasant woman Bertrande de Rols better than she might have in the absence of that commitment (see the introduction to this book).

DEFINING OBJECTIVITY

Of course, we have still not arrived at a definition of objectivity, for we seem to have come down to the not entirely logical view that objectivity is a balancing act between objectivity and commitment. Part of the difficulty, here, lies in the notion of objectivity itself. In fact, objectivity is not a single concept, but a number of different concepts that are not entirely reducible to one basic concept. In recent years a number of commentators have made the point that the meaning of the term *objectivity* is variable. For example, the historian Perez Zagorin suggests that in contemporary discourse, "objectivity" is "mainly used with three principal meanings in mind, all of which are related to one another in the sense of sharing family resemblances." (In Wittgenstein's notion of "family resemblance," two different individuals may have no features in common, and yet be recognized as members of the same family because of features they share with other family members). Another recent commentator, the philosopher Heather Douglas, suggests that there are actually *eight* "operationally accessible and distinct senses of objectivity." She adds that "while there are links among these senses, . . . none of the eight senses is strictly reducible to the others." In consequence, we have to contend with what she refers to as objectivity's "irreducible complexity."[13]

How many concepts of objectivity are there, then? Or at any rate, how many concepts are there that are relevant to history? It is possible to divide up conceptual realities in different ways, and I do not mean in this chapter to dismiss other ways of dividing up the conceptual field of objectivity. My claim is only that the typology that I offer in this chapter will help us think more clearly about objectivity issues than we can without it. For the fact is, the word *objectivity* is too often used as a polemical device, with its meaning left completely unanalyzed. In polemics, the aim is to win the argument. My aim is not to win the argument but to understand things well—and perhaps, in this way, to win all the same.

An objectivity-claim, as understood here, amounts to a claim to possess cognitive or epistemological authority of an intersubjectively testable sort. Note how this characterization eliminates certain territories from the range of our concern. For example, a painter, composer, or other artist, at least if this person operates within the aesthetic dispensation of modernity, is likely to want to make authority-claims for his own work. He is likely to want to establish that his work is somehow "in the moment," a leap beyond what was previously done, technically adept, aesthetically powerful, and so on. These are claims to authority, but they are most likely not objectivity-claims as defined here, for the authority being claimed is usually not cognitive. To be sure, artists often claim a truth of *some* kind for their art, but these truths are most often presented as aesthetic, personal, existential, and so on, and not as methodically testable. In other words, the truth-claims in question are not in the same category as the truth-claims that the natural and social sciences—and history—put forward. These truth-claims demand acceptance by other researchers, who follow commonly agreed-upon procedures of evaluation designed to test the truth of such claims and to minimize the intrusion of error.

Within the general framework of an objectivity-claim as a claim to cognitive authority, it is reasonable and useful to distinguish among four principal senses of objectivity (see figure 5.1). These senses overlap with each other in practice, but we can distinguish them from each other conceptually, and it is often indispensable to do so.

There is, first, a philosophical or *absolute* sense of objectivity, which is deeply rooted in the tradition of modern philosophy from Descartes onward; it is closely connected to (although not quite identical with) the notion that searchers after knowledge are engaged in the enterprise of (in Richard Rorty's phrase) "representing things as they really are."[14] Researchers who are committed to the notion of absolute objectivity aspire to a knowledge so faithful to reality as to suffer no bias, partiality, or distortion. Further, they believe that all inquirers of good will are destined to converge toward the same set of representations, and when this does not happen, they are inclined to suspect the presence of incompetence or mendacity (or both together). Second, there is a *disciplinary* sense of objectivity, which no longer assumes a wholesale convergence, but instead takes consensus among the members of particular research communities as its standard of objectivity. Third, there is an interactional, or *dialectical*, sense, which holds that objects are constituted *as* objects in the course of an interplay between subject and object; thus, unlike the absolute and disciplinary senses, the dialectical sense of objectivity leaves room for the subjectivity of the knower. Finally, there is a *procedural* sense of objectivity, which aims at the practice of an impersonal method of investigation. Here, the suspicion of subjectivity that is prominent in both the absolute and the disciplinary senses of objectivity is pursued in abstraction from the belief that excluding subjectivity necessarily brings truth with it. Here the aim is less to attain truth than to avoid error.

In both theory and practice these four senses of objectivity blur together. They blur together theoretically because, without the others, each of them amounts to nothing. For example, in the absence of commitment to an ideal of truth (however hard to attain in practice), to the goal of illuminating the real character of the objects being investigated, and to good procedure, disciplinary objectivity would amount to one or another variety of "politically correct" orthodoxy. Disciplinary, dialectical, and procedural objectivity cannot be found in their pure forms in reality, and absolute objectivity, which requires a divine level of detachment and insight, is best seen as an ideal lying beyond human attainment (although not beyond human aspiration). Admittedly, in some fields in some periods, we can find *nearly* pure instances of disciplinary, dialectical, and procedural objectivity. But in general this is not the case in historical research and writing, a fact that we may take as a marker of history's impure, hybrid, neither-fish-nor-fowl, contradiction-laden and -tolerant character.

ABSOLUTE OBJECTIVITY. God's-eye view, view from nowhere, aperspectival perspective, Olympian neutrality. Aims to *see* the object as it really is. Values impersonality.	DIALECTICAL OBJECTIVITY. Involves connoisseurship (individual expertise concerning a particular type of object, e.g., Flemish Renaissance paintings). Aims to *interact* with the object and, ideally, to commune with it (and possibly also with its creators).
Seeks to *exclude* subjectivity, except for the objective subjectivity of God.	Seeks to *harness* subjectivity, making it a positive force for the discovery and advance of knowledge.
DISCIPLINARY OBJECTIVITY. Disciplinary consensus is the measure of truth. Hostile to originality-beyond-the-paradigm and to off-center viewpoints generally. Values impersonality.	PROCEDURAL OBJECTIVITY. Values *totally* impersonal procedures (e.g., double-blind experiments), with the intent of avoiding all subjective sources of error. Values avoidance of error as highly as the discovery of truth.
Seeks to *contain* subjectivity: accepts only the (unacknowledged) subjectivity of the discipline (subfield, research network, etc.).	Seeks to exclude *all* subjectivity.

FIGURE 5.1 Four Senses of Objectivity

THE ABSOLUTE SENSE OF OBJECTIVITY

Philosophers have worked longest with objectivity issues. The crucial figure for the philosophical discussion is Kant, whose *Critique of Pure Reason* (1781, 1787) was important in establishing both the term and the concept. To be sure, well before Kant various conceptions of objectivity came into play, although not under the name *objectivity*. Use of *objectivity* (French *objectivité;* German *Objektivität*) in something like the current philosophical sense arose only in the nineteenth century, largely under Kant's influence.[15] Earlier, in scholastic philosophy, *objective* and *subjective* referred, respectively, to objects of consciousness and to things in themselves, usages that are nearly the reverse of current usage.[16]

The absolute sense of objectivity is less a single notion than a set of loosely related notions; in fact, a large part of the history of modern philosophy is implicated in it. We should note first of all the twofold character of the project of "representing things as they really are": ontological (things "as they really are"), and epistemological (since we seek "to represent" things, and can go nowhere without this representation). We can also identify normative and methodological dimensions of absolute objectivity.[17] Further, as Thomas Nagel has pointed out, the notion of absolutely objective knowledge is quite complicated, since by definition absolutely objective knowledge escapes the constraints of subjectivity and partiality—yet if an absolutely objective view of reality is to be all-embracing, it must include the particular, subjective views of reality that exist and thus are *also* part of that reality. Ideally, the objective and the subjective sides of objectivity go together. But they go together only *ideally;* in actual fact, the absolute sense of objectivity comes up against an infinite regress, as Nagel notes. This is why, taken to its extreme, absolute objectivity offers a "view from nowhere": it is a view that we cannot situate, for to be fully comprehensive it would need to view itself viewing, and so on *ad infinitum*.[18]

However, it is misleading to focus too narrowly on the "view from nowhere" conundrum. Much of twentieth-century philosophical discussion presented objectivity less as a matter of "representing things as they really are" than as a matter of arriving at criteria for judging claims to have represented things as they really are. These criteria then help us advance toward knowledge-claims sufficiently authoritative that no rational person, after due investigation, would call them into doubt. And the criteria themselves ought to evoke a similarly universal, rational assent. The knowledge produced would at least *move us in the direction* of the Cartesian (and Baconian) "absolute conception of reality."[19] Of course, we may never actually *arrive* at such a conception, but as rational human beings we can be expected to converge toward an approximation of it. Absolute objectivity, then, presents itself as absolute not in its certitude or infallibility, but rather in the hold that it ought to have on us as rational beings.

Until the 1960s, the dominant assumption in philosophy of science was that rational acceptance or rejection involves bringing to bear the logical weight of observation on specific theoretical statements. This was true equally of Karl Popper and his followers, who maintained that scientific laws can never be verified but only falsified, and of such logical empiricists as Rudolf Carnap and Carl Hempel. The model presupposed that it is possible to test single sentences while leaving aside the question of the validity of the epistemological framework as a whole. Subsequent reflection called into doubt both the logical model and the possibility of singular verification (or falsification). The result was a lively discussion in philosophy. After 1970 or so, much of the discussion took place under the heading "realism" rather than "objectivity," but it embraced a similar range of concerns.[20] Hilary Putnam and Richard Rorty, among many others, were prominent contributors to this philosophical discussion.[21]

Our concern here is much more with the extra-philosophical discussion of objectivity. Yet philosophical concerns are important to many of the extra-philosophical discussions, some of which began as debates with and among philosophers. In particular, philosophers' discussions of *rationality* and of *relativism* had some impact on the wider discussion of objectivity issues from the 1970s onward. Two loci of debate are of special interest because of the issues they raised and the attention they received. One locus, brought into being by the publication in 1962 of Thomas S. Kuhn's *The Structure of Scientific Revolutions,* was centered on the question of the rationality of science; the other, prompted by the process of decolonization that was then going on and by the growing prominence of sociology and anthropology, concerned cultural relativism. In both instances, philosophers were led to say interesting things in part as a result of external engagements—with history of science in the one case, and with sociology and anthropology in the other.

Many philosophers were disturbed by *The Structure of Scientific Revolutions.* They were especially disturbed by Kuhn's account of how a scientific community moves from adherence to one "paradigm," or set of preferred examples, theories, and problems, to adherence to its successor. Since different paradigms are, Kuhn contended, "incommensurable," the reasons that the proponents of a new paradigm put forward for adopting it do not count, he held, for adherents of the currently dominant paradigm. Accordingly, the shift from one paradigm to another is akin, he suggested, to a conversion experience.[22] The shift thus seemed in some deep sense to be irrational. Further, if we take Kuhn's talk of conversion seriously, we must see him as an epistemological relativist, at least insofar as evaluations carried out across paradigms are concerned. That is, we must see him as adhering to the characteristically relativist view that there is no neutral way of choosing between the (two or more) sets of background principles and standards of evaluation that could be used to evaluate (assess, establish) the truth of the competing knowledge-claims in question; in brief, we can find no neutral authoritative view.[23] Little wonder, then, that many philosophers accused Kuhn of being an irrationalist and a relativist. The two charges were closely connected to each other, and both were connected to the alleged impossibility of engaging in the objective evaluation of scientific knowledge-claims. Those philosophers who accused Kuhn of relativism and irrationalism were really accusing him of abandoning objectivity in its absolute, philosophical sense.[24]

The discussion of relativism that took place in the context of the problem of other cultures also connected with the discussion of objectivity in the late twentieth century. Two convenient anthologies provide access to the cultural relativism discussion from the 1960s to the beginning of the 1980s: Bryan Wilson's collection *Rationality* (1970), and Martin Hollis and Steven Lukes's collection *Rationality and Relativism* (1982).[25] The philosophers, sociologists, and anthropologists represented in the two anthologies attempted to come to grips with such matters as cargo cults, magic, and the relation between African traditional thought and Western science. In thus going beyond the purely *theoretical* curiosity of modern philosophy, they anticipated the direction taken by the objectivity discussion in the last two decades of the twentieth century. Yet they did not focus on objectivity *per se,* for their main concern was not with finding criteria that would enable us to judge the correctness of competing beliefs or belief systems. Rather, their concern was with "trans-cultural and trans-theoretical understanding and . . . mutual understanding in general."[26] This problem of "trans-" understanding connects closely with the emergence of the notion of disciplinary objectivity.

THE DISCIPLINARY SENSE OF OBJECTIVITY

Disciplinary objectivity emphasizes not universal criteria of judgment but particular, yet still authoritative, disciplinary criteria. It emphasizes not the eventual convergence of all inquirers of good will but the proximate convergence of accredited inquirers within a given field.[27] To be sure, it is misleading to paint too stark an opposition between absolute and disciplinary objectivity. In practice, there seem to be defensible alternatives between these extremes, and to the extent that this is so, the senses blur into each other.[28] But the blurrings on the conceptual level are countered by institutional separations. Disciplines (subdisciplines, research fields, etc.) exist. Defined institutionally, disciplinary objectivity refers to the claim by practitioners of a particular discipline (subdiscipline, research field, etc.) to have authoritative jurisdiction over its area of competence. Such claims take different forms, with different degrees of explicitness and articulation. The groundings vary from discipline to discipline and from field to field, and they change over time as well. On the most elemental and inarticulate level, disciplinary objectivity-claims appear in, for example, the conviction of historians that historians, rather than sociologists, are able to get at the truth of the past; the conviction of philosophers that they, rather than historians, are able to get at the nature of truth; the conviction of literary scholars that they, rather than historians, are able to get at the truth of literary works; and the conviction of physicists that they, rather than chemists, are able to get at the truth of the physical universe.

Disciplinary objectivity is tied up with the dynamics of the modern academic enterprise, which is sharply divided by discipline and field and fractured by competing claims to authority (this is why boundary disputes, although not always identified as such, come up repeatedly in intellectual discussion). We can, of course, imagine other kinds of intellectual environments, in which people would eschew the making of disciplinary objectivity-claims. They might do so because they believe that they have achieved a *generally* authoritative view: in this case, the claim to disciplinary objectivity would be unnecessary. Or they might do so because they believe that they have developed a special, individual sensitivity to the object of their investigation: for example, the biologist Barbara McClintock saw herself as having "a feeling for the organism," and art historians and critics have often sought to cultivate a similar orientation toward works of art.[29] Here, a claim is being made to dialectical objectivity, involving an interaction between researcher and object; in such a case, connoisseurship might well hold sway over the impersonality that absolute and disciplinary objectivity recommend. Finally, we can imagine investigators so confident of their personal vision or, conversely, so modest about their ability to contribute to knowledge at all, that nothing remotely like a disciplinary objectivity-claim would be made. Edward Gibbon in *The Decline and Fall of the Roman Empire* might be taken as exemplifying the first type; Michel de Montaigne, in his *Essays,* the second.

It is significant that I here evoke two nonacademic authors—writers who did not see themselves as participants in a collective, unified, search for knowledge. Disciplinary objectivity-claims can arise only when such a collective project is in place, for claims of this sort are a way of asserting, at least over a limited domain, the unity of knowledge. But disciplinary objectivity-claims are *also* products of epistemological insecurity. They are likely to arise only when the faith in one indivisible truth that accompanies absolute objectivity seems unsustainable, and when there are doubts about the reliability of personal vision.

Epistemological insecurity among social scientists and humanists helps to explain the enormous impact of Kuhn's *Structure of Scientific Revolutions* beyond its special field: the history, philosophy, and sociology of natural science. As is well known, Kuhn went out of his way to deny that his account of natural science was applicable to the social sciences, let alone to the humanities.[30] Yet by the early 1970s acquaintance with *The Structure of Scientific Revolutions* was *de rigueur* in the social sciences, and was becoming so in the humanities.[31] The historian David Hollinger, writing in the *American Historical Review* in 1973, identified an important reason for the book's appeal: in Hollinger's words, it offered social scientists (including historians) a "sense of validity, or objectivity."[32]

Hollinger's assessment of Kuhn's book will seem strange to some readers, for, as Hollinger noted, many philosophers insisted that Kuhn had "no sense of validity at all"—that he had "so relativized even the developed [that is, natural] sciences as to deny their claims to objectivity."[33] Clearly, to use my terminology, Kuhn denied the notion of *absolute* objectivity; in this regard, Kuhn's "hard" philosophical critics were right in their reaction to his book. But they were wrong in thinking that to deny absolute objectivity is to deny objectivity generally. The paradigm, which holds together the members of a "mature scientific community,"[34] provides a court of appeal that will support objectivity-claims: not an absolute court of appeal, but one that will serve within a particular community at a particular time. If our commitment is to absolute objectivity, the position that Kuhn articulated in *The Structure of Scientific Revolutions* can only appear as an arrant, and errant, relativism. Yet, as Hollinger pointed out, even though historians had long ago forsaken "pretensions to 'scientific history,'" they continued "to term good scholarship 'objective.'" The basis for this continued claim to objectivity lay, Hollinger contended, in the wide degree of intersubjective agreement among professional historians as to the criteria for a successful work of historical scholarship.[35] Kuhn's image of the "normal" scientific community united by a paradigm is simply a more cohesive form of this sort of professional agreement.[36]

Questions of disciplinary objectivity are of compelling importance in our knowledge-making institutions. The system is a multicentered one, in which academic authority is constantly being disputed and reimposed. In the absence of a neutral view, disciplinary objectivity stands as a highly important form of academic authority. After all, the perpetually recurring question, which scholars must answer if they are ever to be heard, is "By what authority do you speak?" The claim to disciplinary objectivity, like the claim to absolute objectivity, offers an answer to this question.

THE DIALECTICAL SENSE OF OBJECTIVITY

Dialectical objectivity offers a different answer. A striking feature of both absolute and disciplinary objectivity is their negative relation to subjectivity. Absolute objectivity seeks to exclude subjectivity, and disciplinary objectivity seeks to contain it. However, the assumed opposition between objectivity and subjectivity emerged historically. In a paper on seventeenth-century conceptions of objectivity, the historian of science Peter Dear has noted the disappearance in the early modern period of the use of the term *objectivity* to refer to a *mental* object, namely, a true representation in the mind, and its use instead to designate the effort to remove from the project of science all features deemed inappropriate to true knowledge. The "inappropriate" features all had to do with subjectivity.[37] Studying nineteenth-century conceptions of scientific objectivity, Daston and Galison similarly note the "negative character" of these conceptions.[38] Phrases like "aperspectival objectivity" and "view from nowhere" rightly draw attention to this negativity.[39] In contrast, dialectical objectivity involves a positive attitude toward subjectivity. The defining feature of dialectical objectivity is the claim that subjectivity is indispensable to the constituting of objects. Associated with this feature is a preference for "doing" over "viewing."

An orientation toward "doing" (practice) permeates a number of different philosophical schools or tendencies, and so it is not surprising that the notion of dialectical objectivity has appeared in a variety of contexts. One early articulation appears in Nietzsche's *On the Uses and Disadvantages of History for Life* (1874). Lamenting that his fellow classicists often had no involvement whatsoever with the Greeks whom they studied, Nietzsche contended that unless the historian already has within himself something of what a particular moment of the past offers, he will fail to see what is being given to him. In other words, *subjectivity* is needed for *objectivity;* or, as Nietzsche put it, "Objectivity is required, but as a positive quality."[40] Working along the same general line, Heidegger in *Being and Time* (1927) argued that objects first become known to us in the course of our action in the world, not through theoretical contemplation.[41] Similar conceptions have also been advanced by a wide variety of other thinkers, often linked to pragmatist, existentialist, or phenomenological tendencies in philosophy.[42]

For a sense of how dialectical objectivity has been thought about in a neighboring discipline to history, anthropology, we can hardly do better than rely on the anthropologist Johannes Fabian's 1991 essay, "Ethnographic Objectivity Revisited: From Rigor to Vigor."[43] Fabian first addressed objectivity in a 1971 paper, "History, Language and Anthropology."[44] He was led to write this earlier paper by his reaction against two views concerning ethnographic objectivity that were then circulating. One view was that the standard for evaluating the objectivity of ethnographic research and writing is "scientific logic."[45] This view, which we can recognize as a version of "absolute" objectivity, came to anthropology from logical empiricist (or "logical positivist") philosophy. The second view, inspired by Kuhn's *Structure of Scientific Revolutions,* was that truly objective knowledge is only possible within the framework of a paradigm. Anthropologists who adhered to this view thought it unfortunate that anthropology was "pre-paradigmatic."[46] This was not Fabian's worry; on the contrary, he declared in his 1971 paper that Kuhn's view "anoints the fetish of professionalism."[47] Reacting against these two views—but especially against the "positivist" view—Fabian argued that objectivity in anthropology needs a foundation in human intersubjectivity, and that such objectivity can only be attained through the communicative interaction that occurs in language.[48]

We can already recognize Fabian's position as dialectical in character, since it emphasizes the notion of interaction. Of course, historians characteristically deal with dead people rather than with the live ones favored by anthropologists, and thus it is not immediately clear how historical research and writing can be dialectical. However, the dialectical interaction that Fabian emphasizes is focused on a problem that has its close analog in historical investigation: How do anthropologists turn their experiences with a given culture into objects of anthropological investigation and reflection? In short, Fabian's concern is with objectivity as *the making of objects*—as "objectification."[49] This is what historians worth their salt do all the time—they make *historical* objects. For example, Fernand Braudel's great achievement was to turn the Mediterranean, which he loved so much, into a historical object (chapter 4).

Fabian came to be interested in objectification as a result of his early fieldwork on a religious movement, the Jamaa movement in Katanga. The problem for the young anthropologist was that Jamaa lacked almost all the usual identifying characteristics of a religious movement. It had none of the "ritual paraphernalia, . . . insignia, biblical attire, communal buildings, etc., typical for so many African religious movements"; its social activities were localized and not especially distinctive; membership was scattered, and its distribution unrevealing; formal organization was lacking; and the founder and prominent followers denied that they had founded a movement.[50] In this situation, Fabian did not find helpful the positivist assumption that objectivity is a product of correct method; indeed, he finally concluded that positivistic approaches conceal everything that is important about objectivity. Positivism wrongly assumed that social scientific knowledge is based on facts that are simply "there"; in consequence, it ignored the problem of how the objects of anthropological investigation are constituted—how, for example, we come to see a particular set of phenomena as "a religious movement."

At first glance, dialectical objectivity may seem antithetical to absolute objectivity. But consider Kant, whose *Critique of Pure Reason* offered an account of how the understanding, through its imposition of the categories of the understanding (unity, plurality, totality, causality, and the like) on the confused manifold of subjective impressions, confers objectivity on those impressions. We can take this account in two ways. Insofar as we stress the *universality* of the categories—their being common to all rational beings—we will see Kant as a theorist of absolute objectivity, an objectivity stripped of everything personal and idiosyncratic. But insofar as we stress the *active* character of the knowing subject, Kant appears as, despite himself, a theorist of dialectical objectivity.[51] Thus, there is a strange and telling symbiosis between absolute objectivity and dialectical objectivity. Indeed, we might even see absolute objectivity as a special case of dialectical objectivity, requiring the construction of a particular *sort* of knowing subject, namely, a subject who is absolutely authoritative.

THE PROCEDURAL SENSE OF OBJECTIVITY

Procedural objectivity, too, has a complex relation with the other types. We can regard it as a modification of absolute objectivity, but a modification that focuses solely on impersonality of procedure, in abstraction from the hoped-for aim of truth; thus, it widens the gap between truth and objectivity that is already present in the discussion of absolute objectivity. Procedural objectivity can also be seen as an application in a particular direction of dialectical objectivity, one in which a rule-bound mode of action requires the construction of subjects appropriate to it—subjects, that is, who can apply, and live by, rules. Yet the governing metaphor of procedural objectivity is not visual, as in absolute objectivity: it does not offer us a "view." Nor does it stress action, as dialectical objectivity does. Rather, its governing metaphor is tactile, in the negative sense of "hands off!" Its motto might well be "untouched by human hands."

To add flesh to these rather abstract assertions, we can usefully evoke the work that the historian of science Theodore M. Porter has done on bureaucratic and scientific standardization.[52] Porter is one of a group of talented historians of science who in the 1980s and 1990s made it their business to write the history—or, perhaps better, the histories—of objectivity.[53] Examining modern bureaucratic administration, Porter shows that objectivity in the bureaucratic sphere is best seen as a set of rules for narrowing the play of subjectivity. The rules provide an alternative to personal judgment exercised by bureaucrats. (The less that bureaucrats are respected and trusted in a particular society, the more detailed the rules. And in societies where judges are not respected or trusted, attempts will be made to reduce them, too, to the status of rule-following minor officials lacking any right to make judgments on their own.) The rules substitute for personal judgment in an entirely negative way, appealing neither to transcendent value (as in absolute objectivity) nor to community standards (as in disciplinary objectivity). In a situation where values are in conflict and consensus elusive, such rules may well be the only thing that permits agreed-upon public action to continue at all.

Historically, the advance of impersonality in scientific practice went along with, and promoted, the progress of standardization (of measurements, categories, etc.). On the one hand, standardization has an *objective* side: categories are imposed on the world of objects, as in the creation of uniform measures and of statistical classifications that define homogeneous classes of people. Less obviously, standardization of *subjects* has also occurred, through the imposition of constraints intended to limit the exercise of personal judgment. For example, rules of statistical inference and rigid interview protocols are designed to make knowledge as independent as possible of the people involved in producing it. Here Porter's research runs along a line also charted out by Daston and Galison, who have shown that suspicion of certain aspects of subjectivity—namely, of "interpretation, selectivity, artistry, and judgment itself"—became in the nineteenth century a prominent feature of objectivity in science.[54]

Porter brilliantly shows how objectivity in the bureaucratic sphere replaces "true" or "best" with "fair." One can find analogous examples in science, in those instances where "true" is replaced by "procedurally correct." For example, researchers often emphasize that they have followed impersonal procedures (e.g., inferential statistics in experimental psychology) without claiming that the procedures guarantee the truth of their findings. We should note the overlap, here, with disciplinary objectivity, for the definition of "correct" procedure is often disciplinary, a matter of conventions arrived at within a particular sphere of research (as when statisticians and others talk about "statistically significant" results). Further, procedural objectivity tries to maintain the letter of absolute objectivity while denying its spirit—using the impersonal means that absolute objectivity recommends, but turning agnostic with regard to the hoped-for end, the attainment of truth. Finally, procedural objectivity has affinities with dialectical objectivity, in that the standardization of objects also brings with it a standardization of subjects.

As readers may already have guessed, procedural objectivity does not exist as a full-fledged orientation in historical research and writing, but only as a tendency. Good historians try to be as careful as they can about their procedures—going to properly verified primary sources, attending to relevant secondary writings, dealing in an analytic and explicitly counterfactual way with matters of causation, putting their evidence and reasoning on the table, and indicating clearly the degree of certainty or speculativeness to be attributed to their claims. But the extreme of *totally* impersonal procedure, as exemplified in the "double-blind" procedures followed in clinical trials in medical science, is alien to historical investigation.

These, then, are the four senses of objectivity—absolute, disciplinary, dialectical, and procedural—that are prominent in current discussion. As I have tried to show, their prominence is no accident, for they have an interrelated logic, each form of objectivity beyond a pure and absolute God's-eye view demanding the presence of the other forms as well. They are conceptual types, but for the reason just noted they overlap in practice. Attentiveness to these conceptual types can help historians think more clearly about the challenges and limits of the work of historical description, explanation, justification, and interpretation. But note that I do not claim that the suggested typology offers some sort of "resolution" to "the problem of objectivity." Those who look for such a resolution are either unaware of the theoretical complexities involved in "the problem of objectivity" or are overconfident as to what theory can accomplish.

At the end of the day, historians must turn from theoretical or quasi-theoretical pronouncements to the hard work of historical investigation itself. They must study specific cases and derive from them what insight they can. It is thus appropriate that the next chapter focuses on a specific case.

A Case Study in Historical Epistemology: What Did the Neighbors Know about Thomas Jefferson and Sally Hemings?

by Steven Shepard, Phillip Honenberger, and Allan Megill

In his *Outlines of the Principles of History*—a work, now almost forgotten, that was in part a treatise on historical epistemology—the nineteenth-century historian and historical theorist J. G. Droysen (1808–84) contended that history needs to make clear to itself "its aims, its means, its foundations."[1] Among the many issues that interested Droysen was the relation between the critical and the constructive dimensions of historical research and writing. As Michael J. MacLean has emphasized, in Droysen's view history is not just a matter of the critical examination of sources (*Kritik*), for source criticism yields only "scattered empirical fragments." The problem is to make the leap from such fragments to, as MacLean puts it, "the durable collective expressions through which men, united in . . . various ethical communities . . . have manifested their concerted acts of will in history."[2]

Droysen lived in a world radically different from ours—the world of German idealist philosophy. His way of conceptualizing the problem of moving from fragmentary source material to a wider picture of past events can no longer be ours. But the problem itself, which he articulates with admirable clarity, is with us still. It is one of the central concerns of this book. Droysen holds that historians *must* speculate. The alternative is to have no history at all, but only collections of facts. Accordingly, the question to be asked is not *Should* historians speculate? Rather, it is *How* should they speculate? Our contention—perhaps naive in its simplicity, and certainly simple in its naïveté—is that they ought to speculate honestly and intelligently. We are persuaded that in the long run it is more intelligent to be honest than deceptive or (worse) self-deceived. Our focus in the present chapter is on how to speculate intelligently; consideration of the ethics of history will be deferred to another work.

A DISPUTED CASE

On September 1, 1802, a journalist and disappointed office-seeker, James Callender, published allegations in the *Richmond Recorder* that the president of the United States, Thomas Jefferson, was involved in a sexual relationship with a slave named Sally. In the two centuries following, the question as to the truth of these allegations was a matter of intermittent discussion. Callender did not further identify the person he called "this wench Sally," but she could only have been Sally Hemings (1773–1835), a household slave. It is likely that she was the half-sister of Jefferson's deceased wife, Martha Wayles Jefferson (1748–82), whose father, John Wayles, had a long-standing sexual relationship with his slave Elizabeth Hemings. (In fact, most historians who have examined the matter consider it a certainty that Sally Hemings was Martha Jefferson's half-sister.)

Among Sally Hemings's descendants there was, and continues to be, an oral tradition that she had been involved in a sexual relationship with Jefferson and that she had borne children by him. However, until recently, almost all historians who considered the matter rejected the notion that there had been any such relationship. They dismissed the idea on a variety of grounds: because Callender was not a disinterested observer but in fact wanted to harm Jefferson; because the accounts of ex-slaves from the Monticello household were inherently unreliable gossip, having no firsthand foundation; because it would have been out of character for Jefferson, a highly moral man, to have engaged in an illicit sexual relationship with a slave; and because Jefferson was too much a racist to have entered into a sexual relationship with a woman of African heritage.

Discussion of the alleged relationship between Hemings and Jefferson intensified in November 1998 when the results of tests of the DNA of nineteen known male descendants of Sally Hemings and of Jefferson's uncle, Field Jefferson, were published. (The testing was organized by Eugene A. Foster, a pathologist, and was carried out by labs in England and the Netherlands.) The tests showed, to an extremely high level of probability, that Sally Hemings's last son, Eston Hemings, was fathered by someone in the Jefferson family line.[3] (It was not possible to test the fatherhood of Sally Hemings's other known children, for the test required an unbroken line of known and surviving male descendants.) Almost a year *before* the DNA test results were published, a law professor named Annette Gordon-Reed had published a book in which she examined the historical evidence for and against a Hemings–Jefferson relationship, and concluded that the evidence for such a relationship was much stronger than had usually been thought. It is hardly surprising, then, that in the wake of the publication of the DNA results an academic conference was organized (by Peter S. Onuf of the University of Virginia) to discuss the significance of the apparent liaison between Jefferson and Hemings.[4]

This chapter began as a response by Shepard to a paper presented by Joshua D. Rothman at that conference, who argued that the newfound certainty of the Jefferson–Hemings relationship obliges us to put greater faith than historians had previously in the reports of James Callender. Specifically, Rothman contended that we ought to believe Callender's claim (in his 1802 *Richmond Recorder* article) that "there is not an individual in the neighbourhood of Charlottesville who does not believe the story; and not a few who know it."[5] In fact, Rothman goes further than Callender, asserting that "some people in Virginia" had known either of the relationship or of the story about the relationship as early as 1790, when Jefferson and his domestic entourage returned from his tour of duty as Minister to France.[6] Deploying epistemological criteria associated with "inference to the best explanation," we argue in this chapter that historians ought to remain agnostic as to whether Jefferson's neighbors really did know that Jefferson and Hemings were sexually involved with each other, because the historical record is not sufficient to show that Rothman's accounting for the historical record is clearly the best accounting.[7]

We became less skeptical of Rothman's claims in the wake of reading his 2003 book, *Notorious in the Neighborhood,* which includes a chapter on Hemings and Jefferson. The wealth of evidence concerning interracial sex in Virginia that Rothman displays in his book to some extent makes up for his lack of evidence concerning the dissemination of rumors of the Hemings–Jefferson case in particular. But in both the 1999 article and the 2003 chapter Rothman does not merely claim that in pre–Civil War Virginia there was a "social knowledge" of the existence of interracial sex; he also claims that there was "social knowledge about Jefferson and Hemings in Albemarle County and among the Virginia gentry long before anything about the couple appeared in the press" (Rothman 2003, 16; see also 37). On this particular point we had—and continue to have—significant doubts about Rothman's attentiveness to historical epistemology.

INFERENCE TO THE BEST EXPLANATION

Supposing that Thomas and Sally did have a sexual relationship, did their neighbors know about that relationship? We believe that the answer to this question ought to be construed as an attempt to make sense of the historical record, and that we ought to incline toward believing whichever answer best makes sense of that record. We further contend that historians are under an obligation to convey to their readers any doubts that remain concerning how the evidence is best interpreted. In our view, all historians ought to have a commitment to seeking *the best way of accounting for the totality of the historical evidence,* found or findable, relevant to the particular issue in question, as well as a commitment to conveying to their readers some sense of the limits of this evidence.

Some persons of hypercritical bent demand that all knowledge be *certain* knowledge. Following established philosophical tradition, they take all certain knowledge to fall into one of two categories. These are, on the one hand, the immediately certain knowledge of one's own experience and, on the other, the logical certainty that is accorded to valid deductive reasoning. Neither of these forms of certainty is attributable to historical knowledge, however. One cannot even know so obvious a fact as that Napoleon Bonaparte existed with absolute certainty in either of these senses. Napoleon himself is no longer "here" to be directly experienced by us, so we cannot know him immediately; and, at the same time, there is no process of reasoning that can establish his existence with logical certainty. Consequently, some people conclude that historians do not really *know* anything about the past.

We agree with such observers that our beliefs about the historical past cannot live up to the traditional philosophical conception of certainty. Accordingly, we contend that certainty in this sense ought to be forever rejected as a criterion of historical knowledge. Instead, insofar as historical knowledge is concerned, we prefer to speak of degrees of certainty. The degree of certainty attributable to a set of beliefs about the past corresponds to *the degree to which adopting those beliefs would serve to make sense of the totality of the historical record* (with a few stipulations to be added below). Although history cannot achieve certainty of either the "immediately experienced" or the "logically deduced" sort, historical accounts can still be judged as more or less likely to be true on the basis of how well they account for the totality of the evidence as compared with alternative accounts.

Where an account is *far* better at accounting for the totality of the data than the alternatives, the historian has every right to claim that such-and-such *was* the case. "Caesar crossed the Rubicon" is so much better an explanation of the data than its negation ("Caesar did not cross the Rubicon") that it may simply be said to be *true,* even though this can never be known immediately or logically. In situations where two or more accounts are viable, however, the responsible historian will clearly indicate that the matter is not beyond dispute. The question of what the neighbors knew about Tom and

Sally is, in our view, an example of such a situation. Of course, there will always be gray areas. The rules and procedures for deciding how we should rank differing accounts, however, are in general specifiable, although we may debate the specific application of these rules. The good historian looks for the account that best "explains" the available evidence; she does not jump to a conclusion on the basis of personal commitments; she does not seek to give the impression that she knows matters that she does not in fact *know;* and if she chooses to work on the basis of an "angular" interpretive perspective (see chapter 5, following note 12, and chapter 4 generally), she does so explicitly and with complete attentiveness to the available evidence.

The techniques for ranking historical accounts as better or worse have been implicitly recognized by historians for centuries. All the same, these techniques may be effectively articulated in a number of different ways. In this chapter, we want to suggest (and show) that historical accounts can be judged better or worse in accordance with what some philosophers and computer scientists have variously called "abduction," "abductive inference," or "inference to the best explanation." In this form of inference, we infer, from the premise that a given hypothesis better accounts for the evidence than does any other hypothesis, the conclusion that the given hypothesis is true.[8]

This form of inference is commonly employed in natural science. In *The Origin of Species* (1859), Charles Darwin supported his argument for evolution by an inference to the best explanation: that is, he claimed that his theory made sense of many more classes of biologically relevant facts than did special creationism, and did so much more simply.[9] Similarly, the eighteenth-century French natural philosopher Antoine Lavoisier defended the theory of oxygen because with it "all the phenomena are explained with an astonishing simplicity."[10]

The American philosopher of science Charles Peirce called this type of reasoning "abduction," suggesting that it be added to deduction and induction as a basic category of logical argument. In his later writings, Peirce portrayed this form of reasoning as follows: "(1) The surprising fact, F, is observed. (2) But if H were true, F would be a matter of course. Hence, (3) there is reason to suspect that H is true."[11] Here Peirce understands abduction as an exploratory method, a logic of discovery that cannot actually serve to evaluate the truth-claims of theories. Abduction proposes a theory, deduction deduces the observable consequences of the theory, and induction empirically verifies (or not) the deduced consequences. In short, in this view abduction has an exclusively *preliminary* status in the conduct of science.

In the messy world of history, however, abduction has roles to play that are broader than the role of a logic of discovery. In history, abduction does more than merely devise hypotheses for further testing. Peirce explicitly pointed to one such role: the establishing of historical facts. Notably, he wrote that "numberless documents refer to a conqueror called Napoleon Bonaparte. Though we have not seen the man, yet we cannot explain what we have seen, namely, all these documents and monuments, without supposing that he really existed."[12] To gloss this: We cannot conclude by deduction that Napoleon existed (or that World War I began in 1914, to take another example). Nor can we arrive at such facts inductively, since they are not empirically observable. Rather, they can only be established abductively, when we observe certain facts about the present-day world (most obviously, the present-day existence of "numberless documents" referring to Napoleon) and then postulate a cause (namely, a really existing Napoleon) that would explain these facts. In other words, the "best explanation" of the multitude of documents referring to Napoleon and his actions is that Napoleon existed and that he actually engaged in these actions.

The computer scientist John R. Josephson relates the truth-establishing species of abduction to inference to the best explanation. He schematizes inference to the best explanation in the following way: "D is a collection of data (facts, observations, givens). H explains D (would, if true, explain D). No other hypothesis can explain D as well as H does. Therefore, H is probably true."[13] Of course, H might imply other statements that we know to be false, in which case H would be a bad hypothesis. But we need not reject out of hand a hypothesis that contradicts previously held beliefs—rather, we might reject those other beliefs. The rejection of established beliefs because of the greater persuasiveness of a new hypothesis is a regular occurrence in human life and human history. Galileo's rejection of the earth-centered view of the universe in favor of the "new" heliocentric hypothesis proposed by Copernicus is an example of a case where a new hypothesis is so much better than the old that it is adopted even at the cost of rejecting a deeply established set of beliefs.

In cases where otherwise tenable hypotheses are at some point in contradiction with each other, we need not wholly reject either hypothesis. It is possible (and quite common among intelligent people) to subscribe tentatively to two or more inconsistent hypotheses while at the same time acknowledging their inconsistency. We believe that such cases of inconsistency are fairly common in historiography. We are inclined to suggest that historians ought to remain agnostic about which of two otherwise tenable hypotheses is in error until further research and argument have settled the issue—*if* in fact they settle the issue.

In applying the logic of "inference to the best explanation" to historical inquiry, we need to be attentive to the different senses of the term *explain*. In a broad and also rather vague sense, to "explain" a set of data is to show how it "makes sense." In this sense, *explain* is more or less synonymous with *elucidate* or *clarify* (a sense of *explain* that was noted, but put to one side, in chapter 4, note 9). Since elucidation or clarification is an elucidation or clarification *for us,* this sense of *explain* is also akin to *interpretation* as defined in chapter 4, where an interpretation is an answer to the question "What is the significance of X, for us, now?" However, to "explain" a historical event or existent in a more specialized sense, the historian needs to do more than offer a hypothesis that makes sense of the presently existing body of evidence; she needs to offer a hypothesis as to what caused this body of evidence to come into being, which usually means that she needs to say what caused the past state of affairs.[14]

The meaning of *explanation* in the phrase "inference to the best explanation" should be understood as akin to but not identical with the meaning given to the term in chapter 4, where an explanation is an answer to the question "What caused X?" Note also that chapter 4 distinguishes between explanation, on the one hand, and argument or justification on the other. This distinction allows historians and their readers to differentiate between *offering an explanation* and *claiming that the explanation is true*. In this chapter, too, we focus on *explanation* in the sense of a proposal as to what caused a particular event or existent, However, in the slightly shifted perspective of this chapter the *explanandum* (the thing to be explained) is as often as not *the evidence itself.*[15]

In abductive inference we offer a *possibly true* account of one or another reality (whether, to take a traditional perspective, this is a supposed reality in the past, or whether it is a body of evidence existing in the present). Going one step further, in attempting infer to the *best* explanation, we offer a justification or justifications for believing that one "explanation" (or description, or interpretation) is better than its competitors. Admittedly, "inference to the best explanation" is a weaker form of justification than are deduction and sense-certainty. Moreover, it is difficult to establish fixed guidelines for deciding when one "explanation" is better than another. The theory of inference to the best explanation is not a magic formula, a skeleton key that will open all doors. All the same, we believe that the theory has much to offer the historian. It provides a way of understanding processes of reasoning that are central to the practice of historical research and that good historians already employ in an intuitive fashion. The "best explanation" is the best account as to what caused something in the past. Alternatively, the "best explanation" offers the best answer to the question "What caused the totality of the evidence to be as it is?"

THAGARD'S THREE CRITERIA

The philosopher of science Paul Thagard has proposed three criteria for deciding which explanation, or which *kind* of explanation, is best in any given case: consilience (the more data explained by an explanation, the better); simplicity (the fewer "auxiliary" hypotheses necessary to make the explanation work, the better); and analogicality (the more analogous an explanation is to other explanations we know to be true, the better).[16] The last criterion—analogicality—is somewhat weaker than the others, and should be used very carefully in historical research and writing. For instance: one might *suppose* that Jefferson ate cornbread for breakfast on the basis of the known fact that many of his contemporaries ate cornbread for breakfast, but such a supposition can only offer a rather low degree of certainty. Any reasonably persuasive evidence to the contrary would blow this supposition to pieces, and a good historian will remain largely agnostic about claims for which analogicality is the only support.

The criterion of consilience is useful when one wants to compare an account that explains data A, B, and C to another that explains data A, B, C, and D (the second theory, all other things being equal, would be better). However, consilience fails as a criterion when two competing accounts make sense of different ranges of data. For example, if we hypothesize that Jefferson fathered Hemings's son Eston, this explains Eston Hemings's descendants carrying the Jefferson Y chromosome, whereas if we hypothesize that it was one of Jefferson's nephews who fathered Eston Hemings, this explains the testimony of Edmund Bacon and T. J. Randolph (Jefferson's overseer and grandson, respectively), both of whom denied that a sexual relationship existed between Jefferson and Hemings. (Conversely, the first hypothesis fails to explain Bacon's and Randolph's testimony, and the second fails to explain the DNA evidence.) Comparing competing explanations is a matter of deciding which evidence matters more, and this decision cannot be based on a quantitative comparison alone.

The criterion of simplicity favors explanations that need fewer auxiliary hypotheses to fit explanations to the circumstances. Auxiliary hypotheses are required whenever we posit past events or objects without evidential support, solely in order to make our theory work. The simplest explanations usually do not require any auxiliary hypotheses. For example, Madison Hemings stated in his 1873 memoir (referred to in note 4, above) that he had an older sister named Harriet. The best explanation of this action (namely, Madison's stating of this claim) is that Madison Hemings *believed* that he had an older sister named Harriet, and that it was this that caused him to make this statement.[17] Our knowledge of Madison Hemings's circumstances justifies assigning him this belief: according to Jefferson's Farm Book and other sources, Sally Hemings gave birth to a daughter named Harriet in 1801.[18] In this simple example, Madison Hemings's action and his circumstances both point to the same state of mind. Therefore, no auxiliary hypotheses are needed to explain this piece of evidence.

Madison Hemings's memoir also describes Thomas Jefferson as having "little taste or care for agricultural pursuits," and yet we know from other sources that Jefferson took great interest in farming. Therefore, a historian interested in establishing the reliability of Madison Hemings's memoir must introduce auxiliary hypotheses—that is, hypotheses that we have no independent basis for taking to be true—in order to make Madison Hemings's beliefs about Jefferson fit in with what we know to have been true of Jefferson. Gordon-Reed suggests that Madison Hemings may have been referring to Thomas Jefferson in the years when he (Hemings) "came of age" at Monticello. In 1819, Madison was fourteen, just apprenticed to his uncle John, and therefore "would have been old enough to pay serious attention." At that time Jefferson was "obsessed, not with his farm, but with building his university" (22). Gordon-Reed has no textual basis for assuming that Hemings was referring only to his formative years; she makes this assumption only to remove the contradiction between, on the one hand, her description of Madison Hemings's memoir as containing statements that Madison believed to be true and, on the other, our knowledge of what was actually true. Here Gordon-Reed employs an auxiliary hypothesis. She posits a historical existent (Madison's state of mind) that cannot be verified on the basis of the available historical record. If there were another explanation of Madison Hemings's statement that accounted for the same data without appeal to an auxiliary hypothesis, this second explanation would have to be preferred, all other things being equal. In the absence of such an explanation, Gordon-Reed's account, while far less than certainly true, may be entertained as the best available explanation.

Thagard's third criterion for judging the quality of an explanation, analogicality, is weak but sometimes useful. For example, in arguing for the existence of a sexual relationship between Thomas Jefferson and Sally Hemings, we might be tempted to draw an analogy between Jefferson and the hundreds of his white contemporaries who had sexual relations with female slaves. But while such an analogy might help us to *interpret* the alleged Hemings–Jefferson relationship—that is, to see it as making sense within the larger context of pre–Civil War Virginia—which would then also make the existence of the alleged relationship more plausible than would otherwise be the case, it cannot *explain* the relationship, in the sense of saying what caused it. Nor, indeed, can it establish, beyond the level of mere supposition, that such a relationship existed in the first place. For remember that we are concerned here with the behavior of a *specific* historical actor (or, at most, of two historical actors). Accordingly, unless we argue that Jefferson altered his actions in order to make them congruent with the actions of the many white Virginia slave-owners who had sex with slaves, we cannot make use of the analogy in explaining Jefferson's actions (assuming, for the sake of the argument, that he actually did have a sexual relationship with Sally Hemings). An overlap between the categories of "white men who owned slaves" and "white men who had sex with slaves" does not, in and of itself, establish a causal relationship, any more than would an overlap between "white men whose surnames began with J" and "white men who spoke French." Thus, analogicality is far from a foolproof way of establishing the best explanation of the historical record. All the same, it appears to have some usefulness for historical thinking, although inferences based solely on analogicality clearly are evidentially weak.

A FOURTH CRITERION

To the useful criteria of consilience and simplicity and the more problematic criterion of analogicality, we add a fourth. Since we human beings are much better at establishing causes than we are at predicting the future—especially where the motivations of other human beings are concerned—we ought to expect history to be firmly rooted in seeking out the causes of known events rather than deducing the consequences of some set of events *in abstracto*. Imagine someone attempting to deduce what would happen in 1938 solely on the basis of her knowledge of the events and existents of 1937 and earlier. Given the contingency of human history, it would be highly surprising if such a person were to succeed in any significant way. On the other hand, a historian in a position to ask the question "What were the causes of such-and-such an event that actually occurred in 1938?" would be able to exploit the historical record in her search for answers. The historian is doing history, whereas his imagined competitor is engaging in futuristic speculation. (This point is further illustrated in chapter 7's discussion of "virtual history.")

As our treatment of auxiliary hypotheses has shown, there is nothing wrong with positing the existence of a historical particular of which one cannot be completely certain—a particular that is not well supported by evidence. In our opinion, of course, a historian is obliged to indicate where he has made a guess. We suggest—in accordance with our fourth criterion—that where historical particulars are posited without knock-down-drag-out evidence, we ought to prefer those guesses that posit *causes* over those that posit *effects*. A historical explanation that starts from a known historical particular (say, the existence of Madison Hemings's memoir) and then seeks out the causes of that particular is in general to be preferred to an explanation that starts from a known historical particular and then deduces the supposed effects of that fact (as in the argument that "Jefferson could not have had sex with Sally Hemings because he was too much of a racist"). As has been shown over and over again, historians' deductions tend to be far less certain than they believe them to be. Thus it seems to us that historians ought in general to *abduce* (posit causes on the basis of effects) rather than *deduce* (posit effects on the basis of causes). We call the first kind of guess an effect-to-cause hypothesis, while the second we call a cause-to-effect hypothesis. The first procedure amounts to proposing explanations, whereas the second is akin to predicting the future. The first procedure is preferable to the second in that it keeps the historian rooted in the real evidence; consciously practiced, it encourages the historian to be clear about which parts of his account are less than certain.

Our fourth criterion, then, is simply this: that in judging historical accounts we ought to remember that explanations in which the reasoning is from effects to causes are preferable to those in which the reasoning is from causes to effects.

Causality in history is an extremely tricky subject. Consider the differences between the following three types of historical realities that might be employed in explaining aspects of the historical record: (1) actions by historical actors; (2) states of mind of historical actors; and (3) historical circumstances. Each of these is highly relevant to the historian's practice of recounting the past. For example, we have before us a letter, putatively written by Jefferson. In inferring that Jefferson was in fact the author of the letter, we might invoke some or all of the following:

1. Action-oriented cause: Jefferson's act of letter-writing caused the letter. At this point we might introduce a handwriting analysis, the letter's provenance, and so on, to establish that it was indeed the product of his act of letter-writing and not of some other act, such as that of a forger.

2. State-of-mind cause: Jefferson's beliefs and desires caused the letter. To establish that the letter was indeed the product of Jefferson's state of mind and of no one else's, we might argue that the letter contains information that only Jefferson could have known, or arguments that only Jefferson was putting forward at the time.[19]

3. Circumstance-oriented cause: The historical circumstances caused Jefferson's state of mind (which in turn caused him to write the letter). Here we might connect a poor harvest on Monticello to the letter's request for an extension of credit.[20]

A rough-and-ready way to think of the possible impact of these three types of historical realities is to regard actions as explaining *what* happened, states of mind as explaining *why* it happened (taking "why" in this instance to be a question as to purposes or intentions), and the evocation of historical circumstances as helping to explain why we believe that such-and-such explanations in terms of actions or states of mind are true. Insofar as the historian decides to treat a historical person as an *agent* or *actor* on the historical scene (that is, as a "character," in the sense that this term has in chapter 4), rather than as a resultant of one or more determinisms, she is obliged to describe what the person's purposes were in acting, and to do so by invoking his or her beliefs and desires at the time of the action as an explanation of the action in question. Although this chapter is concerned with the epistemology involved in *describing* what was the case (Did Jefferson and Hemings have a sexual relationship? Did their neighbors know?), establishing the truth of these descriptions depends in part on the associated explanations as to why the historical actors in question acted as they did.

We believe that this point can be expanded into a rule of thumb: a particular description of the past will be better justified to the degree that the description also offers an explanation of the states of mind of the historical actors involved. For example, Edmund Bacon stated that on Jefferson's orders he gave Harriet Hemings (Sally's youngest daughter) $50 and helped her run away from Monticello (Gordon-Reed, 27). If we assume that Bacon was telling the truth, then we might explain Jefferson's orders by inferring that Jefferson had some attachment to Harriet or some commitment to her mother, and knew that Harriet wanted to leave Monticello. This would be an explanation that reasons from effect (Jefferson's orders) to most likely cause (Jefferson's beliefs and desires). A cause-to-effect explanation, on the other hand, would posit Jefferson's state of mind, both on the basis of his other actions (e.g., his strongly racist assertions in *Notes on the State of Virginia* [referred to in note 4, above] and his demonstrated reluctance to free slaves, especially females) and on the basis of his circumstances (e.g., his mounting financial hardships), and would then argue that Bacon's testimony must be wrong, because Jefferson would never have done such a thing. This is reasoning from *putative cause* (posited beliefs and desires, plus circumstances) to *unobserved effect* (according to which Jefferson gave no orders, and Bacon, for some unknown reason, lied). Cause-to-effect explanations are weaker than effect-to-cause explanations for the same reasons that our predictions of another's actions are less accurate than our understanding of her intentions afterward. It can be extremely difficult to know what a particular human being is thinking, feeling, and wanting at any given moment. In many cases, we cannot predict the actions of our best friend, much less the actions of a long-dead historical figure.

Our fourth criterion applies in the following way to what we have called state-of-mind causes: explanations that posit beliefs and desires that, on the basis of recorded actions, could credibly have been held by the historical actors in question are generally better than explanations that predict unrecorded actions on the basis of posited beliefs and desires. It is useful to name these two contrasting types of explanation (which will become clearer to the reader when we apply them to the Jefferson–Hemings case) "bottom-up" and "top-down." Our claim is that, all other things being equal, bottom-up explanations (which reason from known effect to inferred cause) generally beat top-down explanations (which reason from a putatively known cause to a postulated effect). Since we are much better at understanding other people's past actions than at predicting their future actions, a good historical explanation will tend to build up from the data—that is, it will construct credibly attributable beliefs and desires as a basis for explaining recorded actions, rather than positing unrecorded actions that supposedly followed from a historical actor's postulated beliefs and desires. In other words, it is better for explanations of historical actors' behaviors and states of mind to be bottom-up (starting with what we plausibly *know* to have been the case and seeking out the prior causes) than top-down (moving from a general assertion to an inferred posterior result).[21]

INFERRING THE RELATIONSHIP

In *Thomas Jefferson and Sally Hemings: An American Controversy,* Annette Gordon-Reed exhaustively lays out the evidence concerning Madison Hemings, James Callender, T. J. Randolph (who claimed that Jefferson's nephew Peter Carr was the father of Sally Hemings's children [254–56]), and finally Thomas Jefferson and Sally Hemings themselves. Although Gordon-Reed says nothing in her book about inference to the best explanation, it is in fact an extended argument of precisely this type. On the basis of the available evidence she posits beliefs and desires for each relevant figure, and then she suggests that an account of what happened that assumes a Jefferson–Hemings relationship is evidentially stronger than a competing account that assumes a relationship between Hemings and either Peter Carr or his brother Samuel Carr. (Again, bear in mind that Gordon-Reed reached this conclusion before the appearance of the DNA evidence, which demonstrated to an extremely high degree of certainty that neither of the Carr brothers could have fathered Eston Hemings, since they were not in the Jefferson male line.)

Gordon-Reed showed that the Jefferson–Hemings explanation is more consilient (that is, explains more data) than does the Carr–Hemings explanation. The Jefferson–Hemings explanation accounts for such things as Jefferson's favorable treatment (and ultimately his freeing) of Hemings's children; reports as to the resemblance of Sally Hemings's children to Jefferson; Madison Hemings's claim to be the son of Thomas Jefferson; and the fact that Hemings's conceptions all occurred at times when Jefferson was present at Monticello.[22]

Gordon-Reed also argued persuasively that the Jefferson–Hemings explanation is simpler (that is, makes less use of unsupported auxiliary hypotheses) than is the Carr–Hemings explanation. The Carr–Hemings explanation has to assume that Madison Hemings and Israel Jefferson (Thomas Jefferson's manservant, no family relation) lied when they spoke of the Jefferson–Hemings relationship to S.F. Wetmore, the abolitionist publisher who interviewed them in 1873, or that they allowed him to put words into their mouths. The Jefferson–Hemings explanation, on the other hand, must assume that Edmund Bacon and T. J. Randolph spoke inaccurately when they denied the Jefferson–Hemings relationship. Gordon-Reed showed that this second hypothesis is more supportable than the first, for she was able to question the accuracy of Bacon's knowledge (he arrived at Monticello five years after the events he denied) and to impeach Randolph's reliability (he gave two different accounts of how he came to know that the Carrs were involved). She also noted that both men had a perfectly understandable interest in preserving Jefferson's reputation, while neither Israel Jefferson nor Madison Hemings had much to gain by fabricating their story.

Finally, in an extensive discussion Gordon-Reed exposed the weakness of the top-down explanation that Jefferson's character rendered him incapable of a relationship with Hemings (107–57, 228–34). Agreeing with Gordon-Reed, we are inclined to reduce the problems with the "character" argument to two. First, those who deploy the character argument are appealing to something that is completely unobservable, namely, a posited "inner Jefferson," to which they attribute such-and-such characteristics on what can only amount to highly subjective grounds (hence grounds that are likely to be infected, wittingly or not, by the historian's own unstated and undefended ideological preferences). Second, these persons are also assuming that the said character structure would have made it impossible for Jefferson to engage in such-and-such actions—in this case, to have sex with a slave. In assuming that Jefferson's actions would have had to be consistent, they ignore (or at least discount) the high degree of observable inconsistency in the actions of human beings.

In *An American Controversy* Gordon-Reed did not purport to establish that Thomas Jefferson had a sexual relationship with Sally Hemings. Rather, her claim was that "the quantum of evidence that exists to support the notion [that Jefferson and Hemings did have sex] has been seriously underestimated." She also concluded that the evidence for what was then the dominant alternative theory, namely, that the Carr brothers were responsible, "has been overestimated." (210) In the terminology of inference to the best explanation, Gordon-Reed found that the Jefferson–Hemings explanation was not sufficiently better than the competition to justify accepting it as true unreservedly. She succeeded in demonstrating, however, that the Carr–Hemings explanation was clearly *not* the best.

INFERRING KNOWLEDGE OF THE RELATIONSHIP
IN ALBEMARLE COUNTY

We now apply the epistemological criteria associated with inference to the best explanation to Joshua Rothman's claim that the accuracy of James Callender's allegations concerning the Jefferson household are "remarkable testimony to the extent and transmission of social knowledge about private interracial sexual affairs in Virginia communities" (Rothman 1999, 103; Rothman 2003, 16 [see note 6, above]). More particularly, Rothman claims that Callender's reports testify to the broad circulation in Albemarle County of knowledge concerning the alleged Jefferson–Hemings relationship. Rothman's claim, if true, would make sense of two types of historical data: reports of, and apparent evidence for, pre-1802 rumors about a

Jefferson–Hemings relationship, and the mix of fact and fiction in what Callender says about the alleged relationship. Rothman explains these data by reference to the beliefs and desires of James Callender and of (unnamed) residents of Albemarle County. His account involves four hypotheses:

H1. Before September 1802, many Albemarle County residents believed that Jefferson was involved in a sexual relationship with an enslaved woman, Sally Hemings, and had had children by her (Rothman 1999, 95).

H2. These residents also believed details about the relationship that we now know to be false, such as the existence of a young black "President Tom" (purportedly the eldest child of Jefferson and Hemings, purportedly born about 1790) (Rothman 1999, 102).[23]

H3. Callender thought that the beliefs described in H1 and H2 were true.

H4. Callender desired to report the truth, and desired not to report falsehoods (Rothman 1999, 89 [see also 100–101]; Rothman 2003, 16).[24]

If we are to consider Rothman's account of the situation plausible, we must be able to think of the above-noted beliefs and desires as caused by what we know to have been true about the historical circumstances. Rothman mentions such data (or alleged data) as the following: the proved existence of a Jefferson–Hemings relationship (Rothman 1999, 89); the public actions (that is, statements) of Jefferson related to miscegenation; circumstances at Monticello related to miscegenation; and common feelings about interracial sex among white residents of Albemarle County.

In the following sections we engage in our own examination of the data. We believe that the data support an account of what people believed or said about the alleged Jefferson–Hemings relationship prior to 1802 that is different from Rothman's account. Here are the central elements of our alternative account (AA):

AA1. Before September 1802, almost no residents of Albemarle County had any reason to believe that Jefferson had fathered any of Hemings's children or had any special relationship with her. Indeed, few would have known who Hemings was.[25]

AA2. Residents of Albemarle County knew that Jefferson was circumstantially associated with miscegenation, and therefore may have been willing to believe (suspect?) that he was involved with an enslaved woman.[26]

AA3. Callender thought that he had reason to believe that Jefferson was the father of Hemings's children.

AA4. Aware of AA2, Callender desired to persuade his readers that Jefferson *was* the father of Hemings's children.

AA5. Callender believed that in order to persuade his readers of a Jefferson–Hemings relationship, he needed to make some statements he knew to be false. Specifically, he needed to convert AA2 to the stronger H1 and to fabricate H2.

Our alternative account does not explain how or why Callender thought he had reason to believe that there was a Jefferson–Hemings relationship. He may have had inside information—or, he may merely have *guessed correctly* on the basis of whatever circumstantial information he could gather. Either way, Callender might have thought he had reason to suspect a relationship even if very few people in Albermarle county did.

DIRECT REPORTS OF AND EVIDENCE FOR THE RUMOR

Rothman has five pieces of evidence that directly support his hypothesis H1, namely, that it was widely believed among Jefferson's neighbors prior to Callender's first published accusation in the *Richmond Recorder* of 1 September 1802 that there was a sexual relationship between Jefferson and "this wench Sally." First, Callender himself accompanied his allegation with an assertion that there was "not an individual in the neighborhood of Charlottesville that does not believe the story, and not a few who know it" (Rothman 1999, 87). In the *Recorder* of October 20, 1802, Callender referred to an unnamed "gentleman" who came into the Richmond district court and offered to bet anyone a suit of new clothes that the story was true.[27] In November he added (false) information about Hemings's children, which he tempered with the phrase, "it is said, although we do not give it as gospel" (Rothman 2003, 35, 254, n. 62). Finally, in December he claimed to be able to prove his claims in court with "a dozen witnesses" (Rothman 1999, 99, 111, n. 39; Rothman 2003, 34, 254, n. 59). However, reports postdating September 1, 1802, are highly suspect in this context, because rumors of a Jefferson–Hemings relationship certainly would have existed after Callender's first accusations were published.

A second piece of evidence that Rothman cites for believing that the relationship was bruited about before September 1802 is the existence of a piece of doggerel that appeared in *Port Folio,* a Federalist newspaper published in Philadelphia in July 1802. The imagined black poet proposes switching wives with Jefferson, so that Jefferson would have a "black wife" and the black poet a white wife. But nothing in the doggerel suggests that Jefferson was *already sleeping* with a "black wife."[28]

Third, William Rind, editor of the *Virginia Federalist,* apparently alluded to Jefferson's "depravity" in June 1800. (We have not seen this reference, and Rothman cites it from Callender's September 1, 1802, article rather than directly [Rothman 1999, 94, 110, n. 22; Rothman 2003, 30, 252, n. 42]; thus we have not investigated the context in which this assertion was made—nor, apparently, has Rothman.)

Fourth, after Callender's first piece appeared, the *Gazette of the United States* allegedly stated that while it did not have the corroboration to publish its own story about Jefferson, it had "heard the same subject freely spoken of in Virginia, and by Virginia Gentlemen" (Rothman 1999, 95, 110, n. 24; Rothman 2003, 30, 253, n. 45).[29]

Finally, Henry Randall, an early biographer of Jefferson, wrote in private correspondence in 1856 that Callender was "helped by some of Jefferson's neighbors" (Rothman 1999, 99, 111, n. 40; Rothman 2003, 34, 254, n. 60).

Callender's testimony is suspect because it appears that he would have had a clear motive to inflate a small number of sources into a scandalous rumor in order to bolster his claims (this is our AA4 and AA5). As Rothman notes, Callender was "an angry, bitter, and cynical man who made a career by specializing in invective and character assassination" (Rothman 1999, 88; Rothman 2003, 14). It is true, as Rothman notes, that sometimes Callender may have been concerned that his statements actually be true. After all, some of his statements we know to be true (e.g., that there was a slave named Sally at Monticello; and it is also reasonable to suppose that she had had five children by the time Callender wrote). Further, on one occasion, when he thought that new information might be false, Callender stated that he did not "give it as gospel." Callender's biographer, Michael Durey, and Gordon-Reed both assert that Callender had a good record (for his time) in reporting the basic truth of matters (this is further justification for Rothman's H4, namely, that Callender desired to report the truth and to not report falsehoods).[30]

But did Callender view the alleged common knowledge as another fact to be reported, or did he fabricate it as a tool to heighten the scandal and convince his readers? After all, he fabricated insulting (and inaccurate) descriptions of Sally Hemings, perhaps in order to arouse the stereotypes of his day,[31] and for all we know he may have invented Hemings's twelve-year-old son, "President Tom," for whose existence there is absolutely no evidence. When did Callender consider himself to be reporting fact, and when was he allowing himself to exaggerate in order to rile up his readers? Evidence of pre–September 1802 rumors concerning Jefferson's sexual activities is very thin. Some instances of rumor-spreading are reported only by Callender, and thus are without confirmation. The *Port Folio* doggerel is quite inconclusive as evidence of rumors of Jeffersonian miscegenation. The verses caricature a black slave who wants to "make all like" and "nab" his master's white wife (Jefferson's wife had died in 1782). Could the poem have been meant as a mockery of the enslaved population? Or as a northern gibe at southern miscegenation? Both seem as likely as the suggestion that the piece is a joke aimed specifically at Jefferson and alluding to his sexual relationship with a slave. What satirist, with real information about a sitting president, would mention him only as an afterthought to musings on a slave's desires?[32] In addition, Randall's testimony in 1856 is highly suspect for several reasons. First, it is of late date. Second, his claims are unclear. Did he mean that the neighbors helped Callender discover the story, or did they help by fueling speculation and rumor? Third, Randall said that one of the Carr nephews was the father of Hemings's children (Gordon-Reed, 80–82). Accordingly, any allegations that Jefferson's neighbors might have made to Callender to the effect that Jefferson had fathered children by Hemings would have contradicted the story that Randall told in 1856. If Randall believed his own story, then *he* could not have held that Jefferson's neighbors knew that Jefferson had fathered children by Hemings (since one cannot *know* something that is false, but can only *mistakenly believe* it).

Overall, we find that the best evidence for the pre–September 1, 1802, spread of rumors about Jefferson's alleged sexual activities are the lines in the *Washington Federalist* of September 14, 1801 (see our note 29, above), stating that "a man very high in office" had fathered "a number of yellow children" and was "addicted to golden affections." (Rothman introduces this evidence in his 2003 chapter; he did not discuss it in his 1999 article.) The anonymous author appears to be doing obeisance to the widely held ethical taboo against spreading defamatory gossip, given that he tempers his mention of the allegations by declaring that "if they are false and malicious they ought to be contradicted."

THE QUALITY OF CALLENDER'S REPORTS

Rothman argues that common knowledge of the (alleged) Jefferson–Hemings relationship best explains the mix of fact and fiction in Callender's reports (H1 and H2). After all, *someone* must have told Callender a lot: Hemings's name, her status as a house servant, her trip with Jefferson to France, her (alleged) first pregnancy, and the five children she had borne by 1802. But Callender also seems to have made mistakes, particularly with regard to his fictitious "President Tom," the purportedly twelve-year-old son of Hemings who, Callender claimed, looked like Jefferson and lived at

Monticello. To Rothman, Callender's mix of fact and fiction is proof that he was tapping into a gossip mill in which "the possibilities for exaggeration to become hyperbole as the Jefferson–Hemings story passed from person to person . . . were enormous" (Rothman 1999, 103; see also Rothman 2003, 37). But this explanation seems questionable. One person could have been as wrong as twenty. Or Callender might have added his *own* hyperbole.

Rothman notes another statement by Callender: in December 1802 the journalist offered to prove his allegations in court with "a dozen witnesses." Rothman, seeking to locate the rumor among the Albemarle gentry, seizes on the bluster: "if [Callender] was serious . . . his witnesses would have to have been white"—because Callender's "disgust for African-Americans" (Rothman 1999, 99; Rothman 2003, 34) would have disinclined him to speak to slaves (also, slaves were not permitted to testify in court). But the only contemporaries of Jefferson and Hemings who we can say *unquestionably* knew (or believed they knew, or purported to know) of the relationship were Monticello slaves: Madison Hemings and Israel Jefferson (and Israel, although Jefferson's personal servant for fourteen years, stated that he did not "positively know" about the relationship, but believed it only "from circumstances").

How would white people have learned the details of the alleged relationship? Rothman speculates that "given Callender's disgust for African-Americans, it is unlikely that he spoke directly to any Albemarle slaves." A similar argument was applied for years to Jefferson: Dumas Malone, Virginius Dabney, and John Miller ruled out Jefferson's having had a sexual relationship with Hemings in part on grounds of his racism (Gordon-Reed, 133–34). Such top-down explanations are much too weak to prove either that Jefferson would not have had sex with Hemings or that Callender would not have spoken with slaves. If we permit ourselves to imagine that Callender spoke with slaves, then we no longer have to assume common knowledge among Jefferson's white neighbors in order to explain Callender's reports. After all, the only white "witnesses" known to have commented on the matter (Edmund Bacon and T. J. Randolph, noted above; and one other person, Jefferson's granddaughter Ellen Coolidge) all stated that someone else was the father of Hemings's children (Gordon-Reed, 28, 79). We have no proof that these "witnesses" knew the actual truth. There is much reason to believe that Jefferson and Hemings would have been very, very discreet about their alleged relationship. (Note that Israel Jefferson, in the 1873 memoir published by S. F. Wetmore, is said to have said that he "believe[d] from circumstances" that the Hemings children had been fathered by Jefferson, but that he "d[id] not positively know" it ["Appendix C," in Gordon-Reed,

253].) Perhaps the "witnesses" who denied that Jefferson had fathered Sally Hemings's children really did honestly believe that someone else was the father. It is even possible to imagine that Hemings had a relationship with one or both of the Carrs as well as with Jefferson. We do not *know* one way or the other.

The claim that Callender "probably relied especially on members of the Virginia gentry from Albemarle and counties nearby" for his information (Rothman 1999, 99; Rothman 2003, 34) lacks support from anything Callender said, for Callender did not mention the social status of his sources (although the alleged *Gazette* citation does mention the rumor among "Virginia Gentlemen"). Rothman guesses: "These men . . . might have overheard their slaves discussing the Hemings story" (Rothman 1999, 99; Rothman 2003, 34). And Rothman notes that they "would have been the whites most likely to have visited Jefferson at Monticello . . . (and to have seen Sally Hemings and perhaps her children)" (Rothman 1999, 99; Rothman 2003, 34). But Hemings's oldest child to survive early infancy, Beverly, was just four years old in 1802, and Hemings herself was probably employed as Jefferson's private chambermaid and perhaps as a seamstress. No good reason exists for us to imagine that she or her young children would stand out to white visitors, especially at Monticello, which was home to a large number of light-skinned house slaves (Rothman 1999, 87–88). Even if they had been noticed, it does not seem credible to imagine that they or Jefferson would have given to white visitors any indication of their relationship, especially when we remember that Jefferson's own manservant believed in the relationship only "from circumstances." Nor does it seem likely that any of the white people closest to Jefferson and Hemings would have given away their alleged secret, even assuming (which we have no textual basis for doing) that they possessed the knowledge to do so.

CIRCUMSTANCES AT MONTICELLO: AN UNJUSTIFIED EQUATING OF RUMOR WITH KNOWLEDGE

Rothman, having exhausted the textual evidence, and having attempted to explain the quality of Callender's reports by reference to the quality of the alleged common knowledge among white residents of Albemarle, has a further argument, namely, that the Jefferson–Hemings relationship was common knowledge because circumstances made it easy to believe. In Rothman's words, "Jefferson's particular actions and associations also gave residents of Albemarle County reason to believe the Hemings story" (Rothman 1999, 103; Rothman 2003, 38). Rothman cites the following circumstantial matters: the longstanding presence of "white slaves" at Monticello; Jefferson's father-in-law's long relationship with Betty Hemings, Sally's mother; Jefferson's nephew Samuel Carr's reputed miscegenation (which seems to have been first written about in 1874); and Jefferson's sale, in 1792, of Sally Hemings's sibling Mary Hemings to her white lover, Colonel Thomas Bell (the result of a request by Mary Hemings that Jefferson accommodated).

All these circumstances lead Rothman to conclude that "many people who lived in Jefferson's neighborhood believed the Hemings story because Virginia's slaveholders and Jefferson himself had prepared them to believe it" (Rothman 1999, 104; Rothman 2003, 38). At this point Rothman is no longer arguing bottom-up (from observed effect to hypothesized cause), but top-down (from invisible cause to hypothesized effect). In the absence of any recorded actions by Albemarle residents that are both (*a*) independent of Callender and (*b*) best explained by hypothesis H1, namely, that the relationship was common knowledge, Rothman is arguing that the residents' *environment* caused H1: "Given what Virginians already knew about sex and slavery in their society in general, *they did not need to have heard the details* of Jefferson's relationship with Sally Hemings to believe he might be sexually involved with her" (Rothman 1999, 103 [emphasis added]; Rothman 2003, 37–38 has a slightly different wording).

Here Rothman is in tricky territory. As Edmund Gettier showed in a famous article ("Is Justified True Belief Knowledge?"), a justified true belief is not *necessarily* knowledge. On the contrary, it is knowledge attributable to the person making the assertion in question if and only if, in making the assertion, that person has knowledge of the assertion's actual justification.[33] What if a white resident of Albemarle County, steeped in Virginia's culture of miscegenation, noticed Monticello's light-skinned slaves, winked at his neighbor and said: "I bet there are some young mulatto President Toms running around up there." Such a belief is not *knowledge* of the Jefferson–Hemings relationship (H1), because the belief could have occurred with or without Sally Hemings. This is what we are suggesting in AA2, above.

In his account Rothman invokes the anthropologist's notion of "social knowledge." What constitutes *social* knowledge? We take it that social knowledge is knowledge of the customs of a particular society gained from living within that society. For example, even Virginians who had little contact with the workings of the slave system could not help but infer, from the visible existence of many light-skinned slaves, that a lot of "sex across the color line" was going on. But to apply the designation "social knowledge" to the claim that one particular couple—which in this case would have had to have been remarkably discreet —was having sex is a misapplication. We believe that Rothman has a plausible, although far from evidentially well-founded, case for his claim that rumors of a Hemings–Jefferson relationship circulated in the "neighborhood" that was Albemarle County. But in our view Rothman unjustifiably equates *rumor* and *belief* with *knowledge*. It may well be that some of Jefferson's neighbors had information that would have justified the central rumor in question (namely, that there was a sexual relationship between Hemings and Jefferson). Such information would have converted rumor into knowledge. But Rothman has no evidence at all that Jefferson's neighbors had such information. Moreover, he *knows* that he does not have such evidence, yet fails to recognize the implications for his argument.[34]

A SUMMING UP OF THE DATA

The data to be accounted for can be stated as follows:

D1. In September 1802 Callender asserted that there was a sexual relationship between Thomas Jefferson and Sally Hemings and that it was "well known" that this was so.

D2. The "black wife" poem appeared in the *Port Folio* and the lines about "Mr. J." in the September 14, 1801, *Washington Federalist*.

D3. Henry Randall stated in 1856 that Callender was helped by "some of Jefferson's neighbors."

D4. Callender made correct statements about Sally Hemings.

D5. Callender made some false and exaggerated statements about Sally Hemings.

D6. On occasion, Callender was careful to report the "basic truth."

D7. There is no record of any white contemporary of Callender and Jefferson claiming to know of the alleged Jefferson–Hemings relationship prior to 1802 (with the possible exception of the September 14, 1801, *Washington Federalist* lines). Several reported (long afterward) that they did not believe such a relationship existed.

We note the following circumstantial data that may help explain some of the preceding data:

D8. Jefferson was publicly associated with miscegenation: light-skinned slaves lived at Monticello; Jefferson's father-in-law apparently had a sexual relationship with a black woman, Betty Hemings; one of Jefferson's nephews may have had sexual relations with black women; and Jefferson sold one of his slaves to her white lover.

D9. Jefferson and Hemings were discreet (inferred from Israel Jefferson's statement and from D7).

D10. The ethical norms of white Albemarle society prohibited open discussion of miscegenation.

THE CASE FOR OUR ALTERNATIVE ACCOUNT

Recall Callender's language in his first accusation: "There is not an individual in the neighborhood of Charlottesville who does not believe the story and not a few who know it." Callender draws a distinction between knowledge and belief. Why? What did he mean to imply about those Albemarle residents who merely "believed" in the relationship without "knowing" it? Did any of Jefferson's Albemarle County neighbors in fact *know* anything at all, or were they simply ready to believe whatever rumors might come their way?

After all, aside from Callender's assertions (D1) we have no textual evidence that supports Rothman's claim (H1) that the Jefferson–Hemings relationship was common knowledge. The *Port Folio* poem, the assertions by Rind and the *Gazette,* Henry Randall's recollections, and even the lines in the *Washington Federalist* can all be explained just as well by assuming a common mental association between Jefferson and miscegenation (AA2, above). Further, the circumstantial data (D8), when expanded to include the demonstrated secrecy of the relationship (D9), would surely at most have caused *speculation* that Jefferson was involved with an enslaved woman, not common *knowledge* (H1) that he was so involved.

Further, Rothman's claim that Callender desired to report the truth (H4) does not explain Callender's demonstrated willingness, indeed eagerness, on other occasions to use exaggeration and invention to achieve his goals (D5). If we imagine Callender as willing to use false statements as a means of convincing others of the truth (AA5), this would explain both D1 and D5.

Our alternative account would also explain why no details of the alleged relationship, assuming that there actually was a relationship, were reported, anywhere, before 1802 (D7): the details simply were not known to anyone besides, perhaps, a few people at Monticello (AA1 and AA2). This is a simple bottom-up explanation: lack of action (D7) caused by lack of knowledge (AA1). Rothman must explain D7 (namely, the lack of [any record of] any white contemporary of Callender and Jefferson claiming to *know* of the alleged Jefferson–Hemings relationship prior to 1802) from the top down: that is, he assumes that the ethical norms of Albemarle society (D10) caused people to desire not to discuss their knowledge of the relationship openly.

Both our account and Rothman's account employ auxiliary hypotheses in order to explain how knowledge of the presumed Jefferson–Hemings relationship spread from Monticello. Rothman assumes (without evidence) that knowledge spread from Monticello slaves to the enslaved population of Albemarle, and from the enslaved population to the white gentry (H1), and that somewhere along the line it became corrupted (H2). We assume (also without evidence) that James Callender, desiring to cause Jefferson political harm, investigated a publicly known association between Jefferson and miscegenation (AA2) and in doing so somehow got wind of allegations that were unflattering to Jefferson, as well as of a few pieces of *true* information, most notably the first name of Sally Hemings.[35] He then reported AA2 as H1 (namely, that many Albemarle County residents believed that Jefferson was involved in a sexual relationship with an enslaved woman) in order to convince his readers that his account of the relationship was true (AA5).

How does our auxiliary hypothesis compare to Rothman's? We assume that Callender somehow managed to learn certain (true) details about Jefferson's domestic establishment, which he used as the basis for his story about Jefferson and "this wench Sally." We do not claim to know *how* he learned these details. Rothman assumes that the residents of Albemarle County somehow learned and transmitted specific knowledge of a close and salacious secret without leaving any record at all of doing so. Rothman's account provides a simpler explanation of D1; our account better explains D7. What we know of the Albemarle environment (D8 and D9) seems more likely to have caused our AA2 than Rothman's H1. We believe that neither account is clearly better, and that we ought to remain agnostic about which hypothesis (AA2 or H1) offers the truer account of the states of mind of Albemarle residents.

Historians and other readers are of course free to draw their own conclusions—but if they wish to assert them as true, they are obliged to lay out the grounds for believing them to be true. They are also obliged to indicate as clearly as possible where the boundaries (admittedly sometimes variable) are between fact and speculation. Finally, they are obliged to justify—*as speculations*—the speculations that they offer.

Historians are sometimes careless of the distinction between fact and speculation, a carelessness that tends to lead them to present as unequivocally true claims that are not unequivocally true at all. For example, we consider it a mistake, in the light of the current state of the data, to assert as an unequivocal truth that Jefferson had a sexual relationship with Sally Hemings. At the same time, all three of us believe that he in fact did have such a relationship, for we find that the hypothesis that there was such a relationship offers a "better explanation" of the totality of the extant evidence than does the contrary hypothesis. As for the claim that Thomas Jefferson's alleged relationship with Sally Hemings was common knowledge in the neighborhood of Monticello prior to September 1802 (when Callender published the first of his articles on the subject in the *Richmond Recorder*), unless more evidence comes to light, we must regard this not as unequivocal truth but as arrant speculation. We are of course *not* against speculation (since there is a speculative dimension in all history); we are only against speculation that is not identified as such.

We hope that this chapter has helped to show the relevance of inference to the best explanation and of intelligently employed theory generally to the project of reading, writing, and thinking about history. In regular historical works—as distinguished from demonstration pieces in historical epistemology, such as this chapter—the scaffolding of theory is perhaps best kept in the background. But the historical reader and critic should always have the sense that the historian has thought clearly and well about these issues, even if she chooses to offer only hints of the conceptual thinking that has gone into the construction of the historical work in question. When such thinking is absent, we have little reason to have confidence in the truth of the stories that historians tell, however interesting, exciting, edifying, or politically useful those stories may appear to be.

Counterfactual History: On Niall Ferguson's *Virtual History* and Similar Works

Recently, there has been a minor boom in "counterfactual history," that is, in "history that never happened." To make sense of this phenomenon, we need to get clear about the theoretical issues that counterfactuality raises. We also need to make some distinctions. I would begin with a distinction between two types of counterfactual history, "restrained" and "exuberant." "Restrained" counterfactual history involves an explicit canvassing of alternative possibilities that existed in a real past, whereas "exuberant" counterfactual history deals in past historical outcomes that never in fact came to be.

"Exuberant" counterfactual history diverges radically from normal historical research and writing. This is the kind of counterfactual history that tries to imagine what might have resulted if Britain had intervened in the American Civil War, if an Irish Home Rule Bill had passed the British parliament in 1912, or if Germany had invaded Britain in 1940. All three of these imagined situations appear in Niall Ferguson's edited volume, *Virtual History*.[1] This sort of counterfactual history is indeed better called "virtual history" to emphasize that it addresses no *actual* past — or "imaginary history," to emphasize its lack of groundedness. "Virtual history" evokes "virtual reality." It also evokes the world of historically based game-playing: one thinks, for example, of the well-known board game *Axis & Allies,* now available in a computer version, which attempts to simulate World War II from 1942 onward.[2] Such games allow players to go back to some chosen point in historical time and make decisions that diverge from the decisions made by the real historical actors. What then eventuates, different from what actually happened, results from chance, and also (this is no small matter) from assumptions embedded in the game by its makers. There is no pretension here to be replaying historical reality, at least none that a grown-up could take seriously. It is a *game,* dressed up with certain features of a real past.

When professional historians write virtual history, we ought to treat their claims concerning "what might have been" with about the same distanced skepticism with which we would treat the playing out of World War II by a group of fifteen-year-olds. One can certainly speak of plausibilities, but the plausibilities are far harder to judge than *normal* historical plausibilities, which are tied down to a world that actually existed. When historians imagine what might have happened if John F. Kennedy had not been shot or if the USSR had avoided collapse, they are on shaky epistemological ground. Historians must always speculate (chapter 6), but speculations concerning virtual history are far more deeply permeated by under-supported assumptions about the real nature of the world than is the case when the normal canons of historical method operate. Indeed, quite apart from the specific ideological preferences of the historian or game-maker, virtual history cannot be invented nor the game played without a set of rules that are in large measure arbitrary. These assumptions constitute a "theory" about how the world normally operates that may or may not be true. To make inferences on the basis of such assumptions is to engage in "top-down" inferential reasoning, which, as noted in chapter 6, is epistemologically much more problematic than "bottom-up" inference.

It will clarify matters if we look at virtual history in the light of issues of temporality. The virtual historian cuts into the real past at some particular moment—normally just before one of the historical actors involved made a weighty decision. The virtual historian conceptualizes this moment as one of contingency, in which the decision *could* have been rendered differently and from which, subsequently, matters *might* have gone in a particular other direction. The virtual historian exploits the supposed contingency at the beginning in order to launch his counterfactual history. But contingency cuts two ways. Contingency and the freedom entailed by the very idea of a human capacity to decide give virtual history its opening. But the same contingency that makes virtual history possible also undermines it. If we have contingency in its beginning, we must surely have contingency in its early middle: to paraphrase the sociologist Max Weber, contingency is not a train one can get on or off at will. This means that virtual history cannot follow any definable course at all. More precisely, it can follow a definable course only until the next contingency arises. Although the virtual historian may well try to get away with claiming a normal historian's authority, once past this moment of renewed contingency, he is better thought of as a writer of imaginative literature. This is not necessarily bad, but it is not history.

Virtual history ought not to be confused with counterfactual history in general. Virtual history starts out from a moment in the real past where things might have worked out differently, and then moves *forward* in time, getting ever further from a world that existed. To put this in the terms suggested in chapter 6, it engages in "cause-to-effect" inference, moving from invisible cause to hypothesized effect. As noted in chapter 6, this direction of inference is epistemologically far more questionable than "effect-to-cause" inference, wherein one moves from observed effect to hypothesized cause. (Cause-to-effect inference is of course only a special case of top-down inference, and effect-to-cause inference a special case of bottom-up inference.) "Restrained" counterfactual history moves from observed effect to hypothesized causes. It starts out from an actual event, such as the English Civil War, and then looks back in time, canvassing how it might have come to pass that the Civil War might *not* have occurred (or might have occurred in a sharply different way). In Ferguson's anthology, John Adamson's essay "England without Cromwell: What If Charles I Had Avoided the Civil War?" is in large measure an exercise of this sort. Adamson canvasses a variety of counterfactuals in the years preceding 1642 and speculates as to how things might have worked out differently but did not. Such an effort is quite different from positing a counterfactual at the beginning (Hitler does not invade the USSR) and then imagining a whole new history that would have followed as the effect of that cause.

Whereas the virtual historian is forced to move ever further into the imaginary, the speculations of the restrained counterfactualist are pinned down by what actually did happen in the end. In imagining how things might have been different, the restrained counterfactualist tries to understand better what actually did happen. The restrained counterfactualist moves from known effect to hypothesized cause; the virtual historian exuberantly moves from invisible (but supposed) cause to an effect that never actually happened. The restrained counterfactualist moves from the bottom up, from known evidence to a theory as to why it happened that way; the virtual historian moves from the top down, deducing a hypothetical effect from a speculative theory concerning how the world functions. The less likely the virtual historian is to have thought seriously about this theory, the more likely it is that he will hold it to be indubitable truth.

In his introduction to *Virtual History* Ferguson spends much effort trying to show that counterfactual history amounts to an attack on historical determinism (most notably, on the determinism allegedly promoted by Marxists). According to Ferguson, counterfactual history highlights the possibility of human agency in history. In a critical discussion of *Virtual History,* the historian of modern Germany, Richard Evans, contends that we need to pay more attention than Ferguson does to underlying structural determinants.[3]

But both historians are surely focusing on the wrong issue, for the question "Human beings: do they have freedom or not?" is not a historian's question. Historians can offer no more than stale banalities concerning this question, because their disciplinary project already *assumes* a position, itself a banality—namely, that human beings are both determined and free, both subordinate to external forces and capable of creating and exploiting such forces, both matter and spirit, both beast and angel. No genuine determinist could ever be a true historian: such a person should rather study neuro-chemical, physical, or other forces. The same is true of anyone who believes that human beings soar above their circumstances like transcendental meditators: such a person will never be found contending with the archival muck that historians so avidly explore.

In fact, the fundamental point at issue in the matter of counterfactual history is the character of historical explanation. (Both Evans and Ferguson see this, but in their eagerness to joust with political opponents—allegedly deterministic leftists on the one hand, and the "New Right" on the other—they tend to bury the point.) To return to my discussion in chapter 4, I mean by an *explanation* an attempt to say why something is the case (why it exists or existed, why it happened). One can equally well say that an explanation is an attempt to answer the question, "What causes (or caused) E?" This second wording raises a difficulty, since even at this late date many people—including many historians—adhere to a "regularity" view of causation, according to which our saying that C is the cause of E needs to involve a "constant conjunction" (Hume's term) of some sort connecting C and E. Reacting against the "regularity" view, which was closely associated with the rise of natural science, R. G. Collingwood claimed in *The Idea of History* that historians do not (or at least should not) invoke causes at all. Rather, historians' explanations, Collingwood contended, are a matter of telling a story: the historian says that this happened and this happened and this happened, and from the story an explanation arises. In Collingwood's formulation: "After the historian has ascertained the facts, there is no further process of inquiring into their causes. When he knows what happened, he already knows why it happened."[4] And although Collingwood does not discuss the matter explicitly, his argument in *The Idea of History* strongly implies a rejection of counterfactuality.[5]

As Carl Hempel showed with brilliant clarity in his 1942 paper, "The Function of General Laws in History," historians cannot offer explanations that conform to the regularity view.[6] Without going into the complexities of the discussion that followed the publication of Hempel's paper, let me simply *assert* that the only view of explanation that works for historians is one that focuses on counterfactuality and that allows the regularity criterion to recede into the background. For historians *in principle* cannot subsume their explanations under regularities: Hempel was right about this. Rather, when a historian suggests that, for example, "imperialism caused [or helped cause] World War I," she is *really* saying (if she is saying anything intelligent at all) something like "all other things being equal, if there had been no imperialism, there would have been no World War I." Of course, the historian is probably also saying more than this, for history is a field where multiple causes, at different levels, are assumed to operate. Thus the counterfactual reasoning that the historian deploys must often be quite complex.

In the final section of his 1940 book, *An Essay on Metaphysics,* Collingwood himself offered a pragmatically oriented account of causation, one that has a strongly counterfactual resonance, for he suggests that what we can most readily imagine as *otherwise,* in the situation that actually existed, we tend to promote to the status of a cause. Thus we tend to take as "the" cause of, say, a car accident whatever we, from our own particular perspective, can most readily imagine as something that could have been different. Think how many *possible* causes there might be: the faulty camber of the road, the too-high speed limit, the driver's carelessness in driving so fast, the driver's drinking, the flawed design of the car. Imagining away one or another element, we imagine the accident not happening—which thus establishes that element's causal character. This is a promising line of thinking that Collingwood conspicuously did not pursue in *The Idea of History.*[7]

The fact is, historians *must* engage in counterfactual reasoning (a point that I have particularly emphasized in the introduction to this book and in chapters 4 and 6). Yet I note with dismay that I have encountered, more often than I would have liked, historians to whom this fact appears to be news. But perhaps this is not so surprising. If a historian sees his project as primarily one of describing or interpreting some past historical reality and is not interested in exploring causal relations, there would be no need for counterfactuals used for explanatory purposes (however, as chapter 6 shows in its discussion of "inference to the best explanation," this does not by any means banish all counterfactuals). Some famous historians in the tradition of the French *Annales* school were of this sort, much more interested in description and in suggestive juxtapositions than in causal analysis. The same tends to be true of the most recently dominant historiographic "paradigm," cultural history. One result is that when historians operating in these frameworks *do* try to make causal claims, they sometimes fail completely to understand what kind of reasoning is required for doing so. Likewise, historians who maintain a deep commitment to some particular theory of history (e.g., doctrinaire historical materialism, and especially "dialectical materialism") will also be inclined to bypass counterfactuals: here, the theory tells them that what did happen pretty much *had* to happen. Nor does it seem likely that historians who see themselves as "just telling a story" will normally be inclined to think about how the story might have proceeded differently. In short, large numbers of historians in the recent past have avoided confrontation with counterfactual reasoning. Some of them, because of other, better aspects of their work, have been quite distinguished. We should therefore be grateful to the new counterfactualists for forcing us to think about the important role of counterfactuality in history.

PART IV

Fragmentation

Fragmentation and the Future
of Historiography: On Peter Novick's
That Noble Dream

My aim in this chapter is to point out some implications of Peter Novick's widely noticed book, *That Noble Dream: The "Objectivity Question" and the American Historical Profession.*[1] In particular, let us think about the fourth and final part of Novick's book, entitled "Objectivity in Crisis." There are four chapters in Novick's part 4, bearing the following descriptive titles: "The Collapse of Comity"; "Every Group Its Own Historian"; "The Center Does Not Hold"; and "There Was No King in Israel."

Most professional historians, in reading these headings and the accounts to which they apply, will be inclined to see Novick as portraying a situation that is primarily negative in its implications. For example, in a long review of *That Noble Dream,* the American intellectual historian James Kloppenberg asserted that "in his conclusion, Novick laments that by the 1980s, 'there was no king in Israel,' and, as a result, 'every man did that which was right in his own eyes.'"[2] In a draft response to Kloppenberg that Novick sent to me in February 1990 after I wrote to him asking for a list of the most recent reviews of *That Noble Dream,* Novick conceded that in quoting Judges 2:25 he had committed a "serious rhetorical gaffe," for his actual assessment of the situation in professional historiography was not "apocalyptic," nor did he mean to suggest that present-day professional historiography was in a state of "individualistic anarchy." In fact, while "there was no king in Israel" characterized quite well the state of the historical discipline at the time that Novick wrote, "every man did that which was right in his own eyes" did not. A careful reading of Novick's book does not suggest that he had an apocalyptic view of the fragmented state of historiography, nor does it suggest that he "lamented" that state. If anything, the lament was Kloppenberg's; it was not Novick's.[3]

I am profoundly suspicious of attempts to overcome disciplinary fragmentation. In their most benign form, these attempts usually amount to a promoting of one or another vision of historical synthesis, one or another favored (but ungrounded) paradigm.[4] Belief that synthesis is a virtue and fragmentation a vice is deeply ingrained in the culture of academic historians. Every few years proposals are advanced for some new synthesis or other. Let us be warned, however: all calls for synthesis are attempts to impose an interpretation. It is fair enough to argue for a particular interpretation *as* an interpretation. But it will not do to present a particular interpretation as the synthesizing magic thread. I find no justification—certainly no articulated justification—for taking *fragmentation* as a dispraising term and *synthesis* as a praising one. We can hope to attain clarity of mind on such issues only if we regard these terms as neutral.

Such is the power of academic professionalism that even in those fields that have most contributed to fragmentation, scholars continue to pay lip service to the ideal of unity. For example, in a commentary on a set of five articles dealing with "women's history," published together in an issue of the *American Historical Review,* Kathryn Kish Sklar points to the "notable assets" that have come with the growth of women's history and then observes that "we must nevertheless recognize that our current situation contains all the liabilities associated with rapid growth, especially inadequate integration." But is "inadequate integration" a liability, as long as insight is advanced in other ways? It is not surprising to find that Sklar follows this observation with a plea for her own "paradigm" for understanding women's movements in different countries.[5] Sklar's way of explaining the emergence and development of women's movements may well serve to "integrate" (we might equally well say "synthesize") people's understanding of those movements. But "syntheses" and "integrations" *never* accommodate all possibly significant historical phenomena: that is not the way the world is—or, speaking more precisely, we have no adequate reason for thinking that that is the way the world is. There must surely be issues that Sklar's proposed synthesis fails to accommodate. Other historians may be preoccupied by other issues. Accordingly, the questions to ask of the work of all these historians are How interesting are the issues with which each historian chooses to deal? and How well are these issues addressed? Judgments of quality will depend on the answers to these critical questions and not on the proximity (or not) of the work being evaluated to Sklar's or anyone else's "paradigm."[6] One of the articles that Sklar comments on, by Daniel Walkowitz, deals with the emergence of a professional identity among female social workers in the United States in the 1920s. Walkowitz suggests in his piece that "to tell the full story of twentieth-century social workers' search for identity, historians need to draw on the literatures of consumption, work, and professionalization, for the development of social work as a profession was shaped by cultural conventions and limited by the material realities of the home and the workplace."[7] Walkowitz identifies elements that historians would certainly want to find in an account of "social workers' search for identity." But what justifies the claim that these elements would lead us to "the full story" of that search? The justification, I suggest, lies deeply embedded in the professional identity of historians. Walkowitz's use of the phrase "the full story" is almost certainly offhanded, but the offhandedness makes his use of it all the more significant, all the more a marker of a widely shared historians' bias.

The bias needs to be challenged. Novick's remarkable book helps us to do this, for his wide-ranging, ironic, dispassionate—indeed, in several senses of the term, *objective*—account of the American historical profession calls into question that "absolute" sense of objectivity (see chapter 5 in this volume) according to which there is a "full story" that we historians can uncover.

The most sophisticated observers of the historiographic scene understand well enough the contingency of the faiths that hold professional historiography together. With contingency comes the alleged threat of fragmentation. The sophisticated response to the alleged threat is the pragmatic, Peircean appeal to "communities of the competent."[8] But this won't quite do. A disciplinary blindness prevails within the modernist academy, and not only among historians—the blindness of historians who argue only with other historians, philosophers who argue only with other philosophers, economists who argue only with other economists, and so on. When the universe of argument is restricted in this way—and the disciplinary structure of the university certainly encourages such restriction—it is easy to imagine that we know what competence is.

However, there is no single competence, and there is even less an authoritative consensus among those who are supposedly competent. An argument deemed acceptable by the consensus of competent historians may well be deemed unacceptable by the consensus of competent philosophers or economists—and vice versa. Many historians have in fact never entered into serious argumentative relation with economists or philosophers or literary theorists or students of rhetoric (the converse is also true: practitioners of other disciplines rarely engage with the arguments of historians). Hence the multifariousness of competence is obscured. That the "community of the competent" argument has been taken seriously is one marker of the firmness of disciplinary divisions within our institutions of higher learning.[9] Novick's account of raging controversies among historians, and of the now-discarded assumptions of earlier generations of historians, needs to be set within this wider socio-intellectual context.

Still, professional identity has been important for the development of historical knowledge. As one part of his very large story, Novick shows that the repudiation in the post–World War II period of the relativist critique of objectivity offered by Charles Beard and Carl Becker in the 1930s was closely connected with the conception of history as "an autonomous profession."[10] *Autonomy,* like *synthesis,* is another of those words to which most professional historians, without articulated justification, attribute positive value. Thus when Novick observes that for most women's historians, "the feminist community was at least as salient a reference group as was the profession,"[11] he is likely to be read as saying something bad about women's history. But such a reading of Novick seems quite wrong to me. Novick does not approve of "autonomy," nor does he disapprove of it. On the contrary, here and elsewhere he seems determinedly neutral on the matter. If he is not neutral, he ought to be, for nothing in *That Noble Dream* supports the granting of positive value to autonomy—or negative value, either.

A story will perhaps help to link together these issues of synthesis and autonomy. The story is an encapsulated history of the enterprise of professional historiography. It is not the only story that can encapsulate that history, but it is, I think, an important one. In its broad outlines, my story goes, the history of professional historiography is closely connected to differing attitudes toward what we might call "the project of grand narrative." By "grand narrative," I mean the story that the world would tell if the world itself could tell its story.[12]

"In the beginning"—I mean, of course, in that benighted time before professional historians walked the earth—European intellectuals believed that there existed a grand narrative and that it was possible to tell the grand narrative now. More precisely, it was possible to *re*tell the narrative, for the narrative in question was the story offered in Judaeo-Christian Scripture. Professional historians, with their commitment to *finding* the narrative, were unnecessary.

Somewhat later than the beginning, faith in the scriptural grand narrative diminished. Professional historians arrived on the scene. In the early phase of professional historiography, the dominant view was that a grand narrative exists but that it cannot be told now: it can only be told in the future, after "further research" has been done. Such was Ranke's view—at least most of the time. As the late Leonard Krieger pointed out, this view kept Ranke's well-known concern with historical individualities anchored within the larger framework of universal history.[13] It was Lord Acton's view and J. B. Bury's as well. It was also, I suggest, the view of that vast majority of historians who never reflected on universal history but nonetheless wrote out of a fundamental faith in the validity of Western culture as they understood it.

In a later phase of professional historiography, after World War I, there was yet another change. Now historians became more distanced in their commitment to grand narrative. They continued to believe in the existence of a grand narrative, but it was a peculiar grand narrative—a purely ideal narrative, a narrative that could never actually be told. Under this dispensation, autonomy and synthesis were important values—positive terms in the professional historian's lexicon—but no particular synthesis could ever win the approval of any more than a fraction of the profession. Today, there are signs of a fourth phase or attitude. Novick's book both describes the preconditions for a new attitude and, in part, exemplifies it. Whether it comes to full blossom remains to be seen. In the fourth, "postprofessional" phase, the dominant view would reject grand narrative entirely—but ironically (for an unironic rejection of grand narrative would end up reconstituting it in its preprofessional form). I imagine, here, historians who would no longer see terms like *synthesis, paradigm,* and *autonomy* as possessing positive value (but such terms would also not possess negative value). I imagine historians who would not in any way think that they were telling "the full story." I imagine historians who could turn themselves into economists or philosophers or literary critics, and who could shift back and forth between such conflicting fields (for conflicting they most certainly are). I imagine historians who would also be intellectuals, speaking within the field of historiography and outside it as well. These historians would at the same time be epistemologically responsible in their writing of history, rather than careless or deliberately tendentious.

As someone who has seen, in more than one context, the erosion of previously unquestioned consensus, I see fragmentation as in some ways profoundly disturbing. Yet, if the sociological transformation of the academy continues (and I am inclined to think that it will), consensus of the old sort will have a hard time surviving. Unity on the substantive level—the unity provided by the telling of a single story—can only serve to exclude. Likewise, when disciplines become fragmented and when the cross-cuts between them begin to take on lives of their own, unity on the broad methodological level is undermined. Perhaps the only way, finally, of holding together what once was seen (somewhat misleadingly) as a unified enterprise would be through sustained attention to the histories, sociologies, rhetorics, and normative commitments of historical study—that is, through examining precisely the diversities that have shadowed historiography from the beginning and subjecting them to sympathetic but also critical analysis. In short, unity would come only at a reflective level—if it would come at all.

In the fourth phase, works like Novick's, which fall within the hitherto professionally despised field of historiography, or "historiology," would assume an important integrative role. One can think, too, of other works in a reflective mode, by such writers as R. G. Collingwood, Louis Mink, Michel de Certeau, Hayden White, Paul Veyne, and F. R. Ankersmit, which all offer reflective examinations of the historians' project. Consider, however, the character of the integration—for historians generally would be united mainly by a common recognition of the impossibility of their union (although historians specifically might be temporarily united in more substantive ways). The deep teaching of Novick's wise and learned book is that integration is impossible except through force or forgetfulness, and in consequence is not to be desired.

"Grand Narrative" and the Discipline of History

—— CHAPTER NINE ——

Introducing a collection of essays entitled *New Perspectives on Historical Writing* published in the early 1990s, the British historian Peter Burke noted that "in the last generation or so the universe of historians has been expanding at a dizzying rate."[1] In this chapter I wish to point out limits to the claimed expansion. Long before the rise of the various "new histories" that proliferated in the twentieth century, the mythology of the historical discipline included the idea that history is an absorptive enterprise—that it is capable of embracing all subjects and is peculiarly open to whatever useful methods and approaches it finds in other fields.[2]

I show in this chapter that the discipline's absorptiveness and openness are greatly constrained. A particular assumption—at base, an ontological assumption—underlies and gives force to the belief in history's absorptiveness. In briefest terms, the assumption might be characterized as an assumption of ultimate world unity. Such an assumption lies behind the grand narratives that have prevailed in Western historiography.[3] In this chapter I survey the various modifications of the conception of grand narrative that have arisen in the tradition of modern Western professional historical writing and research. I do so with a view to casting some light on the current situation of historical writing and thinking. The situation in question has both a diachronic aspect, linked to this continuing tradition, and a synchronic aspect, linked to the particular conditions of present-day life and culture.

My aim is to offer an account of the deep intellectual bases for the disciplinization or departmentalization of historical research and writing. What is produced by the historical discipline is not the whole of humanity's legitimate engagement with the past, but it is an important part of that engagement. Because the historical discipline claims a special authority in the interpretation of the past—an authority that, even now, is still most often couched in cognitive terms, as based on better method and sounder insight—it stands in need of epistemological reflection. Disciplines (history included) have boundaries. Scholars who are firmly within a discipline most often do not think about its boundaries. Instead, they feel its constraints as simply those of good scholarship generally.

There are institutional reasons why this is so. It is a matter of community and of modes of socialization into community. Except, sometimes, in a few multi-disciplinary fields, participants in one discipline in the humanities and social sciences usually lack serious engagement with participants in other disciplines. Although they may on occasion borrow from other disciplines, they usually do not have the experience of entering into the modes of argument of those disciplines, let alone of producing work that amounts to a contribution to another discipline. It often appears that the larger or more prestigious the academic institution, the higher the barriers. The institutions in question are most often set up in a heavily disciplinary way, and so is the larger scholarly world. The historian's departmental seminar operates in isolation from other humanities and social-sciences seminars, and each of these operates in isolation as well. Indeed, the departmental seminar is often itself highly fragmented, drawing participants only from a particular geographical, temporal, or thematic specialty or from a particular methodological approach. Often, true seminars do not take place at the departmental level at all, but only within specific subfields of history. Glaring error can easily remain uncorrected when the debate among historians occurs *only* in such specialized and rather provincial communities.

In this chapter I deliberately operate at a high level of generality. I acknowledge that accounts of the historical discipline can be offered at other levels, yielding much more complex and historically specific views.[4] I operate at this "high" level because my aim is to reflect on the conceptual foundations and general character of the discipline of history. More precisely, I reflect on the foundations and character of the discipline that emerged in the early nineteenth century in Germany. To a remarkable degree, the conceptual underpinnings that were established then remain in place—although they are clearly under challenge—even today. I apologize in advance for the abstraction that results from this broad attempt at conceptual history. However, I put this history forward in the context of a discipline that pays practically no attention to conceptual underpinnings at all. I urge the reader to attend carefully to the definitions that are offered: they are both precise and important. Reflection of the sort that I attempt here—while obviously only a small part of what historians can and should do—is indispensable because it brings to light what would otherwise remain unexamined prejudice.

Such reflection obviously has a theoretical significance. But it also has implications for the actual research and writing of history. For example, the question of historical synthesis came up as a seriously discussed historiographic issue in the 1980s, in response to a growing sense that history was becoming fragmented.[5] The place of synthesis in historical writing continues to be a live issue today. So also are matters of literary form: think, for example, of questions about the role of narrative in history and about the legitimacy or not of a fictive element in historical writing. To see how historical synthesis needs always to be proposed but at the same time called into doubt, to see how narrative is underpinned by "interested" assumptions that are often not recognized, and to see how fictiveness is both necessary to the historian's project and a source of great danger—these "seeings" all require a grasp of theoretical underpinnings and implications. My hope is that the conceptual devices offered in this chapter and in this book will be taken seriously both by those who are attempting to read works of history in a critical frame of mind and by those engaged in the difficult task of writing history in an epistemologically responsible mode while trying not to be so paralyzed by the uncertainties of historical knowledge that the historical imagination and the writing hand are impaired.

Obviously, an important issue here, perhaps the crucial one, is that of coherence. We cannot exhaust the subject in a single survey, but we can at least make some important distinctions. It seems useful to think of "coherence" as occupying four distinct levels of conceptualization. These are (1) *narrative proper;* (2) *master narrative,* or synthesis, which claims to offer the authoritative account of some particular segment of history; (3) *grand narrative,* which claims to offer the authoritative account of history generally; and (4) *metanarrative* (most commonly, belief in God or in a rationality somehow immanent in the world), which serves to justify the grand narrative. In the present chapter I focus specifically on the level of grand narrative. I do so because this allows the development of a framework that helps us make sense both of the more specific issues and of the fact that they have arisen *as* issues in the particular time that we inhabit. In essence, my concern is with the claim that "professional" or "disciplinary" historiography makes to a peculiarly authoritative role in the understanding of the past—that is, its claim to "objectivity" in the broadest sense of that term.[6]

FOUR IDEAL-TYPICAL ATTITUDES TOWARD THE OVERALL COHERENCE OF HISTORY

Until fairly recently, observers of and participants in the tradition of modern, Western, professional, historical research and writing generally held that every particular work of history ought to orient itself to history generally—that is, to a single history, which I shall here designate as History.[7] We can plausibly view this tradition as connecting history-writing to History in four different ways. In so doing, it manifested four "attitudes" toward History. We can order these attitudes chronologically, although they are also coexistent, and I would argue that in the best historical writing we can find at least traces of all four attitudes. They are conceptual types. First, one finds commitment to a particular "grand narrative" that claims to make sense of history as a whole. The gist of "attitude 1" is that there is a single coherent History and that it can be told (or retold) now. "Attitude 2" holds that there is a single coherent History, but defers its telling to a later date, after "further research" has been done. "Attitude 3" holds that there is a single coherent History, but that it can never be told. Obviously, if we think in narrativist terms, we will find a paradox here, for a grand narrative that can never be told has nothing at all of the *form* of narrative. Instead, it manifests itself in the commitment of historians to the autonomy of their discipline, a commitment that purports to maintain the discipline's purity and coherence in the absence of any single story to which it converges. "Attitude 4" calls even this form of coherence into question.

It has been largely invisible to historians themselves that professional historiography has presupposed the existence, although not necessarily the telling, of a vision of coherence. Of course, historians are generally well aware of the problem of coherence at more specific levels, whether it is a matter of constructing a single (by definition coherent) narrative, or a matter of addressing the implicit or explicit "master narrative" of some specific historical field (as Geyer and Jarausch have done; see note 5). The issue here, however, is coherence at a "world" level. Because the articulation of conceptual presumptions is a theoretical rather than a historiographic task, only rarely do historians articulate them. Moreover, investigators, including historians of historiography, tend to miss precisely those features of a situation that are most "natural" to them.

Still, *some* historians of historiography—invariably informed by extra-disciplinary studies—have seen what is here pointed out. Reinhart Koselleck, a historian acutely sensitive to the history of concepts, noted the emergence in late eighteenth-century Germany of what he called the "collective singular" use of the term *Geschichte,* a word that means "history" or "story." Only in the late eighteenth century, Koselleck contended, did people come to think of *Geschichte* as a singular rather than as a plural term. Moreover, only then did they begin to use it to mean history *in general,* as distinguished from the history of X, Y, or Z. This "collective singular" sense of history, according to Koselleck, "establishe[d] the terms of all possible individual histories."[8] A reading of literary theory led Robert F. Berkhofer Jr., to find in professional historians' concern with context the assumption that the past is "a complex but unified flow of events," a "Great Story."[9] The philosopher Louis Mink found that the eighteenth-century notion of "universal history" survives in twentieth-century historiography.[10] Finally, working from a Kantian standpoint, Leonard Krieger emphasized professional historiography's persistent search for coherence.[11]

Krieger's account is especially telling. He showed that when historians lack fundamental agreement concerning the character of human history, the coherence of the historiographic enterprise is threatened—and vice versa. Developing Krieger's point, from a present-day viewpoint we can see that professional historiography as it emerged in the nineteenth century was remarkably unified in its attitude toward human history. Whatever their different national and ideological standpoints, almost all professional historians agreed that history was political, European, and male. But in recent years professional historiography has found itself driven into a greater pluralism. This change strains the hope of attaining a unified view of the past, even as it challenges the former homogeneity of the enterprise. It also strains the view that historiography can and ought to be autonomous in relation to other enterprises. Krieger was a professional historian's professional historian, deeply committed to the autonomy of the discipline. He held that the historian, although he should certainly learn from neighboring disciplines, ought nonetheless to function as a "pure historian" (that is, as a historian uncontaminated by other disciplines' modes of thinking), for the coherence of a "distinctively historical knowledge" underwrites "the coherence of the past."[12] Yet Krieger's own emphasis on the relation between the subjective and the objective aspects of history calls into doubt the prospects for a coherent disciplinary vision in any time of social disjunction.

ATTITUDE 1. *There is a single History, and we already know what it is.*

Attitude 1 is embodied in the tradition of "universal history." Universal history is relevant to the issue of disciplinary boundaries because in its secularized form it had an immense impact on professional historiography. Although its roots are to be found as early as the Patristic period, it first became a continuing tradition of scholarship and teaching in Protestant German universities after the Reformation humanist Philipp Melanchthon lectured on the subject at the University of Wittenberg in the mid-sixteenth century. In an age when a nation-state did not develop in Germany, as it did in France and Britain, universal history provided for Protestant Germans a vision of unity and glory that they otherwise lacked.[13]

Christian universal history emphasized the Hebrews and took its chronology and periodization from the Bible. In the course of the early modern period, the biblical focus was challenged, and ultimately abandoned. But the undermining of Christian universal history did not destroy the idea of universal history itself, which continued in secularized (i.e., non-biblical) form. In Germany, of course, the idea was supported by the existence of university chairs devoted to it.

The secularized tradition of universal history is the true beginning of the story that I tell here. Although the secularized tradition accorded no special privilege to the Bible, the basic idea of the earlier, biblically based conception remained in place—namely, the idea that there is finally a single history, whose unity is guaranteed by God. Conceptually, a new problem emerged in the move from universal history based on sacred Scripture to one that, although presupposed by theism, granted no special privilege to Scripture. In the first case, we can tell the grand narrative now because our telling is actually a *re*telling, whereas in the second case the telling has no preexisting model. How are we to discover what the grand narrative is, since it is no longer prescribed by the Bible? Can we in fact *know* the grand narrative? To what degree, and by what means?

Immanuel Kant offered one answer. His essay "Idea for a Universal History from a Cosmopolitan Point of View" (1784) explicitly contributed to the universal history tradition, and Kant returned to the matter in "An Old Question Raised Again: Is the Human Race Constantly Progressing?" (1795).[14] In the earlier essay, Kant suggested that a "philosophical history" of mankind could be written. A philosophical history would show how the apparently chaotic workings of individual human will, when viewed "on a large scale," may be seen as manifesting "a regular progression among freely willed actions," the outcome of which will be "a perfect civil union of mankind." Indeed, the writing of such a history would help to achieve the desired end.[15] But Kant knew that such a history could not be empirically justified and disclaimed any wish "to supersede the task of history proper."[16]

In his 1795 essay Kant again emphasized that "the problem of progress cannot be solved directly from experience"; yet he also contended that "there must be some experience or other" that "might suggest that man has the quality or power of being the *cause* and . . . the *author* of his own improvement."[17] In considering his own time, Kant found just such an empirical indicator in "the attitude of the onlookers" of by far the greatest event of his time, the French Revolution. Observers who had nothing to gain from the Revolution greeted it with near enthusiasm—even in Prussia, where such enthusiasms were dangerous. Their sympathy for the Revolution, Kant held, could have been caused only by a "moral disposition within the human race," the presence of which gives ground for believing that human history is progressive.[18] Hegel, too, claimed to be able to discern and to tell the essential shape of history, which he saw as a progressive realization of freedom: first one person is free, then some, then all.[19]

Yet the telling of the grand narrative carries risks, for future events may diverge from the suggested story line. For example, in May 1789 Friedrich Schiller delivered his inaugural lecture as professor of history at the University of Jena. Inspired by Kant's "Idea for a Universal History," he spoke on the topic "What is universal history and why do we study it ?" Schiller recounted a movement from barbarism, still visible in primitive races, to the civilization of eighteenth-century Europe, where truth, morality, and freedom were growing ever more powerful. In his view, "the European society of states seems transformed into a great family," whose members "may have their feuds, but no longer tear each other limb from limb."[20] Schiller apparently never commented on the discrepancy between his complacent account of European history in the inaugural lecture and the world-shattering events unleashed only two months later in France.[21]

A related problem concerns the level of detail to be included in the grand narrative. In a review of 1772 of August Wilhelm von Schlözer's *Universal-Historie,* Johann Gottfried Herder criticized Schlözer for not having implemented the plan of universal history that his book proposed. Responding, Schlözer agreed with Herder's observation that it is easier to propose something than to do it [*dass sich etwas leichter sagen als thun lasse*], but contended that "where it is a matter of world history . . . it must be *proposed* [*gesagt*] before it is *done* . . . a *plan,* a *theory,* an *ideal* of this science must be drawn up."[22] In other words, Schlözer held that the outline of the story can be told now, but he deferred its *complete* telling until later. Schlözer clearly must have thought of that later telling as a mere amplification of the outline. But what, we might ask, if the later telling were less amplification than correction? In such a case, we could not be said to know already what the single History is.

ATTITUDE 2. *There is a single History, but we can know what it is only after further research has been done.*

Attitude 2 defers the telling of the story. Gaining prominence historically as a response to the upheavals of the Revolutionary and Napoleonic Wars, attitude 2 was intimately connected with the emergence of professional historiography. The canonical founder of the discipline, Leopold von Ranke, was critical of such universal historians as J. C. Gatterer, Johannes Müller, and Friedrich Christoph Schlosser.[23] He was even more critical of such philosophers as Hegel, who attempted to posit *a priori* the course of human history. But he was not critical of universal history as such; on the contrary, it remained a continuing preoccupation for him.[24]

Consider the following passage, from a fragment that Ranke wrote in the 1860s:

> The investigation of the particular, even of a single point, is of value if it is done well. . . . But the investigation of the particular is always related to a larger context. Local history is related to that of a country; a biography is related to a larger event in state and church, to an epoch of national or general history. But all these epochs themselves are, as we have said, again part of the great whole [*Ganzen*] which we call universal history. The greater scope of its investigation has correspondingly greater value. The ultimate goal, not yet attained, will always remain the conception and composition of a history of mankind. . . . Comprehending the whole and yet doing justice to the requirements of research will, of course, always remain an ideal. It would presuppose an understanding on a firm foundation of the totality of human history.[25]

Ranke here envisaged three distinct levels of historical concern. The first, "the investigation of the particular, even of a single point," evokes what historians today call micro-history. The second, which shows how the particular is related to a "larger context," is also visible in present-day historiography. The third level, concerned with "the totality of human history"—with "comprehending the whole"—is hidden, but the *idea* of it is familiar to us: it is the idea of grand narrative, of a unified history of humankind.

In his reference to "the ultimate goal, . . . not yet attained," Ranke acknowledged a deferral of the telling of such a history. Similar statements appear elsewhere in his corpus; for example, in a lecture script of 1867, he wrote that "the science of history is not yet mature enough to reconstruct universal history on new foundations."[26] In fact, insistence on a deferral of the telling of grand narrative was necessary for history's emergence as a discipline. Kant, Schiller, and Hegel believed that they already knew the basic outline of human history—or at any rate they believed that they knew which outline of human history it was best to posit as true. However, their conviction deprived historical research of its rationale, for, persuaded by such accounts, one would "seek only to know to what extent the philosophical principle can be demonstrated in history; . . . it would be of no interest at all to delve into the things that happened . . . or to want to know how men lived and thought at a certain time." Furthermore, "were this procedure [of constructing "the whole of history" on an *a priori* basis] correct, history [*Historie*] would lose all autonomy [*Selbständigkeit*]."[27] If through sacred Scripture, or through knowledge of human nature, or in some other way we are able to tell the story now, what need is there for the supposedly distinctive methods of professional historical research?[28]

Ranke's justification for continuing to believe in the reality of a single History even in the absence of its present telling was religious. God created the world and oversees everything in it, one God creating one History. Hints of this view are to be found in Ranke's "Idea of Universal History," where, in referring to the "conception of totality" (*Auffassung der Totalität*) that is one of the features of universal history, he asserts that it is impossible for us to grasp universal history completely: "Only God knows world history."[29] But the connection between the idea of God and the idea of History's unity was perhaps stated most clearly in a letter that the young Ranke wrote to his brother in 1820:

> God dwells, lives, and can be known in all of history. Every deed attests to Him, every moment preaches His name, but most of all, it seems to me, the connectedness of history in the large. It [the connectedness] stands there like a holy hieroglyph. . . . May we, for our part, decipher this holy hieroglyph! Even so do we serve God. Even so are we priests. Even so are we teachers.[30]

There is thus a manifest continuity between Ranke and earlier, Christian conceptions of universal history.

Adherence to the notion of grand narrative by no means required religious faith, for forms of secular faith could also serve. Consider J. B. Bury's inaugural lecture of 1902 as Regius Professor of Modern History at Cambridge, entitled "The Science of History." Here Bury suggested that

> the idea of the future development of man . . . furnishes . . . the justification of much of the laborious historical work that has been done and is being done today. The gathering of materials bearing upon minute local events, the collation of MSS. and the registry of their small variations, the patient drudgery in archives of states and municipalities, all the microscopic research that is carried on by armies of toiling students. . . .This work, the hewing of wood and the drawing of water,

has to be done in faith—in the faith that a complete assemblage of the smallest facts of human history will tell in the end. The labour is performed for posterity—for remote posterity.[31]

The justification for Bury's faith lay in the late nineteenth-century global expansion of Western civilization and in the ideals of science and cooperation that he thought had made the expansion possible. Bury's stance was structurally identical to Ranke's, despite its secular focus. Like Ranke, Bury adhered to attitude 2, deferring the telling of the grand narrative to the future. Bury's foil was an explicit adherent of attitude 1, Thomas Arnold (father of Matthew Arnold), who in his inaugural lecture of 1841 as Regius Professor of Modern History at Oxford had suggested that the "modern age" coincided with "the last step" in the story of man, bearing marks "of the fulness of time, as if there would be no future history beyond it."[32] Bury demurred, but not because he objected to the idea of a single History *per se*. He believed that it was too soon to know the shape of history, not that there is no single shape to be known.

We might be tempted to think that deferral of its telling would dramatically reduce the relevance of belief in a single History to the writing of history. But its relevance remains, for belief in universal history (albeit a universal history that is as yet untellable) has an important epistemological consequence. The belief allows historians to maintain that the historical account is an objective representation, connected to the standpoint of History itself. As Krieger noted, Ranke's "assurance about the historian's objectivity" was predicated on belief in "a single process" linking past and present.[33] In "The Science of History," Bury made precisely this point. He began by insisting that history is a science—"no less and no more."[34] "Science," for Bury, implied purely objective representation: it "cannot safely be controlled or guided by a subjective interest."[35] Rejecting a relation to his own time and place, the historian claims to relate himself to the historical process as a whole. "Principles of unity and continuity" exist within history, Bury believed.[36] These principles suggest the idea of man's future development, which serves as a "limiting controlling conception" telling the historian what belongs in a historical account and what should be excluded.[37]

ATTITUDE 3. *There is a single History. However, it can never be told. It exists only ideally, as the unreachable end of an autonomous discipline. Coherence is now located not in the told or anticipated Story, but in the unified mode of thinking of the discipline.*

Attitude 3 gives up the notion that the single History will ever be told, without giving up the notion that there is a "single history"—that is, a single authorized mode of investigating the past. The historian and theorist of historiography Johann Gustav Droysen, who from 1852 to 1882 taught the theory and methodology of history, came close to articulating this attitude. Droysen maintained in his lectures that the grand narrative could never be told, at least not on the basis of historical investigation. "The highest end" of history, he asserted, "is not to be discovered by empirical investigation."[38] As the mention of a "highest end" suggests, Droysen believed that a coherent History exists. But whereas Ranke and Bury believed that the historian could discover coherence within the objective historical process, Droysen shifted attention to the subjective sphere. Without denying the existence of an objective coherence, he chose "to establish, not the laws of objective History but the laws of historical investigation and knowledge."[39] One implication of Droysen's position is that historiography must itself be a coherent enterprise—for how else could there be *laws* of historical investigation and knowledge? A further implication is that historiography must be clearly separated from contrary enterprises and concerns. With some justification, Hayden White has suggested that Droysen offered "the most sustained and systematic defense of the autonomy of historical thought ever set forth."[40]

While Ranke also emphasized the autonomy of history and defended the subject against those who would approach it with a ready-made grand narrative borrowed from philosophy, Droysen's insistence on autonomy had an additional role: it protected historiography not only from the first, pre-professional conviction that the story is already known but also from the threat of multiplicity and fragmentation. For a mid-nineteenth-century historian, Droysen (a Prussian nationalist of liberal bent) was remarkably sensitive to the idea that historical reality can be described, explained, and interpreted in vastly different ways. For whatever reasons, he seems to have been aware that adherents of competing identities would be inclined to claim legitimacy for their histories just as he claimed legitimacy for Prussia's.[41] Ranke, on the other hand, was protected from coming to grips with such threats by his conviction that Europe constituted a unified political system and by his belief that the task of historiography is to write the history of that (European) system.[42] More sensitive, it appears, to the conflict of interests and identities, Droysen was correspondingly more able to see multiplicity as a *problem;* he recognized multiplicity as legitimate, but at the same time insisted on containing it.[43]

Attitude 3 abandons the hope of ever articulating an objective grand narrative (that is, an authoritative account of History as a whole), while retaining commitment to coherence at the level of the historiographic enterprise itself, which is seen as united by adherence to common methods and aims. Attitude 3 is an idealized version of what seems to have been the dominant stance of the historical profession in the twentieth century c.1914–1991.[44] After the slaughter of World War I—carried out, it seemed, for naught— most professional historians no longer saw their task as the deciphering of a holy hieroglyph or as the telling of a great story of progress. Even if many continued to believe that history was fundamentally benevolent, they no longer saw it as the *historian's* task to portray this benevolence.[45] Attitude 3 has the advantage of allowing adherence to a single ideal, without requiring that the ideal be embodied in a specific historical content.

Yet attitude 3 is deeply paradoxical and tension-laden, for behind commitment to historiography as a single, coherent enterprise the ghost of a hope for an objective grand narrative persists—yet the grand narrative cannot be told. Because Droysen was deeply influenced by German idealist philosophy, especially Hegelian philosophy, and continued to believe in a "moral world . . . moved by many ends, and finally . . . by the supreme end," we cannot finally see him as embodying attitude 3 in a form that is clearly marked off from attitudes 1 and 2.[46] Among theorists of historiography, R. G. Collingwood best exemplifies attitude 3, and thus best displays its inherent contradictions. (Admittedly, one might also look to Wilhelm Dilthey or Michael Oakeshott, who, like Droysen and Collingwood, focus attention on the subjective dimension, that is, on historians' *thinking*.[47] But Collingwood is the clearest thinker of the lot, and his clarity reveals what remains hidden elsewhere.[48]

Collingwood made two crucial "third-attitude" claims about historiography. Professional historians readily embraced these claims, for they conformed to how historians in the twentieth century "always already" conceived of their enterprise.

First, Collingwood claimed that historiographic coherence has its roots in the mind of the historian. In a general sense, Collingwood's position on this issue was Kantian. Kant accepted David Hume's assertion that we cannot perceive causation (although we can perceive the spatial contiguity, temporal succession, and constant conjunction that are normally associated with causation). Hume's view raised the threat of a totalized skepticism, to which Kant responded by asserting that causation is not something empirically discoverable but is an organizing principle in the mind. When, famously,

Collingwood in *The Idea of History* attacked a passive "scissors-and-paste" history and argued that the historian who depends on the documents to provide coherence will wait forever, he was following out the implications for historiography of Kant's "Copernican Revolution" in philosophy.[49]

Second, Collingwood repeatedly emphasized the "autonomy" of history.[50] In invoking autonomy, he was actually referring to two different notions. In the first place, he was concerned to emphasize that the historian ought to have autonomy in relation to "the sources," making up his own mind about the past rather than relying on the supposed authority of "the sources." This first emphasis is simply another way of saying that coherence is rooted in the mind of the historian. But "autonomy" in Collingwood also denotes a rather different claim, namely, that historians ought to have autonomy in relation to other disciplines. Here, Collingwood's argument is that historiography is an independent discipline with its own rules (different from the rules of other disciplines) that have been worked out over time through a process of trial and error.[51] We can see why he would want to emphasize the autonomy of history in relation to other disciplines, for only if we hold that historiography is a clearly bounded field with its own distinctive set of rules can we expect historical thinking to provide coherence. In other words, the subjectivization of coherence—that is, its relocation into the mind of the historian—placed a premium on the claim that historiography is an autonomous enterprise.

Yet at various points Collingwood undermined, and even directly denied, the notion that historiography ought to be an autonomous enterprise in the sense just noted. For example, in his *Autobiography* he asserted that his life's work, as seen from his fiftieth year, "has been in the main an attempt to bring about a rapprochement between philosophy and history."[52] Collingwood's philosophical opponents of the time made a sharp distinction between historical questions (e.g., What was Aristotle's theory of duty?) and philosophical questions (e.g., Was it true?), and saw only the philosophical questions as important (59). Collingwood attacked the separation of the two enterprises. Further, he contended that "the chief business of twentieth-century philosophy is to reckon with twentieth-century history," a contention that connected with another rapprochement he wanted, namely, between theory and practice (79, 147–67). His position was not only that philosophy should become historical, but also that history should become philosophical, and that both should be written out of a profound concern with present problems—for events, he asserted, had broken up his "pose of a detached professional thinker" and had moved him toward engagement (167).[53]

In *The Idea of History* Collingwood's undercutting of the autonomy of historiography is less evident.[54] Yet the undercutting is clearly *there*. It is manifested, for example, in his otherwise quite puzzling contention that history is "re-enactment of past experience,"[55] a wording that seems intended to emphasize, to a greater degree than mere "re-thinking," the activism of the historian. Similarly, his contention that "every present has a past of its own, and any imaginative reconstruction of the past aims at reconstructing the past of *this* present," has subversive implications that potentially demolish his more conservative assertion that "all history must be consistent with itself."[56]

ATTITUDE 4. *The assumption that there is a single History cannot be maintained, either subjectively as an enterprise or objectively as an actual grand narrative to be told now or in the future. Accordingly, a responsible historiography will call the assumption of a single History into question. Yet we may still entertain attitudes 1, 2, and 3, which assume a single History: regulatively, in the case of attitude 1; heuristically or ironically, in the cases of attitudes 2 and 3.*

Attitude 4 both embraces these other attitudes and calls them into question. Attitude 4 is perhaps best approached by reflection on figure 9.1, which suggests the proximity of each attitude to the others. As ideal types, the four attitudes are distinct from each other. In reality, however, they shade off from one to the other; they can also coexist with each other, with the "later" views taking account of the "earlier" ones. Only a slight incredulity toward the present tellability of History is needed for attitude 1 to shade off into attitude 2, as the exchange between Herder and Schlözer, noted above, shows.[57] Only a slight incredulity toward the future tellability of History is needed for attitude 2 to shade off into attitude 3: recall Ranke, who wrote, in the same fragment, both that the telling of History was "the ultimate goal, not yet attained," and that "comprehending the whole . . . will always remain an ideal."[58] Similarly, in Collingwood, emphasis on the autonomy of historiography, which preserves subjective coherence even in the face of the permanent unreliability of an objective grand narrative, tips over, when pushed hard enough, into the notion that the time within which historical thinking is being done is as important as the time of the past—to such a degree that past time gets reconfigured, at every moment, from the viewpoint of the present. In short, there is a conceptual instability pushing one type over into one or more of the other types.

More accurately, *beyond attitude 1* there is a conceptual instability. Attitude 1 is the only self-consistent position. It arises out of historically localized and scripturally authorized monotheism (Judaism, Christianity, Islam),

ATTITUDE 1. There is a single History, and we know it now.	ATTITUDE 3. There is a single History, namely, the autonomous and coherent discipline of history.
ATTITUDE 2. There is a single History, to be known only after further research has been done.	ATTITUDE 4. A single History is unjustified, but may be entertained. Border-crossing and methodological breaches *may* have justification.

FIGURE 9.1. Four attitudes toward history

and there is no reason for it to collapse as long as its religious justification is secure. But the other attitudes are different. Attitude 2 teeters between the possibility that "further research" will *never* yield an objective universal history, and the heuristically or dogmatically maintained view that we already know, at least in outline, the objective universal history. Attitude 3 is caught between pride in the procedures of the historical discipline and the uneasy worry that the procedures will never reveal an objective universal history. As for attitude 4, it occupies the difficult position of Pyrrhonian or Montaignean skepticism, which strives to be skeptical also of its own skepticism. From the point of view of attitude 3, attitude 4 contradicts the coherent way of thinking that is legitimate historiography. From the point of view of attitude 4, on the other hand, we ought not to exclude any mode of understanding the past on *a priori* grounds, whether those grounds are methodological or ontological. Thus attitude 4 is not an argument against (for example) attitude 3, except insofar as attitude 3 seeks to dismiss attitude 4. Yet attitude 4 is constantly in danger of falling into one version or another of dogmatism—either through dogmatic adherence to the view that "there is no single History" (which is itself a statement about the overall character of History), or through dogmatic rejection of disciplinary standards and conventions.

My focus is of course on conceptual presumptions. Investigations of the institutional bases of the discipline of history would yield a more variegated picture; however, my central argument seems justified on an institutional level as well. The institutional structures of intellectual life include, among other things, professional organizations, disciplinary journals, and the departmental organization of universities, all of which find intellectual justification in the presumption that historians are engaged in a single project. My argument here is that in the current situation we ought to see both the institutional structures and the presumptions justifying them not just as supports for the production of knowledge, which they manifestly are, but as limits as well, and, further, that we ought to consider seriously the character of those limits.

The presumption that historiography is finally a single project has the effect of establishing a bias in favor of work written out of the conviction that there is a single, autonomous, historical mode of thinking—an approach, even a method, that aspires to "unification" in "history and the historical profession" in spite of a manifest disunity at the levels of subjects and subject matters. (I evoke here the theme of the American Historical Association annual meeting of December 1992.[59]) The aim is to "historicize" history's objects—that is, to subject them to the methods of a single historical thinking. The presumption of unity establishes a bias against work whose reflections on the past involve commitments to other modes of understanding than the autonomously historical. Insofar as history so practiced relates to other modes of understanding, it does so by way of "appropriating" them for history. I do not reject such work, for that would be inconsistent with my rejection of *a priori* criteria for judging scholarly work. Rather, I suggest that, because we have worked for so long from the standpoint of the "autonomy" view—attitudes 2 and 3—we must reckon with diminishing marginal returns and consider that in some ways it becomes difficult therein to produce new and surprising knowledge. This is a *suggestion,* not a solid assertion as to fact, for the future of any science is by its nature unpredictable.[60]

We might advance other arguments as well for the partial "de-disciplinization" of history. The other arguments have for the most part already been developed, sometimes in considerable detail, although most often in contexts that historians do not attend to. Looking specifically at historiography, the historian and theorist of historiography F. R. Ankersmit points to what he calls "the present-day overproduction in our discipline. . . . We are all familiar with the fact that . . . an overwhelming number of books and articles is produced annually, making a comprehensive view of them all impossible."[61] The result, Ankersmit argues, has been a move away from "the essentialist tradition within Western historiography," which focused attention on "the trunk of the tree." Instead, one can now see a "pull" toward the margins, manifested in forms of historiography that no longer focus on "meaning" (in French, the word is *sens,* which also means "direction") but instead address themselves to aspects of the past (such as mentalities, gender, and the like) that were formerly seen as mere "notations," without significance for the general plot of history.[62]

Beyond historiography, there exists a philosophical line of argument, preeminently represented in certain aspects of the early writings of Jacques

Derrida, which clearly has implications for the unity-claims of disciplines generally (I think especially of Derrida's notion of "originary difference," or *"différance,"* which we can take as part of an argument against convergence).[63] The analytic philosopher Nicholas Rescher, arguing for the legitimacy of an "orientational pluralism" in philosophy, advanced a notion that seems as applicable to concerns with synthesis in historiography as it is to concerns with consensus in philosophy.[64] The political scientists Mattei Dogan and Robert Pahre argue, on the basis of empirical study, that "hybridization" between disciplines, not specialization within them or unification between them, is currently the most reliable route to new knowledge. The Dogan and Pahre argument implies mixed or hybrid modes coexisting with continued disciplinarity.[65]

All the arguments point toward something much broader than historiography, or even than the human sciences generally. They point toward a cultural condition that in the 1980s was widely identified as "postmodern." This is not the place to survey the immense literature that emerged in an attempt to explicate just what the term and the reality of "the postmodern" meant.[66] The term itself was obviously unsatisfactory, and yet at a certain moment it was also indispensable. A global definition does not seem possible. Nonetheless, one feature of the still current social and cultural situation seems salient to what was once thought of as "postmodern." This feature is the juxtaposition of diversities—of competing identities. It is quite possibly not true that the social and cultural situation is markedly more "diverse" than it was before. Nonetheless, contemporary modes of communication bring the diversities into closer proximity than ever before, so that the general feeling, at least in those societies where the diversities manage not to go to war with each other, is of an amazingly rich variety and disjunctiveness.

There is a close parallel between juxtaposed social diversities and juxtaposed disciplines. In both cases we are dealing with boundaries—boundaries, I contend, that should not be wished away. Incredulity toward the discipline's claim to autonomy (for that is what "incredulity toward grand narrative" finally amounts to) means a questioning but not a denial of boundaries. In short, my argument is not an argument for interdisciplinary unification—for there are limits to "openness." The more we learn about how practitioners of other disciplines argue, through the experience of having argued with them on their own grounds, the less likely we are to think that the different modes of argument are compatible enough for any one person to practice them at the same time.[67] And yet these other modes of argument, when well done, also contribute to knowledge. My argument is rather for the *crossing* of boundaries, for temporary residence in other domains, for attempts to speak or at least to understand the foreign language (a different enterprise from translation), and for explicit recognition of the desirability of such projects *within* the historical discipline, to replace misguided views about the wonderful absorptiveness of professional historiography.[68] It is also an argument for invention of hybrid states, possibly temporary Andorras, between the extant ones.

FOUR POSTULATES SUGGESTED
BY THE PRECEDING ACCOUNT

Since the story offered here ends not in the past, however recent, but in the present and future, it acquires inevitably a prescriptive dimension. To be sure, the only really satisfactory answer to the question "How should science and scholarship be done now?" is to do it, for the answer is always a wager. But several prescriptive postulates do seem to follow from the story. They also have, to a greater or less degree, an embeddedness in the present situation (although it is not my aim to articulate an authoritative description of the present situation, an impossible task in any case).

THE MULTIPLICITY POSTULATE. *"Never assume that there is a single authorized historical method or subject matter."*
     A phenomenon of third-attitude historiography in its most intellectually compelling form was the call for "total history," a call most closely associated with the name of Fernand Braudel. Braudel saw his monumental *Mediterranean and the Mediterranean World* as "an attempt to write" such a history.[69] But the aspiration toward "total history" inevitably generates its opposite.[70] The greatest monument to this failure of unity is the journal *Annales: Économies, Sociétés, Civilisations*. One thinks also of *The Mediterranean and the Mediterranean World* itself, which is finally held together by a massive literary conceit.[71] One thinks too of Braudel's later *Civilization and Capitalism,* a vast collection of loosely-related disparates.[72] Not surprisingly, it became commonplace for observers of the historiographic scene to point to the "multiplication" or "proliferation" of history, its conversion from "history" into "histories."[73]
     Multiplicity gained steam in part because of sociological changes bringing into the historical profession people who were inclined to see as interesting hitherto neglected subjects of investigation. For example, in the United States the emergence of social history was prompted in various important ways by the entry into the profession of people from non-WASP ethnic groups, people whose parents had been excluded from the exercise of politi-

cal power and had devoted their energies to assimilation into and success within American society. The emergence of a gender orientation in history had an obvious connection with the entry into the profession of more women.[74] Previously excluded or discouraged groups were able to find new subjects of investigation interesting in part because personal and family experiences made them receptive to such subjects, whereas earlier historians had focused on a relatively small range of privileged political actors.

Investigators have several strategies available to them for coming to grips with the fact that they are engaged professionally with subject matters connected in a now "obvious" way to their own social interests and experiences (earlier connections were generally not "obvious" because of the lesser degree of social diversity). One strategy is assimilation. Hewing to the "third-attitude" standard of autonomy, historians may indeed acknowledge their social commitments, but claim that in their historiography "objectivity" and professionalism hold sway. Here nothing changes, at least not manifestly. A bolder strategy involves continued adherence to professionalism, but strives to change the "grand" or at least the "master" narrative, improving it by including what was previously excluded—for example, gender. Those adopting that strategy may even claim to be finally producing an authoritative account of the past, "the full story." Here, too, one is clearly within the bounds of attitude 3. Sticking with the example of gender, a further move is from "women's history" to "feminist history," where the authority claimed is less a professional authority than a nonprofessional one. The move to feminist history can involve acceptance of received dogma, as in attitudes 1 and 2, or it can involve a dialectical relation to the past and to its own position. In the latter case, one would be tempted to see it as embracing attitude 4, and attitude 3 to the degree that it remains epistemologically responsible. Think of Natalie Davis's *The Return of Martin Guerre,* discussed in the introduction to this book.

THE HYBRIDIZATION POSTULATE. *"Always establish residences outside the discipline."*

By definition (and readers should recognize that much of my argument here is *per definitionem*), third-attitude history, committed to the autonomy of the discipline, does not *practically* recognize the existence of legitimate forms of argument about the human world other than its own. In attitude 3, other disciplines are seen as, at most, "auxiliary" fields. Thus in the 1950s and 1960s connections developed between history and political science, leading to the importation into history of statistical methods for the study of human behavior, and in the 1970s similar connections developed between history and anthropology, leading to the importation of new, culturally oriented ways of looking at past societies.[75] In both instances the disciplinary boundaries guarding historiography remained unchallenged, whatever the insights brought by these cross-boundary raids.[76] In attitude 3, other disciplines are not seen as forms of argument in their own right, which in their very difference from historical thinking might reveal things that historical thinking cannot see, but as sources of methods and results to be imported into history without fundamentally changing it.

By way of contrast, fourth-attitude history responds to the fragmentation of the discipline and its subject matters with partial or temporary residence in other intellectual communities. Cross-disciplinary hybrids, held together by some combination of theory and experience, emerge. Often these communities are *ad hoc* and local, dependent on accidents of character, geography, and intellectual culture; they are hindered by walls and hierarchy and fostered by sociability and egalitarianism. But they share a concern for bridging the difference between different disciplines in temporary pursuit of some common approach or object of study. Within each such group, a new "language game" emerges, a lingua franca different from the language games of the particular disciplines from which each participant comes (for participation *in* a discipline would still be a precondition for entry into a multi-disciplinary language game).[77] Work of a new type is produced in each "hybrid" field, differing from that done in the contributing disciplines.

Multi-disciplinary interaction of a transformative sort is rare in the human sciences. It is perhaps more characteristic of the physical and biological sciences, where disciplinary boundaries are somewhat more fluid and are quite often altered in response to the emergence of new research problems.[78] It is no accident that the best-known instance of "fourth-attitude" historiography comes from the history of science: Thomas S. Kuhn's *The Structure of Scientific Revolutions*.[79] Written by a physicist who turned himself into a historian of science, it was animated by important issues in the philosophy of science. In breaching disciplinary boundaries, it lost the benefit of disciplinary certitudes; its daring took it into problematic regions. But in part because of this, it also generated important insight; indeed, no other work by a historian writing in the twentieth century did so much to raise new problems and to suggest new approaches to old problems.[80]

THE FICTIONALITY POSTULATE. *"Always confront, in an explicit way, the fictionality implicit in all works of history."*

Collingwood asserted in *The Idea of History* that whereas "purely imaginary worlds cannot clash and need not agree" since "each is a world to itself,"

there "is only one historical world."[81] Taken generally, Collingwood's assertion about the historical world is incorrect (since the one historical world
presupposes an infinity of counterfactual ones), but it is largely correct as an
observation about third-attitude historiography, in which commitment to
one way of thinking tends to generate one kind of historical object and to set
limits on the kinds of explanation that will be entertained. Collingwood's
assertion implies, further, that the more that historians find themselves at a
distance from History, the more the "fictional" aspects of their work come
to the fore.

I touch here on issues that I do not think can be resolved, either in theory
or in practice—but the issues need to be raised. The history/fiction dual-
ism is one of many that is of limited analytical value: it is especially prone to
polemical misuse, both by those who imagine that "anything goes" and by
those who would point with horror at precisely that view. Often, a useful
method when one is confronted by such dualisms is to begin to complexify
them. Even at first glance, it seems clear that within the general territory of
fictionality, we need at the very least to distinguish between what I would
call, respectively, the "literary" and the "fictive." By the "literary," I mean all
those devices of literary craft that we commonly notice when we read works
of fiction but that we often see as abnormal and suspect in historiography,
which in its professional mode has tended to cultivate a neutral voice. By the
"fictive," I mean all those dimensions wherein works of history diverge from
truth in its sense as correspondence to empirical reality. All causal analysis is
fictive in this sense, because all causal analysis presupposes counterfactuals.
All typologization is likewise fictive, because types are always idealizations
of a messier reality. Indeed, given the complexity of reality, definition itself
is fictive in this sense as well. Lest there be some mistake about this, bear in
mind that causality, typologization, and definition are essential parts of *all*
historical research and writing. In other words, all historiography possesses
a fictive, or speculative, dimension.

Much has been written on the literary dimension of history-writing, by
such theorists of historiography as Hayden White, Dominick LaCapra, Stephen Bann, Hans Kellner, Philippe Carrard and F. R. Ankersmit.[82] There
is also a small body of stylistically "experimental" works of history written
since the early 1970s that wittingly or unwittingly fall into a fourth-attitude
mold.[83] "Voice" has been an important issue in many of the more experimental works; other issues include a breaking away from the convention of
the smoothly running narrative and a tendency for the historian to intrude
explicitly into the historical account being told. Such literary experiments
suggest a deeper, ontological point: that the historical object itself is a "fic-

tive" creation, something constituted *as object* by the mind of the historian and her readers. This is not an assertion that "there is no *there* there"; it is an assertion that the historian makes (but not out of nothing) the particular historical objects presented in her work.

THE THEORY POSTULATE. *"Always theorize."*

In a world that no longer believes in a single History, historians can awaken universal interest only insofar as they are able in their work to take account of theoretical issues. For example, in an America that no longer sees its history as following directly from the political and constitutional history of Great Britain, an account of, say, "The Gunpowder Plot of 1605" can have interest only insofar as it raises issues of a theoretical sort, detached from the specific events of 1605. Yet, at the same time, just as the conversion of "history" into "histories" problematizes boundaries between history and fiction, so also it problematizes those between history and theory. Recall Collingwood's hope that philosophy would become historical and that, reciprocally, history would become philosophical. In the present dispensation, which is one of multiplicity and disjunction, no happy synthesis of this sort, no middle road, seems possible. Instead, we envisage connections between history and theory that are more local and limited.

Accordingly, we envisage (1) a historiography capable of bringing (localized) aid to theory, contributing in serious ways to the discussion of theoretical issues.[84] Clearly, *different* histories would be told, depending on the different theoretical ends. We envisage (2) a greater attentiveness of historians to theory; of course, there are different theories and different ways of being attentive to them. We envisage (3) a more self-ironic historiography than the current style, having a greater humility and reflexiveness with regard to the interpretation of the past. In this regard it would find its beginnings more in Herodotus than in Thucydides. In his recounting of the advice of Solon to Croesus, Herodotus laid out a principle—namely, that one cannot know history with certainty until after the moment at which there is no more history to know—for the writing of his own history, and perhaps for ours as well.[85] But it would also have more attentiveness than it does now to its own assumptions, evidence, and arguments, and would be more willing and able than it has been up to now to apply historical epistemology to the problems of a present inured to mendacity and self-deception. Finally, in view of the vast, utterly unmanageable body of *primary* historiography that has been produced, we envisage (4) a historiography more in the manner of meditation or commentary, which, in a Montaignean spirit and in the essay form, would comment on the significance of that body for us, now.

In its meditative and reflective mode, fourth-attitude historiography would engage not in the dredging up of new facts—that is, would not engage in historical research as it is normally understood—but would instead engage in the philosophical task of reflecting on the significance of facts already in some sense "known."

—————————————

Paraphrasing Macaulay, Ranke once wrote, "History begins with chronicle and ends with essay, that is, in reflection on the historical events that there finds special resonance."[86] As Ranke's observation begins to suggest, the four attitudes—which in the Western tradition range from preprofessional chronicle (relying on the coherence of a universal history assumed to be known already) to post-professional essay—are already present in the disciplinary tradition itself. Reading the tradition in a particular way, with a sensitivity to contradiction, we can begin to see its repressed self-questionings. In this sense, we merely develop something that is already there in the past. But the concrete social situation of our own time—in "the West" and beyond—prompts, and lends authority to, such a reading.

Coherence and Incoherence in Historical Studies: From the *Annales* School to the New Cultural History

===⇒ CHAPTER TEN ⇐===

When scholars concern themselves with disciplinary coherence and how it might be brought about, we need to look with a jaundiced eye at the discourse of coherence that results. Such discourses are marked by what I call "coherence propositions." Coherence propositions are easy to recognize, for they involve a common basic statement: "Now, we must all unite around X." X, and the epistemological, even ontological, assumptions that support X, may change from generation to generation, even from decade to decade. But in "advanced" sectors of the historical discipline over the last seventy years or so there has been a great deal of continuity in the way coherence has arisen as an issue. The coherence propositions of "advanced" historians of seventy years ago are paralleled—although decidedly not duplicated—in what is currently the hegemonizing and imperializing fraction of the discipline, the so-called "new cultural history," an orientation that arose in the 1980s as both an extension of and a rebellion against the dominance of social history.[1] Academics make claims about coherence when they are interested in achieving professional advancement and institutional domination. In short, when we see coherence propositions being deployed, we should look around in order to see who is making a grab for academic power, who is attempting to marginalize whom. And yet this is not the only thing we should do, for there are also genuine theoretical problems connected with coherence, problems having to do with disciplinary aims, methods, products, and audiences, as well as with the object of historical investigation, the historical past in its many manifestations. Thus, I contend, coherence propositions should be seen both as grabs for academic power and as attempts to address a genuine problem.

In the historical discipline today there is indeed a problem of coherence. This has not always been the case, for coherence was long regarded not as a problem but as an easily achievable aim. At the end of the nineteenth century and in the early years of the twentieth, intelligent men believed that the then relatively new academic discipline was poised to produce a unified account of the history of humanity, or at least of that part of humanity whose doings were worth recording. Reporting in 1896 to the Syndics of Cambridge University Press on the *Cambridge Modern History* that he had undertaken to edit, Lord Acton admitted that "ultimate history we cannot have in this generation," thus implying that such a history would someday be had. And Acton's successor as Regius Professor of Modern History at Cambridge, J. B. Bury, explicitly claimed in his 1902 Inaugural Lecture that historians ought to be working toward a unified history of the world, and that such a history would indeed come to be written.[2] In short, Acton and Bury were committed to the notion of "grand narrative," to evoke Jean-François Lyotard's useful term.[3] The importance of this disciplinary goal, a unified history of humankind, seems to have been assumed by many other historians who, while not actually articulating it as a goal, went about their own teaching and writing of history as if its validity were axiomatically given.

At the beginning of the twenty-first century, matters stand very differently. Today it is obvious that historical study has not converged, but has instead moved off in a multitude of different directions. It is hardly surprising that this should be so. In Acton and Bury's time the field of history was more constrained than it is now. Most historians focused on the nation-state and on how it had emerged as the central political form. Such concerns as the history of everyday life, of mentalities, and of sexuality did not exist within the discipline. Nor was there anything that can be considered a history of any non-Western peoples: those histories of non-Western regions that did exist were in fact histories of European conquest, occupation, and government. Kipling's "lesser breeds without the law" were widely thought to be also without histories; to be sure, events had occurred in their pasts, but these were not seen as rising to the level of being *historical*. Hegel held that no people without written records and a state could have a history, and on this point historians agreed with him.[4] Today, in contrast, historians write about a far wider range of places and times and a far wider swath of human concerns than did their counterparts of a century ago.

Yet history can hardly be said to have conceptual devices or interpretive perspectives that would let the vast current outpouring of historical scholarship come together into a single coherent picture. Around 1900, the story that was told or projected was of the movement of humankind toward an unproblematically defined liberal freedom. There is no such common narrative now: neither the liberal story nor its Marxian variant survives except marginally, and no persuasive replacement has come onto the scene.

Most casual readers of history, to be sure, are not aware of the failure of the discipline's products to cohere into a single story. If they were, they would hardly care about it, for most people read works of history with the expectation of learning about a specific topic, such as the Third Reich or the Founding Fathers or the Civil War or the San Francisco Earthquake, and not for any wider reason. For their part, most historians, although aware of history's pullulating multiplicity, do not think about it very much, and are bothered by it only when they are assigned the task of teaching courses with the impossibly demanding title "World History." Our concern here, however, is with that interesting minority of historians who have offered cures, or at least antidotes, for the multiplicity, in the form of proposals for one or another historiographic united front.

THE *ANNALES* SCHOOL
AND THE PROBLEM OF COHERENCE

The central question facing all proponents of historical coherence is this: What form can coherence take when, manifestly, the researches and writings of historians go off in a multiplicity of different directions? This question shadowed the most influential single orientation in historical research and writing in the twentieth century, the *Annales* school (so named after its journal), and although it is often unremarked, it persists as an issue in the competitions for hegemony among different "paradigms" in the historical discipline today.[5] To be sure, the term *school* is misleading: the *Annales* was more an orientation than a school, and when in 1975 the École des Hautes Études en Sciences Sociales came into being within its general territory, the EHESS could hardly be *identified* with the *Annales*. We should also note that the unified impulse that originally animated the *Annales* became fragmented as its generations succeeded each other. Today, the very phrase "*Annales* school" has an antiquated ring to it: the *Annales* school has been superseded. But it remains the most important reference we have for the problem of coherence. For one thing, the first two generations of *Annalistes* launched the twentieth century's most sustained and ambitious attempt to arrive at a coherence, of sorts, in historical writing. This would remain true even if the *Annales* had not been influential at all. But in fact it has been influential. Although the *Annales* school is a thing of the past, the *Annales* impulse remains directly and indirectly influential. In particular, the new cultural history has strong roots within the *Annales* tradition, and even where such connections do not exist, there remain significant affinities, of substance and situation, between the original *Annales* school program and the programmatic side of cultural history today.

Annales history goes back to 1929, when two historians at the University of Strasbourg, Lucien Febvre (1878–1956) and Marc Bloch (1886–1944), founded the *Annales d'histoire économique et sociale*.[6] Febvre was the great instigator of the *Annales* project, and his importance was magnified by the disruption that World War II brought to Bloch's life.[7] Fundamental to the *Annales* project was Febvre's insistence on "the necessity of synthesizing all knowledge in a historical framework." He wanted to "abolish the barriers between the human sciences and the social sciences. . . . [He] could not accept barriers between disciplines; he believed in the unity of knowledge."[8] The aim of discovering and displaying the unity of knowledge, in the form of a *single* human science, animated both the founding of the journal and Febvre's intellectual and academic activities generally.

As a student at the École Normale Supérieure from 1899 to 1902, and then as the writer from 1905 onward of a doctoral dissertation, *Philip II and the Franche-Comté: A Study of Political, Religious, and Social History* (defended 1911, published 1912), Febvre had been exposed to the controversies of the time concerning the relations between social science and history. One position in the controversy was vividly represented by Émile Durkheim, who was busily inventing sociology in this period, and who proposed that sociology, with its analysis and concept-building, ought to be the master discipline, with history merely a supplier of raw materials. Similarly, some economists argued that economic theory needed to trump economic history. Febvre was too deeply interested in the human past to be attracted by such subjections of history to theory. For Febvre, coherence was not something that would arise from a set of theoretical concepts. An immensely important model for Febvre's efforts was provided by an older *normalien* and indefatigable academic entrepreneur, Henri Berr, who in 1900 had founded a journal, *Revue de synthèse historique,* that aimed, as its title suggests, at historical synthesis.[9] Berr was a critic of the dominant mode of history-writing at the time, an *histoire historisante* (his term) that he saw as focused narrowly on political events, failing to offer a broad picture of human society. In writing his dissertation, Febvre did not limit himself to the stirring political events of the late sixteenth century (when Philip II of Spain, who ruled the Franche-Comté, was contending with the revolt of the Netherlands against Spanish rule), but also dealt with historical geography and with social and economic history. He included statistical tables representing the income of noble estates, and also examined the views and lifestyles of the nobles and burghers. Febvre's next book, commissioned by Berr, was *Geography and the Evolution of Mankind* (1922). This book was intended, on the one side, as an attack on the geographical determinism of such scholars as the German geographer Friedrich Ratzel. On the other side, it was intended to encourage historians to take geographical factors into account in their study of the past. In short, Febvre opposed both an excessive determinism and an excessive commitment to the view that human beings (or rather, the politically enfranchised subset of human beings) are sufficiently free that they can be understood in isolation from their environments.

Where is the coherence in all this? Let us look at the matter broadly. In the first two generations of the *Annales* school, the search for coherence took place at two distinct levels. The more obvious one was the level of historical representations. *Annales* historians hoped to produce comprehensive accounts of the particular historical realities that they chose to investigate. It is to this aspiration toward coherence that the term *total history,* which became a shibboleth of the *Annalistes,* has usually been applied. We can see this aspiration already in place in *Philip II and the Franche-Comté,* where there is a clear intent to offer something like a comprehensive picture of the historical reality of the Franche-Comté in the second half of the sixteenth century. (That it was Febvre's native region no doubt sustained him in this aspiration.) However, the representational aspect of the *Annalistes'* search for coherence is most famously embodied in what came to be seen as *the* exemplary work of *Annales* historiography, the monumental *The Mediterranean and the Mediterranean World in the Age of Philip II* (1949; rev. ed., 1966), by the man who became the *chef* of the second generation of the *Annales* school, Fernand Braudel (1902–85).[10] In this book, which, truth be said, few have read through from beginning to end, Braudel attempts to give a total picture of the Mediterranean world in the time of Philip II. He divides that world into three levels: "structure," "conjuncture," and "event." Alternatively, one can think of Braudel's book as describing the workings of three separate, although overlapping, temporalities—the long term [*la longue durée*], the medium term, and the short term. At the basic, geographical level, time moves hardly at all; at the conjunctural level, it moves in cycles that may last for many years (on the model of certain kinds of economic cycles); while at the level of events (embracing most politics and warfare) it moves quickly but superficially.

Two points need to be made about Braudel's way of conceptualizing his project. The first is that the total history in question is not total, and cannot be so. Entire categories of human life are left out, and *must* be left out, lest "total history" become even more unreadable than it is. The second point is that the attempt to offer a total representation of a past historical reality is virtually guaranteed to highlight historical *in*coherence—notwithstanding the fact that Braudel insisted on "the unity and coherence of the Mediterranean region."[11] It is notorious, for example, that Braudel's "total" picture of the Mediterranean world simply does not hang together: most obviously, his three temporal levels (embodied in three separate divisions of the book) are only tenuously interconnected.[12]

It seems clear that early in the game, well before Braudel, Febvre understood the difficulty of attaining coherence at the level of representation. It is a basic point, only made obvious when one tries to write an all-embracing history. For one of the central features of historical investigation is precisely the unresolvability of its dialectic—an unresolvability that is perhaps most clearly visible in the obligation that lies upon historians to deal with human beings as both determined and free, but is also evident in their obligation to deal both with particulars (such as Montaillou in the thirteenth century, or the French nation) and with "universals" (such as the medieval rural community, or nationhood). Febvre himself noted, with utter explicitness, that one of the tasks of history is "to negotiate the relation of the Institutional to the Contingent"—a task that he saw as comparable to the task in various other sciences of negotiating "the relation of the Logical and the Empirical [le Réel]."[13]

So it is not surprising that Febvre conceptualized coherence as something to be found primarily in *the practice of historical investigation itself*. More accurately, he conceptualized coherence as something to be brought into being by the creation not just of a unified history but of a unified social science—a social science unified, however, by history, rather than a discipline exterior to history. For Febvre turned himself into a fervent advocate of the unity of science. In the early 1930s, as editor-in-chief of a new, government-sponsored *Encyclopédie française,* he wrote to a geographer who had wondered where geography was to be found in his plan for the encyclopedia, declaring that "I am not producing an Encyclopedia of the Sciences." On the contrary, he asserted, the work was to be an encyclopedia of science in the singular, within which the particular disciplines (geography, ethics, logic, metaphysics, law, aesthetics . . .) would be dissolved. It would be focused on "the unity of the human spirit, the unity of unease in the face of the unknown"; its contributors would be "scholars who think of their sciences in the framework of Science."[14]

Febvre was far from being the only person in his time and generation to hew to the notion of the unity of science—"l'Unité vivante de la Science," as he called it.[15] Also in the 1930s, an international group of logical empiricist philosophers, including Otto Neurath, Rudolf Carnap, Herbert Feigl, Hans Reichenbach, and others, developed the even more ambitious idea of laying out the foundations of a unified science (including social science) in another encyclopedia, to be published as a series of monographs, the never finished (indeed, barely started) *International Encyclopedia of Unified Science*.[16] The difference between Febvre's project and the unifying project of the logical empiricists was that, whereas Febvre's project put history at the center of the unified social science, the logical empiricists excluded it entirely. They did so because, like Durkheim and many others earlier, they held that science needs to be "nomothetic"—that is, it is required to focus on the articulating of laws and theories. History, in contrast, is "idiographic," concerned with describing particular realities. In the logical empiricist framework, history can serve as a source of raw materials for theory-construction but is not itself scientific.

Taking a contrary view, Febvre looked forward to the articulating of an account of the human world that would be coherent and that would also take full account of historical complexity and difference. Febvre was against the attempt of the Durkheimian sociologists, among others, to purchase coherence at the price of leaving out what was living and vital in humanity. On more than one occasion Febvre asserted that history is "the science of man": "*Histoire science de l'Homme, science du passé humain,*" as he declared in his 1933 inaugural lecture at the Collège de France.[17] In a 1941 talk at the École Normale Supérieure (ENS), he made the same point, telling his listeners that history is the study of "the diverse activities and the diverse creations of the men of other times, grasped in their temporal location [*à leur date*], in the framework of the societies, extremely varied and yet capable of being compared with one another (such is the postulate of sociology), with which they have filled the surface of the earth and the succession of ages."[18] Time and again Febvre insisted that this study was a unified enterprise. "There is no economic and social history"; rather, "there is history *tout court,* in its Unity," he said in his ENS talk.[19] Febvre and Bloch made the same point in 1929 in the foreword to the first volume of *Annales,* where they regretted the barriers that separated ancient, medieval, and modern historians from each other, as well as researchers dealing with "so-called civilized societies" from those dealing with so-called "primitive" or "exotic" societies, and so on.[20] Febvre was also very clear about what, in his view, underpinned the unity of the historical study of Man: it was the unity of Man himself.

Of course, it is one thing to proclaim that a coherence exists at a basic ontological level and quite another thing to engineer the production of multiple historical studies, dealing with a wide variety of subjects, that actually cohere. Febvre's repeated insistence on the unity of history was in fact accompanied by a clear and precise recognition that the studies collected in *Annales* hardly cohered at all, *as products.* He viewed with contempt the Buryesque notion that armies of laboring graduate students would produce the bricks of objective, well-verified fact that would eventually be used to construct the great edifice of historical knowledge.[21] In Febvre's view, one could not passively wait for the coherence to emerge: one had to strive for it. As part of this effort, and also as a means of increasing the influence in the academic world of *Annales* history, Febvre—and Bloch, as long as he was available—presided over a number of collective research projects, in which teams of researchers (often amateurs living in the provinces) investigated aspects of French history and society (such as French rural housing).[22] And yet, symptomatically, these large projects tended to produce little in the way of finished, published scholarship, let alone coherent scholarship. It was as if the process of collaboration was a poor substitute for a substantive coherence that could not arrive. Where, then, was the hoped-for coherence to be found?

We do not need to guess at Febvre's views on the matter, for he articulated his views in a number of essays from the early 1930s onward. Perhaps the most interesting essay, entitled "Vers une autre histoire," appeared in 1949 in a well-known intellectual journal, *Revue de métaphysique et de morale,* and was reprinted in 1953 as the concluding essay of his *Combats pour l'histoire.*[23] A review of a posthumously published (and unfinished) book by Bloch, *The Historian's Craft,* it was also a characterization and defense of the project in which Febvre and Bloch had been mutually engaged.

The most important thing to note in the review is Febvre's evoking of the incoherence of historiographic production in a France where no unifying vision for historical research yet existed. Febvre suggests that in France in any given year "four or five original works of history" are published that "are relatively new in their conception" and that have some intellectual merit. One would expect Febvre to be happy, at least, about these four or five works. But he was not, and this was because

> these four or five works deal with subjects that are far removed from one another in time and in space. . . . They arouse curiosity. They make us say of their authors: "How ingenious they are" and of their conclusions, "How novel." Thus they occupy the curiosity of certain intelligent readers who have the fairly rare advantage of being well advised by some new-thinking historian friend, "read this, my fellow, and this as well." That is all it amounts to. (434/38–39)

What was to be done, then? Febvre called for "a new kind of history" that would be the product of coordinated historical research:

> Suppose that every year or two the succeeding chapters of a dozen or so well-organized investigations, on subjects which would seem quite obviously to be of great importance in one's life, in the conduct of

one's affairs, and in the political or cultural decisions one has to take:
coordinated investigations, comprehensive thoughts, launched simultaneously so that any important phenomenon . . . could be studied *in
one and the same spirit* either in civilizations far removed from each
other in time or in civilizations separated in space by great distances.
(434/39; my emphasis)

As Febvre makes clear in "A New Kind of History" (as well as in many
of his other writings), he envisaged a "problem-oriented" history (*histoire-
problème*), in which the historian in his present approaches the past with
the aim of solving problems relevant to that present (as in the passage just
quoted). The aim was not to achieve a single, coherent picture of the human
past, or even of some part of that past. Febvre, a historiographic modernist
if there ever was one, wished to get away from the burdening and distorting
weight of the past. He had a low opinion of what he saw as the practices of
"traditional" societies in this regard. Such societies, he held, "produce an
image of their present life, of its collective aims and of the virtues required
to achieve those aims," and then, in looking to the past, they "project" a
"sort of prefiguration of the same reality, simplified but magnified to a certain extent and adorned with the majesty and incomparable authority of
a tradition" (436/40). There is a coherence in such mythic projections, but
Febvre rejected coherence of this sort. Febvre's conception of history implies
rather a *breaking up* of the past, for how could a coherent representation of
the past arise from sets of different questions posed of the past by successive
presents? Indeed, Febvre judged that history is a *liberation* from the past:
"History is a way of organizing the past so that it does not weigh too heavily
on the shoulders of men" (437/41).

In our own time there has been a growing tendency to equate history
with memory. Febvre, on the contrary, held that "it is essential for human
groups and societies to forget if they wish to survive. We have to live. We
cannot allow ourselves to be crushed under the tremendous, cruel, accumu-
lated weight of all that we inherit" (436/40). But this almost Nietzschean
pragmatism does not mean that Febvre abandoned the notion of historiographic coherence. Instead, he *relocated* coherence, situating it in the collective organization of historical research referred to above—in "coordinated
investigations," in "an organized and concerted group inquiry," in historical
research projects carried out "in one and the same spirit" (434, 436/39, 40).
There was an evident propagandistic intent in this proposal, for Febvre suggested that only if historical research were coordinated in this way would
the "average man" come to understand "the role, importance, and scope of

history" (435/39). But it seems clear that coherence at the level of the research itself, brought about by a deliberate effort at coordination, also served to reassure Febvre of the scientific character of the work being done.

Although it would be tiresome to discuss the matter at length, it is noteworthy that Febvre's successor, Braudel, came to make essentially the same argument about coherence. In *The Mediterranean and the Mediterranean World* Braudel strove for representational coherence but never attained it. William H. McNeill has suggested that Braudel's technique in the first (1949) edition "resembled that of the pointilliste painters . . . who used innumerable separate dots of paint to depict everyday scenes, relying on the eye of the beholder to blend them together into a comprehensible whole." Braudel then spent years trying to improve the work. This involved, among other things, trying to make it more coherent. McNeill suggests that Braudel was thus driven, in the 1966 edition, to fit his "magnificent, multicolored portrait" into "a scientific straitjacket."[24]

After *The Mediterranean,* Braudel continued to write big history that aimed to tie together immense and far-flung aspects of historical reality. But as with Febvre, the focus of Braudel's discourse of coherence came to be not representational coherence, but the project of articulating a unified human science. Moreover, Braudel reaped the institutional payoff of Febvre's tireless effort of propaganda and log-rolling. Following the Liberation, Febvre had been involved in the founding of the Sixth Section (Social and Economic Sciences) of the École Pratique des Hautes Études, and he served as president of the Sixth Section from 1948 to 1956. Febvre was succeeded by Braudel, who was president from 1956 to 1972. Braudel proved to be an even better organizer and operator than Febvre had been. As a highly active editor of the journal, the full title of which was now *Annales: Économies, Sociétés, Civilisations,* he encouraged the conduct and publication of a wide range of scholarship on a wide range of topics. He was deeply involved in the founding of a research library and institute, the Maison des Sciences de l'Homme, of which he became director, and he laid the groundwork for the founding of the École des Hautes Études en Sciences Sociales.

As a result, Braudel, far more than Febvre, had at his disposal an institutional framework within which the coordinated pursuit of the social sciences could take place. Of course, through his own work, through his overseeing of research institutes within which different disciplines with many different research interests competed for resources, and through his editing of a journal whose volumes looked like potpourris, he was well aware that coherence of intellectual products is harder to attain than is coherence of principles for the conduct of the intellectual work that yields those products. Coherence remained a stated goal, but it would increasingly be the coherence of a general social science whose unity, Braudel argued, needed to be brought into being. Thus, in a 1958 article, "History and Sociology," Braudel suggested that these two disciplines constitute "a single adventure of the mind," and he went on to claim that "there can exist no social science, of the kind that interests me, without reconciliation. . . . Setting the social sciences one against the other is easy enough to do, but all these quarrels seem quite dated."[25] In another article, "History and the Social Sciences: *La longue durée,*" also first published in 1958, Braudel suggested that social scientists should stop arguing about what the boundaries of their different disciplines are, or about what social science itself is. Instead, they should "try to spell out, through their investigations, the elements (if elements there are) that could orient our collective research, the themes that would permit us to achieve a preliminary convergence. Myself, I believe these elements are: mathematization, narrowing in on locality, *longue durée.* But I would be curious to know what other specialists propose."[26]

Braudel's preoccupation with "convergence"—presumably involving commitment to a single, unified investigation of Man—persisted until the end of his life. To be sure, he had no illusions about the difficulties of such a convergence. No doubt this is why, in 1958, he referred only to a "pre-liminary" convergence. And it is perhaps significant that in a late interview he did not call for interdisciplinarity, which was then fashionable in some quarters, but for something else—"unitary *interscience.* . . . Let us mix to-gether all the sciences, including the traditional ones, philosophy, philology, etc."[27] The coherence of history, it seems, was to be the coherence of what the great, perhaps last, Braudellian loyalist, Immanuel Wallerstein, speak-ing in 1999, called "a truly unified, singular social science."[28] But in the vi-sion of the later Braudel, the science in question would also include—*how* is never specified—the traditional humanities disciplines as well.

THE *ANNALES* SCHOOL:
FROM CONVERGENCE TO MULTIPLICITY

We are now two decades beyond the death of Braudel. A third generation of *Annales*-influenced historians—that of Emmanuel Le Roy Ladurie and his coevals—has given way to a fourth and later generations. What is evi-dent at this long interval is the persistent failure of a unified social science, or even of a unified history alone, to appear. In his 1999 talk Wallerstein characterized Braudel's project as an attempt to bridge the "great epistemo-logical debate" between the nomothetic disciplines and "more humanistic, or hermeneutic epistemologies" that emphasize "variety, not similarities, in human social behavior." He had to concede, however, that "one sees precious few signs today of Braudel's passion to create a truly unified, singular social science."[29]

This judgment is undoubtedly correct. Indeed, as one acute and skeptical commentator, Gérard Noiriel, has noted, Braudel's statements of commitment to the unity of the human sciences must be juxtaposed to his insistence, elsewhere, that there has been a "fragmentation of history," with the discipline breaking up into a multitude of practices that are irreducible to each other. And yet Braudel continued not only to affirm "the unity of history," but also to claim that history occupies a privileged, central position within the human sciences as a whole. Noiriel identifies a theoretical justification offered by Braudel for granting history this central—and unifying—position. The object of the human sciences is "human beings in time." Only two disciplines, history and sociology, have "a 'generalist' vocation"; thus, history and sociology are privileged over all other disciplines, as sciences dealing with "everything that has to do with humankind." Of the two disciplines, only history is concerned centrally with time; therefore, history and historians are destined to unite the human sciences and give them a "common language."[30]

The logic of Braudel's claims leaves much to be desired. But in fact, neither Braudel's claims nor Febvre's analogous claims earlier should be regarded as primarily guided by logic. Consider Febvre for a moment. Febvre repeatedly claimed that history should escape the spirit of specialization, that it should be without "compartments" [cloisonnements], that the barriers between the social and the human sciences should be overcome, that there is a "living Unity of Science," and so on. But all these claims were put forward in the context of a *combat pour l'histoire* that was, more accurately, a combat for a particular *kind* of history—Febvre's kind. When Febvre spoke of collective research that would be carried out under the regime of an "*histoire dirigée*," there is no doubt that this would indeed be a "directed" history and that Febvre and his allies should be the ones directing it.[31] The same considerations come into play in relation to Braudel. As Noiriel notes, we must situate the claims quoted in the previous paragraph within the context of Braudel's "explicit ambition" to raise history to the role of central and unifying discipline among the human sciences.[32]

In fact, the *Annales* school of the first two generations was always in a state of war against enemies. Among these enemies were the competing social sciences of economics, geography, and sociology. The primary enemy, however, was the mainstream of French historians, "traditional" historians committed to the *"histoire historisante"* against which Henri Berr polemicized as early as 1911. What defined *histoire historisante* in Berr's eyes was its focus on *particular* historical realities and its assumption that once the historian had described and analyzed such a reality, he had completed his work. Building on Berr, Febvre held, on the contrary, that the history needs to be open to general concerns. It must be able to engage in comparison, bringing the particulars of one place and time to bear in the attempt to illuminate those of another place and time, as well as the condition of "Man" in general. It must be attentive to the unmoving or slow-moving substratum of the "history of events" studied by, for example, geographers, which *historiens historisants* rejected as irrelevant. History needs, moreover, to understand the need for "hypotheses, for research programs, even for theory."[33] Although, with Febvre's appointment to the Collège de France in 1933 and Bloch's to the Sorbonne in 1936, the *Annales* orientation could hardly be called marginal, until as late as the end of the 1960s Febvre and his successors continued to polemicize against a benighted, supposedly dominant historical mainstream.[34] The program of an *histoire totale* that would somehow make history a coherent enterprise, along with the insistence on an *histoire-problème* by which problems connected to the present would be brought to bear on the investigation of the past, were the two chief weapons in the propaganda war of the *Annalistes* against their opponents.

Today, of course, it is no longer a matter of *Annales* school history versus its various enemies. First of all, there is no longer such a thing as "the *Annales* school." An important overview was provided by the influential American historian Lynn Hunt, in a 1986 article on "the rise and fall of the *Annales* paradigm."[35] Since Hunt's account is remarkably focused and direct, I can hardly do better than reproduce certain of her central points. She asserts that "the *Annales* paradigm began to disintegrate at the very moment of its triumph," which she identifies as the 1970s (213). In 1970, under Braudel's leadership, the Sixth Section had moved into a brand new, modernist high-rise on the boulevard Raspail; then in 1975 the Sixth Section became an independent institution, the École des Hautes Études en Sciences Sociales (EHESS). But the *Annales* was unified by more than a building, she suggests. For it seemed that there was indeed a "paradigm" involved in *Annales* history. The paradigm was exemplified in Braudel's *Mediterranean,* with its "three-level" model of history, noted earlier. As Hunt observes, this model, which ranged from biology, geography, and climate at the bottom to "political and cultural expressions of specific groups or individuals" at the top, was "widely accepted within the French historical profession in the 1960s and early 1970s"; indeed, even some historians who regretted such an approach acknowledged its dominance (212).

Hunt also notes that as early as the late 1970s various participants within the *Annales* were beginning to see signs of the disintegration of the model. For example, in a 1978 article, "The *Annales*: Continuities and Discontinuities," which appeared in the first volume of Wallerstein's Braudellian journal *Review,* a young *Annaliste* of the fourth generation, who in the 1990s would become president of the EHESS, Jacques Revel, observed that "the identification of stable systems is at the heart" of the *Annales* undertaking, and that it lacks any concern "with a theory of social change or with the shift from one historical model [to] its successor." Revel also contended that the body of common social-scientific knowledge "has been rapidly disintegrating since the beginning of the 1960s. The field of research in the social sciences is splintering. Man, the central figure of the preceding mode of analysis, has ceased to be the basic referent and has become the transitory object, and a dated one, of a particular pattern of scientific discourse." Revel suggested that the *Annales* of circa 1978 emphasized "experimentation and interrogation" rather than a unified approach. He also noted an increase in the space the *Annales* gave to "the analysis of cultural systems," after a period dominated by economic and social history, and he suggested that this amounted less to the exploration of "a sort of third level of knowledge" than to "the raising of a new set of questions."[36]

For his part, the prominent third-generation *Annaliste* François Furet, who was president of the EHESS from 1977 to 1985, suggested in a 1983 article that one had now to think of going beyond the *Annales*. He denied that the *Annales* historians shared a "common and unified concept of the discipline"; rather, they worked "in directions that were too diverse for them to be easily assembled under a single intellectual banner." Perhaps the only common feature among Furet's generation of historians was that they saw in the "almost boundless range of topics and methods" that the *Annales* allowed "a heaven-sent oasis on the path away from Stalino-Marxist historicism." Still, in the conception of history that had animated his generation, Furet discerned a coherent program, embodied in two commitments: "first, that history should add to its subjects and methods by borrowing from neighboring disciplines and even by the temporary abolition of divisions between disciplines; and, second, that it should nevertheless remain an all-embracing and ecumenical discipline, meeting the conditions required for the fullest understanding of social phenomena."[37]

In retrospect, we have to see Furet's 1983 article as representing the last gasp of the classic *Annales* approach to historical—or rather, to historiographic—coherence. For already a shift was taking place that would sharply transform the terms of discussion—a shift that Lynn Hunt identified in 1986 as a shift from social history to cultural history.[38] To be sure, Hunt was only drawing the attention of an English-speaking audience to a shift of interest that Revel and Furet had already commented on. Revel's reference to the analysis of culture has already been noted. For his part, Furet in 1983 had also remarked on a growing concern with culture among *Annalistes*. But Furet, in contrast to Revel, was skeptical of this turn, even hostile to it. Furet favored a "problem-oriented" and also conceptualized form of history; his affinities were with social scientists' interest in the "determinants and limits of action," their concern for "isolating constants, if not laws," and their preference for studying "objective behavior, regardless of the deliberate intentions of the actors."[39] In his view the *histoire des mentalités* (that is, the *Annales* version of cultural history) suffered from three defects. First, it was too close to an "affective commitment," namely, the feeling of nostalgia that Furet claims had been generated in France by the tremendous economic progress of the preceding two decades. Second, it blurred the "classic distinction" between objective behavior and the subjective perception of that behavior, and thus gave rise to the illusion that it was able to grasp both the material infrastructure and the ideational superstructure of society. Finally, the *histoire des mentalités* was likely to generate incoherence—for its "lack of definition . . . leads to the unending pursuit of new research topics, turned up by the accidents of life and having no other basis than a passing intuition, or an ephemeral fashion."[40]

COHERENCE AS A WILLED COMMITMENT

Thus the issue of coherence again asserts itself. A century ago, recall, the basis for history's coherence was held to lie in the possibility of eventually constructing a single, authoritative narrative of human history. When this hope failed, the basis for coherence was held to reside in a shared method. Among "traditional" historians, including the *historiens historisants,* the commitment was to a method that was regarded as *distinctively historiographic*.[41] Among the *Annalistes* from Febvre to Furet, the commitment was not to a distinctive method for history but rather to an investigative process that was seen as broadly social-scientific: among these historians there was always a commitment to a science (or "interscience") that would yield authoritative, although possibly provisional, knowledge.

What is striking now is the degree to which the Febvrean-Braudellian-Furetian version of coherence has become passé. For the assumed basis for history's coherence has changed once again. It is no longer to be found in the articulation of a historically sensitive social science. Rather, coherence is now seen as a matter of *willed commitment* to one or another "paradigm" of historical research. And what characterizes the paradigm notion is that it embraces within itself a distinctly non-negligible degree of arbitrariness—an arbitrariness, moreover, that is often (although far from always) admitted as such.

Within the most highly professionalized circles of the discipline, the last twenty years have witnessed a battle between two competing "paradigms" for the researching and writing of history: social history and cultural history (or rather, the *new* cultural history, since there is also an *old* cultural history).[42] It is a complex story that I can only touch on here. The emergence of the new cultural history was formally announced in Lynn Hunt's 1989 edited collection, *The New Cultural History*.[43] However, its origins go back to various developments in the early 1970s and even before. One source of the new cultural history was the *Annales*' history of *mentalités*. Another stimulus came from the anthropologist Clifford Geertz, whose notion of the interpretation of cultures—and emphasis on "thick description"—resonated with many historians.[44] Still another influence was Michel Foucault, who in various historio-philosophical works touched on such topics as "Labour, Language, Life, Madness, Masturbation, Medicine, Military, Nietzsche, Prison, Psychiatry, Quixote, Sade, and Sex" (to quote a list offered by the philosopher Ian Hacking in 1981).[45] Many of these topics were taken up by the new cultural history, as was, to some degree, Foucault's cynical attitude toward conventional notions of science and objectivity. Yet another stimulus came from the sociology of culture proposed by Pierre Bourdieu, particularly his notions of *habitus* and of cultural capital.[46] Finally, there was the so-called "new historicism" in literary criticism, pioneered by Stephen Greenblatt and others, which blurred the boundaries between literary and historical analysis.[47]

There is no need here to survey the efflorescence of cultural history since the early 1980s. Suffice it to say that, by 1999, it was possible for Victoria Bonnell and Lynn Hunt to publish a new anthology, *Beyond the Cultural Turn*, that was much more substantial than Hunt's earlier *The New Cultural History*.[48] *Beyond the Cultural Turn* is a monument to the triumph—but also to certain of the problems—of cultural history in its new mode. One of the most insightful contributors to the collection, Richard Biernacki, is surely right in asserting that "the new cultural history succeeded some time ago in making its agenda preeminent."[49]

But what is the character of this preeminence, and what is the character of the coherence that it brings to history? As Biernacki notes, the new cultural historians purported to assume, for their work, an underlying ontological unity, for they "followed the social historians in building explanations that

rest on appeals to a 'real' and irreducible ground of history, though that foot-
ing is now cultural and linguistic rather than (or as much as) social and economic" (63). Biernacki suggests that in this assumption about the ground of
history, historians followed some not-well-argued bits of Geertz's account
of culture in *The Interpretation of Cultures,* where Geertz had famously asserted that "culture is not a power, something to which social events, behaviors, institutions, or processes can be causally attributed; it is a context, something within which they can be intelligibly—that is, thickly—described."[50]
Biernacki shows that influential cultural historians—among them, Robert
Darnton, Lynn Hunt, and Roger Chartier—took up Geertz's notion of culture as a "grounding reality," as something that is a "general and necessary
truth rather than . . . a useful construction" (64). Without denying what he
sees as the revelatory, path-breaking, enriching character of such works as
Darnton's *The Great Cat Massacre* and Hunt's *Politics, Language, and Class in
the French Revolution,* Biernacki suggests that "we may have reached a point
at which essentializing the semiotic dimension or 'culture' as a naturally
given dimension of analysis is shutting off reflection and disabling possibly
illuminating interpretations of history" (64–65).[51]

Most relevant to my argument here are two of Biernacki's points. He
shows, first, that the new cultural history rests on an assumed ontological claim, namely, that what is *really* real is culture. "Culture" is defined
here in the Geertzian way, as "webs of meaning" that permeate the life of
a human society. Thus "meaning" (in the Geertzian cultural sense) is assumed to be ontologically fundamental. Second, Biernacki shows that the
new cultural historians' claim to have discovered the "grounding reality" of
society and history is without justification. (Likewise, there was no justification for the ontological view that underlay social history—explicitly in the
case of Marxist or *marxisant* historians, implicitly in other cases—namely,
that the true grounding reality of history is the socioeconomic dimension of
society.)

It follows from this lack of justification that the writing of the new cultural history (as of the old social history) is carried out on the basis of what
is essentially a choice. It is no more than that. And in fact the arbitrariness
of the decision for or against cultural or social history is recognized by the
most self-aware of our advanced historians. Consider Hunt and Bonnell.
Their introduction to *Beyond the Cultural Turn* suggests that "since World
War II *new intellectual fashions* [my emphasis] in the social sciences have
emerged in rapid succession. . . . They generally fell into two broad categories: research paradigms . . . and . . . approaches that belonged to the interpretive and hermeneutic tradition." Hunt and Bonnell also observe that

there is disagreement "about the paradigm *to be chosen* [my emphasis] to organize social scientific research."[52]

Indeed, the very terminology of "paradigm" underscores the element of postulation that is involved. For the paradigm notion, introduced by Kuhn in *The Structure of Scientific Revolutions,* carries with it a strong hint of the arbitrary and unfounded. Kuhn willingly acknowledged this in his 1995 Athens interview, where he states that "a paradigm is what you use when the theory isn't there."[53] To put this another way: if it were justified, it would not be a paradigm. One implication to be drawn from Hunt and Bonnell is that, to justify a particular mode of doing history, there is actually *no need* for an ontological foundation. Another implication, conversely, is that no mode of doing history can establish what is ontologically foundational—if anything at all is. A final implication is that neither approach can justifiably claim priority over the other. We choose and then proceed on the basis of our choice.

The extent to which historians since the early 1970s have taken up the terminology of "paradigm" and applied it to their own discipline is striking. Historians' invocation of Kuhn was already noted by David Hollinger in a widely cited 1973 article, "T. S. Kuhn's Theory of Science and Its Implications for History."[54] The habit of deploying the paradigm notion has grown immensely since 1973. In particular, Kuhn's notions of paradigm and revolution have been repeatedly applied to the *Annales* school, as in Traian Stoianovich's 1976 book, *French Historical Method: The* Annales *Paradigm,* and Peter Burke's 1990 study, *The French Historical Revolution: The* Annales *School, 1929–89,* not to mention Hunt's 1986 article announcing the fall of the *Annales* paradigm.[55] Kuhn's notion has also been routinely applied to the conflict between social history and (new) cultural history.

We must reflect on and also interrogate the paradigm notion, for it offers an important insight into the limits of historiographic coherence. The basic question to be posed is, Is the paradigm notion applicable to historical studies or social science *at all?* From their frequent deployment of the term (and presumably of the notion as well), we must conclude that many historians and historical theorists think that it is not only applicable to history, but that the presence of a paradigm is crucial if historical research is to be done in the right way.[56] Kuhn himself would not have agreed. On the contrary, in *The Structure of Scientific Revolutions* he actually insisted that the paradigm notion does not apply to the social sciences. According to Kuhn, "normally, the members of a mature scientific community work from a single paradigm or from a closely related set." But this is not the case in the social sciences, Kuhn held, because the social sciences—and presumably also history—lack "the unparalleled insulation of mature scientific communities from the demands of the laity and of everyday life. . . . Just because he is working only for an audience of colleagues, an audience that shares his own values and beliefs, the scientist can take a single set of standards for granted."[57]

No doubt, as many commentators have argued, Kuhn vastly overemphasized the degree of separation that natural science has from the social world in which it is located. But this criticism of Kuhn in no way diminishes the point that I am making here—on the contrary, it strengthens that point. For the claim would then be that *even in the natural sciences* pursuers of knowledge are not able to detach themselves entirely from extrascientific considerations—considerations that serve to make cross-cuts through what would otherwise be the purity of their scientific commitment to a paradigm. In Kuhn's view, paradigms cannot be theoretically, let alone ontologically, justified. Rather, they can be justified only on *pragmatic* grounds—and only weakly so at that. In Kuhn's theory, a paradigm has the great advantage of generating solvable puzzles and of making it clear without any great need for hesitation which puzzles these are. According to the theory, because the scientist works for an audience of colleagues that shares his own values and beliefs and is insulated from society, he "can take a single set of standards for granted"; he "can . . . dispose of one problem and get on to the next more quickly than those who work for a more heterodox group"; and he can "concentrate his attention upon problems that he has good reason to believe he will be able to solve," instead of having to focus on problems that "urgently need solution" within society but for which tools conducive to solving those problems efficiently may well not exist.[58]

Undoubtedly, some historians resonate to Kuhn's account of the natural sciences and prefer paradigmatic unity because they think that such unity conduces to solving a coherent set of historical problems—while also raising history's prestige by making it look more like a "real" science. Other historians, clearly, see history as the carrying out of politics by other means; for them, commitment to a paradigm is closely connected to one or another political commitment—indeed, sometimes political commitment seems to serve as a substitute for intelligent debate about different genres, approaches, and research programs, and about the actual merits or demerits of specific works.[59]

This latter, politicizing tendency, which amounts to the imposition of a factitious political coherence on history, strikes me as dangerous, not least because it can easily be hijacked by forces outside the university that are unlikely to encourage work that is in any sense critical of extant political reality. The former, scientizing tendency is somewhat less misguided, especially when the paradigm notion is conceived of narrowly, less as a paradigm in any broad sense than as a subdisciplinary research program. When the notion is deployed in this way, focus on a common set of research problems can contribute to research productivity, most obviously by making it easier for members of the discipline (especially unformed, junior members, such as graduate students) to find research topics.

Yet even here we must be sensitive to the limits and disadvantages of the historiographic coherence that is thus proposed. Of course, it is significant that I have been referring throughout to *historiographic* coherence more than to *historical* coherence, for a point that Leonard Krieger made in his book *Time's Reasons: Philosophies of History Old and New* remains entirely valid. Touching on history-writing from Herodotus to Foucault, Krieger emphasized the persistent "problem of the weakness of historical coherence," and concluded that "there is no simple past whereof a historian can be a pure historian."[60] What this means is that, insofar as there is any coherence at all, it has to be a coherence *that is offered by historians*—not by "historical reality." Moreover, it is clear that the historian's choice of paradigm may well relate less to a decision concerning what set of problems is richest in solvable puzzles than to the historian's own life-world preferences. In view of these facts, two questions acquire a certain force: How seriously should we take this historian-generated coherence? and What other things should historians offer, besides coherence?

These questions, which are closely interconnected, can only be touched upon here (and a comprehensive answer to the second question would require a book of its own). But my basic point is simple: it is a mistake to regard history as an enterprise that ought to be fixated on a search for coherence. On the contrary, part of the function of historical study is to shuffle the cards, showing the various ways in which the past is actually incoherent with itself and with our expectations of it, and also showing how the study of the past relies on conflicting modes of understanding and engagement.[61] While research programs, even "paradigms," may be acceptable as voluntary commitments, the notion that historians ought to be judged according to the degree of their work's accordance with a currently dominant paradigm is a dull idea and, in a literal sense, counterproductive. For example, the mode of "high" intellectual history in which I specialize does not connect well with either the social history or the cultural history paradigm. I have never considered this disconnection to be a liability, and I am inclined to think that the research productivity of some of my age cohort has been impaired by too great a reverence for disciplinary paradigms that do not fit well with their interests and talents. In short, the pursuit of historiographic coherence can diminish productivity and learning, as well as increase it.

But is the primary task of historians to offer coherence in any case? I do not think so, for historians have offered, and continue to offer, many things besides coherence. Indeed, if coherence were their main offspring, they would be mythmakers and fabulists without being historians at all. One of the most important things that historians offer, or ought to offer, is a critical perspective on the past, on the present, and on our present use of the past. Criticism, here, means the revealing of fissures and contradictions—in the past, in historians' representations of the past, in historians' assumptions as they seek to represent the past, and in dominant and perhaps also nondominant assumptions in the present concerning the future, the present, and the past.

Another thing that historians offer, or ought to offer, is a modeling of high epistemological standards. Because historians—at least many of them— deal with matters that, because they are "dead and gone," are susceptible to some measure of dispassionate examination, they have a special opportunity to exercise the utmost care in their treatment of evidence and in their articulation of the arguments that support their claims. In this sense historians are better placed to be epistemologically responsible than are those scholars and social scientists whose business it is to deal with the pressing concerns of the moment. Only if historians can be epistemologically responsible can we even begin to expect such responsibility from our politicians, intelligence agencies, journalists, business persons, therapists, clergy, lawyers, judges, and all the rest. The way that the Iraq War of 2003 was justified to the American—and global—public ought to give us pause.

Finally, besides being "pure" historians, contributing to the articulation of a (now admittedly arbitrary) disciplinary paradigm, historians also have the opportunity to be "hybrid" or "hyphenated" historians, contributing historical knowledge and perspectives to other people besides those who are themselves professional historians. While still remaining historians by virtue of their focus on the past and their commitment to rules of evidence and argument that have stood the test of time, such historians may appear to other historians, who are more focused on the preoccupations of their disciplinary colleagues, almost as foreigners in their midst.

Against Current Fashion

In a much-quoted statement in the preface of his *Histories of the Latin and Germanic Nations* (1824), the young historian Leopold Ranke remarked that "to history has been assigned the office of judging the past, of instructing the present for the benefit of future ages." Ranke rejected this grandiose assignment: *his* work, he declared, "wants only to say what actually happened."[1]

What tasks are assigned to history today? In Ranke's time only a few could do the assigning. Today multitudes crowd the scene, both rulers and *demos,* clad in varied clothing and clamoring loudly. They include state legislators, intent on the proper teaching of history in the schools and colleges of their fine states; federal legislators, shocked—*Shocked!*—at the historical ignorance of college students and the general public; generous donors, intent on establishing a chair for the history of this and a chair for the history of that; Americans proud of their ethnic heritage or religion, who want to make sure that its glories are properly represented and celebrated; veterans of wars, eager to see that the wars in question are both rightly interpreted and piously commemorated; and those persons bereaved by, or perhaps only touched by, all major disasters, from Pearl Harbor to September 11, 2001.

Beyond these persons or groups, who have an entirely explicit and active concern with history, are others whose concern is more diffuse and consumption-oriented. I think here of those who "appreciate" history in the way that one might appreciate an appealing wallpaper pattern or a nicely manicured front lawn—who visit presidential houses, stop at battlefields and other historical sites, perhaps pause in their travels to read historical markers, and in general admire oldish things. Their appreciation sometimes goes so far as to express itself in the assertion, "I have always loved history."

In short, Clio, the muse of history, has many friends and perhaps some lovers. But love and friendship are not without their price. The fans clamoring round ask for more things than the judging and instructing that worried Ranke. The tasks that are today assigned to history seem to be of four types. First and foremost, history is assigned the task of *identifying*—of creating and sustaining identities of various kinds, making "us" who we are. Crucial to this task is the related enterprise of commemorating the actions and sufferings of the groups that are thus identified. Second, history is assigned the task of *evangelizing*—of strengthening our civic religion. Third, history is given the task of *entertaining* us: *Clio! Amuse.* Finally, to history is assigned the task, where possible, of *being useful*. To be sure, we acknowledge that history cannot be quite as useful as engineering, biomedical science, or business administration, and we generally believe as well that some history, usually that which is distant from us in time, space, or culture, cannot be useful at all. Hence this fourth task pales before the other three.

Am I mistaken in thinking that these tasks—especially the tasks of identifying, evangelizing, and entertaining—are widely assigned to history today? I think not. Consider the following advertisements drawn from an Amazon.com e-mail newsletter sent out to history buffs on May 11, 2001:

Pearl Harbor: The Day of Infamy—An Illustrated History by Dan van der Vat. President Franklin D. Roosevelt famously declared December 7, 1941, as "A day that will live in infamy," the day the Japanese attacked Pearl Harbor, pulling the U.S. into World War II. This visually stunning book, by noted historian Dan van der Vat, features groundbreaking research, over 250 images, including previously unpublished personal photos from the perspective of both Americans on the ground and Japanese in the air, as well as a moment-by-moment breakdown of the attack. There are also numerous personal accounts, memorabilia, and illustrations by Tom Freeman. A major achievement.

An Album of Memories: Personal Histories from the Greatest Generation by Tom Brokaw. As he's done in his immensely popular Greatest Generation volumes, Tom Brokaw again celebrates the trials and triumphs of the Americans who experienced the Depression and World War II. *Album of Memories* is a collection of letters written to Brokaw by those who lived during this period, and in some cases, their children. Complete with photographs and memorabilia, the overall emotional impact of these letters is intense. To read them is both a moving experience and an opportunity to experience history at its most intimate.

Disaster! The Great San Francisco Earthquake and Fire of 1906 by Dan Kurzman. Just after 5 a.m. on April 18, 1906, an earthquake measuring 8.3 on the Richter scale ripped through sleeping San Francisco, toppling buildings, exploding gas mains, and trapping thousands of citizens beneath tons of stone, broken wood, and twisted metal. Drawing on meticulously researched and eye-witness accounts, Dan Kurzman re-creates one of the most horrific events of the 20th century. More riveting than fiction but incredibly true, *Disaster!* is unforgettable history—a masterful account of the calamitous demise and astonishing resurrection of an American city.[2]

I do not aim to score cheap points against works that no one expects to live up to the standards of scientific history. I refer to the above book blurbs simply as indicators of a particular way of looking at history that appears to be widespread in American culture today. All three blurbs make a strong appeal to American identity. Judging from the blurbs, all the books evangelize, propagating what can be best described as a can-do faith, one that affirms our capacity to overcome the difficulties that life brings, even earthquakes. And along with the identifying and the evangelizing comes the promise of great entertainment—we are being offered experiences that are "visually stunning," "intense," and "riveting."

The most interesting element in these bits of advertising copy is in this final claim—the claim to offer a particular sort of experience, which we might, in shorthand, call an "immediate" experience. The advertising uniformly suggests that the consumers of these histories will be brought into direct contact with the action. Note how the advertisements focus on personal experience. We are told that "one of the most horrific events of the 20th century"—the San Francisco earthquake of 1906—will be "re-created" by the author. We are told that reading letters written to a news anchor by "Americans who experienced the Depression and World War II" is "both a moving experience and an opportunity to experience history at its most intimate." The photos in *Pearl Harbor,* taken "from the perspective of both Americans on the ground and Japanese in the air," likewise seem to promise a virtual reliving of the attack. The book *Pearl Harbor* was issued at about the time that a "major motion picture" focused on Pearl Harbor came out. The "tie-in" was intended. *Pearl Harbor* the movie was not a historical documentary but a lame love story. Still, it attempted to convey, in its sequence showing the attack on Pearl Harbor, the impression of "you are there."[3]

Consider another entertainment, the 1997 movie *Titanic*—likewise not a historical documentary, but a brilliantly realized tragic romance. The producers of *Titanic* made a self-conscious appeal to historical authenticity, for they went to enormous lengths to duplicate the look of the original ship and its furnishings. Here historical immediacy turns into an aesthesis of history, an attempt to get viewers as close as possible to the sight and sound of historical reality itself. The producers were on to something—they rightly intuited that, for a vast audience, history, if it does not mean "dead and gone, irrelevant," means the immediate representation of objects and experiences from the past.[4]

In the last generation or so such an assumption has come to be widely shared. Consider, for example, Ken and Ric Burns's 1990 television series, *The Civil War*.[5] The Burnses faced the considerable challenge of dealing with a conflict that long preceded the invention of moving pictures. Nonetheless, by an innovative use of thousands of still photographs of civil war soldiers, politicians, agitators, cities, landscapes, battles, and ruins, as well as by an attentiveness to the character of the voices reading the hundreds of texts that we hear over the course of the series, the filmmakers gave to their creation an immediacy and directness that one would not have expected in advance. Indeed, this was precisely their intention: Ken Burns has explicitly stated that he wanted to offer an "emotional archaeology" of the war, that he wanted to get at "the very heart of the American experience," that he wished to hear "the ghosts and echoes of an almost inexpressibly wise past."[6] The Burns's approach can be instructively contrasted with the approach taken in an older generation of historical documentaries, notably in Thames Television's 1973 series on World War II, *The World at War,* where the presentation is much more depersonalized and "objective." *The World at War,* which is narrated by the authoritative-sounding voice of Laurence Olivier, placed little emphasis on how that war "felt" to its participants; the aim of the documentarists was to tell and show what *happened,* with no notion that they ought also to uncover the "emotional archaeology" of the war.[7]

The claim to immediacy can be found almost everywhere. It is not limited to popular history books, or to the history put together by video documentarians, or to the historical aspect of popular entertainments. It is also to be found in the work of professional historians and of others connected with them (most often, museum professionals). This is hardly surprising. After all, *identifying* history is overwhelmingly concerned with what it takes to be "our" identity; *evangelizing* history, with what it takes to be "our" faith. Hence the curators at Colonial Williamsburg, Plimoth Plantation, and other similar sites attempt to reproduce the "look" and "feel" of life in an earlier time. We see the same impulse in some digital "archives," those driven by a concern for making "everything" that exists concerning a given past time and place available in a single set of Web pages, with the aim of enabling the browsing public to enter into the life of a past community or the flux of a set of past events.

Let us leave aside the problems that exist on the evidentiary level—above all, the quaint assumption that all evidence relevant to explaining X in some given time and place is localized within that time and place (whereas the universe of *possibly* relevant evidence is in fact unbounded, its *actual* boundaries only determinable through continuing argument). The deeper problem is the making of a promise that can never be fulfilled. Consider also the growing number of projects that combine, in a single entity, features of the archive, museum, and memorial. No doubt there is a kind of catharsis and reflectiveness that can be achieved by standing in the place of (even taking the number of) a Holocaust victim, and there is perhaps also the confirming of an identity. But the assumption of immediate identification is unjustified, while, on the interpretive level, the stakes of the identification are kept implicit, hence unargued, hence uncontroverted, hence undefended in any full sense of the term. Consider, finally, a certain kind of historical biography, the kind that aims at recreating what we might call "the inner Mr. X" (for "Mr. X" substitute any historical figure). Never mind whether a sense of *Innerlichkeit* is applicable to Mr. X in quite the way that it is applicable to "us," "now."[8]

Historical epistemology urges us to steer clear of such claims to have penetrated into the very heart of the past. The past is a foreign country, but it is an unvisitable and unconquerable foreign country, marking the limits of our epistemological power in something like the way that an unruly foreign territory whose customs we do not share and whose languages we do not speak might mark the limits of our military power. Of course, historical experience *does* exist.[9] But historical experience is not the deluded and blithely arrogant conviction that we have experienced the past as people in the past experienced it. Rather, properly understood, it is the experience of a rift, a break, between what *we are* now and what *others were* then. It is, for example, a certain kind of recognition that arises when one comes across "a vast Palladian villa" among "the cramped alleys" of present-day Calcutta.[10] It is a recognition of something in the now that does not make sense in the now, of something that cannot be accommodated within a "theory of the now." It is this recognition that pushes us toward the shaky, inferential construction of whatever it was that inhabited past time.

In sum, historical experience offers us a recognition of distance. The most insidious, yet at the same time often unremarked, feature of the communication and information technologies that are increasingly dominating our world is how they foster the illusion that the whole of reality is either displayed before us right now, or *could* be displayed before us, if the reach of the technologies and our connectedness to them were only slightly better than they are at this moment. What we are being promised here is the context of total connectedness—which amounts, in fact, to a context of no context, since context only becomes context when there are other contexts that stand in opposition to it. We are in danger of educating a generation of people willing to believe that all of human reality is in principle open to their own oversight and control, if not by themselves directly, then by their chosen political agents. As the historian of medieval Europe, Thomas Bisson, has remarked, historical study properly carried out gives us respite from "the crush of the present." Historical study properly carried out focuses on something other than the insistence "on policy and development (that is, on present and future)" that dominates the great universities—progressive, forward-looking, entrepreneurial, and world-commanding—of the present imperium. It focuses rather on "those distant pasts, humanely imagined and imaginatively reconstructed, that alone can place our fragile present in perspective."[11]

These "distant pasts," to be sure, need not be all that distant in time. "Distance" is psychological, aesthetic, and conceptual and not just temporal. Nor is the thinking that opens the way to these "pasts" confined to the historical discipline. There is a line of thought, running from Leibniz in the seventeenth century to the contemporary philosopher of history F. R. Ankersmit, that is peculiarly open to difference and multiplicity, and that offers a kind of philosophical home base for the historical thinking to which I refer here. Two conceptions in Leibniz are particularly suggestive for historical thinking. One of these is his fundamental ontological principle, the monad. Unlike the atom of the Newtonian tradition, each of which is the same as every other, each monad is different from and independent of every other monad, although at the same time somehow connected with the totality of monads. The other Leibnizian conception that is friendly to historical thinking is the notion that one can imagine an infinite number of worlds different from and alternative to the world that actually exists. From our perspective, the true historian (also, perhaps, the true anthropologist) is an explorer of alternative human worlds. This is not to say that all historians see the matter in this way: in fact, many historians are propagandists for one or another favored social, cultural, or political order, whose history they write. And yet there also exists within the discipline a commitment to understanding the past on something like its own terms. There exists, in short, an impossible-to-fulfill desire for historical objectivity, out of which histori-cal thinking is able to arise.

If anything unites the true historical discipline, it is a residual commit-ment, after all, to objectivity. But it is not a *single* objectivity. It is rather a set of divergent but also interconnected objectivities. There is a disciplinary objectivity, amounting to consensus among subgroups of historians; there is a dialectical objectivity, involving a sensitivity on the part of historians to the peculiarities of the historical objects that they describe, explain, and interpret; there is a procedural objectivity that is primarily methodological in character; and there is, above it all, the unrealizable ideal of absolute objectivity, the world as it would be seen by a single omniscient divinity. Of course, such a god would have no need of history, precisely because his om-niscience allows the embrace of everything human within a single vision, a single *theoria*. Conviction robs history of its rationale: if we know the truth entire, we do not need history. Historians are lesser beings, aware that they cannot attain an absolute view, yet committed still to the ghost or residue of such objectivity.

History's focus on what is dead and gone not only offers us alternative conceptions concerning how we might think and live. It also offers, very of-ten, a respite from the insistent demand that the results of research into the human world be tailored to the political demands of the moment. In 2003, the United States went to war against Iraq—an adventure that was justified on the grounds that Iraq possessed imminently deployable weapons of mass destruction that could be used against the United States and its interests. In fact, the research that supposedly justified this conclusion was defective, corrupted by the wish of some to find a persuasive *casus belli* and by the hesitation of others who were well aware of the weakness of the claims that were being bruited about.[12] A historical discipline focused on "memory" and on being useful for the present is in no position to counter such error. A historical discipline properly attentive to historical epistemology, on the other hand, can serve as a model of honesty and intelligence in the investi-gation of the human world.

NOTES

INTRODUCTION

1   Natalie Z. Davis, *The Return of Martin Guerre* (Cambridge, MA, 1983).

2   Davis's epistemological care is powerfully displayed in "'On the Lame,'" *American Historical Review* 93 (1988):572–603, where she responds to a flat-footed critic. Issues of truth, evidence, and doubt are central to *The Return of Martin Guerre*: see 102, 106–8, 119–22, 125.

3   See Arnaldo Momigliano, "The Place of Herodotus in the History of Historiography," in *Studies in Historiography* (London, 1969), 127–42, as well as the remarkable study by François Hartog, *The Mirror of Herodotus: The Representation of the Other in the Writing of History,* trans. Janet Lloyd (Berkeley, 1988).

4   Herodotus, *The History,* trans. David Grene (Chicago, 1987), 7.152; see also 2.123.

5   Thucydides, *History of the Peloponnesian War,* trans. Rex Warner (Harmondsworth, UK, 1954), 1.21.

6   Daniel Mendelsohn, "Theatres of War," *New Yorker,* 12 January 2004, 82. Note that both Herodotus and Thucydides (not just the former) offer us "many voices"—but they do so in different ways.

7   William G. Thomas III and Edward L. Ayers, "An Overview: The Differences Slavery Made: A Close Analysis of Two American Communities," *American Historical Review* 108, no. 5 (December 2003):1299–1307; the "full electronic version" is available at http://historycooperative.org/ahr/; the associated "digital archive" is at http://valley.vcdh.virginia.edu. (Note that historycooperative.org normally needs to be accessed through a subscribing library.)

8   Thomas and Ayers, "An Overview," 1301. This is a citation to the text that appears in the *American Historical Review* itself: henceforth I cite both the journal and the Web site in the chapter text, using the abbreviation *AHR* to designate the journal. In citing the Internet version, I use the authors' "citation keys" (TAS1, E180, etc.). As the authors note, these "keys" take the reader to a particular piece of the article without having to type out a complicated URL. To use this function, click on the "Tools" button near the top of the Web page at http://www.vcdh.virginai.edu/AHR and then click on "Cita-

tion Locator." You should be aware, also, that after clicking on the "Tools" button, you will see a "Reading Record" option. The Reading Record displays rows of dots that stand for "the individual 'atoms' that make up this publication." If you have "visited" a particular atom, the dot will be red; those you have not "visited" will be black. You can click on the black dots to "visit" additional evidence. (It is odd that the authors refer here to "individual 'atoms' of evidence," since most of the dots lead one to relatively large bodies of information. But perhaps to a mind that eschews analysis, a complex topographical map—for example—is indeed an indivisible atom to be quickly glanced at and then left behind as one continues the sightseeing tour.)

9 The term *data collection* seems more accurate here than the term that the authors prefer, *archive*. The "Valley" Web site bears little resemblance, in its presentation and apparent organizing principles, to archives of the kind that are produced and overseen by professional archivists. Scholars who use professionally organized archives have come to expect that the archivists will make their data available in a disinterested and nondirective way. That is not the case here: the Web site resembles, in its uncommented-upon but evident interpretive dimension, a series of data-rich museum exhibits or a modern "reconstruction" of some past town.

10 Note, however, that a careless reader might well infer a causal claim from this sentence—namely, that white people in Augusta were richer than their counterparts in Franklin *because* of slavery. To be sure, this is not what the authors say, but one wonders whether at some level they wish to insinuate it.

11 This is not the place for a thorough analysis of the relation between Thomas and Ayers's claims and the evidence they offer in support of those claims. Such a task is better left to the critical attention of specialists in nineteenth-century U.S. history. Suffice it to say that their deployment of statistics is sometimes extremely difficult to follow. For example, on the Web page at http://vcdh.virginia.edu/tablesandstats/comparison/estatevalues1860.html, they assert that "Augusta County's massive personal estate valuations represented holdings in human property—slaves," but a figure for "value of slave holdings" did not turn up in a search by myself and by an assistant, Phillip Honenberger. Searches were not easy, since the Internet article and digital database did not appear to be globally searchable, nor did it seem certain when we accessed the database that all search results were actually being displayed. Thus we may have missed data that are in fact "there"—somewhere. We should also note that we did our thorough examination of the "digital archive" in February 2004, and there is no guarantee that the links we followed will still work. Subsequent researchers may have to take other routes into it.

Thomas and Ayers do tell us that whereas in Franklin average per capita property holding (personal property *and* real estate), amounted to $633, in Augusta these amounted to $863 ($1,112 if one counts only the whites in Augusta [E117]). We had to search around for their figures for the "average farmer": these are at E152, which is linked from TAF05, where they give "average personal property" of "farmers and planters." If one considers only personal property, the figures the authors give are $156 per capita in Franklin and $364 per capita (including all residents) in Augusta (E117).

Prima facie, the authors' claim that slavery gave Augusta County "massive personal estate valuations" in comparison to Franklin County is misleading, not only because they are comparing incomparables, but also because they leave out real property in making this claim (they report that per capita real property in Franklin was $476 and in Augusta, $499—figures that are quite close to each other [E117]).

The authors fail to discuss what counted as personal property in the 1860 census, nor how reliable the gathering of these statistics was or what it excluded. (Later, I found on the Bureau of the Census Web site the *Eighth Census, U.S. Instructions, & c.* [Washington, DC, 1860], a document apparently lost until the early 1990s, that answered some of my questions [http://www2.census.gov/prod2/decennial/documents; see items for 1860 (accessed Dec. 2004)].) Strikingly absent, as well, is any discussion of debt and credit. If there was little or no indebtedness in either county, the authors should have stated this explicitly and provided supporting evidence. On the other hand, if the economies in one or both counties were sufficiently "modern" to involve significant mortgage and other indebtedness, then no justifiable claims about wealth in the two counties are possible without bringing indebtedness into account. Consider T. Jefferson of Albemarle County, Virginia, not far from Augusta County, who, at his death in 1826, had debts that closely approached the appraised value of his substantial real property (Dumas Malone, *Jefferson and His Time,* vol. 6, *The Sage of Monticello* [Boston, MA, 1981], 511–12).

12 "The historiography and evidence occupy separate spatial locations. They stand beside the analysis, independent of it" (TI3) Why?

13 Paul Veyne, *Writing History: Essay on Epistemology,* trans. M. Moore-Rinvolucri (Middletown, CT, 1984), 3. The translator incorrectly renders *"un récit véridique"* in the original French as "a true account."

ONE: *History with Memory, History without Memory*

1 Herodotus, *The History,* trans. David Grene (Chicago, 1987), 1.1, p. 33.

2 The controversy was surveyed by a number of writers in *Journal of American History* 82 (1995): 1029–1144: see especially Richard H. Kohn, "History and the Culture Wars: The Case of the Smithsonian Institution's Enola Gay Exhibition," 1026–63. One can assay the heat of the debate by searching the keywords "Smithsonian," "Enola Gay," and "exhibit" on the Web: see especially the Air Force Association site, www.afa.org/media/enolagay. However, it appears that the controversy was not simply a matter of enlightened professionals vs. a self-interested subset of "the public." Some discussion of the case suggests that the museum professionals at the National Air and Space Museum who planned the exhibit, notably its director, Martin Harwit, and his curators, engaged in a selective and tendentious reading of the historical record. See Robert P. Newman, *Enola Gay and the Court of History* (New York, 2004), as well as an article of 2 August 2004 in which Newman, an emeritus professor of political communication from the University of Pittsburgh, summarizes his results: "Remember the Smithsonian's Atomic Bomb Exhibit? You Only Think You Know the Truth," available online

on George Mason University's History News Web site, http://hnn.us. (The article is now cached; enter the words "Remember the Smithsonian" into HNN's search window.) If Newman's claims are true, this shows a shocking incompetence and irresponsibility on the part of the exhibit planners.

3   Jan C. Scruggs and Joel L. Swerdlow, *To Heal a Nation: The Vietnam Veterans Memorial* (New York, 1985), 80–84.

4   For example, Eric Foner, *Who Owns History? Rethinking the Past in a Changing World* (New York, 2002). See also Otis Graham, "Editor's Corner: Who Owns American History?" *Public Historian* 17 (1995): 8–11; and Karen J. Winkler, "Who Owns History?" *Chronicle of Higher Education*, 20 January 1995, A10–11. Many other citations could be added.

5   Foner, *Who Owns History?*, xvii.

6   This is the thesis of Erna Paris, *Long Shadows: Truth, Lies and History* (New York, 2001).

7   For information on the Yad Vashem Holocaust Martyrs' and Heroes' Authority, founded in 1953, see www.yadvashem.org.il/aboutyad/indexabout_yad.html. For Yale University's Fortunoff Video Archive for Holocaust Testimonies, founded in 1982 with the purpose of continuing a project begun in 1979 by the Holocaust Survivors Film Project, see www.library.yale.edu/testimonies. In late 2005 Steven Spielberg's Survivors of the Shoah Foundation, founded in 1994, became the University of Southern California's Shoah Foundation Institute; see www.usc.edu/schools/college/vhi.

8   Allen Johnson summarizes the classic case for the unreliability of eyewitness testimony in his *The Historian and Historical Evidence* (New York, 1926), 26–49.

9   Lawrence P. Douglas, *The Memory of Judgment: Making Law and History in the Trials of the Holocaust* (New Haven, CT, 2001), 196–207. Demjanjuk's conviction and sentencing to death were overturned in 1993 by the Israeli Supreme Court. It should be noted, however, that in a characteristically restrained and careful study, Christopher R. Browning has shown that, where critical comparison is possible, witness testimony can indeed help historians fill in gaps in our historical knowledge of the past; see his *Collected Memories: Holocaust History and Postwar Testimony* (Madison, WI, 2003).

10   Peter Novick, *The Holocaust in American Life* (Boston, 1999), 199–201 and passim.

11   Liddell and Scott, *A Greek-English Lexicon*, new edition, s.v. μῦθος, Μῦθ-ύδριον.

12   Thucydides, *History of the Peloponnesian War*, trans. Rex Warner (Harmondsworth, UK, 1956), 1.21–22.

13   This view is succinctly stated by R. G. Collingwood, *The Idea of History*, rev. ed., with *Lectures 1926–1928*, ed. W. J. van der Dussen (Oxford, 1993), 234–35, 253–53, 366–67.

14   Martin Heidegger, *Being and Time*, trans. Joan Stambaugh (Albany, NY, 1996), §73, 378 ff. (German pagination).

15   Collingwood, *Idea of History*, 366, 252–54.

16   John Silverman, "Gruesome Legacy of Dr. Gross," BBC News Online, 6 May 1999, www.news.bbc.co.uk/1/hi/world/europe/336189.stm. For an account of euthanasia in Vienna during the Third Reich, see Herwig Czech, "Forschen ohne Skrupel: Die wissenschaftliche Verwertung von Opfern der NS-Psychiatriemorde in Wien," in *Von der*

Zwangssterilisierung zur Ermordung. Zur Geschichte der NS-Euthanasie in Wien, Teil 2, ed. Eberhard Gabriel and Wolfgang Neugebauer (Vienna, 2002), 143–64. Dr. Heinrich Gross died on 15 December 2005 at age ninety, as this book was being prepared for the press, without a verdict having been reached in the legal proceedings against him, which were suspended in 2000 because alleged advanced dementia made him unfit for trial. (*New York Times,* 23 December 2005, "Obituaries," A21).

17   The "innocent Austria" myth is most clearly and widely visible in the shape of the Rodgers and Hammerstein musical, *The Sound of Music,* which appeared as an immensely popular movie in 1965. The family portrayed in the movie, the von Trapps (loosely based on an actual Austrian family), demonstrated their inability to come to terms with the Third Reich by leaving Austria at considerable cost to themselves. The nonreflective viewer might well take the von Trapps as representative of Austria in general. The historian, on the other hand, is obliged to ask an epistemological question—namely, what evidence is there that many other Austrians acted, or even only *thought,* as the von Trapps did?

18   Paul Ricoeur, *Time and Narrative,* 1:91–230, 3 vols. (Chicago, 1984–88). Vols. 1 and 2 trans. Kathleen McLaughlin and David Pellauer; vol. 3 trans. Kathleen Blamey and David Pellauer. Some might see Ricoeur's emphasis on the experience of time as overstated. For example, does an archeologist need to take account of the experience of time in order to argue that things must have changed in a particular way in order to account for surviving layers of archeological evidence? I do not think so: the inference could be drawn as an extrapolation from the existing, incomplete data. But Ricoeur's point seems broader than this: it is that the very conception of pastness itself requires memory and the experience of time. This is one of the things that makes history different from paleontology or from an ahistorical political science.

19   Jacques Le Goff, *History and Memory,* trans. Steven Rendell and Elizabeth Claman (New York, 1992), xi.

20   The distinction between traces (*Überreste,* also translatable as "remains") and sources (*Quellen*) is discussed in some detail by the historian and historical theorist J. G. Droysen in his *Outline of the Principles of History,* trans. E. Benjamin Andrews (Boston, 1893; translation of Droysen's *Grundriß der Historik,* 3rd ed. [1882]), §§21–26 . It goes back to J. M. Chladenius's reflections on historical method in his *Allgemeine Geschichtswissenschaft,* first published in 1752.

21   This is noted by Eugene T. Webb et al. in the standard social-scientific study of nonintentional evidence, *Nonreactive Measures in the Social Sciences,* 2d ed. (Boston, 1981), 4.

22   I summarize a scene in Claude Lanzmann's 1985 film *Shoah,* where the historian Raul Hilberg, sitting in his study in Burlington, Vermont, lays out what we can infer from one such train schedule, *Fahrplananordnung* 587: it documents the passage of a full train, fifty freight cars long, to Treblinka, and its departure from Treblinka empty. See Claude Lanzmann, *Shoah: The Complete Text of the Film* (New York, 1985), 138–42.

23   Consider Wolfgang Höpken, "Kriegserinnerung und Nationale Identität(en): Vergangenheitspolitik in Jugoslawien und in den Nachfolgestaaten," *Transit: Europäische Revue* 15 (Fall 1998): 83–99. Writing of conflicting "memories" of World War II in

Greece and Yugoslavia, Höpken observes that "divergent memories not only arose alongside each other, but confronted each other directly as memory conflicts that could only with difficulty—if at all—be resolved in discourse" (85). Examples could be multiplied endlessly.

24 While I was revising this chapter, I received an e-mail from George T. Crafts, an acquisitions specialist in the University of Virginia's Alderman Library (e-mail, headed "Holocaust testimony index," from George T. Crafts to University of Virginia history and religious studies faculty and graduate students, 3 June 2003). Mr. Crafts noted that the "Visual History Foundation" had given the library a free copy of the digital index to fifty-one thousand videotaped interviews with Holocaust survivors from the Spielberg archive. Mr. Crafts also noted that the interviews were "only available for purchase, not for loan" and that the cost was $92.00 per testimony. At that rate, a complete archive of testimonies would cost $4,692,000, a price far beyond the reach of almost any academic library. But presumably many people would be willing to pay $92.00 to see a grandparent interviewed about his or her experience of the Holocaust. This underscores my point here.

Later, in October 2005, it was announced that the "Survivors of the Shoah Visual History Foundation" would become part of an academic environment, the University of Southern California, under the name "USC Shoah Foundation Institute for Visual History and Education" (see www.usc.edu/schools/college/vhi). While this new arrangement will make the current fifty-two thousand testimonies readily available to researchers and others, the move seems to represent as much the memorialization of history as it does the historicalization of memory. Readers are invited to judge for themselves by accessing the Web site.

25 The best entry to the notion of collective memory is still Maurice Halbwachs, *On Collective Memory,* ed. and trans. Lewis A. Coser (Chicago, 1992); see especially Coser's introduction, 1–34.

26 For the German variant of the master narrative, see Georg G. Iggers, *The German Conception of History: The National Tradition of Historical Thought from Herder to the Present,* 2d. ed. (Middletown, CT, 1983). On the grounding of the nineteenth-century historical profession in an ultimately Christian grand narrative, see chapter 9.

27 "Address to the Nation about the Watergate Investigations," www.watergate.info/nixon/73-04-30watergate-speech.shtml.

28 Jean-François Lyotard, *The Postmodern Condition: A Report on Knowledge,* trans. Geoff Bennington and Brian Massumi (Minneapolis, 1984), xxiii.

29 To be sure, grand narrative, if it entirely subordinates historical particulars to the developmental or salvational story that it wishes to tell, can blot out history and historical thinking. This is why Marxism so easily tipped over from history to an illegitimate *science* or *theory* of history, and why the Christian salvation story needed to undergo a secularization before it could offer a basis, in the late eighteenth and early nineteenth centuries, for the emergence of the historical discipline.

30 The Disney proposal was extensively discussed in the press in 1994. Among many other items, see the editorial by David Hackett: "Disney, Leave Virginia Alone; Give Us No Imitation History," *St. Petersburg Times,* 1 June 1994.

31 Perhaps the best-known work in the genre is Studs Terkel, *"The Good War": An Oral History of World War Two* (New York, 1984).

32 Note in particular the almost eight-hundred-page *Handbuch der Geschichtsdidaktik,* 5th ed., ed. Klaus Bergmann et al. (Seelze-Velber, Germany, 1997).

33 See "A Blog Takes Off," *Chronicle of Higher Education,* 6 June 2003, A15, which reports that Eric L. Muller, author of *Free to Die for Their Country: The Story of the Japanese American Draft Resisters in World War II* (Chicago, 2001) made, on his Web log, some widely noticed criticisms of false statements concerning Japanese resettlement in World War II by U.S. Rep. Howard Coble, North Carolina Republican and chairman of the House Judiciary Subcommittee on Crime, Terrorism, and Homeland Security.

34 Immanuel Kant, *The Conflict of the Faculties,* trans. Mary J. Gregor (New York, 1979).

35 Michel de Certeau, "The Historiographical Operation," in *The Writing of History,* trans. Tom Conley (New York, 1988), 56–113.

TWO: *History, Memory, Identity*

1 The classic defense of the methodological unity, and hence universality, of history is R. G. Collingwood, *The Idea of History,* rev. ed., with *Lectures 1926–1928,* ed. W. J. van der Dussen (1946; repr., Oxford, 1993), "Epilegomena," 231–315. On the universal/particular opposition, see, for example, Eric W. Hobsbawm, "The Historian between the Quest for the Universal and the Quest for Identity," *Diogenes* 168 (1994): 51–64.

2 Ian Hacking, *Rewriting the Soul: Multiple Personality Disorder and the Sciences of Memory* (Princeton, NJ, 1995), 213. Two immensely influential books that took the "memory as empowerment" route are Ellen Bass and Laura Davis, *The Courage to Heal: A Guide for Women Survivors of Child Sexual Abuse* (New York, 1988); and Judith Lewis Hermann, *Trauma and Recovery* (New York, 1992). On the "recovered memory" phenomenon generally, see Hacking, *Rewriting the Soul,* chap. 15, "Memoro-Politics," 210–20; and Elaine Showalter, *Hystories: Hysterical Epidemics and Modern Culture* (New York, 1997), chap. 10, "Recovered Memory," 145–58. Nicholas P. Spanos, *Multiple Identities and False Memories: A Sociocognitive Perspective* (Washington, DC, 1996) provides an entry to much of the literature.

3 In *Satan's Silence: Ritual Abuse and the Making of a Modern American Witch Hunt* (New York, 1995), Debbie Nathan and Michael Snedeker survey the plethora of "ritual abuse" cases dealt with in the U.S. legal system in the 1980s and early 1990s: such cases normally involved some form of memory "recovery."

  Elizabeth Loftus and Katherine Ketcham, in *The Myth of Repressed Memory: False Memories and Allegations of Sexual Abuse* (New York, 1994), discuss a number of specific cases, including that of George Franklin, in California, whose conviction for murder, on the basis of so-called recovered memories, was ultimately overturned, and that of Deputy Sheriff Paul Ingram of Olympia, Washington, whose 1989 conviction on six counts of third-degree rape, likewise on the basis of such memories, still stood as of early 2004. (Ingram was finally released on parole in 2003, having served fourteen years of his twenty-year sentence.) Lawrence Wright, in *Remembering Satan* (New York, 1994), offers a devastating account of how the Ingram case was conducted. It is highly probable that Ingram was innocent of the charges against him, but it seems to have served a broader social function in Washington state to sweep this fact under the rug.

4 Tim Judah, *The Serbs: History, Myth, and the Destruction of Yugoslavia* (New Haven, CT, 1997), xi–xii and passim.

5 An important point of entry is Saul Friedlander, ed., *Probing the Limits of Representation: Nazism and the "Final Solution"* (Cambridge, MA, 1992): see especially the essays by Christopher R. Browning, Dominick LaCapra, and Eric L. Santner. Andreas Huyssen deals with the paradoxes of Holocaust memory in "Monuments and Holocaust Memory in a Media Age," in his *Twilight Memories: Marking Time in a Culture of Amnesia* (New York, 1995), 249–60.

6 Charles S. Maier, *The Unmasterable Past: History, Holocaust, and German National Identity* (Cambridge, MA, 1988), esp. chap. 3, "A Holocaust Like the Others? Problems of Comparative History," 66–99.

7 Harold Noonan offers a reliable account of Hume's views in his *Personal Identity* (London, 1989), 77–103.

8 Charles Taylor, *Sources of the Self: The Making of the Modern Identity* (Cambridge, MA: 1989), 25–32 and passim. The earlier, pre-retreat dispensation is well described by J. G. Droysen, *Outline of the Principles of History,* trans. E. Benjamin Andrews (Boston, 1893; translation of *Grundriß der Historik,* 3rd ed., 1882): "The human being is, in essential nature, a totality in himself, but realizes this character only in understanding others and in being understood by them. . . . The individual is only relatively a totality. He understands and is understood only as a specimen and expression of the partnerships whose member he is and in whose essence and development he has a part, himself being but an expression of this essence and development" (sec. 12, p. 14).

9 Cf. Stephen Greenblatt, *Renaissance Self-Fashioning: From More to Shakespeare* (Chicago, 1980). Self-fashioning is one of the key ideas of advanced modernity; our possession of it enables us to discern its analogues in earlier times.

10 Friedrich Nietzsche, "Skirmishes of an Untimely Man," sec. 49, from *Twilight of the Idols,* in *The Portable Nietzsche,* ed. and trans. Walter Kaufmann (New York, 1954), 554.

11 Contrast this with peasant culture as described by John Berger: "Peasants do not *play roles* as urban characters do . . . because the space between what is unknown about a person and what is generally known . . . is too small" (*Pig Earth* [New York, 1979], 10). To be sure, the situation that Berger describes may be more a characteristic of "premodernity" *in the West,* dominated by an authoritative monotheistic religion, than a universal characteristic; I do not know how generalizable Berger's description is.

12 As one literary scholar puts it, "memory stabilizes subjects and constitutes the present. It is the name we give to the faculty that sustains continuity in collective and in individual experience"; Richard Terdiman, *Present Past: Modernity and the Memory Crisis* (Ithaca, NY, 1993), 8.

13 Two early markers of what later became a massive interest in the history–memory relation are by Pierre Nora: "Mémoire de l'historien, mémoire de l'histoire: Entretien avec J.-B. Pontalis," *Nouvelle Revue de psychanalyse* 15 (1977): 221–34, and "La Mémoire collective," in *La nouvelle Histoire,* ed. Jacques Le Goff (Paris, 1978), 398–401. During

the 1980s the trickle became a flood, but see especially Jacques Le Goff, *History and Memory,* trans. Steven Rendall and Elizabeth Claman (New York, 1992; first published in Italian in 1986 and then in French in 1988); and the monumental collective work edited by Pierre Nora, *Les Lieux de mémoire,* 7 vols. (Paris, 1984–92). Many essays from this last work have appeared in English in *Realms of Memory,* ed. Pierre Nora, English language edition ed. Lawrence D. Kritzman, trans. Arthur Goldhammer, 3 vols. (New York, 1996). Nora's "Preface to the English-Language Edition" (1:xv–xxiv) makes clear the close connection between "realms of memory" and issues of (French) identity. See also Amos Funkenstein, "Collective Memory and Historical Consciousness," *History and Memory: Studies in Representation of the Past* 1 (1989): 5–27; and Wulf Kansteiner, "Finding Meaning in Memory: A Methodological Critique of Collective Memory Studies," *History and Theory* 41 (2002): 179–97.

14   Maurice Halbwachs, *Les Cadres sociaux de la mémoire,* postface by Gérard Namer (Paris, 1994); *La Topographie légendaire des évangiles en terre sainte,* 2d ed., preface by Fernand Dumont (Paris, 1971); and *The Collective Memory,* trans. Francis J. Ditter Jr. and Vida Yazdi Ditter, with an introduction by Mary Douglas (New York, 1980). For an abridged translation of *Les Cadres* and a translation of the conclusion of *La Topographie légendaire,* see Halbwachs, *On Collective Memory,* ed. and trans. Lewis A. Coser (Chicago, 1992).

15   Maurice Halbwachs, "Preface" and "Conclusion" to *The Social Frameworks of Memory,* in Halbwachs, *On Collective Memory,* 40, 182.

16   Halbwachs, *The Collective Memory,* 84.

17   Benedict Anderson, *Imagined Communities: Reflections on the Origin and Spread of Nationalism,* rev. ed. (London, 1991; orig. pub. in 1983).

18   The importance of "forgetting" was perhaps first noted by Ernest Renan in his classic lecture, "What Is a Nation?" (1882), where he pointed out that the emergence of the French nation required that the Saint Bartholemew's Day massacre (when Catholics murdered Protestants) needed to recede from view. See Renan, "What Is a Nation?" trans. Martin Thom, in *Nation and Narration,* ed. Homi K. Bhabha (London, 1990), 8–22.

19   In his "General Introduction: Between Memory and History," in *Realms of Memory,* Nora deftly notes this dialectic of nostalgia and memory—or, to put the matter in other terms, between complacent identity and threatened identity: see *Realms of Memory,* 1:5–6. Indeed, it may well be that this dialectic, more than that "between history and memory," is the true axis of this influential work. No doubt a key impulse behind the *lieux de mémoire* project was a feeling that French identity required critical examination precisely because its meaning, by the late 1970s and early 1980s, was no longer as clear as it had seemed before.

20   National History Day, Inc., *National History Day Student Contest Guide* (College Park, MD, 1993), 2.

21   "Strictly speaking an original record would be one which contains the direct testimony of an eyewitness of events. All other accounts derived from this would be secondary sources. Usually, however, accounts secured by contemporaries from eyewitnesses are

treated as original sources. Contemporaneousness becomes the real test." See Allen Johnson, *The Historian and Historical Evidence* (New York, 1926), 61.

22 On the weakness of testimony generally (even that which immediately follows the events reported), Johnson's chapter on "The Basis of Historical Doubt" in *The Historian and Historical Evidence,* 24–49, has never been surpassed; see also his chapter in that volume on "The Nature of Historical Proof," 141–56. Still, as Christopher Browning shows in his use of the testimonies of 173 survivors of the slave labor camps in Starachowice, Poland, if there is an adequately dense sample of testimonies, the historian may be able to learn quite a lot from applying critical procedures to them; see Christopher R. Browning, *Collected Memories: Holocaust History and Postwar Testimony* (Madison, WI, 2003), 59, 60–85.

23 This view is close to what Maurice Mandelbaum refers to as "the doctrine of immediacy," which he suggests "has gained a dominant position in twentieth-century thought"; see Maurice Mandelbaum, *History, Man, and Reason: A Study in Nineteenth-Century Thought* (Baltimore, 1971), 350–64, at 358.

24 Margaret Smith [pseud.], *Ritual Abuse: What It Is, Why It Happens, and How to Help* (New York, 1993). Subsequently cited in the text by page number in parentheses.

25 Hacking, *Rewriting the Soul,* 18. In 1994 the American Psychiatric Association renamed MPD "dissociative identity disorder," but this set of phenomena continued to be widely known under the earlier name or variants thereof. For a description, including diagnostic criteria, see *Diagnostic and Statistical Manual of Mental Disorders,* 4th ed. [*DSM-IV*] (Washington, DC, 1994), 484–87. The name change from "multiple personality disorder" to "dissociative identity disorder" acknowledges that there are not many identities, but one (damaged) identity.

26 The videotapes were produced at the Institute of Law, Psychiatry and Public Policy, University of Virginia, during the early 1990s, with subject permission for training and research purposes.

27 Friedrich Nietzsche, *On the Genealogy of Morality: A Polemic,* trans. Maudemarie Clark and Alan J. Swensen (Indianapolis, 1998), "Second Treatise," sec. 1–2, pp. 35–36. Subsequently cited in the text by page number in parentheses.

28 Sigmund Freud, "On the Psychical Mechanism of Hysterical Phenomena: A Lecture" (1893), in Freud, *The Standard Edition of the Complete Psychological Works,* trans. under the general editorship of James Strachey, 24 vols. (London, 1953–74), 3: 25–39. Other early twentieth-century therapists who shared Freud's wish to help patients overcome memory include Pierre Janet and H. H. Goddard (on whom, see Hacking, *Rewriting the Soul,* 86, 252, 260–61).

29 Hacking, *Rewriting the Soul,* 260.

30 Oliver Sacks, *The Man Who Mistook His Wife for a Hat and Other Clinical Tales* (New York, 1985).

31 Geoffrey H. Hartman, "Judging Paul de Man," in *Minor Prophecies: The Literary Essay in the Culture Wars* (Cambridge, MA, 1991), 123–48: "The aim of judgment in historical or literary-critical discourse . . . is to change history into memory: to make a case for what should be remembered, and how it should be remembered. This responsibility

converts every judgment into a judgment on the person who makes it" (148). This last point is precisely right: the shift from "history" to "memory" entails a shift—from a deliberation concerning what was or was not the case in the past, to the offering of judgments concerning the character, political commitments, and so on of those persons claiming to speak about the past. Let us imagine what quality of academic discussion such a move is likely to occasion. First of all we would need reliable tests of character, political commitment, and the like, and the work done by the persons we are judging would be of secondary importance; cf. the introduction to this book.

32 Eve Kosofsky Sedgwick, "Against Epistemology," in *Questions of Evidence: Proof, Practice, and Persuasion across the Disciplines,* ed. James Chandler, Arnold I. Davidson, and Harry Harootunian (Chicago, 1994), 136. It is not entirely clear what Sedgwick means by an "erotics" of evidence. I take it that the phrase denotes an emphasis on the dramatization of present concerns within a media or other performative context, without much (or any) attention being given to how the precise or literal truth of the dramatization is established.

33 Cf. Johannes Fabian, *Remembering the Present: Painting and Popular History in Zaire,* with narrative and paintings by Tshibumba Kanda Matulu (Berkeley, 1996).

34 For an analysis of this sort of move, and of the opposing "critical" or "revisionist" move, see Steven Knapp, "Collective Memory and the Actual Past," *Representations* no. 26 (Spring 1989): 123–49.

35 Paul Ricoeur, *Time and Narrative,* 3 vols.; vols. 1 and 2 trans. Kathleen McLaughlin and David Pellauer; vol. 3 trans. Kathleen Blamey and David Pellauer (Chicago, 1984–88), 1:ix.

36 Collingwood, *Idea of History,* pt. 5, "Epilegomena," and chap. 3, "Historical Evidence," 249–82. The discussion entitled "Who Killed John Doe?" begins at 266. Subsequently cited in the text by page number in parentheses.

37 Chapter 6 of this volume shows emphatically that this claim is false.

38 Michel de Certeau, *The Writing of History,* trans. Tom Conley (New York, 1988), xxv–xxvi, 5, 39, 46–47, 85, 91, 94, 99–102, 218–26, 246–48, and passim.

39 Hayden White, "The Politics of Historical Interpretation: Discipline and De-Sublimation," in *The Content of the Form: Narrative Discourse and Historical Representation* (Baltimore, 1987), 72.

40 Hayden White, "The Question of Narrative in Contemporary Historical Theory," in *The Content of the Form,* 53.

41 Herodotus, *The History,* trans. David Grene (Chicago: University of Chicago Press, 1987), 7.152, p. 521: "I must tell what is said, but I am not at all bound to believe it, and this comment of mine holds about my whole *History.*"

42 I owe several ideas and formulations in this paragraph and in the next two to Michael B. Guenther.

43 Friedrich Nietzsche, *The Gay Science,* sec. 125, in *The Gay Science, with a Prelude in Rhymes and an Appendix of Songs,* trans. Walter Kaufmann (New York, 1974).

44 Ashis Nandy, "History's Forgotten Doubles," *History and Theory,* Theme Issue 34 (1995): 44–66, at 44, 47–48, 53.

45 Dipesh Chakrabarty, "The Rational and the Magical in Subaltern Studies," lecture delivered in the University of Virginia Theory Seminar, 28 February 1997.

46 On the centrality of *autopsy,* or eyewitnessing, for Herodotus, see François Hartog, *The Mirror of Herodotus: The Representation of the Other in the Writing of History,* trans. Janet Lloyd (Berkeley, 1988), 260–73. The emphasis on the need to supplement witnesses and their testimony (*Quellen*) with material remains (*Überreste*) was most famously articulated by Droysen.

47 See Mark J. Osiel, *Mass Atrocity, Collective Memory, and the Law* (New Brunswick, NJ: Transaction Publishers, 1997). The combined (and necessarily conflicting) aims of truth/justice and reconciliation were most clearly those of the South African Truth and Reconciliation Commission. See South Africa Truth and Reconciliation Commission, *Report,* 7 vols. (Cape Town, 1998). The TRC's home page (www.doj.gov.za/trc/) and related sites also make other material available.

THREE: *Does Narrative Have a Cognitive Value of Its Own?*

1 Louis O. Mink, "Narrative Form as a Cognitive Instrument," in *Historical Understanding,* by Louis O. Mink, ed. Brian Fay, Eugene O. Golob, and Richard T. Vann (Ithaca, NY, 1987), 182–203, at 198 and 186.

2 Louis O. Mink, "On the Writing and Rewriting of History," in Mink, *Historical Understanding,* 89–105, at 91.

3 Hayden White, *Metahistory: The Historical Imagination in Nineteenth-Century Europe* (Baltimore, MD, 1973). Ewa Domanska gives a good sense of White's impact on the field in her interviews with various philosophers of history and historians of historiography: Ewa Domanska, ed., *Encounters: Philosophy of History after Postmodernism* (Charlottesville, VA, 1998).

4 For a particularly clear and comprehensive attempt to describe and elaborate on a so-called "narrative paradigm," see Walter R. Fisher, *Human Communication as Narration: Toward a Philosophy of Reason, Value, and Action* (Columbia, SC, 1987), especially parts 2 and 3.

5 The story/discourse distinction is canonical in structuralist narrative theory. For one famous articulation, see Boris Tomashevsky, "Thématique," in *Théorie de la littérature,* ed. and trans. Tzvetan Todorov (Paris, 1965), 263–307. Seymour Chatman, *Story and Discourse: Narrative Structure in Fiction and Film* (Ithaca, NY, 1978), probably remains the most accessible and useful account for most historians.

6 For a brief survey of the literature questioning the viability of narrative, see Richard Kearney, "The Crisis of Narrative in Contemporary Culture," *Metaphilosophy* 28 (1997): 183–95.

7 Jean-François Lyotard, *The Postmodern Condition: A Report on Knowledge,* trans. Geoff Bennington and Brian Massumi (Minneapolis, 1984), xxiii–xxiv.

8 Pierre Nora makes an analogous point with regard to memory (an existential phenomenon that is closely related to the literary phenomenon of narrative): "The less collective

the experience of memory is, the greater the need for individuals to bear the burden, as if an inner voice were needed to tell each Corsican 'You must be Corsican' and each Breton 'You must be Breton' " ("General Introduction: Between Memory and History," in *Realms of Memory,* ed. Pierre Nora, English-language edition, ed. Lawrence D. Kritzman, trans. Arthur Goldhammer, 3 vols. [New York, 1996], 1 : 1–20, at 11).

9   Lyotard, *Postmodern Condition,* 46–47, 67, and throughout.

10 Walter Benjamin, "The Storyteller: Reflections on the Work of Nicolai Leskov," and "The Work of Art in the Age of Mechanical Reproduction," in *Illuminations,* by Walter Benjamin, ed. Hannah Arendt (New York, 1969), 83–109, 217–51.

11 Although his focus is on memory rather than narrative, Nora also comes close to making such a suggestion in discussing "archival memory," in "Between Memory and History," esp. 8–11.

12 Letter from associate director, Office of International Affairs, University of ———, to A. Megill, dated 3 February 1998, asking for a letter supporting the visa application of Professor Y.

13 Beyond Kafka, Max Weber remains the classic writer on bureaucracy. But for a more specific and up-to-date view, see Theodore M. Porter, *Trust in Numbers: The Pursuit of Objectivity in Science and Public Life* (Princeton, NJ, 1995). Porter describes in great detail the workings of a "mechanical" objectivity that seeks to create uniform categories in terms of which we then class particular phenomena. A characteristic device of this statistical orientation is the questionnaire or table (see, e.g., Porter, *Trust in Numbers,* 35–36), which on its face has little in common with the narrative. See also chapter 5 of this book.

14 See Carl. G. Hempel, "The Function of General Laws in History," in *Theories of History,* ed. Patrick Gardiner (New York, 1959), 344–55, at 346. Orig. pub. in *Journal of Philosophy* 39 [1942]: 35–48.

15 Friedrich Nietzsche, *Human, All-Too-Human: A Book for Free Spirits,* trans. R. J. Hollingdale (Cambridge, 1996), vol. 1, pt.1, sec. 2, p. 13.

16 Michel Foucault, *The Archaeology of Knowledge,* trans. A. M. Sheridan Smith (New York, 1972), 12.

17 Benjamin, "Theses," thesis 18.A, in Benjamin, *Illuminations,* 263.

18 Lyotard, *Postmodern Condition,* 3.

19 An "advanced" Google® search in June 2004 of "Trans World Airlines Flight 800" and "crash" generated 370 hits. The official claim is that Flight 800 was destroyed by a spark in its main fuel tank.

20 Michel Foucault, *The Order of Things: An Archaeology of the Human Sciences,* (New York, 1970), xxii–xxiii, 42–43, 250–53, 386–87.

21 Roland Barthes, "Introduction to the Structural Analysis of Narratives," in *Image, Music, Text* (New York, 1977), 79–124, at 79; Paul Ricoeur, *Time and Narrative,* 3 vols. (Chicago, 1984–88), 1: xi; vols. 1 and 2, trans. Kathleen McLaughlin and David Pellauer, vol. 3, trans. Kathleen Blamey and David Pellauer; Mink, "Narrative Form as a Cognitive Instrument," 186; W. B. Gallie, *Philosophy and the Historical Understanding,*

2d ed. (New York, 1968), esp. chap. 2, "What Is a Story?" 22–50; and Hayden White, "The Value of Narrativity in the Representation of Reality," in *The Content of the Form: Narrative Discourse and Historical Representation* (Baltimore, MD, 1987), 1–25, at 1.

22 Cf. Paul Ricoeur, "Gedächtnis—Vergessen—Geschichte," in *Historische Sinnbildung: Problemstellungen, Zeitkonzepte, Wahrnehmungshorizonte, Darstellungsstrategien,* ed. Klaus E. Müller and Jörn Rüsen (Reinbek bei Hamburg, 1997), 433–54.

23 My former landlady was so far from being alone that her delusion has been identified and named: it is Capgras syndrome, first reported in detail in 1923 by the French psychiatrists Capgras and Reboul-Lachaux. See the invaluable book by Louis R. Franzini and John M. Grossberg, *Eccentric and Bizarre Behaviors* (New York, 1995), chap. 7, 121–38. No doubt if Capgras syndrome were better known, and if it somehow connected with anxieties about identity, it would be much more prevalent than it is.

24 See Terry Castle, "Contagious Folly: *An Adventure* and Its Skeptics," Françoise Meltzer, "For Your Eyes Only: Ghost Citing," and Terry Castle, "A Rejoinder to Françoise Meltzer," all in *Questions of Evidence: Proof, Practice, and Persuasion across the Disciplines,* ed. J. Chandler, A. I. Davidson, and H. Harootunian (Chicago, 1994), 11–42, 43–49, and 50–55 (orig. pub. in *Critical Inquiry* 17 [Summer 1991]). Moberly and Jourdain offered their account pseudonymously in Elizabeth Morison and Frances Lamont, *An Adventure,* 2d ed. (London, 1913; other editions were published in 1911, 1924, 1931, and 1955). Castle returns to Moberly and Jourdain in the chapter, "Marie Antoinette Obsession," in her book, *The Apparitional Lesbian: Female Homosexuality and Modern Culture* (New York, 1993), 107–49.

25 John E. Mack, *Abduction: Human Encounters with Aliens* (New York, 1994). I quote from a background article by Marjorie Rosen, J. D. Podolsky, and S. Avery Brown, "Out of This World," *People* Magazine, 23 May 1994, 38–43, at 40, but his statement here is consistent with what he says in *Abduction* (e.g., at 414, on the aliens' "alien/human hybrid offspring" breeding program). I must note that Prof. Mack maintains a different view in his subsequent book, *Passport to the Cosmos: Human Transformation and Alien Encounters* (New York, 1999), where he asserts that "my purpose in this book is not to establish that alien abductions are real purely in a literal, physical sense"; rather, "my principal interest is in the experiences themselves" (9).

26 On "ritual abuse," see Debbie Nathan and Michael Snedeker, *Satan's Silence: Ritual Abuse and the Making of a Modern American Witch Hunt* (New York, 1995). A characteristic work in the genre is Margaret Smith [pseud.], *Ritual Abuse: What It Is, Why It Happens, and How to Help* (New York, 1993) (discussed in chap. 2, at n. 24). For a time, the "Believe the Children" organization acted as a clearing house for alleged cases of ritual abuse. Many Web sites are devoted to this topic. A Google search done in February 1998 produced 1,187 hits; the same search in June 2004 produced about 30,500 hits.

27 The Ingram case has been extensively discussed in print. See especially Lawrence Wright, *Remembering Satan* (New York, 1994), a book that amounts to an indictment of the way that the Washington State legal system operated in this case. On Ingram's then impending release, see the remarkably flat and unilluminating newspaper article by Brad Shannon, "Man in Notorious Sex Case Finishes Term," *Olympian,* 8 April

2003, "front page," at www.theolympian.com/home/news/20030408/frontpage/38738.
shtml. See also chap. 2, n. 3.

28 R. G. Collingwood, *The Idea of History* (1946), rev. ed., with *Lectures 1926–1928*, ed. W. J.
van der Dussen (Oxford, 1993), 204. Subsequently cited in the text by page number.

29 It would be churlish, however, to imagine that history is somehow above the other
human sciences with regard to epistemology. One thinks of the sophisticated grasp of
statistical methods in such disciplines as political science, and—perhaps not so obvious—of textual methods in literary studies. For an example of an alert textual scholar
catching out a tradition of tendentious carelessness among literary scholars, biographers,
and an unlucky historian, see Julie Bates Dock, with Daphne Ryan Allen, Jennifer
Palais, and Kristen Tracy, " 'But One Expects That': Charlotte Perkins Gilman's 'The
Yellow Wallpaper' and the Shifting Light of Scholarship," *PMLA* 111 (1996): 52–65.

30 Here I diverge from C. Behan McCullagh, who in his nonetheless admirable book *The
Truth of History* (London, 1998) is in my view too persuaded that we humans have "the
possibility of discovering *the* truth about the past [my emphasis]" (309). He confuses, I
think, a God's-eye view with human views.

FOUR: *Narrative and the Four Tasks of History-Writing*

1 Francis Bacon, *The New Organon,* ed. L. Jardine and M. Silverthorne (Cambridge,
2000), bk. 2, aphorism 20, p. 130.

2 The notion of "thick description" (a description attentive to the significance of human action and not just to the bare actuality of what happens) was popularized by
the anthropologist Clifford Geertz. See Geertz, *The Interpretation of Cultures: Selected
Essays* (New York, 1973), esp. chap. 1, "Thick Description: Toward an Interpretive
Theory of Culture," 3–30, as well as his *Local Knowledge: Further Essays in Interpretive
Anthropology* (New York, 1983). Two widely noticed anthologies that highlighted an
"interpretive" turn in social science were Paul Rabinow and William M. Sullivan, eds.,
Interpretive Social Science: A Reader (Berkeley, 1979), and the same editors' *Interpretive
Social Science: A Second Look* (Berkeley, 1987).

3 For an overview of logical empiricism (also known as "logical positivism"), see David
Oldroyd, *The Arch of Knowledge: An Introductory Study of the History of the Philosophy
and Methodology of Science* (New York, 1986), chap. 6, "Logic and Logical Empiricism," 209–63. It is generally agreed that logical empiricism died long ago. One paper
influential in undermining its hold was Willard Van Orman Quine, "Two Dogmas of
Empiricism," originally published in *The Philosophical Review* 60 (1951): 20–43. Also
important in this process was Nelson Goodman's still interesting and readable *Fact,
Fiction, and Forecast,* 4th ed. (Cambridge, MA, 1983; orig. pub. in 1954). But the news
of logical empiricism's death took a long time to spread beyond philosophical circles.

4 The notion of cause has a somewhat problematic standing in the empiricist tradition
in philosophy, but this issue need not concern us here (the problem, for the empiricist,
is that no one actually *sees* causation—one can only *infer* it). For reservations about
"cause," see Bertrand Russell's classic article, "On the Notion of Cause" (1912–13), in

his *Mysticism and Logic, and Other Essays* (New York, 1918), 180–208. For a fastidious refusal to use directly the terms *cause* and *effect,* combined with a constant invocation of these very terms, see Carl G. Hempel's equally classic "The Function of General Laws in History" (1942), in *Theories of History,* ed. Patrick Gardiner (New York, 1959), 344–56.

Note also that the "Why?" question could be taken as asking "To what end did such-and-such an intelligent agent bring such-and-such a state of affairs about?" In short, there is a distinction between a past-driven *causal* sense of the "Why?" question and a future-oriented *purposive* sense. In the present context I intend the causal sense. Bear in mind, however, that embodied purposes can serve as causes—that is, they can serve to explain why such-and-such occurred. (Why did the event happen? Because such-and-such an agent or set of agents *decided* that it should be done, for the attainment of such-and-such an end. Here we see an agent's *purpose* as a *cause* of the occurrence.)

The philosopher and linguist Sylvain Bromberger discusses explanation and "Why?" questions in his *On What We Know We Don't Know: Explanation, Theory, Linguistics, and How Questions Shape Them* (Chicago, 1992). My discussion is less deep and goes in a different direction than Bromberger's, but both the direction and the depth are appropriate to the kinds of investigation historians undertake.

5 See, among countless other works, Carl G. Hempel, *Aspects of Scientific Explanation and Other Essays in the Philosophy of Science* (New York, 1965), especially 245 and 344; Carl G. Hempel, *Philosophy of Natural Science* (Englewood Cliffs, NJ, 1966), 47, 49; Ernest Nagel, *The Structure of Science: Problems in the Logic of Scientific Explanation* (New York, 1961), 15–16; and Wolfgang Stegmüller, *Probleme und Resultate der Wissenschaftstheorie und Analytischen Philosophie,* Band I: *Wissenschaftliche Erklärung und Begründung* (Berlin, 1969), 77.

6 Stinchcombe notes the explanatory function of social theories at vii, 5, and passim; see Arthur L. Stinchcombe, *Constructing Social Theories* (New York, 1968). Among the other works I consulted are Eugene J. Meehan, *Explanation in Social Science: A System Paradigm* (Homewood, IL, 1968); Philippe Van Parijis, *Evolutionary Explanation in the Social Sciences: An Emerging Paradigm* (Totowa, NJ, 1981); Abraham Kaplan, *The Conduct of Inquiry: Methodology for Behavioral Science* (Scranton, PA, 1964); Robert Borger and Frank Cioffi, eds., *Explanation in the Behavioral Sciences* (Cambridge, 1970); Patty Jo Watson, Steven A. LeBlanc, and Charles L. Redman, *Explanation in Archaeology: An Explicitly Scientific Approach* (New York, 1971); David Harvey, *Explanation in Geography* (London, 1969); Paul Kiparsky, *Explanation in Phonology* (Dordrecht, 1982); Willem Doise, *L'Explication en psychologie sociale* (Paris, 1982); Peter D. McClelland, *Causal Explanation and Model Building in History, Economics, and the New Economic History* (Ithaca, NY, 1975); and Christopher Lloyd, *Explanation in Social History* (Oxford, 1986).

7 Miriam Schapiro Grosof and Hyman Sardy, *A Research Primer for the Social and Behavioral Sciences* (Orlando, FL, 1985), 112, 114. One exceptional work, written from a neo-positivist perspective, that does deal with "description" is C. Behan McCullagh, *Justifying Historical Descriptions* (Cambridge, 1984).

8   Lee Benson, "Causation and the American Civil War," in *Toward the Scientific Study of History: Selected Essays* (Philadelphia, 1972), 81−82, making use of E. M. Forster, *Aspects of the Novel* (New York, 1927), 47, 130, and throughout; Edward Hallet Carr, *What Is History?* (1961; repr., New York, 1967), chap. 4, "Causation in History," 113, 130 (see also 111−12, 114, 138); and David Hackett Fischer, *Historians' Fallacies: Toward a Logic of Historical Thought* (New York, 1970), xii, 131.

9   In *Historians' Fallacies,* xv, n. 1, Fischer defined explanation as follows: "To *explain* is merely to make plain, clear, or understandable some problem about past events, so that resultant knowledge will be useful in dealing with future problems." Although Fischer did not notice it, there is a tension between the first and second clauses, since "useful[ness] in dealing with future problems" suggests knowledge of cause-effect relations, hence a causal conception of explanation, whereas in the first clause "explain" simply means "to clarify."

10 Paul Veyne, *Writing History,* trans. Mina Moore-Rinvolucrj (Middletown, CT, 1984), 305 n. 5 (orig. pub. in French, 1971); Paul Ricoeur, *Time and Narrative,* vols. 1 and 2 trans. Kathleen McLaughlin and ; vol. 3 trans. Kathleen Blamey and David Pellauer (Chicago, 1984−88), 1 : 175.

11 See Thomas L. Hankins, *Science and the Enlightenment* (Cambridge, 1985), 9, 20−21, 53; J. L. Heilbron, *Electricity in the Seventeenth and Eighteenth Centuries* (Berkeley, 1979), 6, 87ff., 95, n. 47, 458ff.; and Christa Jungnickel and Russell McCormmach, *Intellectual Mastery of Nature: Theoretical Physics from Ohm to Einstein,* 2 vols. (Chicago, 1986), 1:xxiii and passim. On the classificatory impulse in natural history and elsewhere, see Hankins, *Science and the Enlightenment,* 113, 117, and throughout; and Wolf Lepenies, *Das Ende der Naturgeschichte: Wandel kultureller Selbstverständlichkeiten in den Wissenschaften des 18. und 19. Jahrhunderts* (Munich, 1976), 34, 47−48, 93, 98−102, 122−24.

12 Van Parijis, *Evolutionary Explanation in the Social Sciences,* 6; Stegmüller, *Wissenschaftliche Erklärung und Begründung,* 1. Kapitel, 2.b., "Erklärungen und Beschreibungen," 77; Richard Hofstadter, *The Age of Reform from Bryan to F.D.R.* (New York, 1969), 199−200. See also Lionel Trilling on V. L. Parrington and Theodore Dreiser in "Reality in America," in his *The Liberal Imagination: Essays on Literature and Society* (New York, 1956), 3−21.

13 It seems plausible to suggest that thinkers less committed to the base/superstructure metaphor, or to other metaphors that envisage differentially visible realities, will be less committed to the explanatory project. One social science methodologist has noted that most of Max Weber's "theories" are actually "conceptual schemes and descriptions of 'historical types'" (Jack P. Gibbs, *Sociological Theory Construction* [Hinsdale, IL, 1972], 16). There may well be a relation between Weber's well-known suspicion of the base/superstructure metaphor and the fact that his great achievements seem much more descriptive and interpretive than explanatory.

14 The worst offender may well be economics: see Donald [Deirdre] N. McCloskey, *The Rhetoric of Economics* (Madison, WI, 1985), 7−8. But a survey in May 1987 by J. Morgan Kousser suggested that an "informal positivism" remained prevalent at that time

234 ‡ NOTES TO PAGES 85–87

among historians: see J. Morgan Kousser, "The State of Social Science History in the Late 1980s," *Historical Methods: A Journal of Quantitative and Interdisciplinary History* 22 (1989): 12–20, at 14.

15 Carl G. Hempel and Paul Oppenheim, "Studies in the Logic of Explanation," in *Theories of Explanation,* ed. Joseph C. Pitt (Oxford, 1988), 9 (on the importance of this article, see Ronald N. Giere, *Explaining Science: A Cognitive Approach* [Chicago, 1988], 28); Ernest Nagel, *The Structure of Science: Problems in the Logic of Scientific Explanation* (New York, 1961), 4; Social Science Research Council, Committee on Historiography, *The Social Sciences in Historical Study: A Report* [Bulletin 64] (New York, 1954), 86.

16 Wilhelm Windelband, "History and Natural Science," with an introductory note by Guy Oakes, *History and Theory* 19 (1980): 169–85, esp. 175. See also Georg G. Iggers, *The German Conception of History: The National Tradition of Historical Thought from Herder to the Present,* rev. ed. (Middletown. CT, 1983), 147–52.

17 See William O. Aydelotte's classic paper, "Notes on the Problem of Historical Generalization," in *Generalization in the Writing of History: A Report of the Committee on Historical Analysis,* by the Social Science Research Council, ed. Louis Gottschalk (Chicago, 1963), 145–77 (reprinted in Aydelotte, *Quantification in History* [Reading, MA, 1971], 66–100).

18 Hempel, "Function of General Laws in History," 344–45.

19 Aristotle, *Metaphysics,* trans. W. D. Ross, 982a20–25, in *Complete Works,* ed. Jonathan Barnes, 2 vols. (Princeton, NJ., 1984), 2: 1554; on the "commitment to the generic" in Greek thought generally, see Windelband, "History and Natural Science," 181. Note that there is another side to Aristotle, exemplified in the *Ethics* and *Rhetoric,* where he emphasizes specific cases (of moral judgment or of persuasion); see Stephen Toulmin, "The Recovery of Practical Philosophy," *American Scholar* 57 (1988): 337–52, at 339 and throughout. But modernism looks with disfavor on the ethical-rhetorical strand.

20 Aristotle, *Poetics,* trans. Ingram Bywater, 1451a6–7, in *Rhetoric" and "Poetics,"* with an introduction by Edward P. J. Corbett (New York, 1984), 235.

21 On the idea of universality in modern thought, see, among others, Max Weber, "A Critique of Eduard Meyer's Methodological Views," in *The Methodology of the Social Sciences,* trans. Edward A. Shils and Henry A. Finch (Glencoe, IL, 1949), 163, n. 30; Stanley Rosen, *Hermeneutics as Politics* (New York, 1987), esp. 45, 95; and Richard W. Miller, *Fact and Method: Explanation, Confirmation and Reality in the Natural and the Social Sciences* (Princeton, NJ, 1987), 3–4.

22 Hempel, "Function of General Laws in History," 356; cf. Thomas S. Kuhn, *The Structure of Scientific Revolutions,* 2nd ed. (Chicago, 1970).

23 Richard J. Bernstein, *Beyond Objectivism and Relativism: Science, Hermeneutics, and Praxis* (Philadelphia, 1983), 135–36.

24 See Robert Finlay, "The Refashioning of Martin Guerre," and Natalie Zemon Davis, "'On the Lame,'" *American Historical Review* 93 (1988): 553–71 and 572–603, for an exchange that highlights the need to attend carefully to the different voices and attitudes that manifest themselves in a work of history. Even historians aware of the hermeneutic tradition often resist the self-reflexive implications. Note, for example, Quentin

Skinner's apparently unwitting reduction of post- to pre-Heideggerian hermeneutics in "Hermeneutics and the Role of History," *New Literary History* 7 (1975–76): 209–32.

25 The same complexities arise from the further argumentative or justificatory question: What grounds do we, author and audience, have for believing that such-and-such was the case, and that such-and-such is why it was the case? I leave the justificatory question aside here, but see chapter 6 for a case study in this topic.

26 Lawrence Stone, "The Revival of Narrative: Reflections on a New Old History," *Past and Present* 85 (November 1979): 3–24, at 3–4 (reprinted in Stone, *The Past and the Present* [Boston, 1981], 74–96, at 74). Of course, even "the collective and statistical" does not rise to universality. "The collective and statistical" is itself "particular and specific." For *what* is being collected? Of *what* are the statistics gathered?

27 Francois Furet, "From Narrative History to Problem-Oriented History," in his *In the Workshop of History,* trans. Jonathan Mandelbaum (Chicago, 1982), 54–67, at 56.

28 Furet, "From Narrative History to Problem-Oriented History," 57. See also the introduction to *In the Workshop of History,* 8: "Traditional historical explanation obeys the logic of narrative. What comes first explains what follows."

29 On the unattainability of the goal, see Furet, "From Narrative History to Problem-Oriented History," 66–67. On the connection of Furet's preference for problem-oriented history to the prejudice for universality, see *In the Workshop of History,* 6–7 (the new history becomes, as a "form of knowledge," applicable to any and all societies). See also "From Narrative History to Problem-Oriented History," 60, where historical demography's transformation of "historical individuals" into "interchangeable and measurable units" also points to the presence of the universalizability criterion in Furet's thinking.

30 Roland Barthes, "Introduction to the Structural Analysis of Narratives," in *Image, Music, Text,* trans. Stephen Heath (New York, 1977), 79–124, at 94. Barthes's statement is an intensification of Aristotle's assertion in the *Poetics* 1452a20 that "there is a great difference between a thing happening *propter hoc* and *post hoc.*" Among historians, in addition to Furet, who have linked narrative to a *post hoc, ergo propter hoc* logic are Lawrence Stone, *Social Change and Revolution in England, 1540–1640* (London, 1965), xxii, and Charles Tilly, *As Sociology Meets History* (New York, 1981), 90.

31 Morton White, *Foundations of Historical Knowledge* (New York, 1965), esp. 4, 14, 222–25, at 4, 223, 222.

32 As Seymour Chatman observes, "it requires special effort for films to assert a property or relation"; see "What Novels Can Do That Films Can't (and Vice Versa)," in *On Narrative,* ed. W. J. T. Mitchell (Chicago, 1981), 117–36, at 124.

33 An example: "He had been chain-smoking for weeks. His gums bled at the slightest pressure from the tip of his tongue" (J. D. Salinger, "For Esmé—With Love and Squalor," in *Nine Stories* [New York, 1983], 104). Note how unstable the "confusion" is: the addition of an explicit "because" ("Because he had been chain-smoking for weeks") would be enough to destroy it. On the distinction between paratactic style, which does not spell out ranks and relations, and hypotactic style, which does, see Richard A. Lanham, *Analyzing Prose* (New York, 1983), 33–52.

34 Nathan Rosenberg and L. E. Birdzell Jr., *How the West Grew Rich: The Economic Transformation of the Industrial World* (New York, 1986), 125.

35 After completing my analysis of Furet's contention that historical narrative follows the logic of *post hoc, ergo propter hoc,* I discovered that the philosopher W. H. Dray also attacks Furet on this and other points. See W. H. Dray, "Narrative versus Analysis in History," in *Rationality, Relativism and the Human Sciences,* ed. J. Margolis, M. Krausz, and R. M. Burian (Dordrecht, 1986), 23–42, at 26ff.

36 Arthur Stinchcombe, *Theoretical Methods in Social History* (New York, 1978), 13. Of course, as is evident from my argument so far, tone is only part of the story. The explanatory bias derives more broadly from a certain view of science, from certain metaphors, from a concern in social science with pragmatic aims, and perhaps from other influences as well. Historiography does not exist in isolation from other intellectual and social practices.

37 Fernand Braudel, "La double Faillite 'coloniale' de la France aux XVe et XVIe siècles" (review of Charles-André Julien, *Les Voyages de découverte et les premiers établissements, XVe et XVIe siècles* [Paris, 1948]), *Annales: Économies, Sociétés, Civilisations* 4 (1949): 451–56, at 452, 453.

38 J. H. Hexter, "Fernand Braudel and the *Monde Braudellien* . . . ," *Journal of Modern History,* 44 (1972): 480–539, at 535–38, discussing Edmund S. Morgan, "The Labor Problem at Jamestown, 1607–18," *American Historical Review* 76 (1971): 595–611.

39 Hexter, "Fernand Braudel and the *Monde Braudellien,*" 535.

40 Fernand Braudel, *The Mediterranean and the Mediterranean World in the Age of Philip II,* trans. Siân Reynolds, 2 vols. (New York, 1966), 1: 77, 82, 83. Subsequent page references are given in parentheses in the text.

41 A terminological note: Braudel frequently uses the word *explanation* in the broad sense of "to elucidate." He explicitly connects *expliquer* (explain) and *éclairer* (elucidate, clarify, illuminate) in *La Méditerranée et le monde méditerranéen à l'époque de Philippe II* (Paris, 1949), 307 (this passage, in the introduction to part 2, is omitted from the second edition of Braudel's work and hence does not appear in the English translation, which translates that edition.). Accordingly, when Braudel uses *explanation,* he does not always mean it in the sense in which the term is taken here. For one instance where it seems to mean "elucidation" without specific reference to causes, see *The Mediterranean and the Mediterranean World,* preface to the first edition: "This book is divided into three parts, each of which is itself an essay in general explanation" (1:20).

42 As Samuel Kinser pointed out in "*Annaliste* Paradigm? The Geohistorical Structuralism of Fernand Braudel," *American Historical Review* 86 (1981): 63–105, at 83 and elsewhere, Braudel changed his characterization of the first and second of these levels between the first and second editions of *The Mediterranean and the Mediterranean World.* Nor is Braudel necessarily committed to *three* levels in history. But these inconsistencies do not affect my point here.

43 Hexter, "Fernand Braudel and the *Monde Braudellien,*" 535.

44 Claude Lefort, "Histoire et sociologie dans l'oeuvre de Fernand Braudel," *Cahiers internationaux de sociologie* 13 (1952): 122–31, at 124. On the non-connection of levels in

Braudel, see also Bernard Bailyn, "Braudel's Geohistory—A Reconsideration," *Journal of Economic History* 11 (1951): 277–82, at 279; and H. Stuart Hughes, *The Obstructed Path: French Social Thought in the Years of Desperation* (New York, 1968), 58–59.

45 Hexter, "Fernand Braudel and the *Monde Braudellien*," 530; see also 511.

46 Hans Kellner, "Disorderly Conduct: Braudel's Mediterranean Satire (A Review of Reviews)," *History and Theory,* 18 (1979): 197–222, reprinted in Kellner, *Language and Historical Representation: Getting the Story Crooked* (Madison, WI, 1989), 153–87; Northrop Frye, *Anatomy of Criticism: Four Essays* (Princeton, NJ, 1957), 308–14.

47 Frye, *Anatomy of Criticism,* 309, 310.

48 Stone, "Revival of Narrative," 3.

49 Aristotle, *Poetics,* 1450a2–17, in Aristotle, *"Rhetoric" and "Poetics,"* 231. Even though, strictly speaking, the *Poetics* is concerned with drama, not narrative (representation on stage, not storytelling), its influence far transcends such distinctions.

50 Henry James, "The Art of Fiction" (1884, 1888), in *The Art of Criticism: Henry James on the Theory and the Practice of Fiction,* ed. William Veeder and Susan M. Griffin (Chicago, 1986), 174.

51 See Seymour Chatman, *Story and Discourse: Narrative Structure in Fiction and Film* (Ithaca, NY, 1978), 19, 32, 34, 44–45, 96–145. My formula is an expansion of one proposed by Wallace Martin, *Recent Theories of Narrative* (Ithaca, NY, 1986), 117–18, which in turn is inspired by a rather different formula in Gérard Genette, *Narrative Discourse: An Essay in Method,* trans. Jane E. Lewin (Ithaca, NY, 1972), 166.

52 Lucien Febvre, "Un livre qui grandit: *La Méditerranée et le monde méditerranéen à l'époque de Philippe II,*" *Revue historique* 203 (1950): 218; Hexter, "Fernand Braudel and the *Monde Braudellien* . . . ," 518–19; Kinser, *"Annaliste* Paradigm?" 67–68.

53 For a brief account, with relevant references, see Peter Novick, *That Noble Dream: The "Objectivity Question" and the American Historical Profession* (New York, 1988), 622–23. For a defense of "traditional history" against a largely non-narrative social history, see Gertrude Himmelfarb, *The New History and the Old: Critical Essays and Reappraisals* (Cambridge, MA, 1987).

54 For a subtle meditation on the relation of past and present from a historian's point of view, see J. H. Hexter, "The Historian and His Day," in Hexter, *Reappraisals in History* (Evanston, IL, 1961), 1–13. Hexter emphasizes that there is no single present perspective from which the historian writes. He also emphasizes the professional historian's capacity for immersion in the documents of the past.

55 Edward McNall Burns, Robert E. Lerner, and Standish Meacham, *Western Civilizations: Their History and Their Culture,* 10th ed. (New York, 1984), 927–28.

56 Ibid., 674.

57 There is a large literature on this matter. For a useful survey, see Peter Menzies, "Counterfactual Theories of Causation," in the online *Stanford Encyclopedia of Philosophy* at http://plato.stanford.edu/entries/causation-counterfactual (accessed April 2006). For a wide-ranging collection of articles, see John Collins, Ned Hall, and L. A. Paul, eds., *Causation and Counterfactuals* (Cambridge, MA, 2004). For an account that links counterfactual reasoning to historical research, see Jon Elster's "Counterfactuals and the

New Economic History," in his *Logic and Society: Contradictions and Possible Worlds* (Chichester, UK, 1978), 175–221). See also chapter 7 in this volume.

58 Karl Marx, *The Class Struggles in France: 1848 to 1850,* in *Surveys from Exile,* ed. David Fernbach, vol. 2 of Karl Marx, *Political Writings* (New York 1974), 35–142.

59 For example, see the exchange between James Smith Allen and Dominick LaCapra, *American Historical Review* 88 (1983): 805–7, relating to LaCapra's *Madame Bovary on Trial* (Ithaca, NY, 1982).

60 Furet, "Introduction," *In the Workshop of History,* 13–20. The final quotation is from the version of Furet's introduction that appeared as "Beyond the *Annales,*" *Journal of Modern History* 55 (1983): 389–410, at 409; in the book, Furet recommended "an intellectualist history that builds" (20).

61 Furet, *In the Workshop of History,* 16.

62 Braudel, *Mediterranean World,* 1 : 17.

63 Bailyn, "Braudel's Geohistory," 279, 281.

64 Cf. Bernard Bailyn, "The Challenge of Modern Historiography," *American Historical Review* 87 (1982): 1–24, at 5: "Braudel's *Méditerranée* . . . should be known . . . for its ahistorical structure, which drains the life out of history. For the essence and drama of history lie precisely in the active and continuous relationship between the *underlying conditions* [my italics] that set the boundaries of human existence and the everyday problems with which people consciously struggle." How does Bailyn *know* that this is where the "essence and drama" of history lie? And how does he know which conditions are the *underlying* ones? *Vos preuves, M. Bailyn?*

65 Alexis de Tocqueville, *The Old Regime and the Revolution,* ed. François Furet and Françoise Mélonio, trans. Alan S. Kahan, 2 vols. (Chicago, 1998–2001), 1 : 83; Tocqueville, *L'ancien Régime et la Révolution,* ed. Françoise Mélonio (Paris, 1988), 87.

66 See his assertion in the preface to *The Old Régime and the Revolution* that "the object of this book" was to understand "why this great revolution . . . broke out in France" and "why it was so natural a product of the society it was going to destroy" (85). See also the final chapter, "How the Revolution Came Naturally from What Preceded It" (241–47).

67 Tocqueville, *Old Régime,* 86 I write in the margins of Furet's highly intelligent and illuminating analysis of Tocqueville's book; see François Furet, "De Tocqueville and the Problem of the French Revolution," in *Interpreting the French Revolution,* trans. Elborg Forster (Cambridge, 1981), 132–63. Characteristically, Furet tended to conflate the interpretive dimension of Tocqueville's project, concerned with "the meaning of his own time," with the task of articulating "explanatory theory" (132–33; see also 159–60). But as I have argued, these are two distinct (although related) projects.

68 John E. Toews, "Intellectual History after the Linguistic Turn: The Autonomy of Meaning and the Irreducibility of Experience," *American Historical Review* 92 (1987): 879–907, at 882; cf. David Harlan, "Intellectual History and the Return of Literature," *American Historical Review* 94 (1989): 581–609.

69 See, again, Herodotus, *The History,* trans. David Grene (Chicago, 1987); and Thucydides, *History of the Peloponnesian War,* trans. Rex Warner (Harmondsworth, UK,

1954). Herodotus was more inclined to become caught up in the sheer fascination of what he tells, while Thucydides leaned more toward explaining things. But both historians did both.

FIVE: *Objectivity for Historians*

1   Geoff Eley, "Between Social History and Cultural Studies: Interdisciplinarity and the Practice of the Historian at the End of the Twentieth Century," in *Historians and Social Value,* ed. Joep Leerssen and Ann Rigney (Amsterdam, 2000), 93–109, at 94, 95, 97, 99, 104; Thomas Haskell, "Objectivity: Perspective as Problem and Solution" (review of *Historians and Social Values*), *History and Theory* 43 (2004): 341–59, at 358.

2   Friedrich Nietzsche, *On the Genealogy of Morality: A Polemic,* trans. Maudemarie Clark and Alan J. Swensen (Indianapolis, 1998), "Third Treatise," sec. 12, p. 85.

3   See especially Geoff Eley, *Forging Democracy: The History of the Left in Europe, 1850–2000* (New York, 2000), a substantial academic study that, at the same time, highlights its author's political commitments throughout.

4   Eley, "Between Social History and Cultural Studies," 95, 108.

5   Michel Foucault, *Histoire de la folie à l'âge classique* (Paris, 1961); a very abridged translation was published as *Madness and Civilization: A History of Insanity in the Age of Reason,* trans. Richard Howard (New York, 1965); *Discipline and Punish: Birth of the Prison,* trans. Alan Sheridan (New York, 1977; orig. pub. in French, 1975); and *The Archaeology of Knowledge,* trans. Alan Sheridan (New York, 1972; orig. pub. in French, 1969). On Foucauldian anti-method, and his notion of history as offering useful fictions, see Allan Megill, *Prophets of Extremity: Nietzsche, Heidegger, Foucault, Derrida* (Berkeley, 1985), 227–47.

6   Foucault, *Madness and Civilization,* 8–13; Foucault, *Discipline and Punish,* 3–6; Michel Foucault, *The Order of Things: An Archaeology of the Human Sciences* (New York, 1970; orig. pub. in French, 1966), xv, 387.

7   Thomas Haskell, "Objectivity Is Not Neutrality: Rhetoric versus Practice in Peter Novick's *That Noble Dream,*" in *Objectivity Is Not Neutrality: Explanatory Schemes in History* (Baltimore, 1998), 145–73.

8   Haskell, "Objectivity Is Not Neutrality," 149–51.

9   A Google search on 1 March 2005 for "Fox News Channel" and "'fair and balanced'" yielded 57,700 hits. For one commentary on the Fox News Channel's objectivity-claim, see Seth Ackerman, "The Most Biased Name in News: Fox News Channel's Extraordinary Right-wing Tilt," *Extra!,* July/August 2001, at the "Fairness and Accuracy in Reporting" Web site, http://www.fair.org/index.php?page=1067. Ackerman faults Fox less for being biased than for failing to acknowledge what he regards as its undeniable presentation of "a conservative point of view."

10 Nietzsche, *Genealogy,* "Third Treatise," sec. 12, p. 85.

11 Richard Rorty, "Solidarity or Objectivity?" and "Science as Solidarity," in *Objectivity, Relativism, and Truth,* vol. 1 of *Philosophical Papers* (Cambridge, 1991), 21–34, 35–45.

12 Haskell, "Objectivity: Perspective as Problem and Solution," 359.

13 Perez Zagorin, "Francis Bacon's Concept of Objectivity and the Idols of the Mind," *British Journal for the History of Science* 34 (2001): 379–93, at 379; Heather Douglas, "The Irreducible Complexity of Objectivity," *Synthese* 138 (January–February 2004): 453–73, at 453.

14 Richard Rorty, *Philosophy and the Mirror of Nature* (Princeton, NJ, 1979), 334.

15 On objectivity in Kant, see Henry E. Allison, *Kant's Transcendental Idealism: An Interpretation and Defense* (New Haven, CT, 1983), chap. 7, "Objective Validity and Objective Reality: The Transcendental Deduction of the Categories," 133–72. On natural philosophers' conceptions of objectivity before Kant, see Lorraine Daston, "Baconian Facts, Academic Civility, and the Prehistory of Objectivity," in *Rethinking Objectivity,* ed. Allan Megill (Durham, NC, 1994), 37–63; and Peter Dear, "From Truth to Disinterestedness in the Seventeenth Century," *Social Studies of Science* 22 (1992): 619–31. On changing conceptions of objectivity in nineteenth-century science, see Lorraine Daston, "Objectivity and the Escape from Perspective," *Social Studies of Science* 22 (1992): 597–618; and Lorraine Daston and Peter Galison, "The Image of Objectivity," *Representations* no. 40 (Fall 1992): 81–128.

16 Daston, "Objectivity and the Escape from Perspective," 597–98; Daston, "Baconian Facts." There is, however, some affinity between the scholastic sense of *objective* and dialectical objectivity, since both involve the constituting of mental objects.

17 R. W. Newell notes all four dimensions in *Objectivity, Empiricism and Truth* (London, 1986), chap. 2, "The Two Faces of Objectivity," 16–38.

18 Thomas Nagel, *The View from Nowhere* (New York, 1986), 3–5, 18, and throughout.

19 The phrase "absolute conception of reality" is Bernard Williams's; see his *Descartes: The Project of Pure Enquiry* (Atlantic Highlands, NJ, 1978), esp. 64–67. Francis Bacon's discussion of the four "idols of the mind" is the *locus classicus* for his conception of objectivity; see his *The New Organon,* ed. Lisa Jardine and Michael Silverthorne (Cambridge, 2000), bk. 1, "Aphorisms . . . ," nos. 39–44, pp. 40–42.

20 *The Philosopher's Index* (Bowling Green, OH, 1967–) offers a convenient way of tracing the rise and fall of philosophical terms. I counted instances of the use of the terms *objectivity* and *realism* in the titles of articles indexed in *The Philosopher's Index* over the period 1967–90. Taking the years 1969–71 and 1988–90 as comparison points, use of the term *objectivity* increased 2.8 times between the beginning and the end of the period, whereas use of the term *realism* increased 7.2 times.

21 Hilary Putnam, *Realism with a Human Face,* ed. James Conant (Cambridge, MA, 1990), especially "The Craving for Objectivity" and "Objectivity and the Science/Ethics Distinction," 120–31, 163–78; Richard Rorty, *Objectivity, Relativism, and Truth,* especially "Solidarity or Objectivity?" and "Science as Solidarity," 21–34, 35–45. See also Helen E. Longino, *Science as Social Knowledge: Values and Objectivity in Scientific Inquiry* (Princeton, NJ, 1990), especially chap. 4, "Values and Objectivity," 62–82, which brought philosophical discussions of objectivity to bear on gender issues in science— and vice versa. Note, finally, Richard J. Bernstein, *Beyond Objectivism and Relativism: Science, Hermeneutics, and Praxis* (Philadelphia, 1983).

22 Thomas S. Kuhn, *The Structure of Scientific Revolutions,* 2nd ed. (Chicago, 1970), esp. 103, 109–10, 122, 149–52. I confine myself here to Kuhn's view as articulated in the original (1962) edition, leaving aside the restatements appended to the revised edition.

23 I condense and adapt the definition of epistemological relativism offered by Harvey Siegel, *Relativism Refuted: A Critique of Contemporary Epistemological Relativism* (Dordrecht, 1987), 6.

24 For one characteristic (and influential) early critique along this line, see Israel Scheffler, *Science and Subjectivity* (Indianapolis, 1967), esp. 15–19 and 74–89. *The Philosopher's Index* gives ready access to much of the discussion.

25 Bryan Wilson, ed., *Rationality* (Oxford, 1970); Martin Hollis and Steven Lukes, eds., *Rationality and Relativism* (Oxford, 1982). See also Stuart C. Brown, ed., *Objectivity and Cultural Divergence,* Royal Institute of Philosophy Lecture Series 17, supplement to *Philosophy* 1984 (Cambridge, 1984); and Clifford Geertz, "Anti Anti-Relativism," *American Anthropologist* 86 (1984): 263–78, reprinted in Michael Krausz, ed., *Relativism: Interpretation and Confrontation* (Notre Dame, IN, 1989), 12–34.

26 Steven Lukes, "Relativism in Its Place," in Hollis and Lukes, eds., *Rationality and Relativism,* 261–305, at 261.

27 To refer to this view as "disciplinary" objectivity is in some respects a misnomer, since the convergence at which disciplinary objectivity aims is at least as likely to be situated at more specific levels than at that of the discipline. Still, with its double meaning, *disciplinary* seems the most appropriate term here, although one might alternatively have called it "consensual" objectivity.

28 See, in particular, Longino, *Science as Social Knowledge,* especially the section entitled "Objectivity by Degrees," 76–81. In its emphasis on scientific practice (66–68 and elsewhere), Longino's account has affinities with the dialectical sense of objectivity, discussed below.

29 Evelyn Fox Keller, *A Feeling for the Organism: The Life and Work of Barbara McClintock* (New York, 1983), 197–98. For an account of a paradigmatic art connoisseur, see Ernest Samuels, *Bernard Berenson: The Making of a Connoisseur* (Cambridge, MA, 1979).

30 Kuhn, *Structure of Scientific Revolutions,* 164–65.

31 This claim could be documented and perhaps in part corrected through bibliometric and citational research. In the absence of such an investigation, let the sales figures serve as a stand-in: from its original publication on 5 March 1962 through January 1991, *The Structure of Scientific Revolutions* sold 768,774 copies, an astounding figure for an academic work. It hit 22,500 copies in 1968–69 and in the early 1970s was selling at 40,000 copies per year (around 1990 it was still selling about 25,000 copies per year). I owe these data to Douglas Mitchell, history and sociology editor, University of Chicago Press.

32 David Hollinger, "T. S. Kuhn's Theory of Science and Its Implications for History," in *In the American Province: Studies in the History and Historiography of Ideas* (Bloomington, IN, 1985), 105–29, at 115 (orig. pub. in *American Historical Review* 78 [1973]: 370–93). For a survey of sociologists' (mis)use of Kuhn in the same period, see Douglas Lee Eckberg and Lester Hill Jr., "The Paradigm Concept and Sociology: A Critical

Review," in *Paradigms and Revolutions: Appraisals and Applications of Thomas Kuhn's Philosophy of Science,* ed. Gary Gutting (Notre Dame, IN, 1980), 117–36.

33 Hollinger, "T. S. Kuhn's Theory of Science," 116–17.

34 Kuhn, *Structure of Scientific Revolutions,* 162.

35 Hollinger, "T. S. Kuhn's Theory of Science," 116. For an account of historians' relation to objectivity, see Peter Novick, *That Noble Dream: The "Objectivity Question" and the American Historical Profession* (New York, 1988).

36 Hollinger, "T. S. Kuhn's Theory of Science," 117–19. To be sure, we must distinguish between *paradigm* construed as a generally accepted *viewpoint,* and *paradigm* construed as an instance of scientific *practice* that has turned out to be spectacularly successful at solving problems. If one emphasizes the latter meaning, Kuhn's affinities are with dialectical objectivity. But this side of Kuhn's account was of less interest to social scientists than was his emphasis on consensus.

37 Dear, "From Truth to Disinterestedness," 619–21.

38 Daston and Galison, "The Image of Objectivity," 82.

39 The phrase "aperspectival objectivity" is Lorraine Daston's, from "Objectivity and the Escape from Perspective." Additionally, Dear has suggested that the negative character of [absolute] objectivity is nicely captured by Karl Popper's well-known notion of a "Third World" of objective intelligibility, since (*a*) the Popperian "Third World" is hard to locate in any specific way and (*b*) the ideas in it "do not have to be, in any useful sense, *true.*" In Dear's words, "objective knowledge is characterized by its not being subjective. . . . Truth is beside the point" (Dear, "From Truth to Disinterestedness," 619–20; Karl Popper, *Objective Knowledge: An Evolutionary Approach* [Oxford, 1972], chap. 4, "On the Theory of Objective Mind," 153–90).

40 Friedrich Nietzsche, *On the Uses and Disadvantages of History for Life,* sec. 6, in his *Untimely Meditations,* trans. R. J. Hollingdale, with an introduction by J. P. Stern (Cambridge, 1983), 89–95, at 93.

41 Martin Heidegger, *Being and Time,* trans. Joan Stambaugh (Albany, NY , 1996), §15, pp. 62–67 (German pagination).

42 See, for example, Maurice Merleau-Ponty, *Phenomenology of Perception,* trans. Colin Smith (London, 1962); John Dewey and Arthur F. Bentley, *Knowing and the Known* (Boston, 1949); Michael Polanyi, *Personal Knowledge: Towards a Post-Critical Philosophy* (Chicago, 1958); and Marjorie Grene, *The Knower and the Known* (New York, 1966).

43 Johannes Fabian, "Ethnographic Objectivity Revisited: From Rigor to Vigor," in Megill, ed., *Rethinking Objectivity,* 81–108; orig. pub. in *Annals of Scholarship* 8 (1991): 301–28.

44 Johannes Fabian, "History, Language and Anthropology," *Philosophy of the Social Sciences* 1 (1971): 19–47.

45 Fabian, "Ethnographic Objectivity Revisited," 81. Fabian found this view in J. A. Barnes's *Three Styles in the Study of Kinship* (Berkeley, 1971).

46 Barnes thought so in *Three Styles,* xxi. Of course, we can recognize here a commitment to "disciplinary" objectivity.

47 Fabian, "History, Language and Anthropology," 19. Another way of putting this is to say that Kuhn held that any pursuit of scientific knowledge that is worthy of the name must aim to follow *one* set of methods and arrive at *one* view.

48 Fabian, "History, Language and Anthropology," 25, 27

49 Fabian uses the term *objectification* in a neutral, epistemological sense, rather than pejoratively, as many authors do, to designate the turning of "persons" into "mere objects."

50 Fabian, "History, Language and Anthropology," 22.

51 For further discussion, see Grene, *Knower and the Known,* chap. 5, "Kant: The Knower as Agent," 120–56.

52 See Theodore M. Porter, "Objectivity as Standardization: The Rhetoric of Impersonality in Measurement, Statistics, and Cost-Benefit Analysis," in Megill, ed., *Rethinking Objectivity,* 197–237; and, on a larger scale, Theodore M. Porter, *Trust in Numbers: The Pursuit of Objectivity in Science and Public Life* (Princeton, NJ, 1995).

53 Some of their work is cited in note 15, above. See also Peter Dear, *"Totius in verba:* Rhetoric and Authority in the Early Royal Society," *Isis* 76 (1985): 145–61, and "Jesuit Mathematical Science and the Reconstitution of Experience in the Early Seventeenth Century," *Studies in the History and Philosophy of Science* 18 (1987): 133–75. The sociologists of science Steven Shapin and Simon Schaffer have also contributed to this historical study; see their *Leviathan and the Air-Pump: Hobbes, Boyle, and the Experimental Life* (Princeton, NJ, 1985); and Steven Shapin, "The House of Experiment in Seventeenth-Century England," *Isis* 79 (1988): 373–404, among other publications. See also the chapter, "Numbers Rule the World," in Gerd Gigerenzer . . . [et al.], *The Empire of Chance: How Probability Changed Science and Everyday Life* (New York, 1989), 235–70 (although *The Empire of Chance* was written collaboratively by a team of authors, this chapter was largely the work of Lorraine Daston and Theodore M. Porter). That objectivity became an object of historical investigation—that is, a *historical* object—in the late twentieth century is itself interesting, a measure of the problematization of objectivity in our time. This fact of course illustrates a "dialectical" point.

54 Daston and Galison, "The Image of Objectivity"; Daston, "Objectivity and the Escape from Perspective" (the quotation is from "The Image of Objectivity," 98).

SIX: *A Case Study in Historical Epistemology*

1 Johann Gustav Droysen, *Outline of the Principles of History,* trans. E. Benjamin Andrews (Boston, 1893), 4–5.

2 Michael J. MacLean, "Johann Gustav Droysen and the Development of Historical Hermeneutics," *History and Theory* 21 (1982): 347–65, at 354–56; quotations at 355.

3 Eugene A. Foster, M. A. Jobling, and P. G. Taylor, "Jefferson Fathered Slave's Last Child," *Nature,* 5 November 1998, 27–28. Foster reports with "99 percent certainty" that Eston Hemings was fathered by Jefferson or by one of Jefferson's direct male-line relatives. It should be noted that the title of the article, which was chosen by editors at *Nature* rather than by the authors themselves, is not accurate. The DNA evidence *alone*

proved only that a male in the Jefferson line fathered someone in the Eston Hemings line—not that Thomas Jefferson himself fathered Eston Hemings. All the same, the best explanation of the currently available data seems to be the one that takes Jefferson to be the father of Eston.

4   A brief bibliography is in order. Scot A. French and Edward L. Ayers offer a useful account of some earlier discussions of the Hemings–Jefferson matter (and of Jefferson's relation to race and slavery generally) in their essay, "The Strange Career of Thomas Jefferson: Race and Slavery in American Memory, 1943–1993," in *Jeffersonian Legacies,* ed Peter S. Onuf (Charlottesville, VA, 1993), 418–56. Annette Gordon-Reed, *Thomas Jefferson and Sally Hemings: An American Controversy* (Charlottesville, VA, 1997) surveys the evidence concerning the alleged Hemings–Jefferson relationship as it was known prior to the publication of the DNA results. (This work is subsequently cited by page number parenthetically in the text.) The papers from the March 1999 conference held to discuss the wider implications of the putative Hemings–Jefferson relationship were published in Jan Ellen Lewis and Peter S. Onuf, eds., *Sally Hemings and Thomas Jefferson: History, Memory, and Civic Culture* (Charlottesville, VA, 1999). The Onuf-Lewis volume also includes some source texts: Callender's allegations of 1 September and 20 October 1802; an 1873 memoir by Madison Hemings, one of Sally's children; Jefferson's musings on the character of blacks (from his 1787 book, *Notes on the State of Virginia*); and his speculations, in a letter of 1815, as to how much dilution by white "blood" is needed to produce a white person from mulatto ancestors. The matter was discussed again in "Forum: Thomas Jefferson and Sally Hemings Redux," *William and Mary Quarterly,* 3rd series, 57 (2000): 121–210, with contributions by Jan Lewis, Joseph J. Ellis, Lucia Stanton, Peter S. Onuf, Annette Gordon-Reed, Andrew Burstein, and Fraser D. Neiman. Much material concerning Jefferson and Hemings is to be found on the Thomas Jefferson Foundation Web site: http://www.monticello.org, search "Thomas Jefferson and Sally Hemings."

There is a Web site, edited by Eyler Robert Coates Sr., that is largely devoted to disputing the claim that there was sexual relationship between Hemings and Jefferson: see http://www.geocities.com/Athens/7842/jeffersonians/index.html. Coates has also edited a similarly inflected book, *The Jefferson–Hemings Myth: An American Travesty* (Charlottesville, VA: Thomas Jefferson Heritage Society, 2001). Google searches will no doubt bring to light further discussions of this subject.

For a contemporaneous account of the 1999 conference, see Nicholas Wade, "Taking New Measurements for Jefferson's Pedestal," *New York Times,* Sunday, 7 March 1999, sec. 1.

5   Quoted from appendix B of Lewis and Onuf, eds., *Sally Hemings and Thomas Jefferson,* 259.

6   Joshua D. Rothman, "James Callender and Social Knowledge of Interracial Sex in Antebellum Virginia," in Lewis and Onuf, eds., *Sally Hemings and Thomas Jefferson,* 98, 103, 104. See also the restatements of this thesis in Rothman's *Notorious in the Neighborhood: Sex and Families across the Color Line in Virginia, 1787–1861* (Charlottesville,

VA, 2003), 32–33, 35. We subsequently cite these contributions parenthetically in the text as Rothman 1999 and Rothman 2003.

7   The process of researching and writing the present chapter was as follows: Shepard and Megill were skeptical of Rothman's argument. Rothman was kind enough to make the written version of his paper available to Shepard, who then produced several drafts of a paper clarifying the epistemological issues involved in Rothman's claims. Megill, Honenberger, and Shepard then revised Shepard's paper for inclusion in the present book.

8   See Gilbert Harman, "Inference to the Best Explanation," *Philosophical Review* 74 (1965): 88–95. One might also think of inference to the best explanation as equivalent to reasoning from the effect to the most likely cause.

A further terminological note: the meaning attributed to the word *explanation,* as it is used in the "inference to the best explanation" literature, is not *completely* congruent with the use of *explanation* to denote answers to the question "Why?" (taking this question in the sense of "What caused it?"). The use of *explanation* to denote an answer to a "Why?" question is of course highlighted in chapter 4. In our terminology, "inference to the best explanation" would better have been called "inference to the best account," since, although some of the inferred "best explanations" are explanations in our sense, some are better regarded as descriptions or interpretations. However, there is no need for every philosopher to use words in exactly the same way in every instance, as long as the intended meaning is clear in each particular instance. (For our terminology and the distinctions that support it, see chapter 4, at note 4 and throughout. Also, we return to *explanation* below.)

9   Darwin makes this clear in his conclusion; see Darwin, *The Origin of Species by Means of Natural Selection or The Preservation of Favoured Races in the Struggle for Life,* ed. J. W. Burrow (New York, 1985), 455–58.

10 Quoted by Paul Thagard, "The Best Explanation: Criteria for Theory Choice," *Journal of Philosophy* 75 (1978): 76–92.

11 Quoted by K. T. Fann, *Peirce's Theory of Abduction* (The Hague, 1970), 8. The quotation is taken from an unpublished work of 1903. Since, from all appearances, Fann offers a reasonably reliable account of Peirce's theory of abduction, we use it as a stand-in for Peirce's own writings on the subject. This is acceptable in the present context, since we are not engaged in the historiographic task of reconstructing Peirce's thought but are instead using some ideas that Peirce put forward to illuminate issues of speculation and evidence in history.

12 Quoted by Fann, *Peirce's Theory of Abduction,* 21, from Charles Sanders Peirce, *Collected Papers,* ed. Charles Hartshorne and Paul Weiss (6 vols.; Cambridge, Mass., 1931–35), vol. 2, section 2.625. Peirce returned often to Napoleon and abduction: see also vol. 5, section 589 for another wording.

13 John R. Josephson, with Michael C. Tanner, "Conceptual Analysis of Abduction," in John R. and Susan G. Josephson, eds., *Abductive Inference: Computation, Philosophy, Technology* (New York, 1994), 5.

14 See, again, chapter 4, where explanation is clearly distinguished from the other three tasks of historical research and writing. That chapter's emphasis on the causal sense of explanation is hardly new, for it can be found throughout the positivist philosophical tradition. See, most famously, Carl G. Hempel, "The Function of General Laws in History" (1942), in Patrick Gardiner, ed. *Theories of History* (Glencoe, Ill., 1965), 344–56. (In regard to the discussion of states of mind, below, note that chapter 4 also allows intentions to count as causes—that is, we could legitimately regard Caesar's alleged intention, namely, to challenge the Senate, as causing his crossing of the Rubicon.)

15 In this respect the present chapter has a close affinity with Aviezer Tucker's *Our Knowledge of the Past: A Philosophy of Historiography* (New York, 2004), since Tucker, too, is concerned with looking at how historians "explain the evidence." Like us, Tucker was influenced by the "inference to the best explanation" literature. Tucker's book was published only after we had completed all substantive work on the present chapter. His emphasis on "explaining" the evidence came to us as a welcome confirmation of the fruitfulness of this approach.

   From a more conventional perspective, it may seem odd to see historians as "explaining" the evidence, rather than as offering an account of past events and existents. But from an epistemological point of view, these two operations are equivalent. When historians offer justified accounts of the past, they are also making sense of, even "explaining" (in the strict sense of the term), the evidence. Similarly, in offering his theory of "descent with modification," Darwin "explained" (or gave an account of, or made sense of) the extant evidence relevant to his field—most notably, fossils that diverged in form from living organisms. Lavoisier did exactly the same thing with respect to his field of chemistry.

16 Thagard, "The Best Explanation." Thagard's accounts of consilience and simplicity are much more rigorous than ours. Here, as elsewhere in the present book, philosophical arguments are pursued only as far as is needed to illuminate historical research and writing—and no further.

17 We assume for the sake of this point that the memoir recorded and published in 1873 by S. F. Wetmore is in fact an accurate account of Madison Hemings's statements. See Gordon-Reed's important discussion of this issue, as well as of the issue of Madison Hemings's own veracity, in *An American Controversy,* 7–58. It should be noted that in the course of her discussion Gordon-Reed employs, without naming it as such, the important distinction between "top-down" and "bottom-up" explanations that we introduce below. Some further references to Gordon-Reed's book are given in parentheses in our text.

18 To avoid entangling the reader in needless complexities, we have not considered the inferences necessary to establish our knowledge of Madison's circumstances—such as the inference that the best explanation of the Farm Book entry is that Harriet Hemings was in fact born, and so on.

19 R. G. Collingwood, *An Essay on Metaphysics* (Oxford, 1940), 285–95, describes action-oriented and state-of-mind causes in greater detail than we do here. Note, however,

that Collingwood's typology is not adequate for making sense of all instances of historical explanation. In fact, here as elsewhere, Collingwood is biased toward forms of history that focus on action, especially the actions of individuals (as in traditional forms of political history, where the emphasis is on the actions of statesmen and politicians), or of states treated as if they were individuals. In articulating his theory of historiography (in the "Epilegomena" of his *Idea of History*), Collingwood paid next to no attention to forms of history that focus on describing and interpreting structures, meanings, mentalities, and the like—forms of history that are deployed in such works as Jacob Burckhardt's *Civilization of the Renaissance in Italy* (1860) and Fernand Braudel's then unfinished *The Mediterranean and the Mediterranean World in the Age of Philip II* (1949). See R. G. Collingwood, *The Idea of History* (1946), rev. edition with *Lectures 1926–1928,* ed. W. J. van der Dussen (Oxford, 1993), 231–315.

20   In everyday speech we often make a direct causal connection between circumstances and action: "He robbed the store because he was poor." As we hope we show in this chapter, this can be a dangerously elliptical type of argument.

21   After formulating our top-down/bottom-up distinction, we discovered that C. Behan McCullagh uses an identical terminology in McCullagh, *The Logic of History: Putting Postmodernism in Perspective* (London, 2004), 119.

22   On these points, see especially Gordon-Reed's list of "Items Supporting the Assertion that Thomas Jefferson Fathered Sally Hemings's Children," in Gordon-Reed, *An American Controversy,* 211–23. The "coinciding" point is elaborated on in Fraser D. Neiman, "Coincidence or Causal Connection? The Relationship between Thomas Jefferson's Visits to Monticello and Sally Hemings's Conceptions," *William and Mary Quarterly,* 3rd Series, Vol. 57 (2000): 198–210. On statistical grounds Neiman finds something like a 99% probability that Jefferson was the father of Hemings's children. Unfortunately, Neiman fails to state clearly all of the prior suppositions under which his analysis operates, such as the assumption that all Hemings's children had the same father. Thus we cannot take seriously the high statistical probability that he finds. Still, it is striking, and may well be significant, that the six recorded children of Sally Hemings were all conceived when Jefferson was present at Monticello.

23   There is no documentary record of the existence of such a child in Jefferson's papers, although the names and birth dates of five children born to Sally Hemings do appear in those papers. Further, Sally Hemings's known son, Madison Hemings, did not mention a surviving older sibling named Tom in his 1873 memoir (note 4, above), although he did mention a child born to his mother around 1790 who died in infancy (and who thus could not have been "President Tom").

Among the descendants of an African-American, Thomas C. Woodson (ca. 1790–ca. 1879), there was a long family tradition holding that their ancestor had been born of Sally Hemings and Thomas Jefferson, and when this tradition became known outside the family it was widely assumed that Thomas Woodson was none other than the "President Tom" referred to by Callender. But there is absolutely no documentary record linking Thomas Woodson to Monticello, and the DNA tests on Woodson's descendants showed that they did not carry the Jefferson Y chromosome. These two facts, taken together, appear to torpedo completely the claim that Thomas Woodson was Jefferson's son.

    On Woodson and "President Tom," see Rothman 1999, 102–3; Gordon-Reed, 67–75; and Thomas Jefferson Foundation, "Report of the Research Committee on Thomas Jefferson and Sally Hemings" (January 2000), appendix K, "Assessment of Thomas C. Woodson Connection to Sally Hemings," http://www.monticello.org/plantation/hemingscontro/appendixk.html.

24 Note that a full listing of hypotheses would include many more, for example: "The residents of Albemarle County desired to follow the norms of their society." We have listed only those of Rothman's hypotheses that are controversial and therefore important to determining the best explanation of the evidence.

25 Those at Monticello are an exception, of course. Both slaves and nonslaves at Monticello knew who Sally Hemings was. But we reiterate that both the degree to which they knew about her (alleged) relationship with Jefferson and the degree to which they spoke with other slaves or Jefferson's neighbors have not been established.

26 See below for a detailed description of the circumstantial associations.

27 The texts of 1 September and 20 October 1802 are transcribed in appendix B, pp. 259–61, of Lewis and Onuf, eds., *Sally Hemings and Thomas Jefferson,* the volume where Rothman 1999 of course appears.

28 See *Port Folio* (Philadelphia), 10 July 1802, 216. Rothman cites lines from the poem at Rothman, 1999, 94–95, 110, n. 23, and Rothman 2003, 30, 252, n. 44. The following is the allegedly crucial passage:

> For make all like, let blackee nab
>
> De white womans . . . dat be de track!
>
> Den Quashee [the black man's name] de white wife will hab,
>
> And massa Jef. shall hab de black.

29 See also, on Callender's campaign of allegations against Jefferson, Michael Durey, *With the Hammer of Truth: James Thomson Callender and America's Early National Heroes* (Charlottesville, VA, 1990), 157–63.

    Rothman 2003, 30, also draws attention to a few lines in the *Washington Federalist* in September 1801. The issue of September 14, 1801 (p. 2, col. 1), refers to "a man very high in office" (Jefferson was president at the time) who "has a number of yellow children, and . . . is addicted to golden affections." The report also refers to a "Mr. J." The report suggests that "if they [these allegations] are false and malicious they ought to be contradicted." (We are indebted to Lucia Stanton for giving us a transcription of these lines, and to Mary Hackett for finding and transcribing them).

30 Durey, *With the Hammer of Truth,* 157–60; Gordon-Reed, 62.

31 He referred to Hemings as a "slut as common as the pavement," with "fifteen or thirty" different lovers "of all colours." Her children were a "yellow litter," and Jefferson sent for her from "the kitchen, or perhaps the pigstye" (Rothman 1999, 95, Rothman 2003, 30; and Gordon-Reed, 61–62).

32 To be fair, however, we may consider the fact that satirists often have the freedom to mock politicians for the rumors that surround them, whereas journalists generally

consider themselves bound to speak only of things for which they believe they have adequate verification. Thus it would not be surprising if the *Port Folio* doggerel were written in response to certain *rumors* of miscegenation. However, such rumors would not count as *knowledge* on the part of the doggerel's author, nor do we as historians have strong enough grounds for claiming to be certain of the precise intent of the author of the doggerel.

33 Edmund Gettier, "Is Justified True Belief Knowledge?" *Analysis* 33, no. 6 (June 1963): 121–23. For example, I might say to another person, "Either you have a penny in your pocket or you are flying to Barcelona tomorrow." Suppose I *thought* I saw the person put a penny in his pocket, but it was in fact a dime. Yet, although the person has no pennies, quite by accident it turns out that he is flying to Barcelona tomorrow, where, unbeknown to me, his rich uncle lives. In such a case my statement to the person turns out to be true. But I cannot be said to have *known* that it was true—it only turned out to be true by accident.

34 See the following passage at Rothman 1999, 103, which we here offer in abbreviated form (emphases added): "That Callender got so much of the [Jefferson–Hemings] story right is a remarkable testimony to the extent and transmission of *social knowledge* about private interracial sexual affairs in Virginia communities. . . . Not everyone in Albemarle had *information* for Callender because not everyone had *heard the story,* but we should not doubt Callender's assertion that nearly everyone in the county he mentioned it to *believed* it. Given what Virginians already *knew* about sex and slavery in their society in general, they did not need to have heard the details of Jefferson's relationship with Hemings to *believe* that he *might* be sexually involved with her." Had Rothman thought seriously about what he says in this passage, he might well have gotten beyond its confusions. Knowing that something is a quite common social practice is not equivalent to knowing what such and such a particular person did, nor does *hearing a story* equate to *having information*.

35 Callender was angry with Jefferson because the president would give him neither compensation nor respect for his suffering and imprisonment under the Federalist Alien and Sedition Acts (Rothman 1999, 92–94; also Durey, *With the Hammer of Truth,* 143–57).

SEVEN: Counterfactual History

1 Niall Ferguson, ed., *Virtual History: Alternatives and Counterfactuals* (New York, 1999).
2 Various reviewers discuss *Axis & Allies* at http://www.amazon.com: search "Axis & Allies Board Game."
3 Richard J. Evans, "Telling It Like It Wasn't," *Historically Speaking,* 5, no. 4 (March 2004): 11–14 (reprinted from *BBC History Magazine,* December 2002).
4 R. G. Collingwood, *The Idea of History, with Lectures 1926–1928,* ed. W. J. van der Dussen, rev. ed. (Oxford, 1994), 214.
5 See ibid., 246, where Collingwood declares that "there is only one historical world," and rejects the relevance of "imaginary worlds" to history. Ferguson correctly notes

in his introduction to *Virtual History* that the "idealist position" of Collingwood and Oakeshott "ruled out counterfactualism" (50).

6 Carl G. Hempel, "The Function of General Laws in History," in *Theories of History,* ed. Patrick Gardiner (Glencoe, IL, 1960), 344–56.

7 R. G. Collingwood, *An Essay on Metaphysics* (Oxford, 1940), 296–312, especially 304ff. The car-accident example appears in Collingwood's chapter on "Causation in Practical Natural Science," not in his (disappointing) chapter, "Causation in History."

EIGHT: *Fragmentation and the Future of Historiography*

1 Peter Novick, *That Noble Dream: The "Objectivity Question" and the American Historical Profession* (New York, 1988).

2 James T. Kloppenberg, "Objectivity and Historicism: A Century of American Historical Writing," *American Historical Review* 94 (1989): 1011–30, at 1029.

3 Novick agrees with this interpretation in "My Correct Views on Everything," *American Historical Review* 96 (1991): 699–703, at 702. (In this piece Novick responds to four commentaries on *That Noble Dream* presented at the American Historical Association annual meeting in December 1990. One of the commentaries was an earlier version of this chapter.)

4 Let me correct a possible misreading here: *all* paradigms are ungrounded. If they weren't ungrounded, they wouldn't be paradigms.

5 Kathryn Kish Sklar, "A Call for Comparisons," *American Historical Review* 95 (1990): 1109–14, at 1111.

6 The term *paradigm* needs, in any case, to be viewed with suspicion. All too often it is defined in a loose way that invites a usually unnoticed slippage from the notion of an "explanatory theory" to the much broader notion of an "interpretive perspective." The term goes back to Thomas S. Kuhn, *The Structure of Scientific Revolutions* (Chicago, 1962). Margaret Masterman, in "The Nature of a Paradigm," in *Criticism and the Growth of Knowledge,* ed. Imre Lakatos and Alan Musgrave (Cambridge, 1970), 59–89, pointed out the multiple meanings of the term in Kuhn's study. Not surprisingly, in returning to these matters in the second edition of *Structure,* Kuhn substituted for "paradigm" the more variegated notion of a "disciplinary matrix"; see Thomas S. Kuhn, "Postface—1969," in *The Structure of Scientific Revolutions,* 2nd ed. (Chicago, 1970), 174–210, esp. 183–87.

7 Daniel J. Walkowitz, "The Making of a Feminine Professional Identity: Social Workers in the 1920s," *American Historical Review* 95 (1990): 1051–75, at 1074.

8 This response is most closely associated with Thomas Haskell. See especially Thomas Haskell, "Professionalism *versus* Capitalism: R. H. Tawney, Emile Durkheim, and C. S. Peirce on the Disinterestedness of Professional Communities," in *The Authority of Experts,* ed. Thomas Haskell (Bloomington, IN, 1984), 180–225, especially 207. Essentially the same position is to be found in the writings of a number of other historians who likewise appeal to a disciplinary consensus that would overcome conflicting

positions. For example, see David Hollinger, "T. S. Kuhn's Theory of Science and Its Implications for History," in *Paradigms and Revolutions: Appraisals and Applications of Thomas Kuhn's Philosophy of Science,* ed. Gary Gutting (Notre Dame, IN, 1980), 195–222, at 212–13, 216–17; and Kloppenberg, "Objectivity and Historicism," 1029. For Novick's run-through of these issues, see *That Noble Dream,* 570–72, and 625–28.

9   Lest I be misunderstood, I am not arguing for interdisciplinary unification. The more that one knows, through the experience of having argued with them, about how the practitioners of other disciplines argue, the less likely one is to think that the different modes of argument are compatible enough for any one person to practice them at the same time. Thus I am deeply suspicious of notions of convergence between different disciplines.

10   Novick, *That Noble Dream,* 361–411.

11   Ibid., 496.

12   I borrow the term *grand narrative* from Jean-François Lyotard, although the definition offered here is my own. See Jean-François Lyotard, *The Postmodern Condition: A Report on Knowledge,* trans. Geoff Bennington and Brian Massumi (Minneapolis, 1984), xxiii–xxiv and throughout. See also chapter 9 in this volume.

13   Leonard Krieger, *Ranke: The Meaning of History* (Chicago, 1977), 100–104, 130–31, 160–63, 226–28, and throughout.

NINE: *"Grand Narrative" and the Discipline of History*

1   Peter Burke, "Overture: The New History, Its Past and Its Future," in *New Perspectives on Historical Writing,* ed. Peter Burke (Cambridge, 1991), 1.

2   See, for example, the discussion entitled "History the Great Catch-All," in Jacques Barzun and Henry F. Graff, *The Modern Researcher,* 4th ed. (San Diego, 1985), 8–13.

3   With reservations and modifications, I borrow the term *grand narrative* from Jean-François Lyotard, *The Postmodern Condition: A Report on Knowledge,* trans. Geoff Bennington and Brian Massumi (Minneapolis, 1984), xxiii (orig. pub. in French, 1979). The term might well be taken as designating an all-embracing story, arranged in beginning-middle-end order—the most obvious meaning, given Aristotle's influence on our view of narrative. Without necessarily rejecting the Aristotelian view (for it does fit part of the history recounted here), I intend the term more broadly, to designate a vision of coherence—in particular, a vision of coherence broad enough to support objectivity claims.

4   For example, see Horst Walter Blanke's *Historiographiegeschichte als Historik* (Stuttgart-Bad Cannstatt, 1991), an 809-page account of the German tradition of historiography after 1750. Other surveys of (parts of) the history of modern Western historiography—each on a different scale and with different emphases—include Georg G. Iggers's *Historiography in the Twentieth Century: From Scientific Objectivity to the Postmodern Challenge* (Hanover, NH, 1997), which is in part a polemic against so-called postmodernism; Michael Bentley's *Modern Historiography: An Introduction* (London,

1999), a careful and very condensed survey; and Donald R. Kelley's *Fortunes of History: Historical Inquiry from Herder to Huizinga* (New Haven, CT, 2003), an erudite defense of history as an attempt both to awaken and to assuage our curiosity about the past.

5   Thomas Bender, "Wholes and Parts: The Need for Synthesis in American History," *Journal of American History* 73 (1986): 120–36; responses by Nell Irvin Painter, Richard Wightman Fox, and Roy Rosenzweig, and a response to the responses by Bender were published as "A Round Table: Synthesis in American History," *Journal of American History* 74 (1987): 107–30. See also, on the question of a "master narrative" for German history, Michael Geyer and Konrad H. Jarausch, "The Future of the German Past: Transatlantic Reflections for the 1990s," *Central European History* 22 (1989): 229–59, esp. 234–47.

6   For an account operating on a more specific level, that of American historiography, see Peter Novick, *That Noble Dream: The "Objectivity Question" and the American Historical Profession* (New York, 1988). The present chapter might be read as an attempt to lay out a deep background to Novick's book. See also chapter 8, which is, in part, the "for dummies" version of this chapter.

7   The most striking exception, among historians whom we might otherwise be tempted to designate as professional, is the Swiss historian Jacob Burckhardt. At the beginning of *The Civilization of the Renaissance in Italy* (1860), Burckhardt wrote that "the same studies that have served for this work might easily, in other hands, not only receive a wholly different treatment and application, *but lead also to essentially different conclusions*" (my emphasis). In making this amazing claim to (a kind of) non-authoritativeness, Burckhardt was doing nothing less than denying the notion of History. By the same token, he was allowing the "dialectical" or "object-oriented" objectivity of the art connoisseur to triumph over "absolute" objectivity (see chapter 5 for a discussion of these categories); Jacob Burckhardt, *The Civilization of the Renaissance in Italy*, trans. S. G. C. Middlemore, with a new introduction by Peter Burke and notes by Peter Murray (Harmondsworth, UK, 1990), part 1, "Introduction," 19.

8   Koselleck makes this argument in "Die Entstehung des Kollektivsingulars" (section 5.1.a. of "Geschichte") in *Geschichtliche Grundbegriffe: Historisches Lexikon zur politisch-sozialen Sprache in Deutschland,* ed. Otto Brunner, Werner Conze, and Reinhart Koselleck, 8 vols. (Stuttgart, 1972–1997), 2:647–53, quotation at 652. For a brief account in English, see Reinhart Koselleck, "On the Disposability of History, in *Futures Past: On the Semantics of Historical Time,* trans. Keith Tribe (Cambridge, MA, 1985), 198–212, at 200–202 (cf. note 28, below). Koselleck develops a point made by his teacher Karl Löwith, who contrasted the "substantive singular" character of the German *die Geschichte* with the lack of any equivalent term in Greek (Karl Löwith, "Mensch und Geschichte" (1960), in *Der Mensch inmitten der Geschichte: Philosophische Bilanz des 20. Jahrhunderts,* ed. Bernd Lutz [Stuttgart, 1990], 228).

9   Robert F. Berkhofer Jr., "The Challenge of Poetics to (Normal) Historical Practice," in *The Rhetoric of Interpretation and the Interpretation of Rhetoric,* ed. Paul Hernadi (Durham, NC, 1989), 188–89. How does one get from a concern with context to the notion that there is finally only a *single* context? In practice, it is an easy passage from the

observation that a work of history is "contextually rich" to the conclusion that "every meaningful precinct, person, or decision has been accounted for and integrated" by the story that it tells; see Michael Kammen, "Historical Knowledge and Understanding," in *Selvages and Biases: The Fabric of History in American Culture* (Ithaca, NY, 1987), 37.

10 Louis O. Mink, "Narrative Form as a Cognitive Instrument," in *Historical Understanding*, by Louis O. Mink, ed. Brian Fay, Eugene O. Golob, and Richard T. Vann (Ithaca, NY, 1987), 194–95.

11 Leonard Krieger, *Time's Reasons: Philosophies of History Old and New* (Chicago, 1989), xi and throughout. Krieger's commitment to "the traditional discipline of history" led him into some polemical misreading when he turned to the historiography of the 1960s and 1970s (see especially ix–xii and 1–6), but this is no denial of the larger merits of the book. See also Leonard Krieger, *Ranke: The Meaning of History* (Chicago, 1977), where a similar argument is advanced, although in a less general form.

12 Krieger, *Time's Reasons*, 170.

13 The standard account of universal history in the early modern period is Adalbert Klempt, *Die Säkularisierung der universalhistorischen Auffassung im 16. und 17. Jahrhundert: Zum Wandel des Geschichtsdenkens im 16. und 17. Jahrhundert*, Göttinger Bausteine zur Geschichtswissenschaft, vol. 31 (Göttingen, 1960). See also the discussion entitled "Universal History: A Troubled Tradition" in Ernst Breisach, *Historiography: Ancient, Medieval, and Modern* (Chicago, 1983), 177–85. In the late twentieth century, universal history was revived in a very different, but still quasi-theological context: see Francis Fukuyama, *The End of History and the Last Man* (New York, 1992), especially chap. 5, "An Idea for a Universal History," 55–70.

14 Immanuel Kant, "Idea for a Universal History from a Cosmopolitan Point of View," trans. H. B. Nisbet, and "An Old Question Raised Again: Is the Human Race Constantly Progressing?" trans. H. B. Nisbet, in *Political Writings*, ed. Hans Reiss (Cambridge, 1991), 41–53, and 177–90.

15 Kant, "Idea for a Universal History," 41, 51–53.

16 Ibid., 53.

17 Kant, "An Old Question Raised Again," 180, 181.

18 Ibid., 182. On Kant's attitude toward the French Revolution, see Leonard Krieger, *The German Idea of Freedom* (Boston, 1957), 104–5.

19 For the most detailed statement of this view, see G. W. F. Hegel, *The Philosophy of History*, trans. J. Sibree (New York, 1956). For an abbreviated presentation, see the end of Hegel's *Elements of the Philosophy of Right*, ed. Allan W. Wood, trans. H. B. Nisbet (Cambridge, 1991), §§341–60, pp. 372–80 ("World History"). In Hegel the theological underpinnings of grand narrative are particularly evident; note his famous assertion that "the History of the World . . . is the true *Theodicaea*, the justification of God in History" (*Philosophy of History*, 457). On the role of "Christian theology of history" in Hegel, see Laurence Dickey, *Hegel: Religion, Economics, and the Politics of Spirit, 1770–1807* (Cambridge, 1987), 149.

20 Friedrich von Schiller, "Was heisst und zu welchem Ende studiert man Universalgeschichte?" in *Über das Studium der Geschichte,* ed. Wolfgang Hardtwig (Munich, 1990),

18–36, at 27, available in English as "The Nature and Value of Universal History: An Inaugural Lecture [1789]," *History and Theory* 11 (1972): 321–334, at 327.

21 Mink notes this in "Narrative Form," 189.

22 See Johann Gottfried Herder, "A. L. Schlözers Vorstellung seiner Universal-Historie," in *Sämmtliche Werke,* ed. Bernhard Suphan, 33 vols. (Berlin, 1877–1913), 5:436–40, at 438; and August Wilhelm von Schlözer, *Vorstellung seiner Universal-Historie,* 2 vols. (Göttingen, 1772, 1773), vol. 2, "Vorbericht," as cited in Reill, *The German Enlightenment and the Rise of Historicism,* 47, 232–33, n. 59.

23 See Ranke's excursus, entitled by his editors "Die Universalgeschichtsschreibung seit dem 16 Jahrhundert," appended to the introduction to his course of Summer Semester 1848 ["Erster Teil der Weltgeschichte oder Geschichte der alten Welt"], in *Aus Werk und Nachlass,* by Leopold von Ranke, ed. Walther Peter Fuchs and Theodor Schieder, 4 vols. (Vienna, 1964–75), vol. 4, *Vorlesungseinleitungen,* ed. Volker Dotterweich and Walther Peter Fuchs, 208–10.

24 Krieger establishes this in great detail: see his *Ranke,* 103, 107, 112–15, 124, 151–52, and elsewhere. For documentation of Ranke's concern with universal history, see the entries for "Universalgeschichte, -Historie," in the *Sachregister* of Ranke, *Aus Werk und Nachlass,* 4.

25 Leopold von Ranke, [*Die Notwendigkeit universalgeschichtlicher Betrachtung*], in Ranke, *Aus Werk und Nachlass,* 4:296–98, at 297–98; trans. Wilma A. Iggers as "The Role of the Particular and the General in the Study of Universal History (A Manuscript of the 1860s)," in *The Theory and Practice of History,* by Leopold von Ranke, ed. Georg G. Iggers and Konrad von Moltke, with new translations by Wilma A. Iggers and Konrad von Moltke (New York, 1983), 57–59, at 58–59.

26 Leopold von Ranke, "Neuere Geschichte seit dem Anfang des 17. Jahrhunderts (28. Oktober 1867– 10. März 1868)," [Einleitung], in Ranke, *Aus Werk und Nachlass,* 4:411–32, at 411. As Krieger rightly noted, "repeatedly, [Ranke] insisted that the historian's success in perceiving the objective coherence of universal history was only a matter of time" (*Ranke,* 103).

27 Leopold von Ranke, "Idee der Universalhistorie" [lecture script of 1831–32], in Ranke, *Aus Werk und Nachlass,* 4:72–89, at 74–75; trans., in part, by Wilma A. Iggers as "On the Character of Historical Science (A Manuscript of the 1830s)," in Ranke, *The Theory and Practice of History,* 36.

28 Reinhart Koselleck has argued that the emergence of the term *history (die Geschichte)* as an objectless "collective singular" dates from the late eighteenth century: "Only from around 1780 can one talk of 'history in general,' 'history in and for itself,' and 'history pure and simple,'" as distinguished from the history of X and the history of Y (Reinhart Koselleck, "On the Disposability of History," in *Futures Past* [note 8, above], 200). We might speculate that the growing dominance in the nineteenth century of the "collective singular" notion of history compensated for the deferral to the future of the telling of the grand narrative noted here. When the grand narrative is seen as (re)tellable now, there is no need to insist semantically on History's unity. The situation changed, however, when the telling of the grand narrative was deferred.

29 Ranke, "Idee der Universalhistorie," 82–83; see Ranke, "On the Character of Histori-
    cal Science," 44.

30 Leopold Ranke to Heinrich Ranke, letter of March 1820, in Leopold von Ranke, *Das
    Briefwerk,* ed. Walther Peter Fuchs (Hamburg, 1949), 18 (translation from Krieger,
    Ranke, 361, n. 13).

31 J. B. Bury, "The Science of History," in *The Varieties of History from Voltaire to the
    Present,* ed. Fritz Stern, 2nd ed. (New York, 1972), 219.

32 Ibid., 217, quoting Thomas Arnold, *Lectures on Modern History* (New York, 1874), 46.

33 Krieger, *Ranke,* 242.

34 Bury, "Science of History," 210.

35 Compare this with Ranke's famous statement: "I wished to extinguish, as it were, my
    self, and only to recount those things that powerful forces allowed to appear, that over
    the course of centuries emerged and became strong with and through one another";
    see Leopold von Ranke, *Englische Geschichte, vornehmlich im Siebzehnten Jahrhundert,*
    Fünftes Buch, "Einleitung," in *Sämmtliche Werke,* 2 Aufl. (Leipzig, 1867–1890), 15 : 103.

36 Bury, "Science of History," 213, 216.

37 Ibid., 219.

38 Johann Gustav Droysen, *Outline of the Principles of History,* trans. E. Benjamin An-
    drews (Boston, 1893; translation of Droysen, *Grundriß der Historik,* 3rd ed., 1882), §81,
    p. 47. The *Outline* offers an encapsulated version of reflections that are presented at
    greater length in the posthumously published manuscript of his lectures: see Johann
    Gustav Droysen, *Historik,* ed. Peter Leyh, 3 vols. (Stuttgart, 1977 [vols. 2 and 3 are
    noted as forthcoming, but as of April 2006 this important work has not yet appeared]).
    The Leyh edition includes the text of the 1882 edition of the *Grundriß* (413–88).

39 Droysen, *Outline of the Principles of History,* appendix 2, "Art and Method," 118. Com-
    pare Droysen, *Historik,* 69: "The activities that our science concerns itself with . . . are
    only historical because we conceive of them as historical, not in themselves and objec-
    tively, but rather in and through our examination [*Betrachtung*]" (the passage comes
    from the manuscript of Droysen's lectures of 1857).

40 Hayden White, "Droysen's *Historik*: Historical Writing as a Bourgeois Science," in
    The Content of Form (Baltimore, 1987), 83–103, at 99. See also Jörn Rüsen, *Begriffene
    Geschichte: Genesis und Begründung der Geschichtstheorie J. G. Droysens* (Paderborn,
    Germany, 1969), 119.

41 Note Droysen's statement in the first part of *Outline of the Principles of History,* 6: "Ob-
    servation of the present teaches us how, from different points of view, every matter
    of fact is differently apprehended, described and connected with others; how every
    transaction in private as well as in public life receives explanations of the most various
    kinds. A man who judges carefully will find it difficult to gather out of the plenitude
    of utterances so different, even a moderately safe and permanent picture of what has
    been done and of what has been purposed." See also, on this theme, the manuscript of
    his 1857 lectures, *Historik,* 113–14, 236–38.

    But Droysen's recognition of interpretive multiplicity on a theoretical level did not
    mean that he accepted it in practice: both as a man and as a historian he was a deeply

committed Prussian nationalist. On this point, and on Droysen's "maverick" status in the German historical tradition more generally, see Michael J. MacLean, "Johann Gustav Droysen and the Development of Historical Hermeneutics," *History and Theory* 21 (1982): 347–65.

42 Ranke, "The Great Powers" (1833), trans. Hildegarde Hunt Von Laue, in Ranke, *The Theory and Practice of History* (note 25, above), 65–101, esp. 99–101. Here Ranke contended that "world history does not present such a chaotic tumult, warring, and planless succession of states and peoples as appear at first sight" (100). Ranke's discovery of a basic unity was aided by his insistence, endemic among nineteenth-century European intellectuals, on seeing *European* history as *world* history. On Ranke's universalism generally, see Krieger, "Elements of Early Historicism: Experience, Theory, and History in Ranke," *History and Theory* 14 (1975): 1–14, esp. 9–14. On Droysen's rejection of the concept of a European system of the great powers, see Georg G. Iggers, *The German Conception of History: The National Tradition of Historical Thought from Herder to the Present,* rev. ed. (Middletown, CT, 1983), 106–7.

43 See Droysen, *Outline of the Principles of History,* sec. 73, p. 44: "Even the narrow, the very narrowest of human relations, strivings, activities, etc., have a process, a history, and are for the persons involved, historical. So family histories, local histories, special histories. But over all these and such histories is *History.*"

44 Novick, in *That Noble Dream,* generally supports my claim that twentieth-century professional historians (at least, *American* professional historians) largely conformed to the third attitude. A substantial essay could be written on how this is so, but note the following points: (1) Novick established that insistence on autonomy was widespread in the historical profession (361–411). Insistence on autonomy is perhaps the most characteristic third-attitude position, since it implies that historians are in principle capable of arriving at a view of history untainted by irrelevant external influences, without requiring that they actually do so. (2) He established that historians had a widespread, but consistently thwarted, concern with "convergence" in historical interpretation (206–7, 320–21, 438, 457–8, 465 and passim). Desire for a single authoritative narrative, combined with its perpetual failure to appear, is definitive of the third attitude. (3) He established that fragmentation was widely seen as a bad thing (577–91 and passim). This suggests the view that a single authoritative narrative is a good thing, even if it can never be told. (4) He established the long-standing persistence of "the idea and ideal of 'objectivity'" (1), a notion that historians were perfectly willing to concede could never be realized. Again, grand narrative is relegated to an ideal level.

45 Consider H. G. Wells, *The Outline of History, Being a Plain History of Life and Mankind,* 2 vols. (1920; repr., New York, 1921), which emphatically does not conform to the view just noted (see especially Wells's chap. 41, "The Possible Unification of the World into One Community of Knowledge and Will," 2:579–89). In their embarrassed reaction to Wells, professional historians ever since the 1920s have demonstrated their conviction that this sort of thing *is just not done* in historiography.

46 Droysen, *Outline of the Principles of History,* §15, p. 15. See also Johann Gustav Droysen, *Vorlesung über das Zeitalter der Freiheitskriege,* 2 Aufl., 2 vols. (Gotha, 1886), 1:4: "Our

faith gives us the consolation that a divine hand bears us up, that it directs the fates of great and small. And the science of history has no higher task than to justify this faith: thereby is it science. It seeks and finds in that chaotic ocean [*wüsten Wellengang*] a direction, a goal, a plan." Rüsen, in *Begriffene Geschichte,* particularly stresses Droysen's commitment to a Hegelian grand narrative of freedom (126–30, and passim).

47 See Wilhelm Dilthey, *The Formation of the Historical World in the Human Sciences,* ed. Rudolf Makkreel and Frithjof Rodi (Princeton, NJ, 2002; orig. pub. in German, 1927); Michael Oakeshott, *Experience and Its Modes* (Cambridge, 1933), esp. 92–96; and Michael Oakeshott, "The Activity of Being an Historian," in *Rationalism in Politics and Other Essays* (New York, 1962), 137–67, esp. 166–67.

48 Collingwood's philosophy generally, and his theory of historiography in particular, raise many interesting theoretical and exegetical puzzles that I cannot consider here. Among many other discussions of Collingwood's work, see Louis O. Mink, *Mind, History, and Dialectic: The Philosophy of R. G. Collingwood* (Bloomington, IN, 1969); W. J. van der Dussen, *History as a Science: The Philosophy of R. G. Collingwood* (The Hague, 1981); and William H. Dray, *History as Re-enactment: R. G. Collingwood's Idea of History* (Oxford, 1995).

49 Much of the "Epilegomena" to *The Idea of History* is aimed at arguing out this point: see R. G. Collingwood, *The Idea of History,* rev. ed., with *Lectures 1926–1928,* ed. W. J. van der Dussen (Oxford, 1993), 205–334, esp. 266–302. For a condensed version of the argument, see R. G. Collingwood, *An Autobiography* (Oxford, 1939), chap. 10, "History as the Self-Knowledge of Mind," 107–19. In *The Idea of History* Collingwood notes the Kantian roots of his theory several times (60, 236, 240).

50 For some relevant passages, see Collingwood, *Idea of History,* 109, 136, 156.

51 Ibid., 210, 231.

52 Collingwood, *An Autobiography* (Oxford, 1939), 77. Subsequently cited in the text by page number.

53 In this chapter of *An Autobiography* Collingwood identified three R. G. Collingwoods, one of whom lived "as a professional thinker" (151), while the other two respectively believed in and agitated for the unity of theory and practice.

54 Historians who read Collingwood usually fail to attend to *An Autobiography*. Combined with their third-attitude prejudice for well-defined disciplinary boundaries, this may explain why Collingwood's denials of historiographic autonomy have so often been overlooked. For example, the methodology for the history of political thought associated with Quentin Skinner, J. G. A. Pocock, and several other historians was partly inspired by an "autonomist" reading of Collingwood; see Skinner, "Meaning and Understanding in the History of Ideas," *History and Theory* 8 (1969): 3–53. But when Pocock, for instance, wrote that intercourse between history and theory begets pseudo-history, so that, like owl and eagle, the two ought to "stay out of each other's flight-paths," and that, in another striking simile, they are like ships passing in the night that might exchange information, but are traveling on radically different courses, he articulated a position in sharp opposition to Collingwood's; see Pocock, "Political Theory, History, and Myth: A Salute to John Gunnell," *Annals of Scholarship* 1 (1980), 3–25, at 23, 24. It

is a standard hermeneutic observation that interpreters find in what they interpret only those things that they are ready to see; the observation also happens to be true.

55 Collingwood, *Idea of History,* 282–302.

56 Ibid., 247 (my emphasis), 246.

57 Schlözer, *Universal-Histoire* (note 22 above), vol. 2, "Vorbericht."

58 Ranke, [*Die Notwendigkeit universalgeschichtlicher Betrachtung*] (note 25, above), 297.

59 American Historical Association, *Program of the One Hundred Seventh Annual Meeting, December 27–30, 1992, Washington, D.C.* (Washington, DC, 1992), 40.

60 When I first worked out the above line of argument, in the early 1990s, I did not anticipate the extent to which a Foucauldian commitment to what we might call "paradigm-thinking" would become influential in parts of the historical discipline (see chap. 10, esp. the last two sections). The dogmatism of such commitments marks them as a reversion to attitude 1.

61 F. R. Ankersmit, "Historiography and Postmodernism," *History and Theory* 28 (1989): 137–53, at 137.

62 Ibid., 149. For Ankersmit's reflections on "the pull of the frame," and on "notation," see his "The Reality Effect in the Writing of History: The Dynamics of Historiographical Topology," in *History and Tropology: The Rise and Fall of Metaphor* (Berkeley, 1994), 125–61, at 150–53, 157. On the concept of notation, see Roland Barthes, "The Reality Effect," in *The Rustle of Language,* trans. Richard Howard (New York, 1984), 141–42.

63 See especially Jacques Derrida, "Différance," in *Margins of Philosophy,* trans. Alan Bass (Chicago, 1982), 1–27. The notion of originary difference is distinct from the radical textualism that is sometimes—but I think mostly mistakenly—inferred from Derrida's writings.

64 See Nicholas Rescher, *The Strife of Systems: An Essay on the Grounds and Implications of Philosophical Diversity* (Pittsburgh, 1985), xi, 276–77, and passim.

65 Mattel Dogan and Robert Pahre, *Creative Marginality: Innovation at the Intersections of Social Sciences* (Boulder, CO, 1990). See also Clifford Geertz, "Blurred Genres: The Refiguration of Social Thought," in *Local Knowledge: Further Essays in Interpretive Anthropology* (New York, 1983), 19–35. The term "blurred genres" is potentially misleading, however, since "blurring" might suggest lack of clarity and "genre" that the change is simply a matter of *literary* mode.

66 Perhaps the central text—if *central* is the appropriate term here—is Jean-François Lyotard, *The Postmodern Condition.* For a rather disappointing attempt to survey some of the many uses of the term, see Allan Megill, "What Does the Term 'Postmodern' Mean?" *Annals of Scholarship* 6 (1989): 129–51.

67 See, for example, the comments of a university administrator concerned with matters of tenure, promotion, and review: "We rarely recognize that 'multicultural' tensions can be found not only in matters of ethnicity and race, but also between and among our disciplines. . . . I have been struck by how utterly distinct the world views of faculty members from different disciplines can be." See Raymond J. Rodrigues, "Rethinking the Cultures of Disciplines," *Chronicle of Higher Education* (29 April 1992), B1–2.

68 See, among others, Sharon Traweek, "Border Crossings: Narrative Strategies in Science Studies and among Physicists in Tsukuba Science City, Japan," in *Science as*

Practice and Culture, ed. Andrew Pickering (Chicago, 1992), 429–65. Traweek's theme of marginality, or the condition of being *bachigai* (out of place), is much larger than the title of her article suggests; she offers an entire intellectual itinerary. On the epistemological benefits of concern with marginality, see Sandra Harding, "After the Neutrality Ideal: Science, Politics, and 'Strong Objectivity,'" *Social Research* 59 (1992): 567–87, esp. 577–85.

69 Fernand Braudel, *The Mediterranean and the Mediterranean World in the Age of Philip II,* trans. Siân Reynolds, 2 vols. (New York, 1973), 2:1238.

70 The vaunted third-attitude standard of autonomy also does this. For if the autonomy of history is a value, why not "the autonomy of intellectual history" (Leonard Krieger, "The Autonomy of Intellectual History," *Journal of the History of Ideas* 34 [1973]: 499–516)? And if the autonomy of intellectual history is a value, why not the autonomy of all other histories, such as early modern French or late-modern American?

71 Hans Kellner demonstrates this in "Disorderly Conduct: Braudel's Mediterranean Satire (A Review of Reviews)," *History and Theory,* 18 (1979): 197–222; repr. in Hans Kellner, *Language and Historical Representation: Getting the Story Crooked* (Madison, WI, 1989), 153–87.

72 Fernand Braudel, *Civilization and Capitalism: 15th–18th Century,* trans. Siân Reynolds, 3 vols. (New York, 1981–84).

73 Paul Veyne, *Writing History: Essay on Epistemology,* trans. Mina Moore-Rinvolucri (Middletown, CT, 1984), 26: "History with a capital H . . . does not exist. There only exist 'histories of . . .'" (this is, of course, a reversal of what Koselleck, whose notion of the "collective singular" use of the term *Geschichte* [history] was mentioned earlier in this chapter, saw as happening in the late eighteenth century). See also François Furet, whose move from "narrative history" to "problem-oriented history" was aimed at overcoming the present "proliferation of histories" (François Furet, "Introduction," in *In the Workshop of History,* trans. Jonathan Mandelbaum [Chicago, 1982], 13–20, at 16).

74 On women and the writing of history (both "professional" and "amateur"), see Bonnie G. Smith, *The Gender of History: Men, Women, and Historical Practice* (Cambridge, MA, 1998).

75 For the political science connection, see William O. Aydelotte, Allan G. Bogue, and Robert William Fogel, eds., *The Dimensions of Quantitative Research in History* (Princeton, NJ, 1972), "Introduction," esp. 3–14; for the anthropology connection, see Lynn Hunt, ed., *The New Cultural History* (Berkeley, 1989), "Introduction," esp. 1–12, and chap. 10 in this volume.

76 See Peter Novick, *That Noble Dream,* 591, n. 20, discussing the University of Chicago History Department: "At the University of Chicago . . . as of 1987 fully half of the members . . . also held appointments in other units of the university, and others were heavily involved in area studies programs without appointive powers. Yet for all this, the overwhelming majority would unhesitatingly and unequivocally identify themselves as historians, with other commitments relegated to a subordinate position."

77 Here the work of Lyotard is suggestive: see Lyotard, *The Postmodern Condition,* esp. sec. 13, "Postmodern Science as the Search for Instabilities," 53–60.

78 Consider the following announcement, from the University of Chicago: "As of July 1, [1984] the departments of biochemistry and molecular biology and the department of molecular genetics and cell biology replaced the departments of microbiology, biochemistry, and biophysics and theoretical biology" ("Biological Sciences Reorganization Reflects Current Areas of Study," *University of Chicago Magazine* 7 [Summer 1984]: 3–4, quoted in Novick, *That Noble Dream,* 585, n. 13). Common commitment to "scientific method" makes it easier to move the locations of what are thus perceived as mere *internal* boundaries. See also Gérard Noiriel, "Foucault and History: The Lessons of a Disillusion," *Journal of Modern History* 66 (1994): 547–68, at 567–68.

79 Thomas S. Kuhn, *The Structure of Scientific Revolutions,* 2nd ed. (Chicago, 1970).

80 Since the popularity (or not) of history books sometimes arises as an issue, it is perhaps worth pointing out that *The Structure of Scientific Revolutions* has sold far more copies than any "academic" work by a historian, and more copies than all but a few "popular" works of history. From its original publication on March 5, 1962, through January 1991 it sold 768,774 copies. Moreover, the citation data give clear evidence that many scholars intellectually active from the late 1960s through the 1980s actually *read* the book, at least in part.

81 Collingwood, *Idea of History,* 246. He of course omits to note that the historical world is accompanied by an infinite number of counterfactual ones. On this point, see chaps. 4, 6, and 7 in this volume. The point is interestingly developed in Geoffrey Hawthorn, *Plausible Worlds: Possibility and Understanding in History and the Social Sciences* (Cambridge, 1991), which also deals with issues of necessity and contingency in history.

82 See Hayden White, *Metahistory: The Historical Imagination in Nineteenth-Century Europe* (Baltimore, 1973); Stephen Bann, *The Clothing of Clio: A Study of the Representation of History in Nineteenth-Century Britain and France* (Cambridge, 1984); White, *The Content of the Form* (note 40, above); Kellner, *Language and Historical Representation* (note 71, above); Philippe Carrard, *Poetics of the New History: French Historical Discourse from Braudel to Chartier* (Baltimore, 1992); and, by F. R. Ankersmit, books and articles too numerous to mention, but see, for a short statement of his characteristic position, "The Use of Language in the Writing of History," in *Working with Language: A Multidisciplinary Consideration of Language Use in Work Contexts,* ed. Hywell Coleman (Berlin, 1989), 57–81.

83 See, for example, Jonathan D. Spence, *The Death of Woman Wang* (New York, 1978); Natalie Zemon Davis, *The Return of Martin Guerre* (Cambridge, MA, 1983), and *Fiction in the Archives: Pardon Tales and Their Tellers in Sixteenth-Century France* (Stanford, CA, 1987); Robert A. Rosenstone, *Mirror in the Shrine: American Encounters with Meiji Japan* (Cambridge, MA, 1988); and David Farber, *Chicago '68* (Chicago, 1988).

84 The obvious exemplar is Kuhn, *Structure of Scientific Revolutions.* Bringing aid to theory was a conscious intent on Kuhn's part; see "Introduction: A Role for History," 1–9, at 1: "History, if viewed as a repository for more than anecdote or chronology, could produce a decisive transformation in the image of science by which we are now possessed."

85 Herodotus, *The History,* trans. David Grene (Chicago, 1987), 1.32, pp. 47–48; 1.91, pp. 76–77; and 1.5, p. 35. These passages are worth reading and rereading for the insight they offer into Herodotus as historian. Only after the fall of Croesus, the King

of Lydia, does the full meaning of events happening five generations previously, and of various past oracles, become clear. Because the ups and downs of human affairs cannot be predicted, Herodotus relays to us the stories of both the great and the small, not presuming to know now how events will turn out later.

86 Ranke, "Neuere Geschichte seit dem Anfang des 17. Jahrhunderts (28. Oktober 1867—10. März 1868)," 412: "Geschichte beginnt mit Chronik und endigt mit Essay, das ist, in der Reflexion über die historischen Ereignisse, die dort besonders Anklang findet." Ranke appears to have used this passage as early as the summer semester 1853 offering of the course. Macaulay's actual words were "history begins in novel and ends in essay"; see Thomas Babington Macaulay, "History and Literature" (1828), excerpted in Stern, ed., *Varieties of History* (note 31, above), 73.

TEN: *Coherence and Incoherence in Historical Studies*

1 See Lynn Hunt, ed., *The New Cultural History* (Berkeley, 1989); and Victoria Bonnell and Lynn Hunt, eds., *Beyond the Cultural Turn: New Directions in the Study of Society and Culture* (Berkeley, 1999), especially the editors' introductions. The latter is no. 34 in a book series, "Studies on the History of Society and Culture," that Bonnell and Hunt edited. The list of titles preceding the title page of *Beyond the Cultural Turn* gives a good idea of the range and kind of topics embraced by the new cultural history.

2 *The Cambridge Modern History: An Account of Its Origins, Authorship, and Production* (Cambridge, 1907), quoted in E. H. Carr, *What Is History?* (New York, 1962), 3; J. B. Bury, "The Science of History," excerpted in *The Varieties of History from Voltaire to the Present,* ed. Fritz Stern, 2d ed. (New York, 1973), 209–23, esp. 219–20. Stern also excerpts Lord Acton's 1898 "Letter to the Contributors to the *Cambridge Modern History,*" which runs along a similar track (247–49).

3 Jean-François Lyotard, *The Postmodern Condition: A Report on Knowledge,* trans. Geoff Bennington and Brian Massumi (Minneapolis, 1984). For a discussion of how the notion of a grand narrative (often called "universal history") has shadowed the historical discipline from its beginning, see chapter 9 in this volume. The most erudite and searching discussion of the role of coherence in Western historical writing is Leonard Krieger, *Time's Reasons: Philosophies of History Old and New* (Chicago, 1989). The fulcrum of Krieger's book is the destabilization of historical coherence that occurred around the beginning of the twentieth century (107 and elsewhere); its motive is the need to engage with the academic and political radicalisms that Krieger held had entered into the discipline by the late 1970s and early 1980s.

4 On the need for written records, see G. W. F. Hegel, *Lectures on the Philosophy of World History: Introduction: Reason in History,* trans. H. B. Nisbet (Cambridge, 1975), 13; on the state as required for history, see G. W. F. Hegel, *The Philosophy of History,* trans. J. Sibree, ed. C. J. Friedrich (New York, 1956), 111.

5 For a brief account of the *Annales* school, see Peter Burke, *The French Historical Revolution: The* Annales *School, 1929–89* (Cambridge, 1990).

6 The title of the journal has varied slightly since its founding; it is now called *Annales: Histoire, Sciences Sociales.*

7 Although over fifty, Bloch volunteered for army service in 1939. In the midst of the French collapse, he escaped to England from Dunkirk and then returned home via Brittany. Later, in 1943, he became a Resistance leader in Lyon, for which activity he was shot by the Germans in June 1944. Between military service and the Resistance, his Jewish ancestry led to his exclusion from his teaching position under Vichy's anti-Semitic laws.

8 Ubiratan D'Ambrosio, "Febvre, Lucien," in *Encyclopedia of Historians and Historical Writing,* ed. Kelly Boyd, 2 vols. (London, 1999), 1 : 379.

9 On Berr, see William R. Keylor, *Academy and Community: The Foundation of the French Historical Profession* (Cambridge, MA, 1975), chap. 8, "Henri Berr and the 'Terrible Craving for Synthesis.'"

10 Fernand Braudel, *The Mediterranean and the Mediterranean World in the Age of Philip II,* trans. Siân Reynolds, 2 vols. (New York, 1973).

11 Braudel, *Mediterranean,* 1 : 14.

12 Two of the most insightful readers of *The Mediterranean and the Mediterranean World,* J. H. Hexter and Hans Kellner, emphasize the incoherence of the work: see J. H. Hexter, "Fernand Braudel and the *Monde braudellien* ...," *Journal of Modern History* 44 (1972): 480–539; and Hans Kellner, "Disorderly Conduct: Braudel's Mediterranean Satire (A Review of Reviews)," *History and Theory* 18 (1979): 197–222, repr. in Hans Kellner, *Language and Historical Representation: Getting the Story Crooked* (Madison, WI, 1989), 153–87.

13 Lucien Febvre, "De 1892 à 1933: Examen de conscience d'une histoire et d'un historien: Leçon d'ouverture au Collège de France, 13 décembre 1933," in *Combats pour l'histoire* (Paris, 1992), 16. Orig. pub. in 1953.

14 Lucien Febvre, "Contre l'esprit de spécialité: Une lettre de 1933," in Febvre, *Combats,* 104–6.

15 Febvre, "Leçon d'ouverture," 16.

16 A list of the editors and advisors of the *International Encyclopedia of Unified Science* is given on the verso of the title page of Thomas S. Kuhn, *The Structure of Scientific Revolutions* (Chicago, 1962), which originally appeared as vol. 2, no. 2 of the *Encyclopedia*. The connection to the *Encyclopedia* was still signaled in some, generally early, printings of the book's second edition (Chicago, 1970), before disappearing from sight in later printings. Of course, Kuhn's work completely blew apart the idea of a single, universal foundation for all the sciences.

17 Febvre, "Leçon d'ouverture," 12.

18 Lucien Febvre, "Vivre l'histoire: Propos d'initiation" (talk at the École Normale Supérieure, 1941), in Febvre, *Combats,* 20.

19 Febvre, "Vivre l'histoire," 20.

20 Marc Bloch and Lucien Febvre, "À nos lecteurs," *Annales d'histoire économique et sociale* 1 (1929): 1.

21 See Bury, "Science of History," esp. 219–20. Without specifically mentioning Bury, Febvre attacks this notion of history in his "Leçon d'ouverture," 8.

22 These collective initiatives are the focus of Kelly Ann Mulroney, "Team Research and Interdisciplinarity in French Social Science, 1925–1952" (PhD diss., University of Vir-

ginia, 2000). An important statement is Lucien Febvre, "Pour une histoire dirigée: Les recherches collectives et l'avenir de l'histoire," published in *Revue de synthèse* in 1936 and reprinted in *Combats,* 55–60.

23 See Febvre, *Combats,* 419–38; published in English as "A New Kind of History," in *A New Kind of History and Other Essays,* by Lucien Febvre, ed. Peter Burke, trans. K. Folca (New York, 1973), 27–43. I subsequently cite both versions in the text, French pagination preceding the English.

24 William H. McNeill, "Fernand Braudel, Historian," Instituto Fernand Braudel de Economia Mundial, Braudel Papers, no. 22, online at www.braudel.org.br/paping22 .htm (copyright date 2003, accessed March 2004).

25 Fernand Braudel, "Histoire et sociologie," in *Écrits sur l'histoire* (Paris, 1969), 105, 120–21. For an English translation of this essay, see Braudel, *On History,* trans. Sarah Matthews (Chicago, 1980), 64–82.

26 Braudel, "Histoire et sciences sociales: La longue durée," in Braudel, *Écrits sur l'histoire,* 82–83; for an English translation of this essay, see Braudel, *On History,* 25–54.

27 "Une vie pour l'histoire" (interview with Braudel conducted by François Ewald and Jean-Jacques Brochier), *Magazine littéraire,* no. 212 (November 1984), 22.

28 Immanuel Wallerstein, "Braudel and Interscience: A Preacher to Empty Pews?" (paper for the 5th Journées Braudeliennes, Binghamton University, [Oct. 1–2, 1999], online at www.fbc.binghamton.edu/iwjb.htm (copyright date 1999; accessed September 2003). Wallerstein's article led me efficiently to the previous several quotations.

29 Wallerstein, "Braudel and Interscience."

30 Gérard Noiriel, *Sur la "crise" de l'histoire* (Paris, 1996), 94–96 (the passages in quotation marks are all from Braudel). On the fragmentation theme, see François Dosse, *L'histoire en miettes: Des "Annales" à la "nouvelle histoire"* (Paris, 1987), esp. 161–247.

31 See Febvre, "Pour une histoire dirigée," 55–60.

32 Noiriel, *Sur la "crise,"* 92–100; quotation at 97.

33 I draw here on "Sur une forme d'histoire qui n'est pas la nôtre: L'histoire historisante," in Febvre, *Combats,* 114–18, quotation at 117. For Berr's views, see Henri Berr, *L'histoire traditionnelle et la synthèse historique* (Paris, 1921), which includes a section in chapter 2 entitled "Discussion avec un historien historisant" dating from 1911; cited in Febvre, *Combats,* 115.

34 When in 1969–70 two third-generation *Annalistes,* Pierre Goubert and Robert Mandrou, visited the University of Toronto, the conflict of the *Annalistes* with their supposedly entrenched traditionalist opponents was one topic of conversation. There was some doubt, at Toronto, that the *Annalistes* were as marginal in the French historical profession as they seemed to be claiming (personal recollection). The doubt was justified.

35 Lynn Hunt, "French History in the Last Twenty Years: The Rise and Fall of the *Annales* Paradigm," *Journal of Contemporary History* 21 (1986): 209–24. Subsequent page references are given in the text.

36 Jacques Revel, "The *Annales*: Continuities and Discontinuities," *Review* 1, nos. 3–4 (Winter/Spring 1978), 16, 17, 18. In suggesting a turn away from "Man" as the unifying object of analysis, Revel evokes Michel Foucault's well-known hypothesis of "the death of man."

37 François Furet, "Beyond the *Annales,*" *Journal of Modern History* 55 (1983), 389–410, at 390–92. (I follow Lynn Hunt in focusing on the Revel and Furet articles. The Furet article is a minor variant of the introduction to his book, *In the Workshop of History,* trans. Jonathan Mandelbaum [Chicago, 1984].)

38 Hunt, "Rise and Fall of the *Annales* Paradigm," 215–218.

39 Furet, "Beyond the *Annales,*" 397.

40 Ibid., 404–5.

41 Versions of this position include Ernst Bernheim, *Lehrbuch der Historischen Methode* (Munich, 1889); Charles-Victor Langlois and Charles Seignobos, *Introduction to the Study of History,* trans. G. C. Berry (New York, 1904; orig. pub. in French, 1898); and, certainly best known, R. G. Collingwood, *The Idea of History,* rev. ed., with *Lectures 1926–1928,* ed. Jan van der Dussen (Oxford, 1993; orig. pub. in 1946).

42 In brief, the "old" cultural history was committed to the notion that it is both possible and valuable to write the histories of cultural objects and practices while also maintaining that these objects and practices have some element of aesthetic, moral, or intellectual value that *exceeds* the socio-historical conditions under which they were produced. The new cultural history utterly denies that this can or should be done; indeed, even the possibility of such a project does not appear on its radar screen.

   For one statement of the old cultural history, see Jacques Barzun, "Cultural History: A Synthesis," in *The Varieties of History,* 387–402; for a survey, see Donald R. Kelley, "The Old Cultural History," *History of the Human Sciences* 9 (1996): 101–26.

43 Hunt, ed., *The New Cultural History.*

44 Clifford Geertz, *The Interpretation of Cultures: Selected Essays* (New York, 1973).

45 Ian Hacking, "The Archaeology of Foucault," in *Foucault: A Critical Reader,* ed. David C. Hoy (Oxford, 1986), 27, quoted in Patricia O'Brien, "Michel Foucault's History of Culture," in Hunt, ed., *The New Cultural History,* 45.

46 Pierre Bourdieu, *Outline of a Theory of Practice,* trans. Richard Nice (Cambridge, 1977; orig. pub. in French, 1972]); Pierre Bourdieu, *Distinction: A Social Critique of the Judgement of Taste,* trans. Richard Nice (Cambridge, MA, 1984). Orig. pub. in French, 1979.

47 For an overview, see H. Aram Veeser, ed., *The New Historicism Reader* (New York, 1994).

48 Bonnell and Hunt, eds., *Beyond the Cultural Turn.*

49 Richard Biernacki, "Method and Metaphor after the New Cultural History," in Bonnell and Hunt, eds., *Beyond the Cultural Turn,* 62. Subsequent page references are given in the text.

50 Geertz, *Interpretation of Cultures,* 14, quoted in Biernacki, "Method and Metaphor," 63–64.

51 Robert Darnton, *The Great Cat Massacre and Other Episodes in French Cultural History* (New York, 1984); Lynn Hunt, *Politics, Language, and Class in the French Revolution* (Berkeley, 1984). An earlier commentator who pointed out the all-embracing, and thereby empty, character of the new cultural historians' apparently ontological appeal to "culture" is Marilyn Strathern, "Ubiquities" (review of Hunt, ed., *New Cultural History*), *Annals of Scholarship* 9 (1992): 199–208.

52 Bonnell and Hunt, eds., *Beyond the Cultural Turn,* 1.

53 Thomas S. Kuhn, *The Structure of Scientific Revolutions,* 2nd ed. (Chicago, 1970); Aristides Baltas, Kostas Gavroglu, and Vassiliki Kindi, "A Discussion with Thomas S. Kuhn," in *The Road Since Structure: Philosophical Essays, 1970–1993, with an Autobiographical Interview,* by Thomas Kuhn, ed. James Conant and John Haugeland (Chicago, 2000), 300.

54 David Hollinger, "T. S. Kuhn's Theory of Science and Its Implications for History," in *Paradigms and Revolutions: Appraisals and Applications of Thomas Kuhn's Philosophy of Science,* ed. Gary Gutting (Notre Dame, 1980), 117–36. Orig. pub. in *American Historical Review* 78 (1973): 370–93.

55 Traian Stoianovich, *French Historical Method: The* Annales *Paradigm,* with a foreword by Fernand Braudel (Ithaca, NY, 1976); Burke, *French Historical Revolution.* One could cite many other examples.

56 For one recent instance among historical theorists, see Miguel A. Cabrera, "On Language, Culture, and Social Action," *History and Theory,* Theme Issue 40 (2001): 82–102. Cabrera suggests that history "is currently undergoing a new change of paradigm." This means, of course, that "historians *must* adopt [my emphasis] a new agenda for historical research" (100). He then goes on to outline what this agenda *must* be.

57 Kuhn, *Structure of Scientific Revolutions,* 162, 164.

58 Ibid., 164.

59 Foucault's equation of knowledge with power offers—nefariously, I think—a justification for judging historians according to the supposed authenticity or inauthenticity of their political commitments rather than on grounds of the methodological validity and insight-creating capacity of their work. That such a political mode of judgment actually *is* applied within the present-day American historical profession seems clear from some recent, notorious cases. The best known is the reception of Michael A. Bellesiles's *Arming America: The Origins of a National Gun Culture* (New York, 2000). Bellesiles's work received major prizes, and he was granted tenure at a prestigious university, Emory. He seems to have received these benefits in large measure because early, allegedly expert readers of his work became orgasmic at his claim that private gun ownership in the United States before the Civil War was rare—a claim that could be seen as supporting the campaign for gun control. It appears that, as a result of their passionate political solidarity with Bellesiles, these readers failed to notice something that ought to have been obvious to them: that Bellesiles's evidence did not support his claim. Why worry about evidence when the good political cause is being served?

But eventually the inconvenient truth came out. Bellesiles's tenure at Emory was revoked, as was his Bancroft Prize, sponsored by Columbia University, which had been awarded to him for his having written the best work in American history published in the year 2000. Also, his publisher, Knopf, withdrew the book from circulation. These were almost unprecedented actions, and honorable ones on the part of the institutions concerned. For discussion of the Bellesiles case, see the *Newsletter* of the Organization of American Historians for February 2003 (available on the Web at www.oah.org/pubs/nl/2003feb). The anonymous article, "Columbia University Rescinds Bancroft

Prize," recounts some of the main facts of the case, but the best entry into the issues is provided by the "Report of the Investigative Committee in the matter of Professor Michael Bellesiles," dated 10 July 2002, by Stanley Katz (chair), Hanna H. Gray, and Laurel Thatcher Ulrich, which concludes that "the *best* that can be said [my emphasis]" of Bellesiles's work is that it is "unprofessional and misleading" and "deeply flawed." (The report is available at www.emory.edu/central/NEWS/Releases/Final_Report .pdf; quotations at 18–19.)

The OAH's response to the Bellesiles case has been disturbingly equivocal. In the same issue of the *Newsletter,* it published an article by Professor Jon Wiener, "Emory's Bellesiles Report: A Case of Tunnel Vision," that appeared to be written on the principle that every Left perspective, no matter how poorly grounded, is worthy of support. Also, to my knowledge, the OAH has not yet revoked the Binkley-Stephenson Prize, for best article in the *Journal of American History* for 1996, that it granted to the forerunner of Bellesiles's book, his article, "The Origins of Gun Culture in the United States, 1760–1865," *Journal of American History* 83 (1996): 425–55. The matter of Bellesiles can be pursued through Google searches, or via www.hnn.us or www.h-net.org. A far more responsible study of the history of gun control in the United States is Saul Cornell, *A Well-Regulated Militia: The Founding Fathers and the Origins of Gun Control in America* (New York, 2006).

60 Krieger, *Time's Reasons,* 166–67.

61 See, in this regard, John Higham, "Beyond Consensus: The Historian as Moral Critic," *American Historical Review* 67 (1962): 609–25. Higham suggested that historians ought to activate a distinction between "causal history" and "moral history," entertaining both as "reciprocal modes of understanding, each of which suffers from neglect of the other" (622). I see little of such an orientation in the current blithe talk of historiographic paradigms.

CONCLUSION

1 Leopold Ranke, "Preface to the First Edition of *Histories of the Latin and Germanic Nations,*" in *The Theory and Practice of History,* by Leopold von Ranke, ed. Georg G. Iggers and Konrad von Moltke, trans. Wilma A. Iggers and Konrad von Moltke (New York, 1983), 135–38, at 137 (translation altered).

2 Amazon.com, history e-mail newsletter of 11 May 2001. Amazon.com no longer sends out such e-mails, but some sense of the readers' responses to "popular" history books such as the ones noted above can be gauged from the "customer reviews" that are posted on the major bookseller sites, especially www.amazon.com.

3 *Pearl Harbor* [movie], directed by Michael Bay (Burbank, CA: Touchstone Pictures, 2001).

4 Somewhat ironically, the attempted closeness actually underscored the historical *in*authenticity of *Titanic,* since the characters of the drama—their dress, physiques, bearing, voices, language, class relations, desires, sexual behavior, and aspirations—all had to be calculated according to what a present-day audience would find understand-

able, empathetic, and interesting. The *characters* thus clashed quite dramatically with the *furnishings*. See *Titanic* [movie], directed by James Cameron (Santa Monica, CA: Lightstorm Entertainment, 1997).

5 *The Civil War* [PBS television series], 1990, nine episodes, Ken Burns and Ric Burns, producers (Alexandria, VA: PBS Video, 1989).

6 Commenting on *The Civil War,* Ken Burns highlights its "careful use of archival photographs, live modern cinematography, music, narration, and a chorus of first-person voices that together did more than merely recount a historical story. It was something that also became a kind of 'emotional archaeology,' trying to unearth the very heart of the American experience; listening to the ghosts and echoes of an almost inexpressibly wise past." (Ken Burns, "Why I Decided to Make *The Civil War,*" at the PBS Web site: http://www.pbs.org/civilwar/film/).

7 *The World at War* [Thames Television series], 1973, twenty-six episodes, directed by Ted Childs and Martin Smith VII, produced by Jeremy Isaacs (New York: Home Box Office, 2001).

8 Pity the historical biographer nowadays who discovers that his subject has no *Innerlichkeit* whatsoever. If there is no "there" there, what is one to do? This dilemma may in part explain Edmund Morris's interesting but historiographically disastrous fictionalized biography of Ronald Reagan, *Dutch: A Memoir of Ronald Reagan* (New York, 1999), which invents characters who never existed (and fails to distinguish them from the characters who actually *did* exist). But is Morris's procedure so surprising? Surely, where issues of identity are uppermost, evidence tends to become a matter of mere "local color," intended to add verisimilitude to the narrative rather than to establish that it is true.

9 The foremost theorist of historical experience is F. R. Ankersmit: see his *Sublime Historical Experience* (Stanford, CA, 2005).

10 Maya Jasanoff, *Edge of Empire: Lives, Culture, and Conquest in the East, 1750–1850* (New York, 2005), 1.

11 Thomas H. Bisson, letter to the editor, *Atlantic,* 17 June 2005.

12 See David Barstow, William J. Broad, and Jeff Gerth, "How the White House Embraced Disputed Arms Intelligence," *New York Times,* 3 October 2004, online at http://www.nytimes.com/2004/10/03/international/middleeast/03tube.html (other sites findable via Google); and James Risen, *State of War: The Secret History of the C.I.A. and the Bush Administration* (New York, 2006).

INDEX

vs. decoration, 9–10; "erotics" of,
54; "explaining" of, 128–29, 131,
246n15; intentional (aka sources),
25–26, 29, 72, 124, 125; material, 26,
58; and narrative, 63, 71; National
History Day's view of, 49–50; nonintentional (aka traces), 25–26, 29,
72; omitted from textbooks, 85; testimonial, 19–20, 25–26, 29; wrongful
subordination to politics, 5, 265–
66n59. *See also* argument; epistemology; historical epistemology; justification; memory; source; testimony;
trace
evolution, teaching of, 110
"existents," 4, 24; distinguished from
events, 95
experience, xiv, 24, 28–29, 33, 35; historical, 213–14; lived, as inherently authentic, 50, 53
experimental history, 185
explanans, three types of, 135–36
explanation, 65, 78–79, 93–94, 95, 154;
alleged autonomy of, 81, 101–2; bias
toward, 81–87; "bottom-up" vs.
"top-down," 137; Braudel's loose use
of term, 236n41; and counterfactual
inference, xiii, 7, 13, 85, 100, 154–56;
criteria for evaluating, 132–37; and
description, 78–92, 96–97, 98–100,
102, 103; differing senses of, 79, 81,
131, 154, 245n8; of historical record,
128–29; and metaphors of verticality,
82; senses of, differing, 79, 81, 131, 154,
245n8; by three types of cause, 135–37.
See also causation; cause; description;
interpretation; justification
eyewitnessing, 58, 228n46. *See also*
evidence

Fabian, Johannes, 120–22, 227n33; on
objectification, 121–22

facts, historical, 24, 25, 26–27, 122,
240n15; established abductively,
129–30
fallacies, historians', ix
Fann, K. T., 245n12
Farber, David, 260n83
fate, idea of, 63
Febvre, Lucien, xiv, 95–96, 202; for coordinated research, 194–96; for overcoming past, 196–97; for synthesis,
191; for total history, 192–96. *See also*
coherence
Feigl, Herbert, 193
feminism, 1–2, 111, 162
feminist history, 183
Ferguson, Niall, 151–56
fiction, 65, 76, 90–91, 167, 184–86, 211,
239n5. *See also* counterfactual inference; imaginative literature;
narrative
film action, 90
Finlay, Robert, 234n24
first-attitude historiography, 169–71, 179.
See also narrative, grand: four attitudes
toward
Fischer, David Hackett, ix, 80–81
Fisher, Walter R., 228n4
Fogel, Robert W., 259n75
followability, 71
Foner, Eric, 220n4
forgetting, 44, 48; active, 52; and remembering, 73
Forster, E. M., 80
Fortunoff Video Archive for Holocaust
Testimonies, 220n7
Foster, Eugene A., 126
Foucault, Michel, 13–14, 41, 69, 70, 108,
203, 207, 258n60; "death of man" the-
sis, 263n36; equating of knowledge
and power, 265n59
Foundations of Historical Knowledge
(White), 90

Adjustment and Human Relations

A Lamp Along the Way

TRICIA ALEXANDER

Long Beach City College

Prentice Hall
Upper Saddle River, New Jersey 07458

Library of Congress Cataloging-in-Publication Data

Alexander, Tricia.
   Adjustment and human relations : a lamp along the way / Tricia
Alexander.
     p. cm.
   Includes bibliographical references and index.
   ISBN 0–13–974395–2
   1. Self-actualization (Psychology) I. Title.
  BF637.S4A573 2000
  158—dc 21   99–12587
                                        CIP

Editorial director: Charlyce Jones Owen
Editor-in-chief: Nancy Roberts
Executive editor: Bill Webber
Assistant editor: Jennifer Cohen
AVP, Director of manufacturing and production: Barbara Kittle
Managing editor: Mary Rottino
Production liaison: Fran Russello
Project manager: Bruce Hobart (Pine Tree Composition)
Manufacturing manager: Nick Sklitsis
Prepress and manufacturing buyer: Lynn Pearlman
Creative design director: Leslie Osher
Interior design: Bruce Hobart (Pine Tree Composition)
Art director: Jane Conte
Cover designer: Joe Sengotta
Cover art: Leon Zernitsky/SIS Inc.
Director, image resource center: Melinda Lee Reo
Manager, rights & permissions: Kay Dellosa
Image specialist: Beth Boyd
Photo researcher: Deanna Gongora
Marketing manager: Sharon Cosgrove

This book was set in 10/12 Trump Mediaeval by Pine Tree
Composition, Inc., and was printed and bound by R.R. Donnelley
and Sons Company. The cover was printed by Phoenix Color Corp.

©2000 by Prentice-Hall, Inc.
Upper Saddle River, New Jersey 07458

All rights reserved. No part of this book may be
reproduced, in any form or by any means,
without permission in writing from the publisher.

Printed in the United States of America
10 9 8 7 6 5 4 3 2 1

ISBN 0-13-974395-2

Prentice-Hall International (UK) Limited, *London*
Prentice-Hall of Australia Pty. Limited, *Sydney*
Prentice-Hall Canada Inc., *Toronto*
Prentice-Hall Hispanoamericana, S.A., *Mexico*
Prentice-Hall of India Private Limited, *New Delhi*
Prentice-Hall of Japan, Inc., *Tokyo*
Pearson Education Asia Pte. Ltd., *Singapore*
Editora Prentice-Hall do Brasil, Ltda., *Rio de Janeiro*